Working with Microsoft® FAST™ Search Server 2010 for SharePoint®

Mikael Svenson
Marcus Johansson
Robert Piddocke

Published with the authorization of Microsoft Corporation by:
O'Reilly Media, Inc.
1005 Gravenstein Highway North
Sebastopol, California 95472

ISBN: 978-0-7356-6222-3

1 2 3 4 5 6 7 8 9 LSI 7 6 5 4 3 2

Printed and bound in the United States of America.

Microsoft Press books are available through booksellers and distributors worldwide. If you need support related to this book, email Microsoft Press Book Support at *mspinput@microsoft.com*. Please tell us what you think of this book at *http://www.microsoft.com/learning/booksurvey*.

Microsoft and the trademarks listed at *http://www.microsoft.com/about/legal/en/us/IntellectualProperty/ Trademarks/EN-US.aspx* are trademarks of the Microsoft group of companies. All other marks are property of their respective owners.

The example companies, organizations, products, domain names, email addresses, logos, people, places, and events depicted herein are fictitious. No association with any real company, organization, product, domain name, email address, logo, person, place, or event is intended or should be inferred.

This book expresses the author's views and opinions. The information contained in this book is provided without any express, statutory, or implied warranties. Neither the authors, O'Reilly Media, Inc., Microsoft Corporation, nor its resellers, or distributors will be held liable for any damages caused or alleged to be caused either directly or indirectly by this book.

Acquisitions and Developmental Editor: Russell Jones

Production Editor: Holly Bauer

Editorial Production: Online Training Solutions, Inc.

Technical Reviewer: Thomas Svensen

Copyeditor: Jaime Odell, Online Training Solutions, Inc.

Indexer: Judith McConville

Cover Design: Twist Creative • Seattle

Cover Composition: Karen Montgomery

Illustrator: Jeanne Craver, Online Training Solutions, Inc.

Contents at a Glance

Contents

PART I   WHAT YOU NEED TO KNOW

What do you think of this book? We want to hear from you!

Microsoft is interested in hearing your feedback so we can continually improve our
books and learning resources for you. To participate in a brief online survey, please visit:

microsoft.com/learning/booksurvey

What do you think of this book? We want to hear from you!

Microsoft is interested in hearing your feedback so we can continually improve our
books and learning resources for you. To participate in a brief online survey, please visit:

microsoft.com/learning/booksurvey

Foreword

Should you care about search? The answer is "Yes!" However, the reason you should care constantly changes. Back in 1997 when FAST was founded, most people viewed search as a mature and commoditized technology. AltaVista was the leader in web search and Verity had won the enterprise search race. Internet portals cared about search because it was critical for attracting visitors—but those same portals did not anticipate how search would later transform both online monetization and user experiences at large.

As the leader of FAST, I am very pleased that our product has become so widely used and successful that this book is now a necessity. I hope (and expect) that Microsoft FAST Search Server 2010 for SharePoint (FS4SP) will be further embraced and utilized at an increasing rate because of it.

In 2008 when Microsoft acquired FAST, search had already become one of the most important Internet applications and was in the process of becoming a back-end require-ment for digital advertising. FS4SP is the first release from the combined Microsoft and FAST team. The goal was to make advanced search technology available for the masses. Strong search in the context of the Microsoft SharePoint collaboration suite has numer-ous applications, enabling effective information sharing with customers, partners, and employees.

This book takes a hands-on approach. It combines a bottom-up architectural pre-sentation and explanation with a top-down scenario-driven analysis and examples of how you can take full advantage of FS4SP. You will find classical search pages, ways to enrich search experiences with visualization and navigation, as well as examples on how to build high-value solutions based on search-driven experiences. The example applica-tions are taken from both productivity scenarios inside the firewall and from digital marketing scenarios such as e-commerce.

Search enables organizations to make the critical transition from huge disparate content repositories to highly contextual information that's targeted to each individual user. Such contextual information will make your SharePoint solutions excel. End users should be able to explore and navigate information based on terms they understand and terms that are critical for the task at hand. This book explains a practical approach for reaching those goals.

IT professionals will find information about how to best design and set up FS4SP to cater to the different content sources of their organizations, and SharePoint developers will find information about how to use FS4SP in their customized search solutions and how to take advantage of the new toolset to create best-of-breed search-driven applications and solutions.

The authors of this book are experienced search veterans within the field of enterprise search both in general and specifically using FAST and SharePoint. You will learn the FS4SP product and—through the examples—gain ideas about how you can take most of your own SharePoint deployments to the next level.

Dr. Bjørn Olstad
Distinguished Engineer at Microsoft

Introduction

Microsoft FAST Search Server 2010 for SharePoint (FS4SP) is Microsoft's flagship enterprise search product and one of the most capable enterprise search platforms available. It provides a feature-rich alternative to the limited out-of-the-box search experience in Microsoft SharePoint 2010 and can be extended to meet complex information retrieval requirements. If your organization is looking for a fully configurable and scalable search solution, FS4SP may be right for you.

Working with Microsoft FAST Search Server 2010 for SharePoint provides a thorough introduction to FS4SP. The book introduces the core concepts of FS4SP in addition to some of the key concepts of enterprise search. It then dives deeper into deployment, operations, and development, presenting several "how to" examples of common tasks that most administrators or developers will need to tackle. Although this book does not provide exhaustive coverage of every feature of FS4SP, it does provide a solid foundation for understanding the product thoroughly and explains many necessary tasks and useful ways to use the product.

In addition to its coverage of core aspects of FS4SP, the book includes two basic scenarios that showcase capabilities of FS4SP: intranet and e-commerce deployments. Beyond the explanatory content, most chapters include step-by-step examples and downloadable sample projects that you can explore for yourself.

Who Should Read This Book

We wrote this book for people actively implementing search solutions using FS4SP and for people who simply want to learn more about how FS4SP works. If you are a SharePoint architect or developer implementing FS4SP, this book is for you. If you are already using SharePoint search and want to know what differentiates it from FS4SP, this book explains the additional features available in FS4SP and how you can take advantage of them.

If you are a power user or SharePoint administrator maintaining an FS4SP solution, this book is also for you because it covers how to set up and maintain FS4SP.

This book covers basic FS4SP installation but does *not* discuss the details of how to set up an FS4SP farm; that information is covered in detail at Microsoft TechNet. In this book, we have expanded and filled out the information available on TechNet and MSDN to provide valuable real-life tips.

Assumptions

This book assumes that you have at least a minimal understanding of Microsoft .NET development, SharePoint administration, and general search concepts. Although the FS4SP APIs are accessible from most programming languages, this book includes examples in Windows PowerShell and Microsoft Visual C# only. If you are a complete beginner to programming, you should consider reading John Paul Mueller's *Start Here! Learn Microsoft Visual C# 2010* (Microsoft Press, 2011). If you have programming experience but are not familiar with C#, consider reading John Sharp's *Microsoft Visual C# 2010 Step by Step* (Microsoft Press, 2010). If you are not yet familiar with SharePoint and Windows PowerShell, in addition to the numerous references you'll find cited in the book, you should read Bill English's *Microsoft SharePoint 2010 Administrator's Companion* (Microsoft Press, 2010). *Working with Microsoft FAST Search Server 2010 for SharePoint* uses a lot of XML, so we also assume a basic understanding of XML.

Because of its heavy focus on search and information management concepts such as document and file types and database structures, this book assumes that you have a basic understanding of Microsoft server technologies and have had brief exposure to developing on the Windows platform with Microsoft Visual Studio. To go beyond this book and expand your knowledge of Windows development and SharePoint, other Microsoft Press books offer both complete introductions and comprehensive in-depth information on Visual Studio and SharePoint.

Who Should Not Read This Book

This book is not for information workers or search end users wanting to know how FS4SP can help them in their work or how to specifically use FS4SP search syntax, although some of the examples provide some insight into syntax.

Also, little to no consideration was given to the best practices or requirements of any particular business decision maker. The focus of this book is to teach architects and developers how to get the most out of FS4SP, not whether they should use it at all or how or whether FS4SP will make their business successful. Naturally, though, the book includes a great deal of information that can help business decision makers understand whether FS4SP will meet their needs.

Organization of This Book

Working with Microsoft FAST Search Server 2010 for SharePoint is divided into two parts and 10 chapters. Part I, "What You Need to Know," provides an introduction to FS4SP, common concepts and terminology, FS4SP architecture, deployment scenarios, and operations. Part II, "Creating Search Solutions," covers configuration, indexing, searching, useful tips and tricks, and example search scenarios.

Part I is relevant for anyone working with FS4SP. Part II is primarily relevant for people creating and setting up search solutions.

Finding Your Best Starting Point in This Book

The two parts of *Working with Microsoft FAST Search Server 2010 for SharePoint* are intended to each deliver a slightly different set of information. Therefore, depending on your needs, you may want to focus on specific areas of the book. Use the following table to determine how best to proceed through the book.

If you are	Follow these steps
New to search and need to deploy FS4SP for testing its features	Focus on Part I.
Familiar with FS4SP and have a project to develop a search solution	Briefly skim Part I and Part II if you need a refresher on the core concepts. Focus on Chapter 8, "Querying the Index," and Chapter 9, "Useful Tips and Tricks," in Part II.
Presently using FS4SP and want to get the most out of it	Briefly skim Part I and Part II if you need a refresher on the core concepts. Concentrate on Chapter 5, "Operations," in Part I and study Chapter 10, "Search Scenarios," carefully.
Need to deploy a specific advanced feature outlined in this book	Read the part or specific section that interests you in the book and study the scenario that most closely matches your needs in Chapter 10.

Most of the book's chapters include hands-on examples that you can use to try out the concepts discussed in that chapter. No matter what sections of the book you choose to focus on, be sure to download the code samples for this book. (See the "Code Samples" section later in this Introduction).

Conventions and Features in This Book

This book presents information using conventions designed to make the information readable and easy to follow:

- The code samples in this book are in Windows PowerShell or in C#. You'll also see XML and XSLT examples.

- Boxed elements with labels such as "Note" provide additional information or alternative methods for completing a step successfully.

- Text you should type appears in bold font; for example, values that you must enter into fields.

- Programming elements such as classes, inline code, variable names, and URLs appear in italic font.

System Requirements

To work with FS4SP, you need both SharePoint 2010 and FS4SP installed. Chapter 4, "Deployment," covers how to set up a development environment and provides more detail on system requirements and recommended configurations.

Code Samples

This book features a companion website that makes available to you all the code used in the book. The code samples are organized by chapter, and you can download code files from the companion site at this address:

http://go.microsoft.com/FWLink/?Linkid=242683

Follow the instructions to download the *fs4spbook.zip* file.

Installing the Code Samples

Follow these steps to install the code samples on your computer so that you can use them with the exercises in this book.

1. Unzip the *fs4spbook.zip* file that you downloaded from the book's website.

2. If prompted, review the displayed end user license agreement. If you accept the terms, select the accept option, and then click Next.

Note If the license agreement doesn't appear, you can access it from the same webpage from which you downloaded the *fs4spbook.zip* file.

Using the Code Samples

The content of the zipped file is organized by chapters. You will find separate folders for each chapter, depending on the topic:

- **Windows PowerShell scripts**   These scripts are saved in the *ps1* file format and can be copied to your server and run in the Windows PowerShell command shell window. Alternatively, you can copy the script in whole or in part to your servers and use them in the shell window.

- **XML configuration files**   You can copy these files to replace your existing configuration files, or open them and use them purely as examples for modifying your existing XML configuration files.

- **Visual Studio solutions**   The solution files contain the complete working solution for the associated example. You can open these solutions in Visual Studio and modify them to suit your individual needs.

Acknowledgments from All the Authors

The authors would like to thank all of the people who assisted us in writing this book. If we have accidentally omitted anyone, we apologize in advance. We would like to extend a special thanks to the following people:

- Bas Lijten, Leonardo Souza, Shane Cunnane, Sezai Komur, Daan Seys, Carlos Valcarcel, Johnny Tordgeman, and Ole Kristian Mørch-Storstein for reviewing sample chapters along the way.

- Ivan Neganov, Jørgen Iversen, John Lenker, and Nadeem Ishqair for their help and insight with some of the samples.

- Russell Jones, who picked up the project and got us through the approval process.

- Jaime Odell, for guiding us during the editing phase and making it a great experience.

We also want to thank the people at Microsoft Press and O'Reilly Media who took on the project and helped us along the way to complete the final product.

Finally—and most importantly—we want to thank Thomas Svensen for accepting the job as tech reviewer. We couldn't have done this without him, and we appreciate how much more he did than would have been required for a pure tech review job, including suggesting rewrites and discussing content during the writing and revision process.

Mikael Svenson's Acknowledgments

I want to thank my wife, Hege, for letting me spend our entire summer vacation and numerous evenings and weekends in front of my laptop to write this book. The book took far more time than I ever could have anticipated, but Hege stood by and let me do this. Thank you so much! I also want to thank my coauthors for joining me on this adventure. I would never have been able to pull this off myself. Your expertise and effort made this book possible.

I would also like to thank Puzzlepart for allowing me to spend time on this book during office hours. It's great knowing your employer is backing your hobby!

Marcus Johansson's Acknowledgments

First and foremost, I want to thank my wonderful family for always wholeheartedly supporting me in everything I ever decided to do, for always encouraging me to pursue my often far-fetched dreams, and for never giving up on me no matter what.

Even though I vastly underestimated the effort required to write this book, I would do it again at the drop of a hat, which shows how much I have appreciated working with Mikael and Robert—two of the top subject matter experts in our field (who also happen to be great guys). Thanks to both of you!

And last, a very special thanks to Tnek Nossnahoj, who—perhaps without knowing it himself—made me realize what's important in life. I miss you.

Robert Piddocke's Acknowledgments

I want to thank Mikael and Marcus for inviting me to help them on this book project. It has been a fun and enjoyable experience. I would also like to thank them for their enthusiasm and friendly attitude as well as their technical insight into FS4SP. I feel honored to have been included in this project with two of the foremost experts in the field.

A special thanks goes to my loving and supportive family, Maya, Pavel, and Joanna, for supporting yet another book project and putting up with my absence for many evenings and weekends of writing, rewriting, and reviewing.

Errata & Book Support

We've made every effort to ensure the accuracy of this book and its companion content. Any errors that have been reported since this book was published are listed on our Microsoft Press site at *oreilly.com*:

> *http://go.microsoft.com/FWLink/?Linkid=242685*

If you find an error that is not already listed, you can report it to us through the same page.

If you need additional support, send email to Microsoft Press Book Support at *mspinput@microsoft.com*.

Please note that product support for Microsoft software is not offered through these addresses.

We Want to Hear from You

At Microsoft Press, your satisfaction is our top priority, and your feedback our most valuable asset. Please tell us what you think of this book at:

> *http://www.microsoft.com/learning/booksurvey*

The survey is short, and we read every one of your comments and ideas. Thanks in advance for your input!

Stay in Touch

Let's keep the conversation going! We're on Twitter: *http://twitter.com/MicrosoftPress*.

What You Need to Know

## CHAPTER 1

Introduction to FAST Search Server 2010 for SharePoint

After completing this chapter, you will be able to

- Understand the roots of FAST Search & Transfer and FAST Enterprise Search.

- Understand the differences, advantages, and disadvantages of FSIS, FSIA, and FS4SP.

- Compare and choose the FAST product that best fits your business needs.

This chapter provides an introduction to FAST, and specifically to Microsoft FAST Search Server 2010 for SharePoint (FS4SP). It includes a brief history of FAST Search & Transfer—which eventually became a Microsoft subsidiary before being incorporated as the Microsoft Development Center Norway. The chapter also provides a brief history of the search products developed, what options exist today in the Microsoft product offering, and a comparison of the options with the search capabilities in FS4SP.

Finally, we, the authors, attempt to predict where these products are going and what Microsoft intends to do with them in the future. We also pose some questions that can help address the key decision factors for using a product such as FS4SP and other FAST versions. FS4SP is a great product, but standard Microsoft SharePoint Search is sometimes good enough. Considering that a move to FS4SP requires additional resources, one goal of this book is to showcase the features of FS4SP to help you make the decision about which product to use. Therefore, this chapter includes a flowchart, a score-card, and a cost estimator so that you can perform your due diligence during the move to FS4SP.

With the information in this chapter, you should be able to understand and evaluate the product that might be best for your particular business needs. To a certain extent, you should also gain a better understanding of how choices about enterprise search in your organization can impact you in the future.

What Is FAST?

FAST is both a company and a set of products focused on enterprise information retrieval. FAST and its products were purchased by Microsoft in 2008, but the company was kept essentially intact. FAST continues to develop and support the FAST product line and is working to further integrate it into the Microsoft product set—specifically, into SharePoint. The following sections provide a brief history of the company and the products to help you understand the origins of the tools and then describe where things are now and expectations for the future.

Past

The history of FAST Search & Transfer and the FAST search products is a familiar story in the IT world: a startup initiated by young, ambitious, clever people, driven by investors, and eventually acquired by a larger corporation.

FAST Search & Transfer was founded in Trondheim, Norway in 1997 to develop and market the already popular FTPSearch product developed by Tor Egge at the Norwegian University of Science and Technology (NTNU). FTPSearch purportedly already had a large user base via a web UI hosted at the university, so in the days of the dot-com boom, it was a natural move to create a company to market and commercialize the software.

FAST quickly developed a web strategy and entered the global search engine market in 1997 with *Alltheweb.com*, which at that time boasted that it had the largest index of websites in the world in addition to several features, such as image search, that bested large competitors such as Google and AltaVista. However, the company failed to capture market share, and was sold in 2003 to Overture, which was itself eventually purchased by Yahoo!.

John Markus Lervik, one of the founding members of FAST and then-CEO, had a vision to provide enterprise search solutions for large companies and search projects that required large-scale information retrieval, so he pushed FAST and its technology into the enterprise search market.

In 2000, FAST developed FAST DataSearch (FDS), which it supported until version 4. After that, it rebranded the product suite as FAST Enterprise Search Platform (ESP), which was released on January 27, 2004. FAST ESP released updates until version 5.3, which is the present version.

FAST ESP later became FAST Search for Internet Sites (FSIS), and FAST Search for Internal Applications (FSIA). It was used as the base for the core of FS4SP. FAST ESP enjoyed relative success in the enterprise search market, and FAST gained several key customers.

By 2007, FAST expanded further in the market, acquiring several customers and buying up competitor Convera's RetrievalWare product.

FAST ESP was developed constantly during the period from January 2004 through 2007 and grew rapidly in features and functionality based on demands from its customer base. Some key and unique capabilities include *entity extraction,* which is the extraction of names of companies and locations from the indexed items; and advanced linguistic capabilities such as detecting more than 80 languages and performing lemmatization of the indexed text. The capabilities are explained in more detail in the section "Explanation of Features" later in this chapter.

Present

Since its acquisition by Microsoft, FAST has been rebranded as the Microsoft Development Center Norway, where it is still located. Although the company shrunk slightly shortly after its acquisition, Microsoft now has more than twice as many people working on enterprise search as FAST did before the acquisition. In fact, Microsoft made FAST its flagship search product and split the FAST ESP 5.3 product into two search offerings: FSIS and FSIA. ESP 5.3 was also used as the basis for FS4SP.

Microsoft is actively developing and integrating FAST while continuing to support existing customers. FAST is being actively adopted by Microsoft's vast partner network, which is building offerings for customers worldwide.

Future

Predicting the future is tricky. However, having worked with FAST and Microsoft for several years, we are confident that these predictions are as sound as any predictions can be:

- We expect that Microsoft will continue to develop the FAST products as they were before the acquisition while bringing them into the Microsoft product portfolio.

  Practically speaking, this means that FAST will become a SharePoint product that can be managed via SharePoint administration. In such a scenario, you might think that you would have to buy SharePoint to use FAST; however (as with SharePoint Search Server), in this context, SharePoint itself functions only as an administration and UI provider—capabilities you can get with the free version of SharePoint.

  But we also expect Microsoft to do more; Microsoft will likely continue to port the software from its existing Python and Java code base to the Microsoft .NET Framework and abandon support for Linux and UNIX. (The Linux and UNIX prediction is based on MSDN blog information at *http://blogs.msdn.com/b/enterprisesearch/archive/2010/02/04/ innovation-on-linux-and-unix.aspx*.)

- We expect to see the FAST engine adopted into existing Microsoft products such as Microsoft Exchange Server.

- FS4SP will become the built-in search of SharePoint; the existing SharePoint Search index will be abandoned. This is not a major change for most people because the only practical difference is that FAST has a more robust index. The additional features of FS4SP will become standard SharePoint Search features.

Overall, Microsoft is putting a substantial development effort into FAST, so we expect some extensive modifications to the future product, which include:

- Improved pipeline management and administration with new versions of Interaction Management Services (IMS) and Content Transformation Services (CTS) carried over from FSIS.

- Further integration into SharePoint and a simplified administration experience from SharePoint.

Versions

Since the acquisition of FAST Search & Transfer by Microsoft, the FAST ESP 5.x product was rebranded into two different products. These were essentially licensing structures to fit the way in which the ESP product could be deployed: internally (FSIA) or externally (FSIS). Additionally, a new integration with Microsoft SharePoint gave rise to a third product: FAST Search Server 2010 for SharePoint (FS4SP).

> **Important** FSIA and FSIS have been removed from the product list and are no longer officially for sale to new customers. We will still explain all the product offerings because we expect elements from FSIS to move into FS4SP in later versions.

FSIS

FAST Search Server 2010 for Internet Sites (FSIS) was Microsoft's rebundling of the FAST ESP product, licensed specifically for externally facing websites. This package was produced both to fit the unique demands of high-demand, public-facing websites such as e-commerce sites and public content providers and to meet licensing requirements for—potentially—hundreds of millions of unique visitors. It had a few unique licensing and product specifications that differentiated it from FS4SP and FSIA.

FSIS was licensed solely by server. This accommodated the lack of named users in front-facing public websites, as well as the potential for a large number of unique connections and users who connect to the search by connecting as a single anonymous user account.

To help develop search for Internet sites, FSIS was also bundled with a few new components: Content Transformation Services (CTS), Interaction Management Services (IMS), FAST Search Designer, Search Business Manager, and IMS UI Toolkit.

Besides these new modules, FAST ESP 5.3, with SP3, was bundled within FSIS as is, but was partly hidden from users through the modules mentioned in the previous paragraph.

CTS, IMS, and FAST Search Designer The CTS and IMS modules introduce the concept of "content transformation" and "interaction management" flows; they are used for indexing content, respectively orchestrating search user interfaces. FAST Search Designer, a Microsoft Visual Studio plug-in, allows developers to easily build, test, and debug such flows. CTS, IMS, and FAST Search Designer represent a great leap forward for developers and are actually rumored to be included in upcoming FS4SP releases. And because FSIS has been officially removed from the FAST price list, we expect these modules to be included in the next release of FS4SP that will likely accompany the next version of SharePoint.

As anyone with deep knowledge of FAST ESP will tell you, ESP is a rich platform for content processing, but it is not as easy to work with as it is powerful. CTS extends the existing content processing capabilities of ESP and alleviates those problems by building on a brand-new processing framework that enables drag-and-drop modeling and interactive debugging of flows. Also, instead of working with the content source–driven "pipelines" of ESP, developers can now build flows that connect to source systems themselves and manipulate content as needed before sending content into the index or any other compatible data repository. These flows are easily scheduled for execution using Windows PowerShell cmdlets.

Figure 1-1 shows a simple example content transformation flow as visualized in FAST Search Designer. This particular flow is taken from a set of Sample Flows bundled with FSIS. As is typical for most CTS flows, execution starts in a "reader" operator. In this example, a *FileSystemReader* is used to crawl files on disk. The files are then sent through the flow one by one and immediately parsed into an internal document representation by using the *DocumentParser* operator. Unless the parsing fails, the documents are sent forward to a set of extractors that are converting free text data into high-level metadata suitable for sorting and refinement. Finally, a writer operator (the opposite of a reader) sends each document to FAST ESP for indexing.

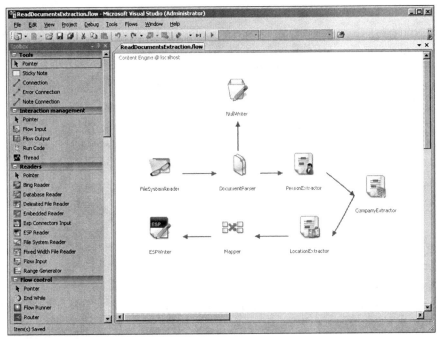

FIGURE 1-1 A sample CTS flow, shown in FAST Search Designer, for indexing files on disk (using the *FileSystemReader*) and enriching the documents by extracting people, companies, and locations into metadata.

Note that it was possible to use any legacy connectors, such as custom connectors developed for use with FAST ESP, with FSIS. Developers could choose to bypass CTS and connect to the internal ESP installation directly, or to use the FSIS Content Distributor Emulator (CDE), which provides an emulated ESP endpoint within CTS that legacy connectors could use—while also reaping the benefits of CTS.

Interaction management flows, or IMS flows, are similar in nature to the content transformation flows (CTS flows), but the set of available operators is quite different. Instead of reading documents from a source system, IMS provides several preexisting operators for calling out to other services, such as the *BingLookup* operator for searching Bing. There is also an *OpenSearchLookup* operator that enables FSIS to federate content from almost any search engine.

IMS flows also differ from CTS flows in the way they are executed. Indexing data can be either a "pull" or a "push" operation, depending on the source system; however, serving queries through an IMS flow is almost always a pull operation. This is where the Search Business Manager comes in handy.

Search Business Manager and IMS UI Toolkit   Search Business Manager is a web-based tool, using the SharePoint look and feel, for managing the wiring between the search application front-end and IMS flows. It contains functionality to map different parts of your search application to different flows, possibly depending on various conditions or on using several IMS flows from within the same search front end. It also contains functionality to conduct A/B testing and functionality for running different IMS flows at predetermined times.

FSIS was also bundled with IMS UI Toolkit, a set of out-of-the-box components and code samples to help web developers and designers create search applications backed by FSIS. You can extend these components with your own code as needed, which gives you a flying start for front-end development.

FSIS was designed for high-demand, public-facing search solutions, so it was extremely configurable to match demanding business needs. The additional licensing and deployment expenses required serious consideration when choosing it; however, when the search required a high level of configurability, FSIS could meet those needs.

The authors are anticipating most, if not all, of these extended capabilities of FSIS to make their way into FS4SP. The only question to be answered is how they will be bundled and licensed.

FSIA

FAST Search for Internal Applications (FSIA) was FAST ESP 5.3 with SP3 but licensed for internal use. As such, FSIA was nothing else than the pre-Microsoft ESP but without the complicated and often confusing features and performance-based license that were used before Microsoft moved FAST over to server-based licenses. This product and its features will not likely reappear in any form because its major capabilities will be covered completely in the next release of FS4SP.

FS4SP

FAST Search Server 2010 for SharePoint, the topic of this book, is a version of FAST ESP 5.*x* integrated with SharePoint. Much of the ESP product has been leveraged and integrated with a SharePoint administration. Because of this integration, some restrictions to the capabilities of FAST ESP were made when devising this product. However, there is a rich administration experience in FS4SP, and most of the core features of FAST are available.

Unique features of FS4SP are native SharePoint content crawling, administration from SharePoint, built-in Web Parts for an enhanced user experience, and support on the Microsoft platform. For SharePoint owners, FS4SP is the best search available at the lowest possible deployment cost.

SharePoint Search vs. Search Server Versions, and FS4SP

The out-of-the-box search in SharePoint has certainly improved greatly over the years and successive releases. Undoubtedly, Microsoft has learned a great deal from first having companies like FAST as competitors in the Enterprise Search space and subsequently having FAST as a subsidiary.

However, there are some major limitations to the standard search in SharePoint and some clear differences where FAST can deliver rich search and SharePoint alone cannot. Additionally, as you saw previously in this chapter, in all likelihood, the standard search index in SharePoint will be replaced in the upcoming version by the FAST core.

In any case, the search products available from Microsoft have some major differences. You're probably reading this book because you're considering FAST for your search needs. There are no fewer than four versions of search available from Microsoft, so you should be extremely careful to choose the one that fits your needs. See "What Should I Choose?," the final section of this chapter, for more guidance on choosing the correct version for you.

Because this book is intended to give you a single source for deploying and customizing FS4SP and is not a guide for SharePoint Search, we do not go into detail about the particulars of each version of Microsoft's search offerings. Alternatively, we just compare what versions of SharePoint Search can do in comparison to those of FS4SP.

Features at a Glance

Table 1-1 through Table 1-3 show what kind of features, experience, and capacity SharePoint and FS4SP provide.

TABLE 1-1 Core search features

Feature	SharePoint	FS4SP
Basic/site search	√	√
Scopes	√	√
Content processing		√
Property extraction	Limited	√
Property mapping	√	√
Relevancy tuning	Limited	√
Administration from SharePoint	√	√
Query federation	√	√
Multiple content sources	√	√
User context–driven search		√

TABLE 1-2 Search experience

Feature	SharePoint	FS4SP
Best bets	√	Visual
Property and rank profile sorting	Limited	√
Scopes	√	√
Query federation	√	√
Query suggestions	√	√
Similar results		√
User context–based promotions/demotions		√
Result refiners	Shallow	Deep

TABLE 1-3 Capacity

Feature	SharePoint	FS4SP
Allowable servers	Unlimited	Unlimited
Number of items in index	100 million	500 million+
Licensing	Per server + Client Access Licenses (CALs)	Per server + CALs

Scalability

Scalability is the first and most important consideration when investigating an enterprise-class search solution. Although most people are familiar with search thanks to the prevalence of global search using search engines such as Bing and Google, the processing power required to run them is often hard to imagine. For web search, where billions of webpages are served to millions of users continuously, the scale is vast. But for enterprise search, the scale can be from a few thousand items for a few hundred users to hundreds of millions of items for thousands of users. This scale gap has a great impact on both the needs of any given organization and the products that can be used. Luckily, as you have seen, Microsoft has an offering for just about every level in that scale. And the enterprise search solution that covers the widest spectrum of needs is FS4SP.

Naturally, if your organization is on the lower end of the scale, standard SharePoint Search may be sufficient. There are even options available that don't require licensing of Microsoft SharePoint Server. However, when your scale approaches certain levels, FS4SP will be a natural decision. Here are several factors to consider when determining what your scalability requirements are:

- Amount of content in SharePoint
- Amount of content in external content sources, including:
  - File Shares
  - Other document repositories

- Line of business (LOB) applications

- Web content

- Email

■ Predicted growth factor of each content source

The built-in SharePoint search is scalable to about 100 million indexed items. However, there are many reasons to move to FS4SP well before this threshold is reached. One hundred million seems like a lot of items, but consider the growing demand to index email, whether in Public Folders, in archive systems, or in private folders connected with a custom connector. The average employee may produce dozens and receive hundreds of email messages a day. Given that an employee receives 200 messages a day and you have 10,000 employees, after five years, the organization could have roughly 400 million email items alone.

Explanation of Features

So that you can better understand the differences between the search capabilities, we outline some unique capabilities of FS4SP. This list is by no means exhaustive, but rather an outline of the features we think are useful to consider.

Item Processing

Item processing is the mechanism by which crawled content is analyzed, modified, and enriched before it is stored in the search index. All search engines perform some sort of item processing between the crawl process and the indexing process. This allows them to take a stream of text and make some sense of it, eventually making it searchable. Different search products have different levels of complexity when it comes to how they process information. Sometimes, processing is simply dividing the text into words and storing those words in the database with a matching reference to the item in which they were found. Other times, such as with FS4SP, the process is much more complex and multi-staged. However, most do not allow for manipulation or customization of this item processing as FS4SP does. FS4SP item processing capabilities include mapping crawled properties such as physical documents or tagged properties to managed properties, identifying and extracting properties from unstructured and structured text data, and linguistics processing modules such as word stemming and language detection, among others. Crawled properties and managed properties are explained in Chapter 2, "Search Concepts and Terminology," and in Chapter 6, "Search Configuration."

In FS4SP, the item processing model is a staged approach. This staged approach is known as the *indexing pipeline* because the item's content passes through the stages as if it is passing through one linear unidirectional pipe. There is only one pipeline, and all content passes through this pipeline's various stages sequentially. Each stage performs its own task on the crawled content. Sometimes, a particular stage does not apply to the particular content and does not modify it; however, it is still passed through that particular stage.

The indexing pipeline cannot be modified in FS4SP. However, it can be configured in two important ways:

- You may map managed properties in the FAST Query Search Service Application to expose metadata for search.

- You may configure a particular stage of the pipeline to execute a custom process for extracting properties or some other task by using external code. What this means is that a stage cannot be added to the indexing pipeline, but there are stages that can be configured in FS4SP and stages that can call external code to add processing outside of the pipeline for that particular stage.

Note The indexing pipeline can be edited, but there is no official documentation on how to do this and it will leave your system in an unsupported state.

The indexing pipeline contains several default stages and some optional stages. Additionally, there is an extensibility stage where custom actions may be performed.

FS4SP performs the following fixed sequence of stages in its default indexing pipeline:

1. **Document Processing/Format Conversion** Documents are converted from their proprietary formats to plain text and property values by using IFilters or the advanced filter pack (if enabled).

2. **Language/Encoding Detection** The language or page encoding is detected either from the text or from metadata on the page or document.

3. **Property Extraction** Properties are extracted from the body text of items and included as crawled properties.

4. **Extensibility Stage** External code can be called to perform custom tasks on the text.

5. **Vectorizer** A "search vector" for terms is created, which shows a physical relationship to terms in the item and is used for "show similar" search functionality.

6. **Properties Mapper** Crawled properties are mapped to managed properties.

7. **Properties Reporter** Properties that are mapped are reported in the Property Mapper.

8. **Tokenizer** The stream of text received from items by the crawler is broken into individual words. Compound words are broken up into simpler terms.

9. **Lemmatizer** Individual words are broken into their lemmas and inflected forms are grouped together.

10. **Date/Time Normalizer** Various date and time formats are converted to a single format.

11. **Web Analyzer** Web content is scraped for HTML links and anchor text.

Figure 1-2 shows a diagram of these stages.

Additionally, there are a number of optional stages that can be enabled or disabled as needed:

- **Person Name Extractor**   A property extractor used specifically for identifying people's names and creating name properties from them.

- **XML Mapper**   A stage that maps properties from an XML file to crawled properties, allowing them to be enriched by custom values.

- **Offensive Content Filter**   A stage that can remove items that are deemed offensive or pornographic.

- **FFDDumper**   A stage that allows inspecting the data of items being processed in the indexing pipeline.

- **Whole Word Extractors and Word Part Extractors**   Enables you to automatically extract entities or concepts from the visible text content of an item.

- **Metadata Extraction**   A custom title extractor for Microsoft Word documents that force-generates titles from Word documents and ignores document title metadata. After SP1, this stage is actually "on" by default but may be turned off.

- **Search Export Converter**   The stage that calls the advanced filter pack for converting a large number of document formats.

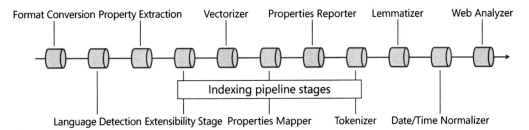

FIGURE 1-2 Stages of the FS4SP indexing pipeline.

Document Processing/Format Conversion

Document Processing is an essential stage to search indexing. Different file types are stored in different proprietary formats, and the content of those documents is not easily read by other programs. Some programs can open other formats, and some formats are based on standards that can be opened and read by other programs. However, to a search crawler, which is a relatively simple document reader, these formats are generally inaccessible. Therefore, either some built-in conversion process or an external library of converters is necessary to convert document formats into plain text that can be managed by the search indexing process.

Windows has a built-in feature called *IFilters*, which provides document converters for several standard Microsoft formats. SharePoint comes with an IFilter pack to handle all Microsoft Office documents. When invoked, IFilters convert the documents and store the text and some properties found in those documents in a cache on the server that is readable by the crawler. Additional IFilters can be downloaded for free (for example, Adobe PDF) or purchased from third-party vendors to handle a large number of document formats. Using IFilter for PDF is, however, not necessary because FS4SP comes with a built-in PDF converter.

FS4SP comes with an additional document processing library licensed from Oracle that is based on a document conversion library developed by a search vendor previously known as *Stellant*. The technology, known as *Outside In*, is what is known as the *Advanced Filter Pack for FS4SP* and is activated by enabling the Search Export Converter. Several hundred different file types are supported. See Chapter 9, "Useful Tips and Tricks," for a more detailed explanation and how to enable the Advanced Filter Pack.

Property Extraction

FS4SP has the capability to extract properties from item content. This extraction is an automatic detection tool for identifying particular text in an item as a type of information that may be used as a property. Previously, this was known as *entity extraction* in FAST jargon. FS4SP has three built-in property extractors: names (people), locations (physical), and companies (company names). The Names extractor is not enabled by default in FS4SP. This is because SharePoint does not rely on FS4SP for People Search and author properties are mapped from a separate crawled property. However, enabling this property extractor may be desirable to enrich social association to items.

Advanced Query Language (FQL)

FS4SP also supports an advanced query language known as FAST Query Language (FQL). This query language allows for more complicated search syntax and queries against the search index in order to facilitate more complicated searches such as advanced property and parametric search.

Duplicate Collapsing

During indexing, FS4SP generates a signature per item, which can be used to group identical items in the search results. The default behavior is to use the full extracted title and the first 1,024 characters from the text and then generate a 64-bit checksum. The checksum is used for the collapsing or grouping of the items. This default behavior will, in many cases, treat different items as the same because of the limited number of characters used. Fortunately, you can create your own checksum algorithm with a custom extensibility module and collapse on a managed property of your own choosing. See Chapter 9 for an example of how to implement this.

Linguistics

FS4SP has a strong multilingual framework. More than 80 languages are supported for a number of features, including automatic detection, stemming, anti-phrasing, and offensive content filtering. Any corpus with more than one language can benefit greatly from language handling. Supported features are described in the following list:

- **Language detection**   Many languages are automatically detected by FS4SP. This allows searches to be scoped by a specific language, providing users with a single language focus to filter out unwanted content.

- **Lemmatization**   This can expand queries by finding the root of a term based not only on the characters in the term but also on inflected forms of the term. Lemmatization allows the search engine to find content that may be relevant even if an inflected form has no other resemblance to the original term (for example, *bad* and *worse*, *see* and *saw*, or *bring* and *brought*).

- **Spell checking**   FS4SP supports two forms of spell-checking mechanisms. The first is a match against a dictionary. Terms entered into search are checked and potentially corrected against a dictionary for the specific language. In addition, spell checking is automatically tuned based on terms in the index.

- **Anti-phrasing**   Most search engines have a list of terms that are ignored, or *stop words*. Stop words are valuable to remove terms that carry only grammatical meaning such as *and*, *this*, *that*, and *or*, and for terms that are too common to be of searchable value (such as your company name). Anti-phrasing is more advanced compared to stop words. Phrases are removed as opposed to trimming single terms. This provides a much more accurate filtering because phrases are less ambiguous than single words and can be removed from the query more safely.

- **Property extraction**   The built-in property extractors for names and places function differently depending on the language detected. It is important to be language-sensitive to names, especially when dealing with different character sets. FS4SP supports language-specific property extraction for several languages.

- **Offensive content filtering**   Many organizations have compliance requirements for removing content that is not acceptable or becoming of the organization. Offensive content filtering prevents items that contain offensive words in the specific language from being indexed.

Table 1-4 outlines the supported features for each language.

TABLE 1-4 Linguistics features per language

Language	Language detection	Stemming	Spell checking: dictionary	Spell checking: tuned	Anti-phrasing	Property extraction	Offensive content filtering
Afrikaans	√						
Albanian	√						
Arabic	√	√	√	√	√	√	√
Armenian	√						
Azeri	√						
Bangla	√	√					
Basque	√						
Bosnian	√	√					

Language	Language detection	Stemming	Spell checking: dictionary	Spell checking: tuned	Anti-phrasing	Property extraction	Offensive content filtering
Breton	√						
Bulgarian	√	√		√			
Belarusian	√						
Catalan	√	√		√			
Chinese Simplified	√				√		√
Chinese Traditional	√				√		√
Croatian	√	√		√			
Czech	√	√	√	√	√		√
Danish	√	√	√	√	√		
Dutch	√	√	√	√	√	√	
English	√	√	√	√	√	√	√
Esperanto	√						
Estonian	√	√	√	√	√		
Faeroese	√						
Farsi	√						
Filipino	√						
Finnish	√	√	√	√	√		√
French	√	√	√	√	√	√	√
Frisian	√						
Galician	√						
Georgian	√						
German	√	√	√	√	√	√	√
Greek	√	√	√	√	√		
Greenlandic	√						
Gujarati	√	√					
Hausa	√						

Language	Language detection	Stemming	Spell checking: dictionary	Spell checking: tuned	Anti-phrasing	Property extraction	Offensive content filtering
Hebrew	√	√	√	√	√		
Hindi	√	√	√	√	√		√
Hungarian	√	√	√	√	√		
Icelandic	√	√		√	√		
Indonesian	√	√		√			
Irish Gaelic	√						
Italian	√	√	√	√	√	√	√
Japanese	√				√	√	√
Kannada	√	√					
Kazakh	√						
Kirghiz	√						
Korean	√	√	√	√	√		√
Kurdish	√						
Latin	√						
Latvian	√	√	√	√	√		
Letzeburgesch	√						
Lithuanian	√	√	√	√	√		√
Macedonian	√						
Malay	√	√		√			
Malayalam	√	√					
Maltese	√						
Maori	√						
Marathi	√	√					
Mongolian	√						
Norwegian	√	√	√	√	√	√	√
Pashto	√						

Language	Language detection	Stemming	Spell checking: dictionary	Spell checking: tuned	Anti-phrasing	Property extraction	Offensive content filtering
Polish	√	√	√	√	√		
Portuguese	√	√	√	√	√	√	√
Punjabi	√	√					
Rhaeto-Romance	√						
Romanian	√	√	√	√	√		
Russian	√	√	√	√	√	√	√
Sami Northern	√						
Serbian	√			√			
Slovak	√	√	√	√	√		
Slovenian	√	√		√			
Sorbian	√						
Spanish	√	√	√	√	√	√	√
Swahili	√						
Swedish	√	√	√	√	√		√
Tamil	√	√					
Telugu	√	√					
Thai	√						
Turkish	√	√	√	√	√		√
Ukrainian	√	√	√	√	√		
Urdu	√	√		√			
Uzbek	√						
Vietnamese	√						
Welsh	√						
Yiddish	√						
Zulu	√						

Refiners

Refiners, also known as *facets*, *filters*, or *drill-down categories*, is a feature of search whereby a list of common properties for a given result set are displayed alongside the result set; users may click these properties to isolate only items with that common property. This feature is becoming more common in both enterprise and site search solutions. The ability to narrow a result set based on item properties helps users to more easily find the exact information they are looking for by removing unwanted results and focusing on the more relevant information.

Although SharePoint supports a refinement panel, the refiners are shallow refiners. This means the number of items analyzed for common properties is limited based on the first 50 results by default, leaving out potential navigation routes in the result set. With FS4SP, refiners are deep refiners, where all items are analyzed and the refiner count is exact. Although only 10 results are displayed on a single result page, all possible results for the given query are analyzed for common properties, and the number of items with each property is displayed with an exact number. This level of accuracy can greatly improve the ability to isolate a single item out of thousands or hundreds of thousands of relevant hits.

What Should I Choose?

Many people would believe that scalability is the most important reason to choose FS4SP. However, although the FS4SP scaling capabilities are a core feature, there are several other factors that can lead you to FS4SP. For example, the power of item processing can be an essential element to making search work within your organization, allowing you to modify seemingly meaningless documents into purposeful business assets. Configurable ranking and the ability to query the index with FQL for custom search applications can mean the difference between search success and failure by allowing content to be queried and returned with more meaning than a plain search experience. And FS4SP performance capabilities can help avoid user frustration and drive adoption. Some of these factors were laid out earlier in Table 1-1 through Table 1-3 but can often be difficult to understand and see the value of. Therefore, the following sections describe some tools to help you decide whether FS4SP is the right choice for you.

First, you'll look at the core decisions for choosing FS4SP. Search is a vast area and many vendors sell solutions, many of which work with SharePoint. A clear advantage of FS4SP in this realm is its integration with SharePoint, its clear future in Microsoft, and ongoing support and development.

Evaluating Search Needs

Assuming that you understand your search requirements, the flowchart in Figure 1-3 will help you get a very rough idea of what product will suit your needs. The scorecard will help you evaluate the worth of each feature for your organization, and the cost estimator should help you get an idea of not just licensing costs, but also resource costs associated with each option. But as a precursor to that, look at some of the questions you should ask before deciding on those tools. Answering these questions honestly will help you use the tools provided.

Environment

The general environment plays a part when choosing a search solution. Consider the following questions when planning your search.

How many users do you have and how often do you expect each one to search?   More users with access to a portal does not always mean the need for more complex search. A common experience is that small groups of high-demand users (for example, an engineering team) will require a more complex search experience given a complex and large corpus.

What type of and how much content do you have?   Specific information that drives or is driven by business processes may require a more honed search experience. Finding the right document in thousands of similar documents is a different and more demanding experience than finding a unique document in a corpus of largely unrelated content. This specialization within business data can push the requirement for more sophisticated search experiences. Additionally, a relatively small corpus will not require such complex search needs because simple search can often make good matches in small document sets.

How can you make your users take action on the search results?   Data that has clear processes directly attached to it, such as workflows or form fulfillment, may require more specialized treatment. Data used largely for reference to complete exterior tasks or to produce reports is often well serviced by more basic search.

Where are you coming from and where do you want to go?   One of the largest motivations for improved enterprise search is poor experience with existing search. This is a good motivator. Obvious shortcomings should be addressed. The question to ask is, "What are the real shortcomings and what should be done to address these shortcomings?" More search functionality is not always the solution to poor content or faulty business processes.

How skilled are your users at searching?   Most users are not experienced beyond Bing or Google search, and you should be sensitive to that. With that said, a good, well-thought-out tool will be easy to adopt, and dedicated users will find clear advantage to improving their search skills. However, too much unfamiliarity can inhibit user adoption, and it is sometimes wise to deploy search features in a staged approach.

Corpus

The corpus, or collection of items, you are planning to index has to be considered when planning your search solution.

How much content do you have to search?   In addition to scalability concerns, the amount of content also surfaces concerns about findability. Many organizations enter a search project hoping to make *all* available data searchable. The web's success with a global search scale has given people the perception that "more is better" when it comes to search. But often, the opposite is true. A good principle is to make all *valuable* content searchable but also *only* valuable content searchable.

Many search solutions have crawl limitations and search performance considerations, and SharePoint is no exception. Although 100 million items may seem like a ludicrous amount, this number can be reached easily when you include all content repositories—especially if you include items such as email or database records in the index. Projected growth should be considered, and if the resulting number seems reachable within a chronological threshold (say, five years or the lifespan of the product), FS4SP will be necessary and should be considered early on to avoid growth and scale problems.

Does everything need to be searchable?   The old computer adage of Garbage In, Garbage Out (GIGO) is seldom as poignantly apparent as with search. So, you should consider carefully when deciding whether to include content sources. Additionally, you can create crawl rules to filter out unnecessary content from crawl operations. Reducing corpus size can both greatly improve search quality and reduce costs.

Are there multiple content sources?   Usually, organizations have more than just SharePoint to contend with. In addition, many people considering FS4SP are new to SharePoint. This means that other content sources almost always come into play. What these content sources may be (for example, file shares, email, Lotus Notes, and Documentum files) and how the data from those content sources is handled will play a large role in which product to choose.

How much and in what divisions is the different content being consumed?   Often, information makes more sense in a particular context. Information is created and divided to fit into different silos based on its purpose. Often, these divisions are removed during search crawling and not preserved in the search experience. Having a clear understanding of the natural divisions and the business processes behind these divisions can help determine how that information should be collected and eventually divided in search. The capabilities to crawl this content separately or make logical divisions when crawling undivided content can affect which product you require.

Content

After you identify the items you want to index, analyzing the content of the items is the next step in planning the search solution.

What is the quality of the content?   Content quality is a major consideration. Being able to process content at indexing can be a major influence when determining which product your search deployment will require. Some factors that determine content quality are: text quality (text or images), metadata quality (good titles, properties), freshness (age), correctness, completeness, and format (document types).

Is there rich metadata?   *Metadata* is data about data. Metadata is most commonly encountered as sets of simple terms or keywords that describe what a particular item is about. In SharePoint, metadata is usually referred to as *properties*. These can be physical document properties, such as document type or size; attached properties, such as title, date, and author; or associated properties from custom property definitions in SharePoint. Having rich metadata helps identify items that are not otherwise easily recognized based solely on their text content. Rich metadata can help improve search in a number of ways: by helping to improve the return of items without queried terms in their content, by improving ranking, by allowing for advanced parametric search queries, and by grouping items by common properties using refiners.

Having good metadata is rare, and unfortunately, the lack of good metadata almost always adversely affects search quality. Choosing a search solution that can automatically identify and expose metadata can improve search quality vastly and should be a serious consideration when deciding on what type of search solution to use. One caveat is that enriching items with metadata—whether by content editing or by content processing with search—is not a trivial or an inexpensive task. Luckily, content processing with FS4SP is much more economical and effective than the alternatives.

What document types are there?   Documents come in hundreds of different formats. Most software programs save their files in a proprietary format, which allows them to apply custom formatting, protect themselves from competition and piracy, and help the operating system associate the program and the documents. In addition, rapid changes in IT over the last few decades mean that information assets are now stored in a myriad of different file types. Being able to access these file types without mass conversion can be a critical search feature.

Investigating which file types are used and their relative value is an essential aspect to consider when choosing a search solution. Not all search engines can index all file types. Even the availability of conversion tools such as IFilters may fall short of some requirements. However, some file types, even though they exist, may not be of sufficient value to justify additional expense. Even in such cases, the existence of special file types can necessitate a more advanced product. FS4SP has a much broader range of file type conversion capabilities than is available with standard SharePoint Search, so specific attention to required file type conversion should be a key factor to consider. See the downloadable scorecard for help evaluating file type requirements.

 Note IFilters are components that can be called to convert documents from their original formats to plain text. See Chapter 2 for more information about IFilters.

Organization

The way content is organized also has a bearing on which search solution might be best suited for that content. You should consider the following issues when planning your search solution.

Does the content have an existing organization (taxonomy, site structure)?   Well-organized content can help greatly with findability. In some cases, well-organized sites with thousands of items may not even require search. But when a site reaches a certain size threshold, even good organization becomes less useful in finding information, and search and automatic classification become essential.

Having a good taxonomy or model for classifying content can also help greatly with findability. Tagging items provides content with richer meaning and can improve findability. If your organization has a good structure and taxonomy, out-of-the-box search will function much better. However, if either or both of these are lacking, a search solution such as FS4SP that can automate tagging and classification will help greatly.

How difficult is it to navigate to the most relevant content vs. search? A key factor that leads users to the search box is poor navigation. Coupled with corpus size, navigation quality is a major factor for the popularity of search. Instead of ignoring this effect, it is wise to embrace search as a viable alternative and improve it to empower the users. In cases where navigation is obviously frustrating, improvements in search are logical. Sites with poor or complex navigation should consider search enhancements.

Decision Flowchart

When evaluating whether you should move up to FS4SP from the built-in SharePoint Search, you should ask yourself some key questions. Figure 1-3 shows a flowchart to aid you in the decision based on key functionality offered in FS4SP.

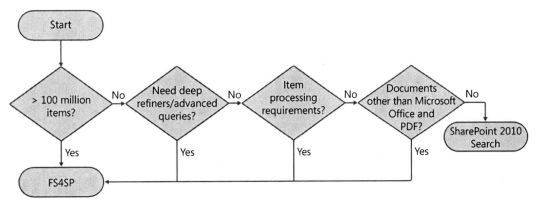

FIGURE 1-3 Decision flowcharts can be used to pick the right product.

Features Scorecard

As an additional aid, we created a scorecard (see Table 1-5) to help you determine which features are valuable for your organization.

 More Info A more complex scorecard form is available from the authors' website at *http://www.fs4spbook.com/scorecard*.

To use the scorecard, fill in your specific determined need for each feature in the My Score column by entering a value on a scale from 0–3, where 0 represents no need, and 3 represents an acute need. Tally your score and compare it with our estimate of each product's functionality. The downloadable scorecard provides additional sheets to help you estimate need for content sources, file types, and languages.

TABLE 1-5 Scorecard for features

Feature	Explanation	SharePoint Score	FS4SP	My Score
Content collection		**1 to 3**		
Crawl SharePoint	Is crawling SharePoint content a priority?	3	3	
Crawl webpages	Are there webpages other than those in SharePoint to crawl, perhaps from an internal website or a public website?	1	3	
Crawl Lotus Notes	Do you need to crawl Lotus Notes?	1	2	
Crawl databases	Do you have database content to crawl?	1	3	
Crawl Documentum	Do you need to crawl Documentum?	1	2	
Crawl other LOB systems	Do you have other LOB systems to crawl?	1	1	
Crawl CMS	Do you have Microsoft Content Management Server (MCMS) 2002 or Vignette to crawl?	1	1	
Content processing				
File types*	Do you need to index content from other critical document types besides Office?	1	3	
Property extraction	Do you want to extract properties from unstructured document content such as company names and locations? Or something more?	0	2	
Custom processing	Do you have a custom process that you want applied to the content to enrich it?	0	2	
Reorder the indexing pipeline	Do you need to reorder the indexing pipeline or add steps in the pipeline?	0	0	

Feature	Explanation	SharePoint	FS4SP	My Score
		Score		
Language handling				
Language detection	Do you have more than one language? Do they need to be detected and searched separately?	0	2	
Stemming	Will expanding queries by searching for stemmed forms be valuable for different languages?	0	2	
Spell checking	Will spell checking in different languages help end users?	0	2	
Anti-phrasing	Would removing terms or phrases that are not valuable to search improve result relevancy?	0	2	
Offensive content filtering	Do you have a requirement to remove offensive terms from the search content?	0	2	
Property extraction	Do you need language-specific property extraction?	0	2	
UI				
Best bets	Do you want text best bets at the top of search results for a given query?	1	1	
Visual best bets	Is there significant value in displaying best bets with images?	0	1	
Sorting	Will sorting on properties or rank profiles make it easier to find information in the search results?	0	1	
Scope filtering	Will it make sense to divide the content for different groups or different search experiences?	1	2	
Context-driven search	Is it a requirement that different users have different search experiences such as custom best bets, result promotions, or demotions based on user groups?	1	3	
Query federation	Does other content from an external system need to be federated into the result page at search time?	1	1	
Query suggestions	Will users benefit from having their queries completed?	1	1	

Feature	Explanation	SharePoint Score	FS4SP	My Score
Similarity search	Would finding similar items in the result set be of value?	0	1	
Result refiners	Will refining on the result list be useful to find the correct result? Can numbered deep refiners have a greater impact than shallow refiners?	1	3	
Document preview	Can seeing an image of the first page of Word documents and a full preview of Microsoft PowerPoint documents help identify them in the result list?	0	2	
People Search	Will searching for people be valuable?	3	3	
Administration				
Administer from SharePoint	Is easy, code-free administration from SharePoint required?	3	2	
Microsoft-based technology	Do you need to stick to Microsoft technology, avoiding other platforms?	3	2	
		25	56	

Cost Estimator

FS4SP is licensed on a per-server instance basis. This means that Microsoft counts a single server, whether physical or virtual, as a licensable entity regardless of the hardware configuration. In other words, each running instance of FS4SP requires a server license. Additionally, each user accessing the FS4SP capabilities requires a SharePoint Enterprise Client Access License (ECAL), whether that is in a search center or in a search-based application that accesses a search server.

You can use Table 1-6 as a cost estimator. This estimator will help give you a rough idea of the costs associated with deploying each search technology. All prices are in U.S. dollars and are estimates for farms of different-sized deployments. Where one server is listed, the price is for one server. When two or more servers are listed, the price is multiplied to match the number of servers. Along with other information in this chapter, this table should give you a rough idea of what the price for the type of farm you require will be.

Note These prices are up to date as of August 2011 and are based on a partial retail cost estimator located at *https://partner.microsoft.com/US/licensing/40141877*. Discounts are usually available for government agencies, nonprofit organizations, educational institutions, and enterprise customers. Please contact Microsoft for exact pricing.

Prices for licensing and Microsoft Software Assurance (SA) are listed separately. There is usually a discount when you purchase these together, but we listed them separately so as not to confuse consecutive year costs and total cost of ownership calculations.

In Table 1-6, SharePoint Server 2010 is listed simply as a comparison to what a stand-alone SharePoint Search Server deployment would cost. Naturally, customers using FS4SP will already have SharePoint licensed and will likely have sufficient CALs for all users.

Pricing for FSIS and FSIA is not included as of the time of this writing (August 2011). We were informed by Microsoft that they no longer sell FSIA or FSIS. We expect FS4SP will be expanded to include any missing functionality.

TABLE 1-6 Cost estimator

	SharePoint Server 2010		FS4SP	
	Licensing costs	Maintenance costs	Licensing costs	Maintenance costs
Minimal environment				
1 search server	$15,961	$7,981	$22,113	$11,057
Totals:	$15,961	$7,981	$22,113	$11,057
1st-year total cost of ownership (TCO)		$23,942		$33,170
Small farm				
1 index server*	$15,961	$7,981	$22,113	$11,057
1 query server	$15,961	$7,981	$22,113	$11,057
Totals:	$31,922	$15,962	$44,226	$22,114
1st-year TCO		$47,844		$66,340
Medium farm				
2 index servers	$31,922	$15,962	$44,226	$22,114
2 query servers	$31,922	$15,962	$44,226	$22,114
Totals:	$63,844	$31,924	$88,452	$44,228
1st-year TCO		$95,768		$132,680

	SharePoint Server 2010		FS4SP	
	Licensing costs	Maintenance costs	Licensing costs	Maintenance costs
Large farm				
4 index servers	$63,844	$31,924	$88,452	$44,228
4 query servers	$63,844	$31,924	$88,452	$44,228
Totals:	$127,688	$63,848	$176,904	$88,456
1st-year TCO:		$191,536		$265,360
1 CAL	$83	$42	$83	$42
Internet connector	40,000		40,000	

* FS4SP uses Index Servers but requires SharePoint to handle the crawl mechanism. SharePoint Server 2010 uses a crawl server and stores the index on the Query Server.

Conclusion

This chapter reviewed the history of FAST, both as a company and as a product. You've seen a brief overview of the development of the product and how it achieved its present form for SharePoint. We made some predictions about where we think the product is heading and what you, as a customer, should expect, which may help prepare you for managing your solution today and prepare for the future.

The chapter explained the different search products available from Microsoft and provided a brief overview of the standard versions of SharePoint Search. You should now have a good idea of what FS4SP can do and how it differs from standard SharePoint Search and other available versions of FAST.

Finally, the chapter explained many of the unique features that FS4SP makes available, and provided several tools to help you determine whether FS4SP is the right choice for your organization.

## CHAPTER 2

Search Concepts and Terminology

After completing this chapter, you will be able to

- Understand how the term *relevancy* applies to search engines.

- Understand the terminology used to describe search architecture.

- Understand search engine features such as linguistic handling and query syntax.

The field of search consists of several key concepts. People who work with Microsoft FAST Search Server 2010 for SharePoint (FS4SP) or any other search engine should know the complete data flow: from retrieving content, enriching and organizing it into searchable pieces, to displaying it for end users using either manual or automated queries. Understanding how content is collected can help you debug problems with search quality and determine the applicability and value of adding content to the corpus.

You should also understand how the quality of search can be improved by processing unstructured text, enriching that text, and by associating it with metadata. Knowing these processes and concepts can help you to implement and optimize a search solution with FS4SP more effectively.

This chapter outlines the basic concepts of Enterprise Search engines and introduces the key concepts for understanding how a search engine works. It also investigates the concepts that are unique to FAST and how they have been merged with Microsoft SharePoint to create FS4SP.

Overview

The goal of any search engine is simple: For any given query, the search engine should list the result(s) that the user is looking for at the top of the result list. Unfortunately, accomplishing that goal is much more difficult than it seems. As a result, search engines rely on a number of complex processes and features to achieve the best result for any query. Understanding *relevancy*—how items are considered relevant and eventually ranked in a result set—will help you determine how to tune FS4SP to achieve the goal of placing the best results at the top of the result list.

All search engines have two main operations: content processing and query processing. *Content processing* includes content collection, content enrichment, and indexing. *Query processing* includes receiving queries from the users, enriching the queries with additional query parameters or logical delineation, matching result items in the search index, and returning the result set to the end user.

To achieve the goal of relevant results, both query processing and content processing enrich the content, the queries, and the process of matching the queries in the index. To understand how these work together, let's first look at relevancy.

Relevancy

Relevancy is a measure of precision in a search engine and refers to how accurately the returned results match the user's query and intent. Users who search for a given term expect to see the item they are looking for or an item containing the information they are looking for at the top of the result list. They consider useful matches as relevant. Relevancy tuning techniques can improve precision by ranking the matches in the result set in a manner that more accurately matches the user's intent. Relevancy is calculated using a number of factors and is determined by the item's rank in the result set.

Recall and Precision

Recall and precision are two factors that determine the quality and effectiveness of a search engine. *Recall* refers to the number of results a search engine returns for a specific query, and *precision* refers to how precisely the results match the search user's intent. You must make a compromise between recall and precision. If recall is too large, you essentially flood the result set with noise, and precision suffers. On the other hand, when recall is too small, you run the risk of missing useful results, so the item(s) the user is looking for may not appear in the result set; again, precision suffers. The goal of any search engine is to get adequate recall while giving high precision so that, for any given query, the correct result is at the top of the search results.

You can see the tradeoff between recall and precision in Figure 2-1, where the corpus is represented as the total body of all items and the result set is the set of retrieved items. The items returned in the result set consist of a set of matches to the specific query. The search engine relies on the query to return items that match the user's intentions. Items that are relevant may not match the given query, and irrelevant items may match that query. Increasing the number of items in the retrieved result set improves recall but can hamper precision; adding more items and increasing the size of the result set effectively reduces the overlap of relevant items and retrieved items. For example, if a user searches for the term *job*, a search engine will usually return all items where the term *job* appears. However, relevant items may exist that use the terms *jobs*, *occupation*, or *career* instead. Likewise, the term *job* may appear in items that do not match the user's goal of finding employment. Recall can be improved by including terms that are considered synonyms (*career*, *occupation*) or by expanding the query with other methods, such as stemming (*jobs*). But this may also introduce results that the search user never intended to be included, and may thus reduce precision.

You can choose from several methods to improve recall and precision in the search index. You can also add features that users can use to expand queries or filter result sets, enabling the users to adjust recall and precision themselves. This chapter explains these features and discusses, where possible, how these features and methods improve either recall or precision or affect the balance of the two.

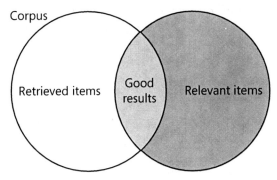

FIGURE 2-1 An overlap of retrieved items and relevant items represents good results.

Improving the quality of the content to be searched can help the search engine improve both recall and precision. The old computer adage of "Garbage In, Garbage Out" also applies to a search engine, which relies on indexed content to return an appropriate result set. *Item processing* is the process of enriching the crawled content before it is indexed. Several different operations are applied during item processing in FS4SP, some of which are optional. These stages detect language, separate text streams into words, extract metadata, and expand terms, among other tasks.

Processing the content before indexing takes place can add important information to the items in the index. This improves recall and supports more precise matches in the result set, for example, expanding a product number to the full product name.

Query Expansion

Query expansion techniques improve recall by expanding the search term or terms based on specific rules to find more possible matches in the corpus and return them in the result set. Some standard techniques are as follows:

- **Lemmatization**   This is a method by which terms are expanded based on their *lemma* (the canonical form of the term). By finding the lemma, the search engine can associate all inflections of the term and add those to the index. In this way, for example, the term *fishy* can be morphed into the lemma *fish*, enabling the search to match *fishing, fishes, fished*, and so on. This expands the result set to include items containing any of the associated terms. Lemmatization can expand queries beyond the literal values of the text because it can identify lemmas that don't actually appear in the given search term. For example, the lemma for the term *better* is *good*. Contrast this with *stemming*, which merely substitutes endings on an identified term root (such as *run, runs, running*—but not *ran*).

> **Note** Because of a common API with SharePoint search, FS4SP lemmatization is referred to as *stemming* in TechNet documentation. FS4SP always performs lemmatization during configuration, even though it uses the term *stemming*.

- **Synonyms**   These are an effective way to expand queries by associating known terms that are the same or similar to those in the query. This kind of expansion can be used to associate true synonyms or to correct spelling mistakes or simple misunderstandings about the content. Jargon can often be replaced with accepted terms and common language usage, and organizational terminology can be aligned.

- **Best bets**   These are promoted results on the SharePoint Search result page. Best bets are usually a link to the content that the site collection administrator thinks is best for the particular search term. The link and a description are placed at the top of the result page for a given query.

FS4SP takes this concept a step forward by allowing the site collection administrator to use a visual best bet—that is, a link and description with an image or some other HTML content (see Figure 2-2). This type of result is much more eye-catching for end users, and can help a great deal to lead them to the promoted content.

FIGURE 2-2 A visual best bet for FS4SP.

Corpus

Corpus is the Latin term for *body*. In search engine terminology, it refers to all items to be indexed. Items may be documents such as Microsoft Word or Microsoft PowerPoint, Adobe PDF documents, webpages, text files, rich text format files, or any number of other file formats. They may also be records from tables in a database or other content captured through Business Connectivity Services (BCS) in SharePoint. Each one of these unique files or pages and all of its associated metadata and security information is considered to be an item in the corpus.

Rank Tuning

Ranking is the method by which a value is applied to a given item to place it in a position of relevance in the result set. The ranking value is applied with a mathematical algorithm against the content of the item and its associated metadata. In FS4SP, several methods can be used for modifying the ranking values of items in a result set. Two of these methods are static rank tuning and dynamic rank tuning, discussed in the following sections.

Static rank tuning *Static rank* is the rank value applied to items in the index independent of the specific query. This is also known as *quality rank*. Four factors are taken into consideration, by default, to determine this rank:

- URL depth rank

- Doc rank

- Site rank

- Hardwired boost (HW boost)

URL depth rank gives a higher ranking value to more shallow items—that is, items that have a shorter URL with few slashes (/). The number of slashes roughly indicates how many clicks a user had to make from the entry point of the site to get to the content. How close an item is to the top of the site may be a good indication of value because users typically organize important content near the entry level of the page and store less important content in deeper libraries and folders. *Doc rank* is a Google PageRank–like evaluation that gives higher value to items that have a larger number of links pointing to it. Similarly, *site rank* gives additional weighting based on the number of links pointing to items on a site. Finally, *HW boost* is a default item property for adding quality rank. Rank values can be tuned for static rank by using Windows PowerShell to add or remove static rank values.

> **More Info** See Chapter 6, "Search Configuration," for an example of modifying the static rank of the rank profile. For more information about static rank tuning, go to *http://technet.microsoft.com/en-us/library/ff453906.aspx*.

Dynamic rank tuning The *dynamic ranking value* is calculated based on the query terms and their relation to the items in the result set. The factors taken into consideration are managed property context, proximity weight, managed property field boost, anchor text weight, click-through weight, and stop-word thresholds.

> **More Info** For more information about dynamic rank tuning, go to *http://technet.microsoft.com/en-us/library/ff453912.aspx*.

Linguistics

To make sense of languages, search engines perform a number of language-specific tasks on the data as it is being indexed. FS4SP has several features that break text streams into language-specific words; recognize those languages; expand them with lemmatization; and apply anti-phrasing, spell-checking, and synonyms.

FS4SP can automatically recognize 80 different languages in all common document encodings. The detected language is then used to further process the text and apply language-specific rules to it, such as property extraction and offensive language filtering.

More Info For more information about linguistic features, go to *http://technet.microsoft.com/en-us/library/ff793354.aspx.*

Tokenization *Tokenization* is an important element for identifying terms in a search engine. The crawler delivers a stream of information to the indexing pipeline. The job of the indexing pipeline is to make sense of that information and make it storable to in the search engine. *Tokenization* is the process of breaking apart the stream of text received from the document converters and identifying individual terms. Depending on the language detected, the stream of text picked up by the crawler may be tokenized (broken into unique words) in a different manner.

Keyword rank *Keyword rank* boosts the value of specific documents when a certain keyword is searched for. This can be done by specifying keywords and assigning document and site promotions to the keyword.

Document promotion is a useful and effective method of forcing ranking on specific items for specific keywords. Alternatively, best bets can be used to place a specific hit or information above the result list.

More Info See more information about best bets in the "Query Expansion" section earlier in this chapter. For an example of document promotions, see the section "Keyword, Synonym, and Best Bet Management" in Chapter 6. For information about keyword rank tuning, go to *http://technet.microsoft.com/en-us/library/ff453900.aspx.*

Rank Profiles

Rank profiles are a part of the FS4SP index schema that provides a mechanism for defining how ranking values for each item in the result set is determined. FS4SP has a default Rank Profile with settings that may be adjusted by using Windows PowerShell (see Figure 2-3). New Rank Profiles may be created with Windows PowerShell and custom weights applied to a number of components, including freshness, proximity, authority, query authority, context, and managed properties. A number of rank profiles may be created and exposed for the end user to choose from depending on their search intent.

```
Administrator: Microsoft FAST Search Server 2010 for SharePoint          _ □ ×
PS C:\temp> $RankProfile = Get-FASTSearchMetadataRankProfile -Name default
PS C:\temp> $RankProfile.GetQualityComponents()


ManagedPropertyReference : hwboost
Weight                   : 0

ManagedPropertyReference : docrank
Weight                   : 70

ManagedPropertyReference : siterank
Weight                   : 100

ManagedPropertyReference : urldepthrank
Weight                   : 100


PS C:\temp>
```

FIGURE 2-3 Viewing the default rank profile with Windows PowerShell.

Note Overall, the ranking algorithms applied by default with FS4SP are very good and require little tuning. They are a built to return the best results for the greatest variety of searches. Rank tuning in FS4SP is intended for well-thought-out, advanced search scenarios.

SharePoint Components

An FS4SP installation, naturally, relies on and requires SharePoint. Most readers already know and understand most of the core concepts of SharePoint before looking into FS4SP. However, knowing SharePoint or how to take advantage of its other capabilities is not a requirement to use FS4SP as an Enterprise Search solution. Therefore, the topics in this section define some of the core concepts of SharePoint that FS4SP relies on.

Web Front End

A *web front end* (WFE) is a SharePoint term used to describe a server with a web application role. For the most part, WFEs are web servers that handle user requests and deliver web content for the GUI, in addition to delivering other requests to the appropriate service applications in SharePoint. However, a WFE server can host other server roles if necessary. A WFE can also be set as a dedicated server for handling requests from the crawler. In such a case, the WFE should be excluded from the Network Load Balancer, and the crawl server should be set to crawl only the WFE. In large deployments, a dedicated set of WFE servers can be used for crawling.

More Info The term *web front end* is not an official Microsoft term and is no longer used in Microsoft documentation since Microsoft Office SharePoint Server 2007 (MOSS). However, the term is still widely used in the SharePoint community and is an accepted term to refer to servers with the web application role. For more information about servers with the web application role, go to *http://technet.microsoft.com/en-us/library/cc261752.aspx*.

Central Administration

Central Administration is the administrative interface of SharePoint. It is the central location for modifying and monitoring most operations of the SharePoint farm. For FS4SP, Central Administration displays the FAST Query Search Service Application (SSA) and FAST Content SSA. Central Administration is a SharePoint Site Collection itself with preconfigured menus for settings pages. Figure 2-4 shows the SharePoint Central Administration site.

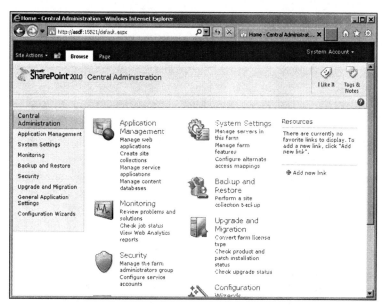

FIGURE 2-4 SharePoint Central Administration.

Search Service Applications

In SharePoint, service applications control much of the service-based functionality in a SharePoint farm. In SharePoint Search, the Search Service Application handles crawling, indexing, and querying of its own search index. In FS4SP, because we are connecting to an external search farm and because the People Search capability is still handled by a SharePoint index, two Search Service Applications need to be provisioned to make search work. See Chapter 4, "Deployment," for more details about the following two SSAs:

- **FAST Query Search Service Application (FAST Query SSA)** The FAST Query Search Service Application hosts the query processing part of FS4SP search in addition to a separate index for People Search. Depending on whether search is being submitted from the People Search scope or from another scope, the FAST Query SSA directs the query to the appropriate index. If the search is directed to FS4SP, the QR Proxy takes the query and handles it on the FS4SP farm, passing it to the QR Server after resolving security claims.

- **FAST Content Service Application (FAST Content SSA)** The FAST Content Service Application handles the crawling of content sources via the built-in connectors. The content crawled by the FAST Content SSA is passed to the content distributor on the FS4SP farm for processing and indexing.

Federated Search Object Model

The *Federated Search Object Model* is an application programming interface designed to query and return results from multiple search engines. Search Centers in SharePoint use this query API when executing search queries. Federated Search Object Model usage is explained in Chapter 8, "Querying the Index."

Query Web Service

To support remote access by client applications, SharePoint—and therefore, FS4SP—also supports SOAP Web Service access to the Query Object Model via the Query Web Service. When SharePoint is installed, the Query Web Service can be found at *http://server/[site collection/]_vti_bin/search.asmx*.

The Query Web Service can allow external applications to pass a standard XML-based query to the Query Object Model and receive results. This is especially powerful for integrating legacy applications and external systems with FS4SP.

 More Info For more information about using the Query Web Service, see Chapter 8 and go to *http://msdn.microsoft.com/en-us/library/ee872313.aspx*.

Query RSS Feed

An RSS feed is provided for very simple queries to the Query Object Model. The RSS feed takes a simple search query and returns a result set by using the RSS standard. This standard may also be called to apply a simple federated search from one farm to another.

Query Object Model

The Query Object Model is the core object model that passes the query on to the SSA. The keywords and any attributes needed to satisfy the search are executed using the *KeywordQuery* class. Figure 2-5 shows a diagram of the path the query takes to the Query Object Model and beyond.

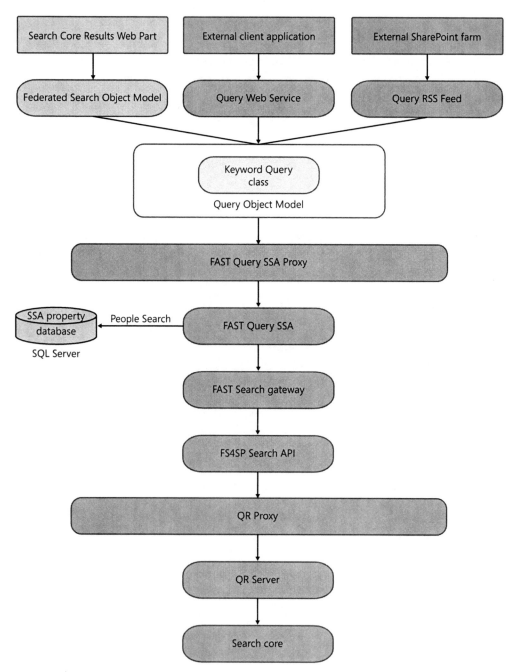

FIGURE 2-5 The query flow in FS4SP.

Web Parts

SharePoint uses Web Parts in its webpages to display content, retrieve information from users, and allow for interaction with the various functions of the platform. Web Parts are essentially web-based applications that are ASP.NET server controls embedded into Web Part zones in SharePoint. The Search Centers (both FS4SP and standard search) in SharePoint use a number of Web Parts that interact with the FAST Query SSA to query the index and display results, refiners, sorting mechanisms, and a variety of other search features.

The most important Web Part in an FS4SP Search Center is the Search Core Results Web Part, which handles both sending queries to the query mechanisms and displaying the results returned to the Search Center. The Search Core Results Web Part sends the user's query via the Federated Search Object Model, which in turn sends it to the Query Object Model, which passes it to the FAST Query SSA, which then sends it on to FS4SP. A detailed diagram showing the path of the query is shown in Figure 2-6.

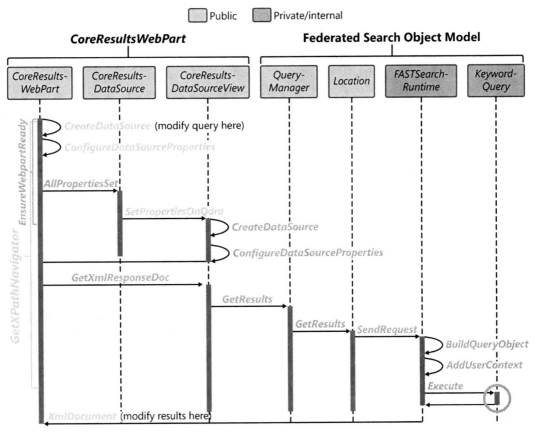

FIGURE 2-6 The path a query and result set take from the Search Core Results Web Part to FS4SP. (Image courtesy of Thomas Svensen.)

People Search

SharePoint has a feature-rich, built-in expertise and People Search functionality. This functionality is built not only on imported users from a directory service but also from enriched user information from SharePoint MySites. Therefore, SharePoint People Search is used in FS4SP; a separate people index that uses FS4SP is not available.

It is the utilization of the SharePoint People Search capability that requires two separate Search Service Applications in an FS4SP deployment. The FAST Content SSA is used for crawling content sent to the FS4SP farm; the FAST Query SSA crawls people content by using the SharePoint index and directs queries appropriately (either to the FS4SP farm or to the SharePoint index for People Search queries).

Content Processing

Content processing includes all the parts of the search engine that perform the collection, enrichment, and indexing of the items in the corpus.

Content Sources

Content sources are crawler definitions that specify the type of content to be crawled and where crawling should begin. A single content source may have a number of start addresses but only one kind of content is defined. That is, if you choose a SharePoint content source, only SharePoint sites can be crawled by adding start addresses to them; if you choose a file share content source, only addresses of file shares are crawled. This is because the content sources define which code is used to request the content from that source. Content sources are sometimes referred to as *connectors*, but connectors are actually the binaries that are executed when accessing the source systems defined in the content sources. FS4SP has built-in connectors that are set in the content source when it is created. After creating a content source in the FAST Content SSA in SharePoint, you can add or remove start addresses but you may not change the connector type.

> **Note** Content sources should not be confused with Content Collections. *Content Collections* are logical separations of content in the index where the content is tagged as belonging to a specific collection. Read more about content sources in Chapter 5, "Operations."

Crawling and Indexing

Although often used interchangeably, crawling and indexing are two separate stages for a search engine. *Crawling* is the process in which requests are made to content sources and the received content is collected and passed on for further processing. For example, in the case of a web crawler, a request is sent asking a web server for the webpage, the same way a browser would request the page. The retrieved data consists of all the information the web server returns, including the HTML content and HTTP headers from the web server. For other content sources, such as databases or a document management system, a query is made to the content source and whatever is returned by the source system is passed on by the crawler for processing and indexing. Depending on the logic of the connector to the content source, the crawled item can include metadata.

Indexing

Indexing is the process of organizing the extracted terms from the content and storing them in a searchable index with references to the source documents or pages. FS4SP has an intermediary stage called *Item Processing*, which implements a number of stages known as the *indexing pipeline*. This pipeline is where the documents are converted, broken into individual terms, recognized for language, enriched with metadata, and associated with properties, among several other stages.

The type of content indexed depends on what content sources can be effectively crawled and if the content received from those content sources can be converted into storable data. All collected content is effectively normalized into plain text terms, properties, and document references, which are then stored in the index. So, to be able to index content, the content must first be collected by a content source connector or protocol handler and then processed in the indexing pipeline.

Federated Search

Federated Search is the method by which results from another, external search engine are displayed on the result page together with the result set of a search engine. In many cases, it would be ideal for the federated results to be combined with the existing result set and normalized for ranking. But this would require a benchmark value for both indexes, so usually federated results are displayed side by side with the core results.

Federated search in FS4SP supports the OpenSearch 1.1 standard. This standard defines an XML format by which search results should be delivered and is supported by most global search engines and popular websites with search capabilities, for example, Bing. A noteworthy exception is Google, which does not expose an OpenSearch interface as of this writing. A Federated Search using Bing as the source is shown in Figure 2-7.

 More Info For more information about OpenSearch, go to *http://www.opensearch.org*.

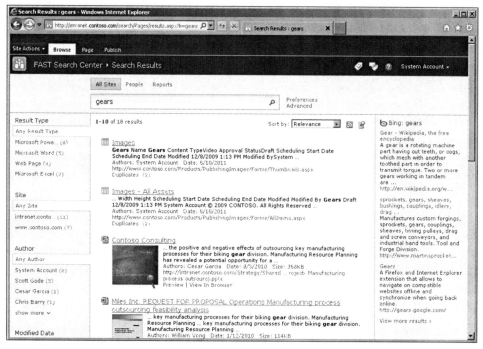

FIGURE 2-7 An example of a Federated Search result from Bing alongside the search result from FS4SP.

Document Processor

The *document processor* takes the content that the crawler has collected and sent via the content distributor and organizes it into searchable text by sending the content through the indexing pipeline. As such, the document processor is the mechanism that pushes items through the pipeline in which different processors perform different, specific tasks on the content. Document processors can perform many tasks, such as extracting text from files, breaking the text into words, identifying languages, and extracting entities. By the end of the indexing pipeline, several unique processors are passed and the text is in a format that can be stored in the index and made searchable.

Documents can be converted using IFilters or some other document conversion filter. The IFilter interface is a mechanism for handling document conversion filters that are built into Windows operating systems. IFilters themselves are either added with a search engine like those installed by the Microsoft Office Filter Pack or added individually from third-party vendors. They can be called to convert a variety of document types. FS4SP comes with additional document conversion filters in the Advanced Filter Pack, which can be enabled via Windows PowerShell.

> **More Info** For more information about the IFilter interface, go to *http://msdn.microsoft.com/en-us/library/ms691105*.

FIXML

After the crawled items run through the document processors in the indexing pipeline, intermediate XML files with a data structure containing items prepared for indexing are created. The XML file is in an internal format called *FIXML*, which is described in detail at *http://msdn.microsoft.com/en-us/library/ee628758(office.12).aspx*. All data and metadata about the items are present in the files.

The FIXML files are stored below *<FASTSearchFolder>\data\data_fixml* and the files are processed by the indexing component in FS4SP.

Indexing Dispatcher

The Indexing Dispatchers route the processed items to Index servers. A dispatcher is required because an FS4SP installation may distribute the index over several servers. The index dispatcher needs to know which server to send which items to.

Metadata

Metadata is data about data, that is, information that describes another piece of information. Generally, metadata appears as properties or meta tags that describe an item. A simple example is a keywords meta tag on a webpage. The keywords are placed in the meta tag in the HTML of the page to let search engines understand, in a few words, what the webpage is about.

Metadata can come from several different sources. *Physical* metadata is data about the item that accompanies the item and is often reported by the source system. This can be file type, file size, mime type, or date. Defined metadata can come from within the document or in files or properties associated with the item in the source system. For example, SharePoint has columns associated with every document in a document library. Custom columns can also be added to extend associated properties. FS4SP indexes this metadata in addition to any metadata found on the document.

Another type of potential metadata is *extracted properties* (also known as *entities*). These are properties that are extracted from the body of the document or item. Properties such as person names or place names are common extracted properties.

Any metadata that is picked up by the crawler is stored as crawled properties. This does not make the metadata automatically searchable. In order for metadata to be searchable, either it must be mapped from a crawled property to a managed property, or the crawled property has to be marked as searchable by itself. This is done in the FAST Query SSA in SharePoint Central Administration or with Windows PowerShell. For more information about mapping properties, see Chapter 6.

Index Schema

An index schema is a model of how the index is created and what elements are part of that model. FS4SP has four basic parts to the index schema. These are crawled properties, managed properties, full-text indexes, and rank profiles. The diagram shown in Figure 2-8 illustrates the hierarchy of these parts in the index schema.

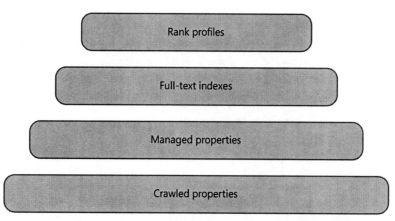

FIGURE 2-8 A hierarchical overview of the key concepts of the index schema.

A *crawled property* is any document property that FS4SP knows about. It might be a column from a database, the last modified date of a Microsoft Excel spreadsheet, or a title from a crawled blog post—in short, any document metadata that has entered FS4SP during content crawling or that has been extracted in the indexing pipeline. As such, these crawled properties are not yet available in the index and are not searchable. They are simply what they are called: crawled. However, you can set a flag on the crawled property to make it searchable from the full-text index. This is default behavior for all SharePoint columns.

Managed properties, on the other hand, are available in the index and are searchable. These properties are chosen from the set of crawled properties and are made members of the index. After mapping managed properties from crawled properties, you can use managed properties to construct targeted queries, use them for sorting, or use them as refiners.

A *full-text index* is actually a property containing many managed properties. Indeed, in previous FAST technology, it was referred to as a *composite field*. A full-text index is what FS4SP uses behind the scenes when you run an untargeted query. Just like you can map crawled properties into managed properties, you define a full-text index by mapping managed properties into it. You also set different levels of importance on each managed property that you map into a full-text index. These levels are used when FS4SP is calculating a given item's relevance against a certain search query.

The last key concept of the index schema is the *rank profile*. A rank profile is referenced by a full-text index and defines more specifically how the different managed properties in the full-text index should contribute to rank calculations.

Query Processing

Query processing is the stage of the search where the query is received from (for example, the Search Center) and is processed to apply certain rules or expansion before being matched to the content of the index. Query processing in FS4SP is a set of components (QR Proxy, QR Server, and Topfdispatch) that receive the query from the FAST Query SSA, process it, and pass it onto the Query Matching component. The query dispatching part (Topfdispatch) passes the query to the index columns and eventually to any index partitions.

QR Server

The *Query & Results Server* (QR Server) is the component on the search server that is responsible for executing searches in FS4SP. The QR Server also provides its own web-based interface that is mainly intended for testing FAST Query Language (FQL) expressions and debugging any potential issues with FS4SP. Read more about FQL in the "Query Language" section later in this chapter.

Refiners (Faceted Search)

Refiners are clickable terms on the search result page that allow users to narrow a search based on common properties in a result set. This method of displaying the most prevalent common properties from metadata on items has also been known as *faceted search*, which refers to the similar "faces," or properties, of the items in the result set. Faceted search is a poor linguistic association, and the new Microsoft terminology of *refiners* is a better description of what is actually happening: The result set is getting refined to a purer set of results by focusing in on items with desirable properties.

> **Note** You might also hear refiners being referred to as *navigators*. This term was used in FAST ESP.

FS4SP is capable of providing both *shallow* and *deep* refiners. Deep refiners are refiners that are listed based on the entire result set. Shallow refiners include only a limited number of results. Sometimes that result set can be very large and the number of common properties also very large. FS4SP has the ability to analyze the entire result set (regardless of size), display the refiners, and report the exact number of matching items for each. In contrast, standard SharePoint search can analyze only a very shallow set of results (up to 500).

Query Language

FS4SP supports a robust search syntax. Users can add query syntax to the search query, or that syntax can be added programmatically. The query language can be used to fetch a custom and specific result set. The query language is required to make sense of the keywords that users search for, in addition to any refinement the users may apply. Predefined queries using complex query language may also be desirable for building custom search experiences or search-based applications.

SharePoint has its own query language, the *Keyword Query Syntax*. This is also known as *KQL* (Keyword Query Language), where *K* stands for *keyword* and is the parameter used for passing keyword queries to SharePoint. FS4SP also has its own query language, which is known as *FQL* or *FAST Query Language*. However, users of SharePoint will not see FQL because KQL works on both SharePoint search and FS4SP. The QR Server does the job of translating KQL into the appropriate platform-specific query languages and receiving the correct results. However, in some cases, a developer may want to use the added functionality of FQL to pass more complicated queries and retrieve specialized result sets. Some examples may be when adjusting ranking order or custom sorting is desirable. See Chapter 8 for a detailed explanation of the query languages in FS4SP.

 More Info For more information about query languages in SharePoint and FS4SP, go to *http://msdn.microsoft.com/en-us/library/hh144966.aspx.*

Token Expressions

Token expressions are the simplest queries of words, phrases, numbers, or identification values that may be expected to return a specific item in the index. Token expressions can be a single word, multiple words, or a phrase. They can also be numbers or letter-number combinations that represent a title or document ID.

Property Specifications

Properties or metadata are often more useful to search for than free text in the body of a document. *Properties* are often applied to describe a document and fill in information missing from the body of the document. In FS4SP, properties can also be searched for independently of token expressions. Specifying a property and its value can return all documents with the matching property and property value, regardless of text within the item.

Boolean Operators

George Boole was an English mathematician who invented Boolean logic, which has conjunction, disjunction, and negation operators. For search engines, these operators are applied as Boolean *AND*, *OR*, and *NOT* operators. A Boolean *AND* operator, which is the default operator for most search engines, provides a result set with only items that match all of the terms searched. For example, if a search user enters the query *Swedish meatballs*, only items with both the term *Swedish* and the term *meatballs* are returned. Alternatively, an *OR* operator returns all items with either *Swedish* or *meatballs* in them.

The *NOT* operator returns only items that do not contain the term immediately following the *NOT* operator. For example, if the search user searches for *Swedish meatballs NOT Chefs*, the search engine should return items that contain both *Swedish* and *meatballs* (not necessarily together) and do not contain the term *Chefs*.

The default operator when querying against FS4SP from the Search Center or via the API is the *AND* operator. This means that when two or more terms are searched for, only items with all of the terms are returned. This allows for refinement of the search results by adding terms to the search query. This is what most users expect from a search engine. If a user wants to get all documents with any of the terms, that user is required to manually enter the *OR* operator in the search query field. An example of an *AND* search with a *NOT* operator can be seen in Figure 2-9.

FIGURE 2-9 A complex query using Boolean operators. *AND* is implied by default.

> **More Info** For more information about using operators in keyword queries, go to *http://msdn.microsoft.com/en-us/library/ee872310.aspx*. A complete reference can be found at *http://msdn.microsoft.com/en-us/library/ff394462.aspx*. Using Keyword Query Syntax and FAST Query Language is discussed in more detail in Chapter 8.

Search Scopes

Search scopes are a SharePoint concept of delimiting search result sets prior to query. Essentially, a search scope is a logical separation of the search index based on a property query. The property query is added to the search terms at query time and the entire search is submitted to the index, retrieving only results that match the terms searched for and all rules in the scope.

Scopes help users search in a subset of the index and can be set on specific search pages or search-based applications to limit the scope of the search regardless of the query syntax. Scopes can also be made available through drop-down menus next to the search box, allowing users to select the section of the site or search index they want to query. This is very useful for building search interfaces that query only a specific site or level of a site in a portal. Users may not even know that the index contains information from other sites because they receive only results within that specific site. Scopes can also be used in certain circumstances to filter the result set in order to remove noise or improve ranking by forcing the inclusion or exclusion of content to queries.

> **Note** Scopes are appended to search queries as a logical *AND* operation, which means the matching result set applies your query in addition to any rules set in the scope and returns only those results that match all the criteria. Several scopes can even be applied to a single search result Web Part by using an *AND* operator to separate them. However, the scopes setting only supports *AND* settings, not *OR* or *AND NOT* operators.

Those familiar with SharePoint search know that scopes can be set in the SSA or in Site Collection Administration on the Site Settings of the Site Collection, and then applied to the Search Centers. Scopes in SharePoint allow for rules by address (folder, host name, or domain), by property queries, or by content source. In FS4SP, these scopes are limited to address (folder, host name, or domain) and property queries; however, because the scope rules are property filters that are defined in FQL, the query can be set to virtually any available property as long as that property is mapped as a managed property in the Metadata Property mappings in the FAST Query SSA or with Windows PowerShell. If the Scopes user interface in SharePoint is used, the FQL statements are autogenerated by SharePoint.

If Windows PowerShell is used, the administrator can define his or her own FQL. This makes scope usage in FS4SP very powerful.

> **More Info** For information about using Windows PowerShell to define an FQL, go to *http://technet.microsoft.com/en-us/library/ff453895.aspx#BKMK_ReviewSearchScopesIncludingFQL.*

A typical use of scopes in FS4SP is to create separate search tabs in the search UI and set a specific scope for each tab. This gives the users a different search page for each type of search or section of the site. This is seen in the Search Center with All Sites and People Search tabs (see Figure 2-9). These submit different scopes and, as described previously, the People Search scope is captured and passed to a different index. Additionally, it is not too difficult to create an image tab, a site tab, or tabs for different departments or document types. Analyzing business needs and user behavior before creating different search tabs that submit to different scopes can be helpful in determining which scopes to define.

As shown in Figure 2-10, the SharePoint interface has two scope rule types:

- **Web Address** Any URL that can be set. The path and all subdirectories are automatically included in the rule.

- **Property Query** A property query defined with allowable syntax in a property query field.

The default rules have three basic behaviors:

- **Include** Include all the content that matches the path or property rule specified in the rule definition. A good example is when you are building a sub site–specific search and including only items from the path and subdirectories of a specific site. For a property, you may want to include all the items that match a specific property (for example, approved items).

- **Require** This rule is similar to the inclusion rule but is stricter insofar as all items must match any rule defined with this behavior. This rule behavior is usually used for properties that must match all items.

- **Exclusion** Anything matching a rule with this behavior is excluded from the scope.

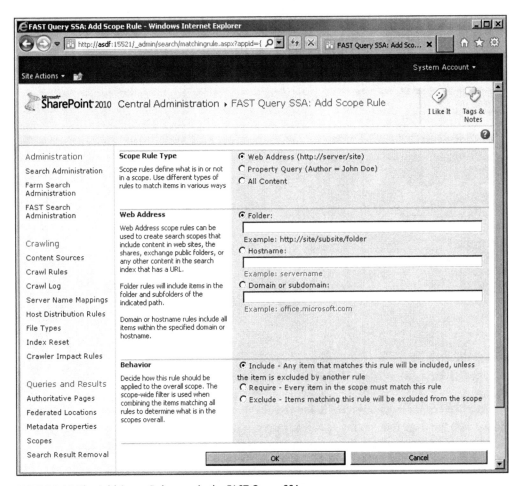

FIGURE 2-10 The Add Scope Rule page in the FAST Query SSA.

After a scope is set up and defined, it can be set on the Search Result Web Part or used in a search box. To delimit a search result page with a scope, you should edit the result page and then edit the Search Core Results Web Part. Scopes can be defined in the Location Properties section, shown in Figure 2-11.

FIGURE 2-11 Setting a scope in the Search Core Results Web Part.

To add a Scopes drop-down list to the search query box so that users can select a predefined scope, edit the page that has the search box on it and then edit the Search Box Web Part. The top section allows for a number of scope drop-down settings, as shown in Figure 2-12.

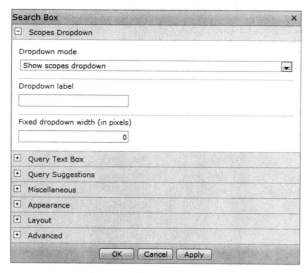

FIGURE 2-12 Setting a Scopes Dropdown in the Search Box Settings dialog box.

Scopes are a useful and user-friendly feature of SharePoint and FS4SP. Consideration must be given as to how to appropriately implement them on a site, but they can quickly and easily add value for the search user by helping them delimit search results without additional query terms or property filters.

Security Trimming

Security trimming is an important part of an Enterprise Search Solution. The result set given to any specific user should contain only results that user has rights to view.

When content is indexed, a property that is picked up and added to each item in the index is its *authorization token*. This is usually in the form of an Access Control List (ACL) that is returned with the item by the source system to the user defined to crawl (Content Access Account). Having this information stored in the index with the content is essential to being able to match the search user's own logged information with that stored ACL.

> **More Info** For more information about security tokens, go to *http://msdn.microsoft.com/en-us/library/aa379570(VS.85).aspx* and *http://msdn.microsoft.com/en-us/library/aa374872(VS.85).aspx*.

When a search is performed, the Security Identifier (SID) of the user performing the search is passed with the query to the search engine. The SID is then matched with the authorization properties of the items in the index, usually with the aid of a directory system like Active Directory or a Lightweight Directory Access Protocol (LDAP) server. All items that do not have a matching authorization property—and therefore should not be viewable by the user—are filtered out.

FS4SP trims the result set by interacting with the FAST Search Authorization (FSA) component. The FSA component in turn communicates with the Claims Services, Active Directory Services, or another LDAP service to identify the user doing the searching and compare that user's SID to those associated with the items in the result set. The main task of the QR Proxy, which passes the queries forward to the QR Server from the FS4SP Search API, is to capture the User Claims that it receives with the query and pass them to the FSA Worker process. The FSA Worker process returns the SID to the QR Proxy, which passes the entire query forward to the QR Server for processing.

Within the QR Server is a Security stage that again communicates with the FSA worker after a set of query enrichment stages to match that SID with the user's associated access rights. This includes all groups or associated privileges that the user may have on specific content. This entire query, including these access rights, is then submitted to the search core; items that satisfy all the parameters, including security access, are then returned.

> **Note** A requirement for FS4SP to filter result sets based on security is the availability of authenticated user tokens. FS4SP does not itself authenticate users. This task is performed by SharePoint, and the user's claims information is passed to FS4SP. If authentication is not performed, if the user is not logged in (for example, anonymous access is enabled), or if the security filter of the QR Server is disabled, security trimming may not perform as expected.

Claims-Based Authentication

Support for claims-based authentication is available in SharePoint 2010. Claims-based authentication is an alternative authentication model whereby users are not directly authenticated by Active Directory but a claim is made to some other system that is trusted to authenticate that user. This can be useful when the directory service or user permissions of a particular system are not supported by SharePoint directly. FS4SP is specifically powerful because it can support these claims and authenticate against external systems. Figure 2-13 shows the interactions with which security information is added to the query in FS4SP.

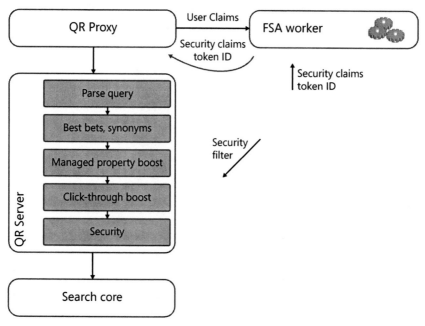

FIGURE 2-13 Interacting with the FSA worker to perform security enrichment of the query. (Image courtesy of Thomas Svensen.)

Conclusion

The terms used in search terminology are new to many people. This chapter serves as an introduction to give you a better understanding of what constitutes a search engine—in particular, FS4SP.

In this chapter, you looked at how search engines return results and how the concepts of recall and precision are balanced to deliver good search results to end users. You explored content processing and query processing and the concepts within each of these areas in an FS4SP deployment. The chapter also explained key terminology related to search engines, such as linguistics, refiners, and metadata. Finally, you looked at the index schema in FS4SP and the relationship of its elements.

FS4SP Architecture

After completing this chapter, you will be able to

- Understand the relationship between FS4SP and your existing SharePoint architecture.

- Set up and use Search Service Applications in SharePoint to communicate with FS4SP.

- Understand the main internal components of FS4SP and their roles.

- Understand the column and row architecture of the FS4SP search index.

Every search system is built from several components. This chapter describes how Microsoft FAST Search Server 2010 for SharePoint (FS4SP) works on a component level and how it fits into the Microsoft SharePoint 2010 architecture. When setting up a new system, you need to consider how the system will be used day to day. A thorough understanding of the SharePoint/FS4SP architecture will help you to meet your scale, system load, and high-availability needs.

Overview

A SharePoint Server farm is one SharePoint deployment potentially consisting of a number of servers performing the same or unique roles, but sharing the same Central Administration. Each new SharePoint farm, by default, includes the built-in SharePoint enterprise search components. However, FS4SP is deployed and configured as a separate farm—the FS4SP farm. This is not to be confused with a dedicated SharePoint search farm for the built-in SharePoint search.

More Info For more information about the components included in different editions of SharePoint, go to *http://sharepoint.microsoft.com/en-us/buy/Pages/Editions-Comparison .aspx?Capability=Search*. For more information about dedicated SharePoint search farms, go to *http://technet.microsoft.com/en-us/library/cc262936.aspx#section9*.

The FS4SP farm is a separate installation that builds on top of the SharePoint farm and extends it with more advanced search capabilities. Although the SharePoint farm can stand on its own, the FS4SP farm requires a SharePoint farm and cannot exist by itself. What this means is that the integration points for communicating with the FS4SP farm are exposed by using Search Service Applications (SSAs) via the Service Application architecture of the SharePoint farm. You cannot communicate directly with an FS4SP server when you want to search content; communication is performed via a SharePoint server, which uses authenticated calls to the FS4SP farm (Figure 3-1). People Search does not use FS4SP; this will be discussed in more detail in the "FAST Search Query/Query SSA" section later in this chapter.

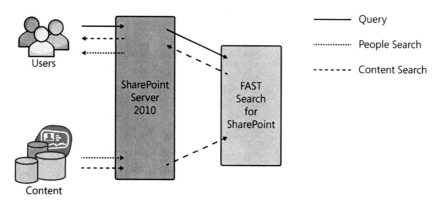

FIGURE 3-1 FS4SP extends SharePoint Server. The superset of capabilities includes common base functionality and a platform.

 Note When indexing content, you would usually do so via a Search Service Application on the SharePoint farm, but you can also index content directly to the FS4SP farm by using the Content API together with a certificate or via the FAST Search–specific connectors. See Chapter 7, "Content Processing," for more information.

Although you technically can install FS4SP on the same servers as you install SharePoint, this setup is not a supported production environment. In a production environment, you would not install any SharePoint-specific components on the FS4SP servers, and you would not install FS4SP on a Windows Domain Controller. You also need separate licenses for your FS4SP servers and cannot save on the license cost by bundling FS4SP on the same servers that SharePoint is on.

 More Info For information about hardware and software requirements for FS4SP, go to *http://technet.microsoft.com/en-us/library/ff381239.aspx.*

In a development or test scenario, you can install everything on the same machine to ease development. You'll learn about this in Chapter 4, "Deployment," which covers deployment scenarios for both development/testing and production environments.

Microsoft does not state the reason why SharePoint and FS4SP are not supported on the same server, but both SharePoint and FS4SP use significant hardware resources, so they would most likely interfere with each other in a production scenario. This would make it hard to troubleshoot potential issues you might encounter.

After installing FS4SP, you must configure the SharePoint farm to use the index and search capabilities of FS4SP instead of the SharePoint built-in versions. You accomplish this via two special SSAs within SharePoint that redirect indexing and search queries to the FS4SP farm instead of to the built-in SharePoint Search Service Application.

FS4SP and the built-in SharePoint Search share the same connectors and indexing API in addition to a common query API. This commonality makes it easy to upgrade from the internal SharePoint search capabilities to FS4SP. Your existing search solutions will continue to work as before, but you can change them to take advantage of the extra capabilities that FS4SP offers on top of the built-in search.

Important You need to reindex your content if you migrate from the built-in SharePoint Search over to FS4SP, but your search solutions should work without the need for a lot of changes.

With the built-in SharePoint search, you have only one SSA handling both indexing of content and the search queries on that content.

Important People Search uses the built-in search from SharePoint, which is not a component of FS4SP. People Search uses the phonetic and nickname capabilities of Microsoft Speech Server—capabilities not included in FS4SP.

Both FAST Search for Intranet Applications (FSIA) and FAST Search for Internet Sites (FSIS) have phonetic capabilities as part of their feature sets, but this has been removed in FS4SP.

Communication between SharePoint and FS4SP occurs via Windows Communication Foundation (WCF) services, which acts as a bridge between SharePoint and FS4SP. On the FS4SP side, service calls are proxied over to FS4SP internal services, which handle the execution of the calls. Figure 3-2 shows the SSA architecture and how the SharePoint farm communicates with the FS4SP farm.

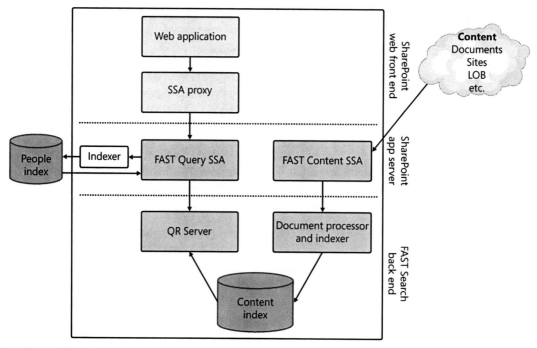

FIGURE 3-2 SharePoint Search Service architecture with the FAST Query SSA and FAST Content SSA running on a SharePoint application server.

Server Roles and Components

FS4SP is composed of many components. Some of these are located in the SharePoint farm in the form of Service Applications and index and query APIs, and some in the FS4SP farm, where the components constitute the FS4SP search engine.

Depending on your usage scenario, you can keep all the SharePoint components on one SharePoint server, and all the FS4SP components on one FS4SP server. When you have special requirements for high availability, indexing, and query speed, or when your content volume exceeds the capabilities of one server, you can scale many of the components out to additional servers on both the SharePoint farm and the FS4SP farm.

> **Tip** For a company that has two SharePoint servers on its farm—one front-end server and one back-end server—for running services, you would install a Search Center site on the front-end server and the SSAs on the back-end server. If the company has fewer than about 15 million documents to index, you could make do by setting up a single-server FS4SP farm, which would handle both indexing and search queries.

The SharePoint farm handles the crawling of content and the search queries going into the system, whereas the FS4SP farm builds and stores the search index, executes search queries against the index, and returns the hit list.

> **Note** It is possible to crawl data outside of the SharePoint crawling framework. FS4SP comes with several custom connectors that run outside of the SharePoint crawling framework. These are covered in more detail in Chapter 7. You can also index content directly using the Content API for FS4SP, also covered in Chapter 7.

The following sections dig deeper into all the different parts that make up the FS4SP architecture and their exact roles.

FS4SP Architecture

FS4SP consists conceptually of four main areas: Content Gathering, Item Processing, Search, and Administration, as shown in Figure 3-3 and described in the list that follows the figure.

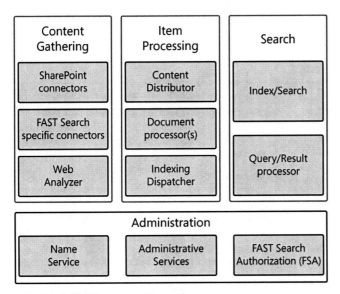

FIGURE 3-3 FS4SP component overview.

- **Content Gathering** As the name implies, the Content Gathering components are the modules that retrieve content to be indexed. On the SharePoint farm, this is the Content SSA, which gathers content and sends that content to the FS4SP farm. There are also some FAST Search specific connectors for FS4SP (see Chapter 7) running outside of the SharePoint connector framework that can be used to gather content. When a connector has retrieved content from the source system, that content is passed on to the Content Distributor for further processing.

- **Item Processing**   This starts with the Content Distributor component, which receives data to be indexed from the connectors. The Content Distributor then sends the data to the Document processors. This is also known as the *indexing pipeline.* After the data is processed by the Document processors, it is sent to the Indexing Dispatcher, which determines which indexing component in FS4SP should receive the data. If you have only one FS4SP server, you will have one indexing component.

- **Search**   This includes both the indexing component that stores the search index to disk, and the search component that reads the stored index data when you execute a search. It also holds the Query/Result processor (QR Server), which contains a pipeline for incoming search queries, and another pipeline for outgoing results. Some modules in the search pipeline handle spell checking, search suggestions based on the query language, and security enforcement on the search results.

- **Administration**   This holds the FS4SP Name service; WCF services to remotely administer FS4SP components such as the index schema; custom dictionaries and keywords functionality (synonyms, best bets, promotions); and the FAST Search Authorization (FSA) security module, which is the component in charge of making sure a user gets only those results to which he or she is supposed to have access.

Table 3-1 summarizes the FS4SP processes and the areas they belong to.

TABLE 3-1 FS4SP internal process overview

Process name	Associated with	Role
configserver	Administration	Handles the internal configuration files in FS4SP
nameservice	Administration	Name service
nctrl	Administration	Node controller
samadmin	Administration	Item-level security
samworker	Administration	Query processing component handling item-level security
spelltuner	Administration	The process that iteratively improves the dynamically built spell-check dictionary
browserengine	Content Gathering	A component of the FAST Search Web crawler that emulates a real browser in order to evaluate JavaScript on the crawled pages
crawler	Content Gathering	The main component of the FAST Search Web crawler
sprel	Content Gathering	A component handling search click-through analysis
walinkstorerreceiver	Content Gathering	A component of the Web Analyzer that receives the anchor link information from the document processing pipeline
walookupdb0	Content Gathering	A component of the Web Analyzer that stores the anchor link information in an internal database
webanalyzer	Content Gathering	The main component of the Web Analyzer
contentdistributor	Item Processing	Receives content from the FAST Search specific connectors or from SharePoint, and sends it to the registered Document processors
indexingdispatcher	Item Processing	Receives processed content from the Document processors and sends it to the indexers

Process name	Associated with	Role
procserver_n	Item Processing	Instances of the indexing pipeline
indexer	Search	The process that creates the FS4SP index
qrproxy	Search	Query processing component that interfaces with the FAST Query SSA
qrSserver	Search	Main query-processing component
search_n	Search	Query matching process for searching through a local index column
topfdispatch	Search	Top-level query dispatcher running on the query processing server

Figure 3-4 illustrates the basic flow of indexing and searching and how data flows between the SharePoint farm and the FS4SP farm.

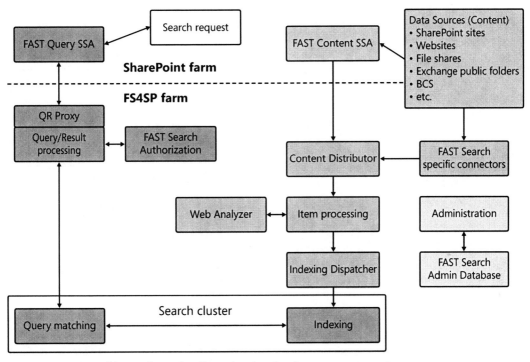

FIGURE 3-4 FS4SP architectural overview illustrating data flow between components.

SharePoint Search Service Applications

In SharePoint, search is handled by a single Search Service Application, which takes care of both indexing and searching of content. In FS4SP, this functionality has been split into two different service applications:

- FAST Search Connector (FAST Content SSA)
- FAST Search Query (FAST Query SSA)

More Info You can read more about the Service Application Architecture in SharePoint at Microsoft TechNet. Go to *http://technet.microsoft.com/en-us/library/ee704547.aspx*.

In FS4SP, the responsibilities for indexing and searching are cleanly divided between the two SSAs. One handles the crawling of content, sending it over to the FS4SP farm, and the other handles search queries.

FAST Search Connector (FAST Content SSA)

The FAST Search Connector (often referred to as the *FAST Content SSA*) is where you can add content sources, and it is responsible for content acquisition. Out of the box, it supports connectors for SharePoint sites, websites, file shares, Microsoft Exchange Server public folders, and line of business (LOB) data via Business Connectivity Services (BCS) and BCS custom-developed connectors. This list is exactly the same as for the built-in SharePoint search, and thus the administrative experience is the same for FS4SP when it comes to administrating content sources.

After content has been acquired by a connector, it is fed from the FAST Content SSA to one of the registered Content Distributors in FS4SP, which in turn passes it on to the Document processors. Figure 3-5 outlines the data flow during indexing.

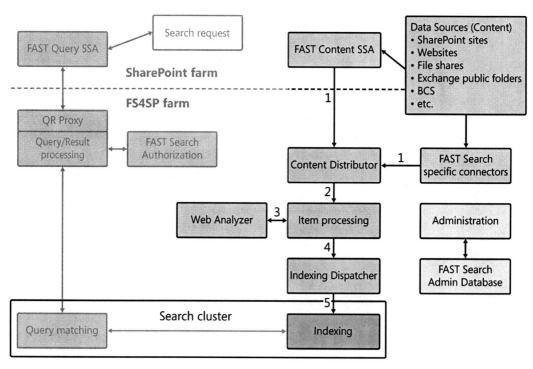

FIGURE 3-5 Content feeding from SharePoint to FS4SP.

Here's a more detailed description of the steps shown in Figure 3-5:

1. Content is crawled by a connector on the FAST Content SSA or from a FAST Search specific connector and is sent over to the Content Distributor in the FS4SP farm.

2. Content is then sent for item processing in the indexing pipeline.

3. During item processing, the content is passed on to the Web Analyzer.

4. After item processing completes, it is passed on to the Indexing Dispatcher.

5. The Indexing Dispatcher sends the content to an indexing server for inclusion in the index.

The administration page for the FAST Content SSA resembles one of the regular Search Service Applications for SharePoint, which you can see in the next screenshot. However, if you look closely, you can see that several links are missing. Links to Authoritative Pages, Federated Locations, Metadata Properties, Scopes, and Search Result Removal are all missing. All links related to searching have been removed, and you can configure only items related to indexing data in the FAST Content SSA. Items related to searching have been separated out to the FAST Query SSA instead.

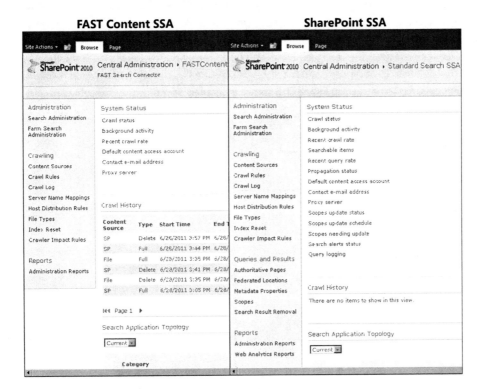

Note Microsoft TechNet states not to deploy more than one FAST Content SSA with your FS4SP farm. Go to *http://technet.microsoft.com/en-us/library/ff599525.aspx#ContentSSARedundancyAndAvailability*.

If you have multiple SharePoint farms, it is tempting to deploy one FAST Content SSA to each farm and have them share a single FS4SP farm. The primary reason this is an unsupported scenario is that the click-through relevancy and link-relevancy have a chance of generating identical item IDs when run on two farms. This can lead to incorrect relevancy in the search results. Also, having two FAST Content SSAs can generate identical item IDs if the FAST Content SSAs both index to the same content collection (for example, "sp"), and content can be accidentally overwritten or deleted in the search index.

FAST Search Query (FAST Query SSA)

The FAST Search Query module (often referred to as the *FAST Query SSA*) is responsible for querying the search index. When a user executes a search from a search center or via one of the search APIs, the query is sent to the FAST Query SSA and then over to one of the registered Query/Result (QR) Proxies in FS4SP, which in turn passes it on to the internal Query/Result (QR) Server service in FS4SP. The QR Server then executes the query pipeline, and upon receiving the results from the index, passes the results through the result pipeline. After the result pipeline has completed, the final result is sent back and rendered for the end user. Figure 3-6 shows a detailed flow of query execution.

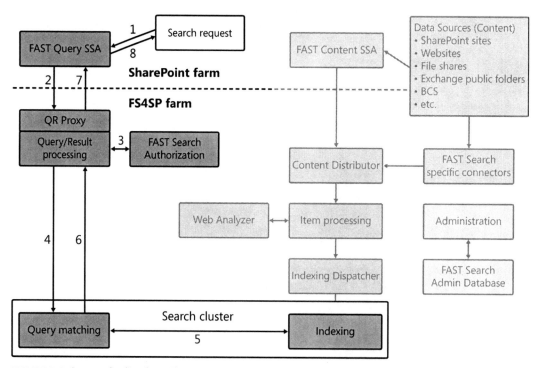

FIGURE 3-6 Content feeding from SharePoint to FS4SP.

Here's a more detailed description of the steps shown in Figure 3-6:

1. A search request is submitted.

2. Queries are sent via the FAST Query SSA over to the QR Proxy (WCF service), which in turn sends the query to the QR Server.

3. Authentication tokens are added to the search query as a claims token.

4. The QR Server runs the query through a query pipeline and sends it to a search server for query matching.

5. The search result is retrieved from the search index.

6. The search result is passed back to the QR Server and run through the result pipeline.

7. A search result set is generated and passed back to the Query SSA.

8. The end-user application that initiated the search operation receives the final ranked, sorted, and paged result.

The Query SSA is where you also configure changes to scopes and metadata.

An FS4SP installation has to have at least one FAST Query SSA, but you can scale out to more servers for performance and failover. Because the FAST Query SSA doesn't do much processing (except for People Search), having two instances so that you can handle failovers should be sufficient in most cases.

If you examine the administration page for both the FAST Content SSA and FAST Query SSA, you will notice that they both have a section for crawling. Although this makes sense for the FAST Content SSA that handles content acquisition, you might wonder why the FAST Query SSA also has this section.

There is a perfectly reasonable explanation: People Search does not go through FS4SP but instead uses the built-in SharePoint Search. When the FAST Query SSA receives the queries, it sends queries regarding people to the People Search module in SharePoint and sends all other queries over to FS4SP. The only content source you should ever need to add to the FAST Query SSA is a SharePoint site with the *sps3://servername* protocol.

Note It is possible to add other content sources to the FAST Query SSA. The FAST Query SSA then behaves like the normal Search Service Application in SharePoint for searches configured to go against the SharePoint search index and not FS4SP.

If you have FS4SP installed, there is no reason to do this unless you need to create a head-to-head comparison of the two search engines.

One important point about the FAST Query SSA administration page is as follows: Metadata configuration is handled via the FAST Search Administration link, as seen in the upper-left column in Figure 3-7, and not via the Metadata Properties link below the Queries And Results header. The Metadata Properties link at the bottom is for People Search only.

Metadata configuration

FIGURE 3-7 The FAST Query SSA page in Central Administration.

Under the Queries And Results header in the left menu is a link called Federated Locations. Clicking that link opens the Manage Federated Locations page, shown in Figure 3-8.

The *federated locations* are configurations for sending the search queries to the correct search engine. They also contain default XSLT transformations for the result rendering in the search Web Parts included with SharePoint. If a search location is not specified for a search query by the Search Center or one of the search APIs in SharePoint, the search is directed to the Local FAST Search Results location.

The definition of *federated search* is to allow simultaneous search of multiple searchable resources. A single search query request is distributed to all search engines participating in the federation, and the results are (in the case of the FAST Query SSA) aggregated before being returned to the requestor.

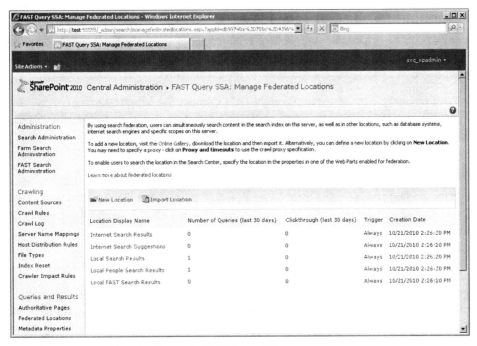

FIGURE 3-8 Federated location list on the FAST Query SSA.

By default, a FAST Search Center executes searches against FS4SP and People Search (both listed in Figure 3-8). If you add a Web Part that sends queries to an external search service—for example, Flickr—this source would also participate in the federated search. Figure 3-9 shows how this would work.

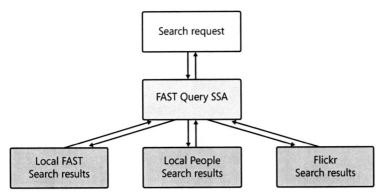

FIGURE 3-9 The query is sent from the Query SSA to three different search engines, and the results are aggregated before being sent back to the UI.

Crawl Components and Crawl Databases

Crawl components are responsible for crawling content sources and adding information about the content sources and their crawl schedules to the crawl components' associated crawl databases. A crawl component also passes the crawled items to the FS4SP farm.

When adding multiple content sources on the FAST Content SSA, you might experience that crawling takes a long time or that the crawl server has load issues. This can be remedied by adding more crawl components to your SharePoint farm in order to distribute the crawling load across your SharePoint farm servers.

Each crawl component is associated with a crawl database. The crawl component stores metadata related to the content sources in the crawl database. Crawl schedules and other information related to the crawl operations from the FAST Content SSA are also stored in the crawler database. Typically, this is information about when an item was last crawled and whether the item changed since the last crawl. Note that there is no indexed content stored in the crawl database because this is stored in the FS4SP indexes.

The crawl databases can also be scaled out. No guidelines are available for scaling the crawl database in regard to FS4SP, but Table 3-2 shows the limitations for the different search components related to the built-in SharePoint Search. The built-in SharePoint Search can handle 10 databases, each with 25 million items, for a total of 250 million items. We know FS4SP can scale way beyond that and that the crawler database also stores much less information when used with FS4SP. This leads us to estimate that you can safely have at least 50 million items per crawler database, giving a maximum of 500 million items.

TechNet shows you an installation scenario with 500 million items at *http://technet.microsoft.com/ en-us/library/hh147946.aspx*. This scenario uses four crawl components and 12 crawl databases, which would yield approximately 42 million items per crawl database, which is well within our proposed limits.

It is also possible to assign a content source to be handled by a specific crawler component and database by adding host distribution rules. This allows a particular server to index certain content, instead of distributing the indexing in a round-robin fashion.

More Info Detailed information about how to set up multiple server deployment of the FAST Content SSA can be found at Microsoft TechNet. Go to *http://technet.microsoft.com/ en-us/library/ff599537.aspx*.

TABLE 3-2 Scaling of crawl components and crawl databases*

Limit	Maximum value	Limit type	Notes
Crawl databases and database items	10 crawl databases per search service application	Threshold	The crawl database stores the crawl data (time/status, etc.) about all items that have been crawled. The supported limit is 10 crawl databases per SharePoint Search service application.
	25 million items per crawl database		The recommended limit is 25 million items per crawl database (or a total of four crawl databases per search service application).
Crawl components	16 per search service application	Threshold	The recommended limit per application is 16 total crawl components, with two per crawl database and two per server, assuming the server has at least eight processors (cores).
			The total number of crawl components per server must be fewer than 128/ (total query components) to minimize propagation I/O degradation. Exceeding the recommended limit may not increase crawl performance; in fact, crawl performance may decrease based on available resources on the crawl server, database, and content host.
Crawl log entries	100 million per search application	Supported	This is the number of individual log entries in the crawl log. It will follow the Indexed items limit.

* http://technet.microsoft.com/en-us/library/cc262787.aspx#Search

Search Rows, Columns, and Clusters

A search cluster is the grouping of indexing and query components in an FS4SP farm. These components can be scaled in a matrix of rows and columns, where each component is one physical FS4SP server, as shown in the cluster topology in Figure 3-10.

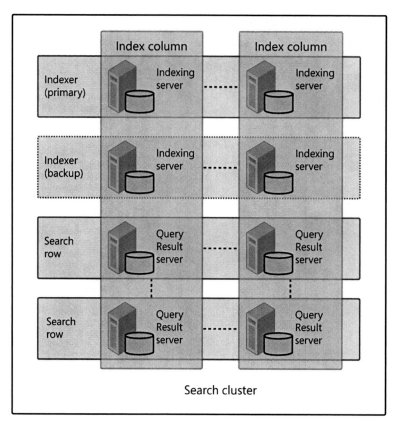

FIGURE 3-10 FS4SP search cluster architecture.

The indexing service scales out according to the number of items. If the indexing service runs on a single server, both the number of items it can handle per second and the total number of items it can include in the index are limited. To scale out the indexing service, you can deploy it across more than one index column. Each index column will contain one part of the index, and the combined set of index columns will form the complete index. In this case, each indexing server handles only a part of the whole index, which allows it to scale out both the number of items that can be indexed per second and the total number of items. Additionally, backup indexing servers can provide fault tolerance. The following list explains the process in Figure 3-10.

- **Index column** In a single server FS4SP installation, you have only one index column because all content is stored on one server. If the total index is too large to reside on one server, you can add more columns (servers) and distribute the data across all the columns. You can also add more columns to increase the indexing throughput because indexing gradually slows down as more data is added. Note that adding columns to a running system involves recrawling all your content. (See Chapter 5, "Operations," for how to modify the FS4SP farm topology.) The complete index is the total of all the index columns. When a search is being executed, it is evaluated against all the index columns within the search cluster, and the results from each index column are merged by the Topfdispatch process (see Table 3-1) into the final result set.

- **Search row**   For each index column in the search cluster, you have a corresponding search server. A search row is the collection of the search servers matching the index columns for the cluster. A given search row can handle a set amount of queries per second (QPS), and you can add multiple search rows to handle more queries as individual queries are distributed among the available search rows. Search rows can also be added for fault tolerance. Any additional search rows on non-indexer servers pull copies of the binary index from indexer servers in the same column.

- **Primary and backup indexer**   To provide fault tolerance on the indexing side, you can configure a backup indexer. You then have a backup indexing row. The two indexers produce identical indexes, but it is the primary indexer that distributes the indexes to the search servers.

> **Important** The primary and backup indexer servers are specified as *indexer rows* in the deployment configuration file (*deployment.xml*). Search rows and indexer rows use the same row numbering in the deployment configuration file.
>
> The number of columns in the query-matching service always equals the number of columns in the indexer service. The reason is that the index columns represent a partitioning of the index, and each query-matching servers can handle only one such partition of the index.

Scenario

One server can hold 15 million documents, and you have 25 million documents to index.

> **Note** The supported limit per column is 15 million. Capacity per server is explained in detail in Chapter 4.

The minimum number of servers needed to achieve this is two servers. You would need two index columns in order to hold 25 million documents, and they would be distributed equally during indexing among those two columns. You would also have room for growth. The same two servers that hold the index columns would also double as search servers.

If you want fault tolerance for serving search queries, you would have to add an additional row made up of two more servers mirroring the original row of indexed content, one per indexing column. This new row could also act as a backup indexer to achieve high availability on indexing.

> **Note** A physical server can act as the roles of both index column and search server, but keep in mind that search performance will be degraded if you index at the same time as you are executing search queries.

FS4SP Index Servers

In Table 3-1, there is a process called *indexer* running in FS4SP. This is the internal process that creates the binary index on disk. The binary index is in a propriety format and is not stored in a relational database. The index is optimized for full text searching while also allowing for all other advanced index features of FS4SP. Each index column, holding a part of the index, will have this process running.

The indexing component on FS4SP consists of the previously mentioned indexer process, but also a process called the *Indexing Dispatcher*. If you have more than one index column in your FS4SP farm, the Indexing Dispatcher will route items to the index columns based on a hash algorithm, distributing the items evenly to the *indexer* process on all the index columns.

After the indexer receives an item from the Indexing Dispatcher, it creates binary indexes in the data folder on disk. These binary indexes are then sent to the query matching component and are used during query evaluation during searching.

The indexing dispatcher can also be scaled out on several servers for fault tolerance. Usually, the indexing dispatcher is installed on the same machine as the primary indexer.

Note One server represents one index column (index server) and/or only one search server. Often an index column is referred to as an *index server* and a search server as a *query server*. You can, however, share an instance of the index server and the search server on the same physical server.

FS4SP Query Result Servers/QR Server

On your FS4SP farm, you will have one or several servers acting as a query and result server.

More Info For information about how to scale your FS4SP farm, see the section "Production Environments" in Chapter 4.

The role of the FS4SP Query Result Server (QR Server) is to provide query processing prior to submitting the queries to the search engine and also processing of the returned results before they are sent back to the FAST Query SSA in SharePoint. The QR Server component has a built-in software load balancer to even out the query load on your QR Servers.

The QR Server receives queries from the FAST Query SSA (via the QR Proxy Service) and then runs them through a query processing pipeline that analyzes, and, if required, transforms them. Typical stages being run are as follows:

- Converting queries from SharePoint Keyword Query Syntax to FAST Query Language (FQL)

- Linguistic query processing such as spell checking and anti-phrasing

- Result Clustering

- Navigation

- Find Similar

- Did You Mean

- Dynamic Duplicate Removal

- Query syntax validation

- Adding security descriptors to the query for the user executing the search

- Adding boost values based on content freshness

After passing the user query through the query pipeline, the query is distributed to the appropriate search servers (see the search_n process in Table 3-1) to retrieve the actual results. When the search servers return the result set, the QR Server creates a query analysis result report for that particular query and the returned result. Based on configuration, this result report is either returned to the FAST Query SSA and the end user or used for automatic resubmission.

 Note A result report contains all parts of a result, including did-you-mean, search suggestion, refiners, and the search hits.

Conclusion

FS4SP consists of many components, both on the SharePoint farm and on the FS4SP farm. The complexity can be overwhelming at first. It will take time to get used to the different components and their particular roles, including which parts reside on the SharePoint farm and what parts reside on the FS4SP farm.

Two Search Service Applications run on a SharePoint application server: the FAST Content SSA and the FAST Query SSA. One is for retrieving content for inclusion into the search index and one is for getting the content back out. There is also the mental obstacle to overcome: The FAST Query SSA handles not only queries but also the indexing of SharePoint User Profiles. The FAST Query SSA is also responsible for the legacy SharePoint behavior of People Search, whereas FS4SP does not get involved at all. This is because the user profiles are stored in the SharePoint Search index and not in the FS4SP index.

After content leaves the FAST Content SSA, that content is sent over to the FS4SP farm for processing, going through different steps before being written to disk in a binary index.

The binary index is split up over one or more rows and columns. The row and column layout provides for scaling for more data, increased indexing speed, and increased search speeds, and it also provides fault tolerance and failover.

When a query enters FS4SP from the FAST Query SSA, it goes through a number of processing steps before it can be used to access the binary index to return search results.

## CHAPTER 4

Deployment

After completing this chapter, you will be able to

- Understand the FS4SP hardware and software requirements and best practices.

- Deploy and configure your own development environment.

- Plan and scale your production FS4SP farm according to your usage scenario.

When you install enterprise software such as Microsoft SharePoint and Microsoft FAST Search Server 2010 for SharePoint (FS4SP), being familiar with network and hardware setup is a necessity. Both SharePoint and FS4SP require substantial hardware resources when running in a production environment; planning which internal FS4SP component should run on what hardware is key when optimizing your FS4SP deployment.

This chapter describes the hardware and software requirements for an FS4SP farm and goes over some of the important points about installing FS4SP in a development environment. It also covers various scaling strategies in production environments.

Overview

Developing for FS4SP is very similar to developing for SharePoint. For efficiency and stability reasons, it is often recommended to configure separate environments for development, testing, staging, and production. By using multiple environments, developers can safely test new features without interrupting the live production environment. Typically, each of these environments has its own characteristics; a development environment often consists of one machine only, but the number of servers increases as you move your solution over to the testing, staging, and production environments. As such, a SharePoint farm shares similarities with an FS4SP farm.

In practice, when using FS4SP, each developer often runs the development environment locally, has one or two server test installations—perhaps virtualized—and the production environment. When FS4SP is installed in addition to SharePoint Server 2010, a fully deployed FS4SP solution consists of both a SharePoint farm and an FS4SP farm.

Hardware Requirements

FS4SP is hardware-intensive, requiring fast CPUs, a lot of RAM, and low-latency disks. CPU and RAM are the most important factors when indexing content, whereas disk speed is a limiting factor for query latency and throughput. RAM is also important for searches, depending on which and how many index features you have enabled. The following list provides an easy-to-remember—although crude—rule of thumb of FS4SP's relationship to hardware:

- **Faster CPU** The system can index data faster.

- **More RAM** The system can handle more item processing and more index features, such as refiners and sortable properties.

- **Faster disk** The system can handle more queries per second (QPS) and execute complex and heavier queries faster.

A good principle is to allocate 2 GB of RAM per CPU core. This allocation provides high CPU usage processes with enough memory for the processing they do. Additionally, because more RAM allows the operating system to cache disk reads and writes, FS4SP performance generally improves across the board.

Complementing these general guidelines is a list of performance effects, provided by Microsoft TechNet, for enabling a certain index feature. You can find this list at *http://technet.microsoft.com/ en-us/library/gg702611.aspx*. Refer to this list when designing solutions in which high query through-put is anticipated.

The general hardware requirements from Microsoft are listed in Table 4-1. Keep in mind that a multi-server farm can benefit from heterogeneous hardware depending on which FS4SP services, such as item processing or indexing, run on each server.

TABLE 4-1 Official FS4SP hardware requirements

Minimum	Recommended
4 GB of RAM	16 GB of RAM
4 CPU cores, 2.0 GHz CPU	8 CPU cores, 2.0 GHz CPU
50-GB disk	1 TB of disk space on RAID across six spindles or more

Storage Considerations

When you set up storage for the servers storing the search index, you can find multiple options available from hardware vendors. Should you use local disks or a storage area network (SAN), and what disk characteristics are important? This section outlines what you need to consider when deciding on your storage approach for FS4SP.

Disk Speed

FS4SP is very I/O intensive; the nature of a full-text index gives rise to lots of random disk access operations. As such, disk latency is a very important factor for achieving good performance during indexing and searching. In general, a faster disk means lower latency and is usually a good investment when equipping FS4SP servers. SAS disks are preferred over SATA disks, and 15,000 RPM disks are preferred over 10,000 RPM disks.

Today, more options are available for using solid-state drives (SSD) in server environments. The main characteristic of an SSD is low latency on random access because of its use of memory chips instead of mechanical components. You should consider using SSDs in your FS4SP deployment if you have the option; they can cut down on the number of columns used in your deployment. The more items you store per server, the more data the search engine must evaluate for each search query. Because using SSDs cuts down the disk latency compared to regular disks, you can evaluate more data in the same amount of time, meaning that you can store all your content in fewer columns.

 Note Within a fixed power and cost budget, it is better to get a larger number of 10,000 RPM disks compared to fewer 15,000 RPM disks. For example, if you have two 15,000 RPM disks and a particular operation requires 100 disk reads, you would have 50 reads per disk. If you have five 10,000 RPM disks instead, the operation would require 20 reads per disk. All read operations are executed simultaneously, so the 20 read operations would be faster even though the disks themselves are slower.

Disk Layout

If you are planning to use local disks, FS4SP benefits from partitioning the physical disks similarly to how you would partition a Microsoft SQL Server database: using the three separate volumes shown in Table 4-2. By keeping data and log files away from the operating system partition, you will prevent the operating system drive from filling up and potentially crashing your system. Storing the data files on a high-performance volume configured for high availability is good production practice; likewise, you should keep the log files on a smaller volume (approximately 30 GB) because they consume less space.

TABLE 4-2 FS4SP volume layout

Volume	Contains	Physical disk layout
1	Operating system, FS4SP program files	RAID 1
2	FS4SP data files (binary index, dictionaries)	RAID 10 (1+0), RAID 5, or RAID 50 (5+0)
3	FS4SP log files	RAID 1

If you have a large number of drives available for the data files volume, RAID 50 is usually preferred over RAID 10 because the storage capacity is almost doubled on the same number of disks.

Note FS4SP uses predefined locations for data files and log files. If you want to partition your drives as per Table 4-2, see the section "Changing the Location of Data and Log Files" in Chapter 5, "Operations."

More Info Read more about the different RAID levels and how to combine them at *http://en.wikipedia.org/wiki/RAID*. The level that is available to you depends on your disk controller.

If you are storing your FS4SP files on a SAN, network-attached storage (NAS), or SSD disks, other rules apply than what was just outlined; the following sections discuss these storage technologies.

Using a SAN

Because company server farms are often streamlined for storage operational efficiency, you might not have the option to use local disks on an FS4SP server in your deployment. The company might have standardized on a SAN storage or even a NAS storage for its data usage.

When you use a SAN, multiple servers share a centralized storage pool, shown in Figure 4-1. This storage pool facilitates data exchange between the servers connected to the SAN. Each server is connected to the SAN by using a dedicated Fibre Channel and has its own storage area on the SAN where they can access data in much the same fashion as when using local disks.

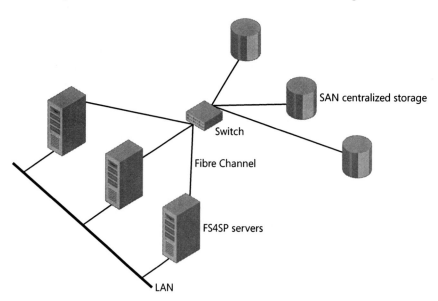

FIGURE 4-1 Storage area network (SAN).

Tests by Microsoft have shown that a sufficiently powerful SAN will not be the bottleneck in an FS4SP farm if the SAN is properly configured with dedicated disks. The key metrics for determining whether your SAN's performance is enough for FS4SP are as follows:

- 2,000–3,000 I/O operations per second (IOPS)

- 50–100 KB average block size

- Less than 10 milliseconds (ms) average read latency

> **More Info** You can read more about performance characteristics of different deployment configurations at *http://technet.microsoft.com/en-us/library/ff599526.aspx*. Both the extra-small and medium scenarios describe configurations with SSD disks.

If you have five servers in your FS4SP farm, the SAN must be able to serve 10,000–15,000 IOPS to the FS4SP farm alone, regardless of other servers using the same SAN.

> **More Info** You can use a tool called *SQLIO* to measure the raw I/O performance of your storage system. Go to *http://technet.microsoft.com/en-us/library/gg604775.aspx* for information about how to obtain and use SQLIO on an FS4SP server.

Using NAS

NAS, shown in Figure 4-2, operates similarly to a SAN except the traffic is carried over a standard high-speed local network rather than over a dedicated Fibre Channel.

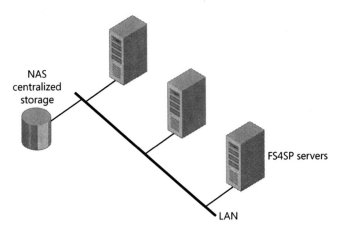

FIGURE 4-2 Network-attached storage (NAS).

NAS does not scale as well as either SAN or local disks because it shares bandwidth with the centralized storage instead of having dedicated connections. In addition to sharing bandwidth, the NAS bandwidth of a network connection is lower compared to Fibre Channel and local disks: 125 MBps for network 1 Gbps, 250 MBps for Fibre Channel 2 Gbps, and 320 MBps for local disks. The network becomes the limiting factor after you add more servers. Because FS4SP is I/O-intensive, you want disk operations to be as fast as possible, so using the network as the main I/O transport is just not a good idea.

Important The only NAS usage you should consider with FS4SP is to store log files or to do backup because NAS hinders search and indexing performance.

Using SSD

A solid-state drive (SSD) uses solid-state memory instead of magnetic platters to store persistent data. As such, an SSD has no moving parts like a traditional hard drive and does not require spin-up time. Disk access is typically around 0.1 ms—many times faster than a mechanical hard drive. This faster disk access provides improved I/O performance and very fast random disk access, which helps FS4SP perform better across the board.

High-query volume scenarios are ideal for using solid-state drives. Although a 15,000-RPM SAS disk can deliver around 200 IOPS on random read/write, an SSD drive can deliver from 5,000 IOPS to more than 1 million IOPS depending on your hardware. A test performed by Microsoft shows that two SSDs perform the same as seven 10,000-RPM SAS disks; both setups deliver more than 60 QPS while crawling is idle. To maintain a high QPS during crawling, you need to set up a dedicated search row.

More Info For more information about IOPS and to see where the numbers just referenced came from, go to *http://en.wikipedia.org/wiki/IOPS*. To see the results of the Microsoft test, go to *http://technet.microsoft.com/en-us/library/gg512814.aspx*.

FS4SP and Virtualization

For several years, there has been a shift toward setting up virtualized servers instead of physical ones and using a SAN instead of physical disks. The typical use case for virtualizing a server is to use hardware resources more efficiently and make it easier to scale a particular server's allotted resources. By hosting several servers on the same physical hardware, you also are able to cut utility costs: Because fewer physical servers require less cooling, using fewer servers by itself is cheaper to host and requires less maintenance.

Even though FS4SP supports virtualization with Microsoft Hyper-V and VMware server products, Microsoft recommends that you only use virtualized servers for FS4SP in nonproduction environments with one exception. The exception occurs when you have a separate administration server, which *can* be virtualized because the I/O requirements are low for the administration services. Tests by Microsoft have shown a general decrease of 30 percent to 40 percent in overall performance when running on virtualized servers; this decrease most likely results from the heavy use of CPU and disk I/O by FS4SP.

> **More Info** You can read more about setting up FS4SP in a virtualized environment at *http://technet.microsoft.com/en-us/library/gg702612.aspx*. To see the recommendations resulting from the Microsoft tests, go to *http://technet.microsoft.com/en-us/library/gg702612.aspx*.

When discussing virtual machines, we talk about virtual CPUs (vCPUs). A vCPU is what the guest operating system sees as an available CPU. A vCPU maps to a physical CPU *core*, not a physical CPU. Virtual machines have access to only a limited number of vCPUs—four vCPUs with Hyper-V and eight vCPUs with VMware. This low access to vCPUs limits the resources you can assign to the virtual FS4SP server, even though the physical hardware may have more available. The following provides the pros and cons of virtualization:

- **Pros** If you are a small- or medium-sized organization and have fewer than 8 million items to index, tests from Microsoft show that you can get close to 10 QPS on a single-server FS4SP farm running on Hyper-V. For a small- or medium-sized organization, 10 QPS can be enough to serve queries from a Search Center in SharePoint.

- **Cons** An issue with virtualization is redundancy. An FS4SP farm can be scaled to multiple rows to provide a hot failover of indexing and search; however, if the farm is running on the same virtual infrastructure, the entire solution could fail if the host server goes down.

To put this all into perspective, our experience shows that typical intranet scenarios peak at around 3 QPS for normal out-of-the-box FS4SP usage, well within what a virtual server can deliver. If you build a lot of search-driven applications and rely heavily on search for data retrieval on your site, the query latency will increase. When the latency per query rises above what you deem acceptable, you should move to physical hardware to scale better.

Software Requirements

You will not install any SharePoint components on the FS4SP servers, but FS4SP requires either SharePoint 2010 with Enterprise Client Access Licenses (ECAL) or a SharePoint Server 2010 for Internet Sites Enterprise Edition license in order to run. This is because all search queries pass through SharePoint, as explained in Chapter 3, "FS4SP Architecture."

> **More Info** You can find information about the software and hardware requirements for SharePoint at *http://technet.microsoft.com/en-us/library/cc262485.aspx*.

You can install FS4SP on the following operating systems:

- Windows Server 2008 R2 x64

- Windows Server 2008 SP2 x64 (Standard, Enterprise, and Datacenter versions are supported.)

You should fully update the server with the latest service pack and updates before you install FS4SP. In addition, you must install Microsoft .NET Framework 3.5 SP1 on each FS4SP server before installing the FS4SP software. You can download .NET Framework 3.5 SP1 from *http://www.microsoft.com/ download/en/details.aspx?id=22.*

Note You may use .NET Framework 4 for Pipeline Extensibility stages because an External Item Processor can be any executable and installing .NET Framework 4 will not interfere with the older versions of .NET installed on the server.

Installation Guidelines

This section does not contain detailed step-by-step installation instructions for FS4SP; instead, it focuses on what you need to do *before* installing FS4SP and on the parts of the installation that require close attention.

More Info For a complete installation guide for FS4SP, go to *http://technet.microsoft.com/ en-us/library/ff381243.aspx.*

FS4SP can be set up and configured in numerous ways, from a single server installation to a farm handling several hundred million documents. Adding to the complexity of having many servers, each server can also host several internal FS4SP components in a multitude of configurations. If the complexity of the SharePoint farm and IT infrastructure is included, you are bound to encounter issues that are not covered directly in the deployment guides provided by Microsoft. It's impossible to cover everything, but this section tries to outline what you should think about before deploying FS4SP and what you need to pay extra attention to during the installation. Table 4-3 lists some good resources that may help when you encounter an issue you do not find an immediate solution to.

TABLE 4-3 Troubleshooting resources

Resource title	Link
"Troubleshooting (FAST Search Server 2010 for SharePoint)"	*http://technet.microsoft.com/en-us/library/ff393753.aspx*
"Microsoft Search Server 2010 and Microsoft FAST Search Server 2010 Known Issues/ReadMe"	*http://office.microsoft.com/en-us/search-server-help/ microsoft-search-server-2010-and-microsoft-fast-search-server-2010-known-issues-readme-HA101793221.aspx*
"Survival Guide: FAST Search Server 2010 for SharePoint"	*http://social.technet.microsoft.com/wiki/contents/ articles/2149.aspx*
"FAST Search for SharePoint" (forum)	*http://social.technet.microsoft.com/Forums/en-US/ fastsharepoint/threads*

Before You Start

To successfully install FS4SP, you must fulfill several requirements. Use the information in Table 4-4 as a checklist before and during the installation. This information is also available as a separate down-loadable document (PDF file) at *http://fs4spbook.com/fs4sp-install-checklist*.

TABLE 4-4 Installation checklist

Category	Requirement	Notes
Accounts	The user running the installer must be a member of the local Administrators group.	Administration rights are needed to perform certain operations during installation.
Accounts	The user running the installer must have the Allow Log On Locally permission.	This permission is assigned during installation and should not be removed. Make sure you don't have any policies that will change this on reboot.
Accounts	Create a domain account to run FS4SP under, for example, sp_fastservice. The user needs the following rights: <ul><li>dbcreator role on the SQL server</li><li>Log on as a service</li><li>Allow logon locally</li></ul>	Make sure the user account is not a local administrator and not a domain administrator because this is unnecessary and increases security risks. Also make sure you don't have Group Policies overwriting the account rights.
Accounts	To simplify the process of adding more search administrators, create a domain group, for example, FASTSearchAdmin. Add this group to a local group named FASTSearchAdministrators on every FS4SP server. You can also manually create a local group called FASTSearchKeywordAdministrators and add user accounts that should have access only to keyword administration.	By using a domain group, you can add new search administrators in one place instead of on all servers. Only user accounts that are added via a domain group or directly to the local group named FASTSearchAdministrators are able to execute commands against FS4SP.

Category	Requirement	Notes
Accounts	Add all users who will administer the FS4SP installation to your domain search administrators group FASTSearchAdmin.	If you didn't create a domain group, you must add the users directly to the local FASTSearchAdministrators group on each FS4SP server, as stated earlier in this table.
Accounts	Add the user who runs the Application Pool for the web application hosting your search services to your domain search administrators group FASTSearchAdmin. Typically, the application pool is named Web Application Pool - SharePoint - 80 or something similar.	The user account running the Application Pool for the web application is needed to communicate with the FS4SP administration server. If you didn't create a domain group, you must add the user accounts directly to the local FASTSearchAdministrators group on each FS4SP server, as stated earlier in this table.
Antivirus	Exclude all FS4SP folders from antivirus scans. This includes the installation folder of FS4SP, the location of your data and log files, and any folder you have created for pipeline extensibility modules.	This prevents the antivirus software from falsely identifying FS4SP files as malware and ensures that performance is not affected by virus scans.
Antivirus	Exclude the following FS4SP binaries from antivirus scans: ■ cobra.exe ■ contentdistributor.exe ■ create_attribute_files.exe ■ docexport.exe ■ fastsearch.exe ■ fastsearchexec.exe ■ fdispatch.exe ■ fdmworker.exe ■ fixmlindex.exe ■ fsearch.exe ■ fsearchctrl.exe ■ ifilter2html.exe ■ indexer.exe ■ indexingdispatcher.exe ■ jsort2.exe ■ make_pu_diff.exe ■ monitoringservice.exe ■ pdftotext.exe ■ procserver.exe ■ qrserver.exe ■ spelltuner.exe ■ truncate_anchorinfo.exe ■ walinkstorerreceiver.exe ■ walookupdb.exe ■ webanalyzer.exe	All binaries reside in the <FASTSearchFolder>\bin folder.
Database	Verify that the main SQL Server service and the SQL Server Browser service are running.	SQL Server and SQL Server Browser have to be running in order for the installer to detect the SQL Server instance.
Database	In SQL Server Network Configuration, verify that TCP/IP is enabled under Protocols for your running instance.	FS4SP communicates with SQL Server over the TCP/IP protocol.

Category	Requirement	Notes
Database	Make sure your FS4SP service account is given the dbcreator role.	This role is needed for the installer to be able to create the admin database.
Network	Verify that all servers in the FS4SP farm have Windows Firewall turned on.	You can check the status of the Windows Firewall via Windows PowerShell with Get-Service MpsSvc. You can start the Windows Firewall service via Windows PowerShell by using Start-Service MpsSvc.*
Network	The FS4SP installer uses the computer's default settings for Internet Protocol security (IPsec) key exchange, data protection, and authentication.	If you do not use the default settings for IPsec—for example, because of domain Group Policies or the computer's local policies—ensure that the custom global firewall IPsec settings provide sufficient security. Also, ensure that the global IPsec settings are the same for all servers in the deployment.
Network	Make sure you are using static IP addresses.	Make sure that all FS4SP servers have static IP addresses to enable the installer to automatically configure IPsec in the firewall during the installation.
Network	Make sure port 13390 is open for connection on the FS4SP administration server, and make sure the other FS4SP server can connect to the port.	Non-administration servers communicate default on port 13390 to the administration server.
Network	During installation, FS4SP adds the port range 13000–13499 to the Windows Firewall settings.	If you change the base port from 13000, the range and ports are adjusted accordingly.
Network	The following default ports should be accessible from the SharePoint farm to the FS4SP farm (assuming the base port is 13000): ■ 13255: Resource Store (HTTP) ■ 13257: Administration Service (HTTP) ■ 13287: Query Service (HTTP) ■ 13391: Content Distributor	You have the option of securing the query and administration traffic by using HTTPS. The following default ports should be accessible when using HTTPS: ■ 13258: Administration Service (HTTPS) ■ 13286: Query Service (HTTPS)
Network	Make sure the TCP/IP offloading engine (TOE) is disabled.	In a multi-server FS4SP farm, the non-administration servers communicate with the administration server via IPsec and IPsec does not work correctly with TOE. This can lead to issues with the Kerberos sessions and with the FS4SP servers not being able to communicate with each other.**
Network	Make sure your database server can accept connections on port 1433.	The FS4SP administration server accesses the database server via TCP/IP on port 1433 by default. You must make sure port 1433 is added to the SQL Server firewall rules.***
Operating system	Make sure you are running either Windows Server 2008 SP2 64 bit or Windows Server 2008 R2 64 bit.	Standard, Enterprise, and Datacenter editions are supported for Windows Server 2008 SP2.
Security	Make sure you do not have a Group Policy that restricts the Kerberos Maximum Token Size. Also make sure you do not have a Group Policy that restricts Kerberos to use only User Datagram Protocol (UDP).	Changing these default values prevents FS4SP servers from communicating with each other.
Server	The server name of your FS4SP server cannot exceed 15 characters.	This is a limitation within some FS4SP components.

Category	Requirement	Notes
Server	If possible, use lowercase letters for your server name and fully qualified domain name (FQDN). Make sure you use the same casing when entering the FQDN during installation.	Some components of FS4SP require the correct casing of server names even though Windows itself is not case sensitive.**** If you can use lowercase letters everywhere instead of mixed capitalization, you are less prone to errors. As an example, use fast.contoso.com instead of FAST.contoso.com.
Server	Make sure your machine is part of a domain.	FS4SP requires your servers to be part of a domain.
Server	Turn off automatic Windows updating.	Plan to install updates after a controlled shutdown of FS4SP to avoid any possible data corruption.
Server	Disable automatic adjustment of daylight saving time (DST).	If DST adjustment is enabled, query timeouts may occur for a brief period around midnight on the date of DST adjustment.
Server	Verify that the clocks on the servers in the FS4SP farm and the SharePoint Server farm are synchronized on minute level.	The DST setting on the servers in the SharePoint Server farm is allowed to differ from the DST setting on the servers in the FS4SP farm.
Server	Activate the following features on your SharePoint farm: ■ SharePoint Server Publishing Infrastructure ■ SharePoint Server Enterprise Site Collections	By activating these SharePoint features, you can create a search center based on the FAST Search Center site template.
Server	Make sure you apply SP1 before running the configuration if you have more than four CPU cores enabled during installation.	The RTM version of FS4SP has a known bug that makes the installation of FS4SP fail if you have too many CPU cores in your system.*****
Server	Make sure the Windows service called Secondary Logon is running.	This service is often disabled during hardening of the operating system but is needed by the FS4SP configuration.
Software	Install .NET Framework 3.5 SP1	Handled by the prerequisites installer.
Software	SharePoint software is not installed on the server.	Although you can have SharePoint installed on the same server(s) as FS4SP, this setup is not a supported scenario by Microsoft. In a development scenario, it is acceptable to host SharePoint and FS4SP on the same server.
Software	The server is not a domain controller.	Although FS4SP works on a domain controller, this is not a supported scenario by Microsoft. In a development scenario, it is acceptable to host FS4SP on a domain controller.

* Even if you intend to run without a firewall in production—for example, to improve performance—you must have it turned on during installation.

** For support information about communication issues between Kerberos sessions and the FS4SP servers, go to *http://support.microsoft.com/ kb/2570111.*

*** For information about how to configure a Windows Firewall for Database Engine access, go to *http://msdn.microsoft.com/en-us/library/ ms175043.aspx.*

**** For more information about case sensitivity, go to *http://support.microsoft.com/kb/2585922.*

***** For more information about this bug, go to *http://support.microsoft.com/kb/2449600.*

Software Prerequisites

Before installing FS4SP, you must prepare the server with some additional software components. The FS4SP installer bundle contains a prerequisites installer that takes care of downloading and installing these components for you.

If your server is not connected to the Internet during installation, you need to download the software prerequisites manually. You can install them in two ways:

- Install them manually, one by one.

- Launch the prerequisites installer by using the appropriate parameters from a command-line prompt. Then have them installed for you by the prerequisites installer, described in the sidebar "Installing Predownloaded Prerequisites As Part of the Prerequisites Installer" later in this chapter.

Table 4-5 lists the software prerequisites for installing FS4SP, and Listing 4-1 provides a script for installing the components via the prerequisites installer. Using a script is well suited for unattended installation.

TABLE 4-5 Prerequisites and download links

Software component	Download link	Command-line option
Web Server (IIS) Role	Operating system feature	
Mimefilt.dll	Operating system feature	
Distributed Transaction Support	Operating system feature	
Windows Communication Foundation (WCF) Activation Components	Operating system feature	
XPS Viewer	Included with .NET Framework 3.5 SP1 redistributable package	
Microsoft .NET Framework 3.5 SP1	*http://go.microsoft.com/ FWLink/?Linkid=188659*	/NETFX35SP1:file
Microsoft .NET Framework 3.5 SP1 Hotfix*	*http://go.microsoft.com/ FWLink/?Linkid=166368*	/KB976394:file
WCF Hotfix**	*http://go.microsoft.com/ FWLink/?Linkid=166369*	/KB976462:file
Windows PowerShell 2.0	Included with Windows Server 2008 R2.	
	Windows Server 2008 SP2 x64: *http:// go.microsoft.com/FWLink/?Linkid=161023*	/PowerShell:file
Windows Identity Foundation	Windows Server 2008 SP1: *http:// go.microsoft.com/FWLink/?Linkid=160381*	/IDFX:file
	Windows Server 2008 R2: *http:// go.microsoft.com/FWLink/?Linkid=166363*	/IDFXR2:file
Microsoft Primary Interoperability Assemblies 2005	Included with the FS4SP installer	/VSInteropAssembly:file
Microsoft Visual C++ 2008 SP1 Redistributable Package (x64)	*http://go.microsoft.com/ FWLink/?Linkid=188658*	/VCCRedistPack:file
Microsoft Filter Pack 2	Included with the FS4SP installer	/FilterPack:file

* Required for Windows Server 2008 SP2 only

** Required for Windows Server 2008 R2 only

Installing Predownloaded Prerequisites As Part of the Prerequisites Installer

To run the prerequisites installer with your downloaded components, you can use the following procedure and code shown in Listing 4-1. The sample code can be used both for Windows Server 2008 SP2 and Windows Server 2008 R2.

1. On drive C, create a folder called **FASTprereq** to host the prerequisites files.

   The FS4SP installation media is in drive D, shown in Figure 4-3.

2. In the FASTprereq folder, create a file named **prereq-install.cmd**.

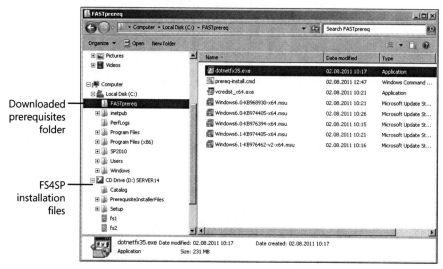

FIGURE 4-3 FS4SP installation folder and downloaded prerequisites folder.

3. Copy the code in Listing 4-1 to the newly created file.

4. Launch *prereq-install.cmd*.

   LISTING 4-1 Prerequisites installer code

```
@echo off
set PREREQ_DIR=C:\FASTprereq
set FS4SP_INSTALL=D:\
cd /D %FS4SP_INSTALL%
PrerequisiteInstaller.exe /IDFX:%PREREQ_DIR%\Windows6.0-KB974405-x64.msu /
IDFXR2:%PREREQ_DIR%\Windows6.1-KB974405-x64.msu /VCCRedistPack:%PREREQ_DIR%\
vcredist_x64.exe /NETFX35SP1:%PREREQ_DIR%\dotnetfx35.exe /PowerShell:%PREREQ_
DIR%\Windows6.0-KB968930-x64.msu /KB976394:%PREREQ_DIR%\Windows6.0-KB976394-x64.
msu /KB976462:%PREREQ_DIR%\Windows6.1-KB976462-v2-x64.msu /unattended
if ERRORLEVEL 0 goto Success
echo Something went wrong. Code %ERRORLEVEL%
goto End
:Success
echo Prerequisites installed
:End
```

FS4SP Preinstallation Configuration

Before installing FS4SP, you need to change the execution policy of Windows PowerShell scripts. This is to ensure that the Configuration Wizard you run later is able to run Windows PowerShell scripts during configuration. To change the execution policy, open a Windows PowerShell command window as an administrator. At the Windows PowerShell prompt, run the following code.

```
Set-ExecutionPolicy RemoteSigned
```

You can install the FS4SP binaries in two ways:

- Via the GUI by starting the installer from the splash screen or by manually executing *fsserver.msi*

- Unattended by using the following command.

```
Msiexec /i fsserver.msi /q FASTSEARCHSERVERINSTALLLOCATION="<InstallDir>" /l <LogFile>
```

<InstallDir> is the location where you want to install the FS4SP binaries. *<LogFile>* is the path and file name of the installation log file. You can omit the */q* parameter if you want to see progress while installing. For example:

```
Msiexec /i fsserver.msi /q FASTSEARCHSERVERINSTALLLOCATION="C:\FASTSearch" /l C:\fastinstall.log
```

After you install the binaries, continue with the post-setup configuration and be sure to add your FAST admin users to the local FASTSearchAdministrators group before rebooting the server.

> **Important** If you are using SQL authentication between your FS4SP farm and SQL Server, you must configure FS4SP via Windows PowerShell and cannot use the Microsoft FAST Search Server 2010 For SharePoint Configuration Wizard.

FS4SP Update Installation

After you complete the initial FS4SP configuration and setup, Microsoft recommends that you install the latest service pack and/or cumulative updates for FS4SP. Note that fixes for FS4SP occur both on the SharePoint farm and on the FS4SP farm. Use the following links to find information on the latest updates:

- See "Update Center for Microsoft Office, Office Server, and Related Products" at *http://technet.microsoft.com/en-US/office/ee748587.aspx* for the latest updates about SharePoint.

- See "Updates for Enterprise Search Products" at *http://technet.microsoft.com/en-US/enterprisesearch/gg176677.aspx* for the latest updates about FS4SP.

  You can also find a wiki page that describes the FS4SP updates in more detail at *http://social.technet.microsoft.com/wiki/contents/articles/fast-search-for-sharepoint-cumulative-updates.aspx*.

Opening FS4SP Shells or SharePoint Management Shells with Administrative Privileges

You can use the following procedures to open an FS4SP shell or a SharePoint Management Shell.

To open an FS4SP shell with administrative privileges:

■ On the Start menu, click All Programs, click Microsoft FAST Search Server 2010 For SharePoint, right-click Microsoft FAST Search Server 2010 For SharePoint Shell, and then select Run As Administrator.

To open a SharePoint Management Shell with administrative privileges:

■ On the Start menu, click All Programs, click Microsoft SharePoint 2010 Products, right-click SharePoint 2010 Management Shell, and then select Run As Administrator.

When applying updates to a running system, you need to address a couple of points:

■ **Have you added a custom Pipeline Extensibility module?**   See Chapter 7, "Content Processing," for more information about how to extend the indexing pipeline.

■ **Have you increased the content capacity to support more than 30 million items per column?**   See Chapter 5 for more information about how to increase the content capacity.

If you answered "yes" to one or both questions, make sure you back up the changed configuration files before running the post-setup configuration script. If you don't, there is a high probability the files will be overwritten during the patch process and you will lose your customizations. See the section "Manual and Automatic Synchronization of Configuration Changes" later in this chapter for a list of files that are overwritten during configuration changes.

Best practice with FS4SP is to make a copy of any configuration file you have edited manually before applying an update. After applying an update and running the post-setup configuration script in patch mode, compare the backed-up files with the live ones to ensure all your edits are still in place.

Run the post-setup configuration script in patch mode

An update may include updates to configuration files, and these updates are usually patched into the existing files. As such, you need to run the post-setup configuration script in patch mode to apply the patches to your system.

1.   Open an FS4SP shell.

2.   Browse to *<FASTSearchFolder>*\installer\scripts, where *<FASTSearchFolder>* is the path of the folder in which you have installed FAST Search Server 2010 for SharePoint, for example, C:\FASTSearch.

3. Type the following command to run the post-setup configuration script in patch mode.

```
.\psconfig.ps1 -action p.
```

 More Info For a detailed description about how to apply a software update to FS4SP in a single-server or multi-server farm, go to *http://technet.microsoft.com/en-us/library/hh285624.aspx*.

FS4SP Slipstream Installation

There is no official documentation on slipstreaming in service packs or cumulative updates with the installation of FS4SP, but because service packs and cumulative updates contain Windows Installer patch files (.msp files), you can use the patch parameter of Windows Installer to also install the updates during installation.

Using service pack 1 as an example, execute the following command from a command prompt to unpack the .msp files from the service pack. The same procedure can be applied to cumulative updates. Type the following command, where *x:\installfolder* is the destination drive and folder location where you unpack the service pack.

```
fastsearchserver2010sp1-kb2460039-x64-fullfile-en-us.exe /extract:x:\installfolder
```

Next, save the script in Listing 4-2 to a file named **fs4spslipstream.cmd**.

LISTING 4-2 Slipstream installation script

```
@echo off
if "%1" == "" goto error
if "%2" == "" goto error
setlocal enabledelayedexpansion
set patches=
for %%i In ("%2\*.msp") DO set patches=!patches!%%i ;
%1\fsserver.msi /update "%patches%"
goto end
:error
echo.
echo Usage: fs4spslipstream.cmd [fs4sp install files folder] [patch files folder]
echo.
echo Example: fs4spslipstream.cmd d:\ c:\patches
echo.
:end
```

If your FS4SP installation files reside in d:\ and your extracted patches in c:\patches, you can do a slipstream installation by using the following command from a command prompt.

```
fs4spslipstream.cmd d:\ c:\patches
```

After the installation, you need to run the post-setup configuration as normal.

Single-Server FS4SP Farm Configuration

This section covers the steps of the Microsoft FAST Search Server 2010 For SharePoint Configuration Wizard. (We refer to this wizard throughout the rest of the chapter as just the *Configuration Wizard*.) The section also explains the different options found in the Configuration Wizard. The same options must be set in a scripted configuration.

Configure a single-server FS4SP farm by using the Configuration Wizard

1. When you configure FS4SP as a single-server FS4SP farm, choose the Single Server (Stand-Alone) option in the Configuration Wizard, shown in Figure 4-4. (The other two options are used for deploying a multi-server farm.)

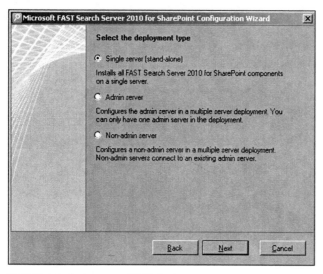

FIGURE 4-4 Single-server FS4SP deployment.

2. On the next page of the wizard, enter the user name and password that your FS4SP service will run under, as shown in Figure 4-5. (See Table 4-4 for the account requirements.)

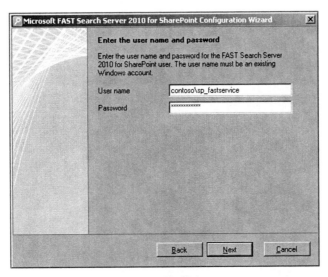

FIGURE 4-5 FS4SP service user credentials.

3. On the next page of the wizard, enter a password for the self-signed certificate, as shown in Figure 4-6. This password is needed when installing the certificate on the SharePoint farm (if you decide to go with the self-signed certificate for your deployment).

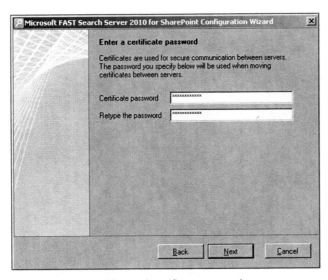

FIGURE 4-6 FS4SP self-signed certificate password.

4. On the Server Settings page of the Configuration Wizard, shown in Figure 4-7, you can either use a default deployment configuration file or provide a custom one. See the section "Deployment Configuration" later in this chapter for more information about the default deployment configuration file.

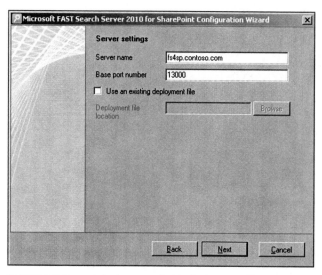

FIGURE 4-7 Use a default or an existing deployment file.

5. On the next page of the wizard, enter the database settings for where FS4SP stores the administration database, as shown in Figure 4-8.

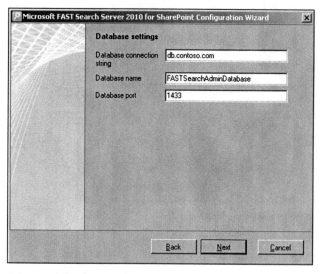

FIGURE 4-8 Database settings.

6. Click-through relevancy is a feature that gives an additional boost to items that are frequently opened from the search results. Over time, this feature helps identify high-value and important items, ensuring they are moved up the result list.

If you want to enable click-through relevancy, on the Click-Through Relevancy Settings page, choose either Standalone or Server Farm depending on the installation mode of SharePoint Server, as shown in Figure 4-9. If you set up SharePoint Server as a farm, enter the user name of the user running the Microsoft SharePoint 2010 Timer Service.

Note When you enable click-through relevancy, SharePoint logs all clicks for results on the search page in a SharePoint Search Center site. These logs are then transferred to your FS4SP server at specific intervals for processing.

The more clicks a result item receives from your users on a given search term, the higher ranked the result item will be for that search term. The result item is given a boost for future queries, potentially moving it higher up the result list as more users click it.

If you decide not to install click-through relevancy during the initial configuration, you can enable it afterward by following the steps outlined at this link: *http://technet.microsoft.com/en-us/library/ff384289*.

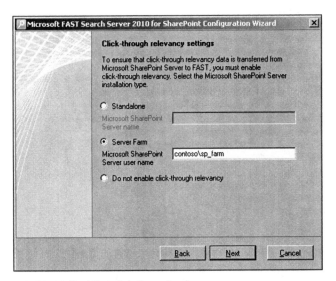

FIGURE 4-9 Enabling click-through relevancy.

7. The last page of the wizard shows a summary of your choices. Click Configure to finish the configuration.

Deployment Configuration

When using the default deployment configuration, the following components are installed on your server:

- Administration services
- Document processors (four instances)
- Content Distributor
- Indexing Dispatcher
- FAST Search Web crawler
- Web Analyzer
- Indexer
- QR Server

The deployment configuration file in use after an initial configuration with the default file *deployment.xml* is located at *<FASTSearchFolder>\etc\config_data\deployment\deployment.xml*. The deployment configuration file is identical in configuration to the single-server sample deployment configuration located at *<FASTSearchFolder>\etc\deployment.sample.single.xml*.

The following code shows a sample file for single-server deployment.

```
<?xml version="1.0" encoding="utf-8" ?>
<deployment version="14" modifiedBy="" modifiedTime="2010-06-21T14:39:17+01:00" comment="FAST
Search Server single node deployment example" xmlns="http://www.microsoft.com/enterprisesearch"
xmlns:xsi="http://www.w3.org/2001/XMLSchema-instance" xsi:schemaLocation="http://www.microsoft.
com/enterprisesearch deployment.xsd">
  <!-- Logical name for entire installation - replace with suitable name after own wishes -->
  <instanceid>FAST Search Server Single Node</instanceid>
  <!-- Used by connectors - replace with correct values -->
  <connector-databaseconnectionstring><![CDATA[jdbc:sqlserver://sqlservername\instancename:portn
uber;DatabaseName=dbname]]></connector-databaseconnectionstring>
  <!-- Single node, replace name of host with correct hostname -->
  <host name="single01.search.microsoft.com">
    <admin />
    <!-- Set with number of document processors needed -->
    <document-processor processes="4" />
    <content-distributor id="0" />
    <indexing-dispatcher />
    <!-- replace organization name and email if crawler will be used, this information is left
behind at  sites the crawler visits. This tag can be removed if the crawler will not be used -->
    <crawler role="single" />
    <!-- Max targets is the number of CPU's the web analyzer utilizes -->
    <webanalyzer server="true" max-targets="1" link-processing="true" lookup-db="true" />
    <searchengine row="0" column="0" />
    <query />
  </host>
  <searchcluster>
    <row id="0" index="primary" search="true" />
  </searchcluster>
</deployment>
```

Multi-Server FS4SP Farm Configuration

When configuring a multi-server farm, you use a deployment configuration file very similar to the one used for single-server deployment. The difference is that you define more host servers where you spread out the different components, as described in Chapter 3. Inside the deployment configuration file, you define the configuration for all the servers building up your FS4SP farm, and you use the same configuration file on all machines. The first server to be configured in a multi-server farm is the server that holds the administration component.

Listing 4-3 shows configuration for a two-server deployment, where *multi01.contoso.com* hosts the administration component and, thus, must be installed first as an administration server by using the option *Admin server*, shown in bold in Listing 4-3. The other server, *multi02.contoso.com*, uses the *Non-admin server* option, also shown in Listing 4-3.

LISTING 4-3 Deployment configuration file for two servers

```xml
<?xml version="1.0" encoding="utf-8" ?>
<deployment xmlns="http://www.microsoft.com/enterprisesearch">
  <instanceid>FAST Search Server Multi Node 1</instanceid>
  <connector-databaseconnectionstring><![CDATA[jdbc:sqlserver://sqlservername\instancename:portn
uber;DatabaseName=dbname]]></connector-databaseconnectionstring>
  <host name="multi01.contoso.com">
    <admin />
    <document-processor processes="8" />
    <content-distributor />
    <indexing-dispatcher />
    <webanalyzer server="true" link-processing="true" lookup-db="true" max-targets="4" />
    <searchengine row="0" column="0" />
    <query />
  </host>
  <host name="multi02.contoso.com">
    <document-processor processes="4" />
    <searchengine row="1" column="0" />
    <query />
  </host>
  <searchcluster>
    <row id="0" index="primary" search="true" />
    <row id="1" index="none" search="true" />
  </searchcluster>
</deployment>
```

Your FS4SP installation comes with three reference sample deployment files located in *<FASTSearchFolder>\etc*:

- A single-server farm (*deployment.sample.single.xml*)

- A two-server farm (*deployment.sample.multi1.xml*)

- A five-server farm (*deployment.samlple.multi2.xml*)

> **More Info** A detailed explanation about all settings of the *deployment.xml* file can be found at *http://technet.microsoft.com/en-us/library/ff354931.aspx*.

Manual and Automatic Synchronization of Configuration Changes

When setting up a multi-server FS4SP farm, make sure all servers performing specific roles are configured in the same way. You can change some settings on the administration server and they will be automatically copied over to the other servers; with other settings, you have to manually execute on the different servers.

Table 4-6 outlines the different configuration files in FS4SP that you can edit, on which server or servers you have to edit the files, and if you need to take special actions on the files when applying an FS4SP service pack or cumulative update.

TABLE 4-6 Supported configuration files

File	Where to update	Comment	File location
loggerconfig.xml	All servers	This file is overwritten when you apply updates and service packs.*	*<FASTSearchFolder>\etc*
logserverconfig.xml	All servers		*<FASTSearchFolder>\etc*
monitoringservice.xml	All servers		*<FASTSearchFolder>\etc*
custompropertyextractors.xml	Administration server		*<FASTSearchFolder>\etc\ config_data\ DocumentProcessor*
deployment.xml	Administration server		*<FASTSearchFolder>\etc\ config_data\deployment*
optionalprocessing.xml	Administration server		*<FASTSearchFolder>\etc\ config_data\ DocumentProcessor*
user_converter_rules.xml	Administration server	This file is overwritten when applying updates and service packs.*	*<FASTSearchFolder>\etc\ config_data\ DocumentProcessor\ formatdetector*
xmlmapper.xml	Administration server		*<FASTSearchFolder>\etc\ config_data\ DocumentProcessor*
pipelineextensibility.xml	Servers running a document processor	This file is overwritten when applying updates and service packs.*	*<FASTSearchFolder>\etc*
Third-party IFilters	Servers running a document processor	You must install the IFilters on all servers.	
All custom pipeline extensibility modules	Servers running a document processor	You must deploy your custom modules to all servers.	
jdbctemplate.xml	Servers running the FAST Database connector	You should always make a copy of this file and not use the template.	*<FASTSearchFolder>\etc*

File	Where to update	Comment	File location
beconfig.xml	Servers running the FAST Enterprise Web crawler		*<FASTSearchFolder>\etc*
crawlercollectiondefaults.xml	Servers running the FAST Enterprise Web crawler	This file is overwritten when you apply updates and service packs.*	*<FASTSearchFolder>\etc*
crawlerglobaldefaults.xml	Servers running the FAST Enterprise Web crawler	This file is overwritten when you apply updates and service packs.*	*<FASTSearchFolder>\etc*
cctklog4j.xml	Servers running the FAST Search Database connector and Servers running the FAST Search Lotus Notes connector	This file is overwritten when you apply updates and service packs.*	*<FASTSearchFolder>\etc*
lotusnotessecuritytemplate.xml	Servers running the FAST Search Lotus Notes connector	You should always make a copy of this file and not use the template.	*<FASTSearchFolder>\etc*
lotusnotestemplate.xml	Servers running the FAST Search Lotus Notes connector	You should always make a copy of this file and not use the template.	*<FASTSearchFolder>\etc*
rtsearchrc.xml	Servers that are part of the search cluster	This file is overwritten when you apply updates and service packs.*	*<FASTSearchFolder>\etc\ config_data\RTSearch\ webcluster*

* When you run the post-setup configuration script in patch mode after installing an update or a service pack, the script executes the FS4SP cmdlet *Set-FASTSearchConfiguration*, which overwrites the file.

Certificates and Security

Certificates are used for authenticating traffic between FS4SP and SharePoint and for authenticating traffic between servers in a multi-server FS4SP farm. In addition, certificates are used to encrypt traffic when you use Secure Socket Layer (SSL) communication between the SharePoint farm and the FS4SP farm over the optional HTTPS protocol for query traffic and administration traffic (for example, when adding best bets).

Each server in an FS4SP farm potentially has three certificates that serve different functions and must be configured and replaced separately. The first two certificates can be combined into one certificate if you do not have a requirement to use HTTPS for the query and administration services traffic:

- A general purpose FS4SP certificate that is used for internal communication, administration services, and when indexing content via SharePoint (FAST Content SSA).

- A server-specific certificate for query traffic that uses HTTPS. This is needed only on query servers that have HTTPS query traffic enabled.

- A Claims certificate, which is a certificate that you export from your SharePoint farm to the FS4SP servers running as QR Servers.

By using certificates issued by a common certification authority (CA) for authentication and for traffic encryption over HTTPS, FS4SP can provide a very high level of security if needed. This ensures that no one can access sensitive information that is contained in the query traffic; best practice is to use HTTPS if your documents contain highly sensitive information.

 Important Even though traffic is encrypted when you use HTTPS, the query logs are still accessible in clear text on the FS4SP servers for users that have access to those servers.

During the initial installation, FS4SP generates a self-signed certificate. This certificate has a one-year expiration date from the date of installation and is meant to be used in test and development environments. If you decide to use the self-signed certificate in production and don't want to replace the certificate every year, you can modify the certificate creation script in FS4SP in order to extend the expiration date to, for example, 100 years. See Chapter 9, "Useful Tips and Tricks," for information about how to extend the default certificate.

To verify that your certificate is registered correctly, you can execute the following Windows PowerShell cmdlet. This cmdlet checks whether the SharePoint server can connect to a content distributor on the FS4SP farm.

```
Ping-SPEnterpriseSearchContentService
```

Follow these steps:

1. Open a SharePoint Management Shell as an administrator.

2. Type the following command, where *<hostname>:<port>* is the host name and port number for your content distributor found in *<FASTSearchFolder>\Install_Info.txt*.

   ```
   Ping-SPEnterpriseSearchContentService -HostName <hostname>:<port>
   ```

The command output should list *ConnectionSuccess* as *True* for your certificate, shown in Figure 4-10. If all lines read *False*, the certificate is not correctly set up.

Certificate used between the FAST Content SSA and the Content Distributor

FIGURE 4-10 Successfully installed FS4SP self-signed certificate in SharePoint.

Security Considerations

Using certificates and encrypting traffic are both important contributions for guarding against unauthorized access to information in your FS4SP deployment. When deciding whether you need a CA-issued certificate for your servers or need to encrypt traffic with HTTPS, you should coordinate these needs with the security guidelines in your organization and how you evaluate the threat level in your network environment.

 Note From our experience, deploying FS4SP with HTTPS-enabled and CA-issued certificates often hits many bumps. The time used to get it to work should be weighed against the added security it brings.

Traffic between servers in a production environment is often secured with firewall settings that prevent unauthorized monitoring of data traffic. If you do not have special requirements for using certificates and encrypted traffic within your organization, you can use the self-signed certificate in production.

The importance of security should not be downplayed in an FS4SP deployment, but you have to evaluate the maintenance and complexity of using CA-issued certificates in your deployment against the security gained. Also, remember that a user with local access to an FS4SP server can have access to all indexed data in clear text via the intermediate FIXML files and the query logs, depending on the rights assigned to those files.

 More Info For information about the use of certificates, additional IPsec setup for encrypting inter-FS4SP farm communication, proxy settings, antivirus settings, and user account requirements, go to *http://technet.microsoft.com/en-us/library/ff599535.aspx*.

Creating FAST Content SSAs and FAST Query SSAs

As described in Chapter 3, FS4SP requires two Search Service Applications (SSAs). The FAST Query SSA handles all incoming search requests as well as the search index for People Search, and the FAST Content SSA handles the content sources and indexing.

 More Info Setting up the FAST Content SSA is described in a TechNet article at *http://technet.microsoft.com/en-us/library/ff381261.aspx*. Setting up the FAST Query SSA is described in a TechNet article at *http://technet.microsoft.com/en-us/library/ff381251.aspx*.

When you create the SSAs, both have one crawler component assigned, and each crawler component is associated with one crawler database. Adding crawler components to additional farm servers is done to distribute the crawl load. With FS4SP, the crawl components use fewer system resources compared to the built-in SharePoint search because of the architecture: Items are sent over to the FS4SP farm for processing instead of being processed on the SharePoint server. However, during monitoring of your system, if it is peaking on CPU usage during crawling or the crawler database on the SQL Server is showing reduced performance, adding an additional crawler component and optional crawler database can improve the situation.

To provide failover for search queries, you can add additional query components in the same fashion that you add crawler components. Because the FS4SP farm handles the actual query processing and the load associated with it, you should never need more than two query components in your SharePoint farm.

 Important You must configure each server that hosts a crawl component to use an SSL certificate for FS4SP. If you used the self-signed certificate when you enabled SSL communication for the FAST Content SSA, you must use the same certificate on the server with the added crawler component. If you instead used a CA-issued certificate, you must use a certificate issued by the same CA as the original certificate on the server with the added crawler component.

A detailed description about how to add and remove crawler components and the required certificates can be found at *http://technet.microsoft.com/en-us/library/ff599534.aspx*.

Enabling Queries from SharePoint to FS4SP

Queries from SharePoint are sent over to the FS4SP farm by using claims-based authentication with certificates. To set up claims-based authentication, you export a certificate from the SharePoint farm and install it on all QR Servers in the FS4SP farm. The traffic is, by default, sent over HTTP, but you can optionally secure this traffic further by using SSL certificates over HTTPS.

 More Info Detailed steps about installing the certificates can be found at *http://technet.microsoft.com/en-us/library/ff381253.aspx*.

Creating a Search Center

After you set up the FAST Content SSA for crawling, the FAST Query SSA for handling search queries, and the communication between the SharePoint farm and the FS4SP farm, you can set up a Search Center on your SharePoint farm. This Search Center can be used to execute queries against the FAST Query SSA. The Search Center is a SharePoint site based on the FAST Search Center site template. Customizations and configurations of the Search Center are covered in depth in Part II of this book.

More Info Detailed steps about setting up a Search Center site can be found at *http://technet.microsoft.com/en-us/library/ff381248.aspx*.

Scripted Installation

When you install FS4SP, particularly in larger deployments, you are often required to automate and streamline the deployment procedure. With FS4SP, this can be achieved for both the installer and the post-configuration process because they can be run in unattended mode. The included offering requires you to manually start the installation and configuration in unattended mode locally on each server; however, it is possible to automate this process even further by creating custom Windows PowerShell scripts that use remoting to install and configure FS4SP on all servers.

After you install and configure FS4SP, you still must manually execute the certificate procedures between the FS4SP farm and the SharePoint farm, set up the FAST Content SSA and the FAST Query SSA on the SharePoint farm, and create a Search Center. These tasks are outside the scope of the scripts included with FS4SP but can be automated with custom scripts.

More Info You can read more about scripted installation and configuration of FS4SP at *http://technet.microsoft.com/en-us/library/ff381263.aspx*.

Advanced Filter Pack

Out of the box, FS4SP supports extracting text from the file formats listed in Table 4-7. The default text extraction is provided by the Microsoft Filter Pack, one of the prerequisites when installing FS4SP.

TABLE 4-7 File types included by default

File name extension	Comment
.pdf	Adobe Portable Document Format file
.html (and all other HTML files, regardless of file name extension)	Hypertext Markup Language file
.mht	MHTML web archive
.eml	Microsoft email message
.xlb	Microsoft Excel binary spreadsheet (Excel 2003 and earlier)
.xlsb	Excel binary spreadsheet (Excel 2010 and Excel 2007)
.xlm	Excel macro-enabled spreadsheet (Excel 2003 and earlier)
.xlsm	Excel Open XML macro-enabled spreadsheet (Excel 2010 and Excel 2007)
.xlsx	Excel Open XML spreadsheet (Excel 2010 and Excel 2007)
.xls	Excel spreadsheet (Excel 2003 and earlier)

File name extension	Comment
.xlc	Excel spreadsheet chart file
.xlt	Excel template
.one	Microsoft OneNote document
.msg	Microsoft Outlook mail message
.pptm	Microsoft PowerPoint Open XML macro-enabled presentation (PowerPoint 2010 and PowerPoint 2007)
.pptx	PowerPoint Open XML presentation (PowerPoint 2010 and PowerPoint 2007)
.ppsx*	PowerPoint Open XML slide show (PowerPoint 2010 and PowerPoint 2007)
.ppt	PowerPoint presentation
.pps	PowerPoint slide show
.pot	PowerPoint template
.pub	Microsoft Publisher document
.vsd	Microsoft Visio drawing file
.vdw	Visio Graphics Service file
.vss	Visio stencil file
.vsx	Visio stencil XML file
.vst	Visio template
.vtx	Visio template XML file
.doc	Microsoft Word document (Word 2003 and earlier)
.dot	Word document template (Word 2003 and earlier)
.docx	Word Open XML document (Word 2010 and Word 2007)
.dotx	Word Open XML document template (Word 2010 and Word 2007)
.docm	Word Open XML macro-enabled document (Word 2010 and Word 2007)
.xps	Microsoft XML Paper Specification file
.mhtml	MIME HTML file
.odp	OpenDocument presentation
.ods	OpenDocument spreadsheet
.odt	OpenDocument text document
.txt (and all other plain text files, regardless of file name extension)	Plain text file
.rtf	Rich Text Format file
.nws	Windows Live Mail newsgroup file
.zip	Zipped file

* Support for this format requires that you have installed Microsoft Office 2010 Filter Pack Service Pack 1, which is available at *http://support.microsoft.com/kb/2460041*.

FS4SP comes with an option named the *Advanced Filter Pack*. With the Advanced Filter Pack, you can extract text and metadata from several hundred additional document formats. These formats complement those included with the Microsoft Filter Pack.

> **More Info** You can see the complete list of files supported by the Advanced Filter Pack by opening the file *<FASTSearchFolder>\etc\formatdetector\converter_rules.xml* in a text editor.

Before purchasing a third-party IFilter for metadata and text extraction, you should see whether the Advanced Filter Pack already supports your document format. The Advanced Filter Pack is turned off by default but is easily enabled by using Windows PowerShell. See Chapter 9 for information about enabling or disabling the Advanced Filter Pack.

> **Important** Remember to activate the Advanced Filter Pack on all servers that have the document processor component installed.

IFilter

If you have a file format that is not covered by the Microsoft Filter Pack or the Advanced Filter Pack, you can obtain and install a third-party IFilter that handles the document conversion. You can find several vendors of third-party IFilters; you can also develop your own.

When installing a third-party IFilter, you should pay attention to the following points:

- Only 64-bit versions of IFilters work with FS4SP.

- The IFilter has to be installed on all FS4SP servers hosting the document processor component.

- Make sure the file extension that your new IFilter handles is *not* listed in the File Types list on your FAST Content SSA. The File Types list includes all extensions *not* to be crawled.

- Edit *<FASTSearchFolder>\etc\config_data\DocumentProcessor\formatdetector\user_converter_rules.xml* on the FS4SP administration server to include the extension for the file handled by the IFilter.

> **More Info** For information about configuring FS4SP to use a third-party IFilter, go to *http://msdn.microsoft.com/en-us/library/ff795798.aspx*.

- Issue **psctrl reset** in order for the document processors to pick up and use the new IFilter.

Replacing the Existing SharePoint Search with FS4SP

Depending on your content volume, doing a full crawl can take a lot of time. Fortunately, if you are upgrading to FS4SP from an existing SharePoint deployment, you can keep your existing SharePoint search while you deploy FS4SP and get it up and running.

SharePoint Central Administration has a section where you configure which service applications are associated with your current web application. The SharePoint Search Service Application is set as the default SSA in the application proxy group.

As long as you keep your existing SSA and include it in the application proxy group, SharePoint redirects any search queries to the existing search. When you are finished setting up the FAST Content SSA and the FAST Query SSA, you associate the FAST Query SSA as your new SSA in the application proxy group instead of your existing one.

 More Info You can read more about the application proxy group and how to add and remove service applications to a web application at *http://technet.microsoft.com/en-us/ library/ee704550.aspx*.

To ease the transition of moving your crawler setup from your existing SSA to the FAST Content SSA, you can use the export and import Windows PowerShell scripts at the following locations:

- **Import** *http://gallery.technet.microsoft.com/scriptcenter/ 3a942068-e84a-4349-8eb7-019cc29542a9*

- **Export** *http://gallery.technet.microsoft.com/scriptcenter/ 5ce9297e-90e6-4439-a584-04182b12dd43*

Another approach is to upgrade your existing SSA to a FAST Query SSA. See Chapter 9 for information about how you can upgrade your existing SSA to ease the migration process.

Development Environments

When developing for FS4SP, you need both SharePoint and FS4SP installed. Because you may often change configurations in both environments, the most suitable development environment has everything installed on the same machine. This is not a supported production environment but works fine for a single-user development setup.

For a single-server FS4SP development setup, you start off with a domain controller that has SQL Server and SharePoint installed, and you continue with installing FS4SP on the same machine. If you develop pipeline extensibility stages or custom Web Parts in your solution, you also have to install Microsoft Visual Studio on your machine.

More Info For information about setting up the development environment for SharePoint on Windows Vista, Windows 7, and Windows Server 2008, go to *http://msdn.microsoft.com/ en-us/library/ee554869.aspx*.

FS4SP supports SharePoint in both stand-alone and farm mode, but it requires SharePoint to be installed with an Enterprise license to enable the FS4SP features.

Single-Server Farm Setup

As explained earlier, FS4SP is a disk I/O–intensive application. The same goes for SharePoint because most operations require database access. When bundling SQL Server, SharePoint, and FS4SP on the same machine, disk I/O quickly becomes the bottleneck.

Desktop computers have room for setting up multiple disks in RAID and can increase the disk I/O throughput that way; however, laptops usually have room for only one or two hard drives, which are also slower than the desktop counterparts because of the smaller form factor.

Using an SSD disk is key to setting up an optimal single-server development environment for FS4SP. This yields far better performance compared to mechanical drives, even when the mechanical drives are set up in RAID. If you have the option to use SSD disks, you can save a lot of waiting time during development and test cycles, and you will become a more effective developer.

When it comes to RAM, 4 GB is sufficient when combined with an SSD disk but should be increased if you don't have SSD as an option.

To sum it up, the faster the disk is and the more memory you have, the more responsive your development environment will be.

Multi-Server Farm Setup

If you develop modules for both the SharePoint environment and the FS4SP environment, best practice is to have both SharePoint and FS4SP installed on the same server; equal to the single-server setup described in the previous section.

By adding a second server, you can move the domain controller role and SQL Server over to that machine. This move reduces the disk I/O on your development machine.

If you develop modules for either SharePoint or FS4SP only, you can add a third server and move out the system you are not targeting in your development to that server. This leaves the most re-sources to the server you are working on for your development, ensuring that your environment is as effective as possible.

Physical Machines

If you have a dedicated machine for development, install Windows Server 2008 SP2 or Windows Server 2008 R2 as your operating system and install SharePoint and FS4SP afterward, just like you would when setting up a development server for SharePoint. This allows your setup to have full access to disk, RAM, and CPU.

Virtual Machines

If you don't have a dedicated FS4SP development machine but have to host FS4SP on an existing machine that runs your day-to-day applications like Microsoft Exchange Server or Active Directory directory services, a better option is to use a virtual machine. A virtual machine does not have direct access to your disk, RAM, and CPU and will have a performance overhead, most noticeably on the disk.

If you must use solely Microsoft products, your only option for running a virtual machine is to use Windows Server 2008 R2 with Hyper-V as your desktop operating system. Microsoft Virtual PC is not an option because it does not support running guest operating systems in 64 bit, a requirement for SharePoint and FS4SP.

Other alternatives are to use the free VMware Player, the commercial VMware Workstation, or Oracle VirtualBox. All of these support 64-bit guest operating systems, for example, Windows Server 2008 R2.

Booting from a VHD

An alternative to running a full virtual server is to only virtualize the disk and use dual boot. With dual booting, you can have several operating systems installed side by side on different disk partitions or on Hyper-V virtual disks and pick which operating system to start when you turn on your computer.

Both Windows 7 and Windows 2008 R2 come with a feature that you can use to boot the operating system from a virtual hard file (VHD). This boot option has the benefit that only the disk subsystem is virtualized while the CPU and RAM are accessed directly. This way, you can run your FS4SP development setup side by side with your day-to-day machine setup but at the expense of having to reboot in order to switch between the environments.

 More Info TechNet has a video on how to set up dual-boot with Windows 7 and Windows Server 2008 R2 at *http://technet.microsoft.com/en-us/edge/Video/ff710851*.

Production Environments

Setting up a production environment for FS4SP involves careful planning and consideration to match your search requirements. This section highlights important areas that affect how you set up your production environment.

More Info TechNet has a thorough explanation on performance and capacity planning from both a business perspective and system architectural perspective at *http:// technet.microsoft.com/en-us/library/gg604780.aspx*.

Content Volume

When you start to plan your FS4SP farm, the first thing you should consider is how much content you intend to index. *Content* includes objects such as documents, webpages, SharePoint list items, and database records.

In our opinion, it is better to know how many files of different file formats you want to index instead of knowing the disk usage of the raw data, for example, 2 TB. There are a couple of reasons to use the number-of-items approach instead of the disk space approach. One reason is that a file server usually contains a wide variety of files, many of which consume a lot of space but are not interesting for indexing. Log files, backups, and company event pictures are such examples and often consume a large part of a file server's total volume. The second reason is the default absolute maximum limit for the number of items in one index column of 30 million items, as mentioned earlier; when exceeding the recommended 15 million items, indexing goes slower and slower until you hit 30 million. At this point, the index column stops accepting more items.

More Info For recommendations about content volume capacity for FS4SP, go to *http:// technet.microsoft.com/en-us/library/gg702617.aspx*.

The 30-million item limit exists regardless of the item size because FS4SP internally is configured with six internal partitions, each holding 5 million items. During indexing, items are moved between the partitions; when you start filling them up, you generate more disk I/O, which accounts for the degradation in indexing speed. Also, searching over a larger index size requires more disk I/O per search. That said, size is not unimportant, and it is important to know what data the 2 TB contains and how many unique items it represents. Indexing 100,000 list rows in SharePoint generates a smaller index on disk compared to indexing 100,000 Word documents. Hence, searching across the 100,000 list items performs faster compared to the Word documents for the same reason.

Note The 15-million item limit can be extended to 40 million by using high density mode. For more information, go to *http://technet.microsoft.com/en-us/library/gg482017.aspx*.

Ideally, you would be able to add more servers as your content grows; however, there is currently no automatic distribution of the already-indexed content to new servers. You must either perform an index reset and full crawl when extending the index capacity or see the section "Server Topology Management" in Chapter 5, which discusses how to redistribute the internal FIXML files. If downtime of your search solution is acceptable, you can go for the first approach, which is easier to perform.

The second approach—redistributing the FIXML files—only causes downtime for indexing new content and is the most desirable when adding servers to accommodate content growth. For most businesses, however, search has become a vital part of the information infrastructure, and you should plan and estimate your content growth for the next two to three years in order to provide a search solution without downtime or partial results.

As an example, if you have 7 million items today and expect an annual growth of 30 percent, you will hit 15 million items in three years' time. Although one server would accommodate your needs for this timespan, using two would be better because you can grow even more. With two servers, you also mitigate the risk that your content volume grows faster than planned while potentially improving performance.

Even though you can extend the capacity to 40 million items per server, you are better off following the 15-million item recommendation for performance reasons. If you follow the 15 million items per server recommendation, two index servers would be the best choice for the previous example. Content is distributed on all index servers in your FS4SP farm, and you get an added speed benefit.

 Important When you add a new index column, you must reindex all your content. There is no automatic distribution of the already-indexed items to the newly added index column. With this information in mind, you should plan your FS4SP farm in regard to content growth as well as what you have today.

Failover and High Availability

After you have scaled your FS4SP farm for content volume, you have to think about failover capabilities. If you need failover for search queries, you can add more search rows. If you want failover on indexing, you have to add a row with a backup indexer. The backup indexer does not provide an automatic failover like search does, and you must manually configure your deployment to start using the backup indexer.

In the previously mentioned example, you used three servers (columns). In order to add failover capabilities, you must add at least three more servers to add a new row to the deployment. Depending on your budget, you may want to start with two servers in a one-column, two-row layout where you can store up to 30 million items per server, and have failover for the items. The cost of using fewer servers is speed degradation over time, search downtime, and a full crawl performance when you add more index servers.

Query Throughput

After you decide on what content you want to index, you have to plan for how this content is going to be used in search scenarios. The number of queries your solution needs to handle is largely dependent on how many users you have and how often those users issue search queries. Many Internet retailers are dependent on search to drive the user interface. Retailers typically have thousands of concurrent users around the clock, all with completely different characteristics, and with most searches happening during work hours.

In cases where you don't know what query volume you have to serve, we recommend that you start out simple with a one-row or two-row deployment and increase the query capacity as you go along by adding more search rows. You also need to determine how important search is in your organization. Again, for an Internet retailer, search is what drives the website, and you have to set up your system for redundancy and high availability. But for a small company, search might not be considered that important; the company might be able to tolerate several hours of downtime for the search system because it won't affect day-to-day operations in the same way as for the Internet retailer.

In a one-row setup, your servers handle both indexing and search queries. During crawling, the search performance may degrade because of increased disk I/O. If your current search row is not able to serve the incoming query traffic, you can add more search rows to your FS4SP farm.

When scaling the query throughput with additional search rows, the search queries are distributed among the rows. Adding search rows improves performance in a linear fashion: If one search row can deliver 5 QPS, then two rows can deliver 10 and three rows can deliver 15 QPS. Adding new search rows does not require downtime. How many queries per second you can get from one search row depends on how many items you have, how many managed properties are searchable, and the number of refiners returned for your search query. More items increase query latency because more items have to be evaluated before returning the result.

More Info Query latency is measured as the average round-trip delay from the point where a query is issued until a query result is returned.

The query latency can be reduced by limiting the number of items per column or by adding one or more dedicated search rows, or both. By adding search rows, you avoid having the indexing load affect the query latency, and you also achieve increased query availability. We recommend that you add a separate search row when the query latency must be kept low. Also, quicker disks reduce query latency, as mentioned earlier in this chapter.

The FAST Query SSA is what handles the search queries on the SharePoint farm. You can achieve high availability for the SharePoint farm by adding an additional query component to the FAST Query SSA.

Important Do not deploy more than one FAST Query SSA associated with your FS4SP farm. For information about FAST Query SSA redundancy and availability, go to *http://technet.microsoft.com/en-us/library/ff599525.aspx#QuerySSARedundancyAndAvailability.*

See "Performance Monitoring" in Chapter 5 for information about how to identify where your bottlenecks are and for recommendations about adding more columns or rows to your FS4SP farm.

Freshness

Content freshness refers to how long an item appears in the search results after it is created or updated. When a user adds a new document to a SharePoint document library, does it need to be accessible in search results right away, or is waiting 15 minutes or until tomorrow sufficient? Because SharePoint uses schedule-based crawling, the theoretical minimum time from when an item is created to when it is searchable is around 2 minutes, but 10–15 minutes is a more realistic number to tell your users.

The answer to the freshness question varies depending on the data you index and is something you must take into account when setting up crawl schedules for your content. The more often you crawl, the fresher your content, but also the more load you put on the source systems and the FS4SP indexer servers. You might find that crawling at off-peak hours is sufficient for some sources and near-instant search is needed for other items.

Balancing your freshness requirements against the load these requirements will put on the different systems impacted by crawling is something you have to monitor and adjust accordingly when deploying FS4SP.

> **More Info** For detailed information about how to plan your FS4SP topology, go to *http://technet.microsoft.com/en-us/library/ff599528.aspx*.

Disk Sizing

When setting up your FS4SP servers and the SSAs on the SharePoint farm, you have to plan for how much disk space is needed for your deployment.

> **More Info** The following tables are based on the "Performance and capacity results" scenarios from TechNet at *http://technet.microsoft.com/en-us/library/ff599526.aspx*. The scenarios use a mix of SharePoint containing file server and web content and mimic what you would find in a typical intranet scenario.

In Table 4-8 and Table 4-9, we have listed the disk usage characteristics for each scenario. Only the medium scenario had actual numbers for Web Analyzer disk usage. For the other two scenarios, this number has been increased to account for more realistic numbers in a production environment. Also, note that the extra-large scenario uses two search rows, effectively doubling the disk space needed.

> **More Info** A note for the medium scenario states that the disk value is somewhat lower than the recommended dimensioning. For more information, go to *http://technet.microsoft.com/en-us/library/ff599532.aspx*.

TABLE 4-8 FS4SP disk sizing

Scenario	Number of items (million)	Original data size (TB)	Rows	Web Analyzer/million items peak (GB)	Index size (TB)	Total index size (TB)
Medium	44.0	11.0	1	1.63	2.2	2.3
Large	105.0	28.0	1	3.00	5.0	5.3
Extra-large	518.0	121.0	2	3.00	44.2	45.8

TABLE 4-9 Crawler database sizing

Crawl database data + log (GB)
149.0
369.0
4400.0

> **Note** One crawler database can hold approximately 50 million items. You can read about crawl components and crawl databases in the "FS4SP Architecture" section of Chapter 3.

When breaking down the numbers in space needed per item (per search row), we get the values in Table 4-10.

TABLE 4-10 Per-item size (KB)

Original data size	Index size	Crawler database
250.00	51.63	3.39
266.67	50.62	3.51
233.59	44.16	8.49

If we compare the numbers in Table 4-10 to a test in which you indexed 100,000 HTML files in 20 different languages, you get per-item size shown in Table 4-11.

TABLE 4-11 Per-item size (KB)

Original data size	Index size	Crawler database
2.08	19.93	2.50

For the intranet scenarios, we have a ratio of approximately 1:5 on raw data to indexed data, whereas the small HTML files have a ratio of 10:1 on raw data to indexed data. Seeing how different the index size can be compared to the raw data shows the importance of doing a test indexing of a representative sample of data; by doing so, you can properly estimate how much disk space is needed on your FS4SP servers.

Server Load Bottleneck Planning

When you index content, many integration points come into play. You can look in several places for bottlenecks. Figure 4-11 provides a graphical overview of bottleneck points between the different components. The following list describes some of the typical bottlenecks seen with FS4SP deployment and provides suggestions about how you should prepare and plan to avoid them:

- **Content sources** How long does it take to do a full or incremental crawl of a particular content source? If you want to decrease this time, you first have to see whether the connector in use is working as fast as possible or if it's the source system that is not able to deliver content fast enough. As long as the content source is able to deliver data without maxing out the hardware limit or the bandwidth available, or without disturbing normal operations, you can increase the number of simultaneous requests a connector issues to the content source. By adding more connector threads, you can decrease the time you use to retrieve all items.

- **Document processors** After the FAST Content SSA has sent the data over to the FS4SP farm, each item has to be run through the indexing pipeline. If you don't have enough document processors in your system to handle the data coming in, there is no need to add crawler impact rules to speed up crawling of the content sources.

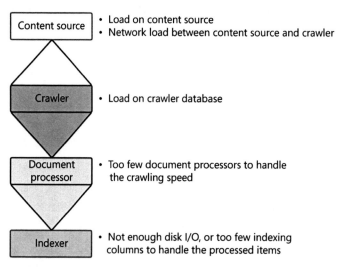

FIGURE 4-11 Load bottleneck points in FS4SP.

When monitoring your FS4SP farm, if you see that the document processors are not running at full capacity during indexing, you can add crawler impact rules on the content source to speed up crawling. If doing so, you have to check that the source system can handle the increased load. As a rule, you should not add crawler impact rules to speed up crawling if you have fewer than 100 document processors in your FS4SP farm because the crawlers will most likely fetch data quicker than the document processors can handle. By default, the FAST Content SSA sends a maximum of 100 batches at a time to the Content Distributor, and each batch is further sent to a document processor. The FAST Content SSA throttles the crawls if the FS4SP farm cannot handle all items being sent over without queuing them up. Throttling starts if FS4SP takes more time to process the items it receives than it takes for the crawling to put more items in the queue.

> **Note** When adding more document processors, make sure the indexer can keep up with the data coming in to prevent moving the bottleneck from the document processors to the indexer. Also, pay close attention to whether the source system you are indexing can handle the crawl load.

> **More Info** For more information about performance and capacity tuning, go to *http://technet.microsoft.com/en-us/library/gg604781.aspx*. Also, see the section "Performance Monitoring" in Chapter 5 for information about how to monitor your FS4SP deployment to find potential performance bottlenecks.

- **Network**   Determine how much bandwidth is available between the content sources and SharePoint, between SharePoint and FS4SP, and between the different FS4SP servers. Planning and monitoring this is key to having an optimized search system. If you have reached your maximum bandwidth, latency will start increasing, and you might consider using dedicated network cards and switches between key components.

- **Dedicated Search Rows**   When building the search indexes, the FS4SP indexing servers use a lot of hardware resources. If you also have the search component on the same server, this is affected by indexing, thus lowering the queries per second the search row can deliver. By having one or more dedicated search rows, you have control over the queries per second your FS4SP farm can deliver without being affected by the indexing.

Conclusion

When you set out to deploy FS4SP, you should know your content and have a good idea of how you want to search against it. What type of items you have, what content sources they come from, and how many of them you will index are key factors that will determine hardware and structural considerations. The more questions you can answer up front, the easier it is to make the right decisions when you plan your initial deployment.

Factors like content volume, query freshness, and redundancy are important to consider when you start sketching out how your SharePoint and FS4SP farms should be deployed and how much and what type of hardware to deploy. Discussing the farm topologies with your IT administrator is another important part of your deployment in order to get all domain policies and service accounts set up correctly.

Also keep in mind which scenarios you may have to prepare for in the future. Be aware that adding new search columns to your deployment requires you to plan ahead to reduce potential downtime. If you set up a large farm, you should consider how to script the installation in order to more quickly move changes between environments, or consider changing the FS4SP topology itself.

The goal of this chapter has been to help you surface the proper questions, understand the hardware and software requirements of FS4SP, and be ready to deploy the solution in the most efficient and problem-free way.

## CHAPTER 5

Operations

After completing this chapter, you will be able to

- Manage the day-to-day operations of FS4SP.

- Modify the FS4SP farm topology.

- Configure logging and do basic monitoring and system health analysis.

- Back up your FS4SP solution, and recover it when disaster strikes.

You can manage many features of Microsoft FAST Search Server 2010 for SharePoint (FS4SP) in Microsoft SharePoint directly. But many more FS4SP toggles and settings are not immediately apparent nor available from the SharePoint GUI. In this chapter, you explore the importance of Windows PowerShell and delve into how you can manage your search engine on a daily basis. Additionally, you go through the tools available for monitoring and analyzing system health and learn what you should do to back up your solution properly.

Introduction to FS4SP Operations

Operations are an essential element of any IT platform. The concept of "set it and forget it" is entirely foreign to Enterprise Search. Search is a constant three-party dance between content sources, the search engine, and the users. Keeping a constant eye on your search engine's health and performance and all its components makes the difference between success and failure.

Compared to previous FAST technology, monitoring is now three-tiered. You have Windows-based event logging for simple identification of critical errors and monitoring via performance counters and Systems Center Operations Manager (SCOM). You can perform more in-depth investigations using the detailed FAST logs. Finally, you also have logs accessible in SharePoint.

On a high level, FS4SP administration has four main methods. Table 5-1 briefly describes these four methods, which are covered in more detail in the following sections of this chapter.

TABLE 5-1 Four main administration methods

Administration method	Example of typical operation
SharePoint	Examine crawl logs and search usage via Central Administration.
Windows PowerShell	Change FS4SP farm topology, apply patches, and modify the index schema.
Configuration files	Modify low-level settings, and edit FAST Search specific connector configurations.
Command-line tools	Start or stop internal FS4SP processes, and retrieve statistics of search servers.

Administration in SharePoint

Via Central Administration, you have access to information regarding crawling and searching, based on the activity of the Content Search Service Application (SSA) and FAST Query SSA. Timer jobs are run at regular intervals to check the health of the crawler database and will trigger alerts in SharePoint Central Administration when something is wrong.

Administration in Windows PowerShell

You can execute most of the FS4SP Windows PowerShell commands in the Microsoft FAST Search Server 2010 for SharePoint shell (FS4SP shell), but you must run a few commands from the SharePoint 2010 Management Shell.

In general, if a cmdlet contains the word *FAST* as part of its name, you execute it in an FS4SP shell on an FS4SP server; otherwise, you should execute it in a SharePoint Management Shell on a SharePoint server.

> **Note** Some of the command-line utilities and Windows PowerShell scripts in FS4SP require elevated privileges to run. Opening your shells by using *Run as Administrator* provides the appropriate rights. Alternatively, modifying the shortcut so that it always runs as a user that has administrative privileges eases management because you will always have the required permissions to execute any FS4SP-related command or script.
>
> Also make sure the logged-in user executing the Windows PowerShell cmdlets is a member of the FASTSearchAdministrators local group on the server as specified during installation.

More than 80 different FS4SP-related Windows PowerShell cmdlets are available. These commands are roughly divided into five categories:

- *Administration* cmdlets
- *Index schema* cmdlets
- *Installation* cmdlets
- *Spell-tuning* cmdlets
- *Security* cmdlets

More Info For more information about Windows PowerShell cmdlets, go to
http://technet.microsoft.com/en-us/library/ff393782.aspx.

Other Means of Administration

You can perform administrative tasks for FS4SP in a couple more ways, as the following topics explain.

Using Configuration Files

If you are moving from an older FAST incarnation to FS4SP, you might notice that the number of configuration files has gone down drastically. Many low-level settings are still available only by editing files, whether plain text or XML, but there are only 16 configuration files, of which 6 are related to the FAST Search specific connectors; you may edit any of these 16 configuration files without leaving your system in an unsupported state. The 6 FAST Search specific connectors are all XML files.

More Info For more information about FS4SP configuration files, go to
http://msdn.microsoft.com/en-us/library/ff354943.aspx.

There are several more important files, and you'll learn more about a few of them in this chapter.

Using Command-Line Tools

You run and control some FS4SP operations using command-line tools (.exe files). These tools live in the *<FASTSearchFolder>*\bin folder and are available from the FS4SP shell. All in all, there are 25 of these tools. Throughout this book, you'll become familiar with the most critical of these tools. You should understand the difference between these command-line tools and the Windows PowerShell cmdlets mentioned in the preceding section, "Administration in Windows PowerShell." An example of a command-line tool operation is *nctrl restart (nctrl.exe)*, which restarts the local FS4SP installation. An example of a Windows PowerShell cmdlet is *Get-FASTSearchMetadataManagedProperty*, which displays information about managed properties.

More Info For a complete list of FS4SP command-line tools, go to
http://msdn.microsoft.com/en-us/library/ee943520.aspx.

Basic Operations

When working with FS4SP, as with any larger system, you need to be able to control it in a safe manner. Even though the internal processes have safeguards in place, it is never a good idea to abruptly end one of the internal processes. If you do, the best case scenario is that you will temporarily lose some functionality. In the worst case, you can corrupt your index and cause the system to become nonfunctional. This section describes how to safely start, stop, suspend, and resume FS4SP or any of its internal components.

The Node Controller

Chapter 3, "FS4SP Architecture," lists and describes all the FS4SP internal processes in Table 3-1. Depending on how many servers you're using in your solution, these internal processes might be spread out or duplicated across the servers. The tool you use to safely manage these processes is called the *Node Controller*, which is an internal process just like any other in FS4SP except that the Node Controller is always running on all servers in your FS4SP farm.

You use the Node Controller to start, stop, suspend, resume, and dynamically scale up certain internal processes. Its command-line interface is called *nctrl.exe*. You find it in the *<FASTSearchFolder>* bin folder. This tool is one of the command-line tools mentioned in the previous section, "Administration in Windows PowerShell."

From an FS4SP shell, you can invoke the Node Controller with the command *nctrl status*. This returns a list of all internal FS4SP processes and their status on the local machine, as shown in Figure 5-1. Running this command is a good first step when you want to check the status of FS4SP. However, when troubleshooting FS4SP, a process marked as *Running* does not necessarily mean it is running correctly and without any problems.

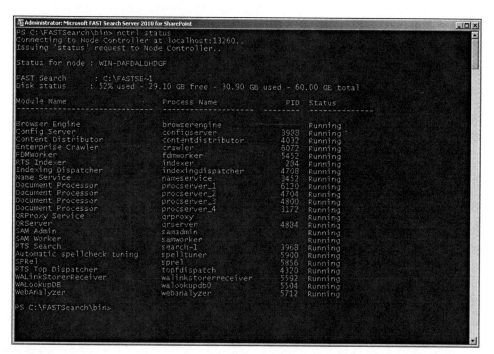

FIGURE 5-1 Output from issuing the command *nctrl status* in a single-server FS4SP installation.

Starting and Stopping a Single-Server Installation

To shut down a local single-server installation in a controlled and safe manner, run the command *nctrl stop* from an FS4SP shell. Subsequently, you can bring the server back up again using the command *nctrl start*. If you want to restart FS4SP immediately after a shut down, you can save yourself some typing using the command *nctrl restart*.

> **Important** Microsoft recommends that you suspend all crawls before shutting down FS4SP. This is also recommended when using the FAST Search specific connectors.

When running *nctrl stop*, the order in which FS4SP shuts down its internal processes is predefined according to the Node Controller's configuration file. See the section "A Note on Node Controller Internals" later in this chapter for more information about this.

> **Important** If you need to reboot the whole server, Microsoft recommends that you shut down FS4SP manually before doing so, because FS4SP does not adequately shut down its internal processes when Windows is shutting down. Read more about this in the section "Relationship Between the Node Controller and the FS4SP Windows Services" later in this chapter.

Starting and Stopping a Multi-Server Installation

If your FS4SP installation is spread out over several servers, starting and stopping the solution works in the same manner for each server as it does in a single-server installation. To shut down the entire installation, you have to manually (or by using remote scripting) issue the *nctrl* command on each server. Follow the procedure described in the previous section, "Starting and Stopping a Single-Server Installation."

Depending on your farm configuration, the order in which you shut down the servers can be important. On a standard multi-server installation, you should follow this procedure:

1. Suspend all crawls and content feeding.

2. Stop all FAST Search specific connectors.

3. Shut down all servers configured to run document processors.

4. Shut down all servers configured with the indexer component.

5. Shut down all servers configured as QR Servers.

6. Shut down all remaining servers; the FS4SP administration server should be the last one to shut down.

Even though a healthy FS4SP installation should have no problem being shut down in a different order than just listed, this strategy minimizes the risk of ending up with an index in an unknown or invalid state. It also minimizes the number of warnings that the FS4SP internal processes inevitably emit when other processes become unavailable.

During startup, you start the servers in the reverse order—proceeding from item 6 to item 2 in the previous list—and then resume all relevant crawls.

> **More Info** Microsoft has published a farm version of *nctrl* that you can use to start or stop any FS4SP server remotely from the administration server, making it considerably easier to manage large farms. Go to *http://gallery.technet.microsoft.com/scriptcenter/ cc2f9dc4-2af8-4176-98d2-f7341d0d5b39* for more information.

Starting and Stopping Internal Processes

To stop an individual FS4SP process, run *nctrl stop [process name]*, for example, *nctrl stop indexer*. This puts the specified process into a "User Suspended" status, meaning that you have to manually bring it back up by running *nctrl start [process name]*. If you do not, the process remains in the "User Suspended" state even after an *nctrl restart*, or server reboot.

FS4SP also provides the psctrl.exe tool, which can control all available document processors in the solution—regardless of which server they run on. Among other things, you can use it to restart all available document processors without having to log on to every server in the farm. You do this by issuing a *psctrl stop* command from any FS4SP server in the farm. Confusingly, there is no start command, because FS4SP automatically restarts the document processors shortly after they shut down.

> **More Info** For more information about the *psctrl.exe* tool, go to *http://technet.microsoft.com/ en-us/library/ee943506.aspx*.

Relationship Between the Node Controller and the FS4SP Windows Services

As the boxed area in Figure 5-2 shows, six Windows services are related to FS4SP. There is an overlap between the Node Controller and these services. In fact, if you compare the services in Figure 5-2 to the processes shown in Figure 5-1, you will notice that five of the six services are also defined in the Node Controller.

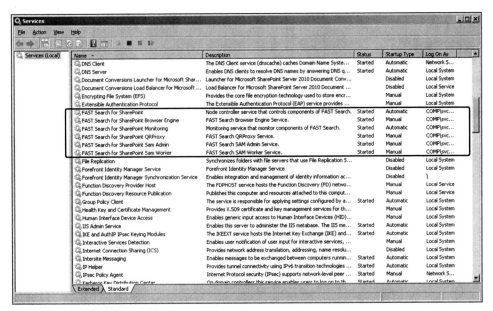

FIGURE 5-2 The FS4SP services. All services except FAST Search for SharePoint Monitoring are defined in the Node Controller. Note that this screenshot shows a single-server installation, and the content may differ for a multi-server installation.

This overlap of services means that instead of shutting down the FAST Search for SharePoint Browser Engine service through the GUI, you can run *nctrl stop browserengine*. This applies to all FS4SP services except the FAST Search for SharePoint Monitoring service, which exists only as a Windows service. Because it is a monitoring tool, it is of course crucial to never shut down the FAST Search for SharePoint Monitoring service unless stated otherwise in the documentation, even though the rest of FS4SP is shut down using the *nctrl stop* command.

Restarting the most important Windows service, FAST Search for SharePoint, is the equivalent of running *nctrl restart*. Doing so also shuts down all five other services—all but the monitoring service. Choose whichever method you prefer; there are no differences between the two. If the monitoring service is already stopped when you issue an *nctrl start* or when you start the FAST Search for SharePoint service, the monitoring service automatically starts.

Notice that the Windows services (and consequently the internal processes) running on a particular server in a multi-server installation vary, depending on your deployment. A larger FS4SP multi-server deployment might have dedicated servers for the indexer, document processors, and so on. See Chapter 3 and Chapter 4, "Deployment," for more information.

Stopping F24SP Gracefully at Server Shutdown

The FAST Search for SharePoint service has a not-so-obvious problem: If you shut down the entire server, Windows automatically shuts down this service as well. In theory, this shut down should also stop all internal FS4SP processes wrapped by the service. However, that doesn't happen.

You can double-check this by manually shutting down the server and inspecting the Node Controller log file *<FASTSearchFolder>*\var\log\nodecontroller\nodecontroller.log after bringing the server back up again. You will notice that there are no messages about any processes shutting down. Because the processes are not allowed to shut down gracefully, there is a small but nonnegligible risk of running into problems.

You can circumvent these problems either by always shutting down the FAST Search for SharePoint service manually (or by running *nctrl stop*) or by using the following steps to add a Group Policy to shut it down for you automatically:

1. On the Start menu, select Run, and then type **gpedit.msc** to open the Group Policy Editor.

2. In the left panel, expand Computer Configuration and Windows Settings.

3. Double-click the Scripts (Startup/Shutdown) item.

4. Click the Add button.

5. In the Script Name field, specify **<FASTSearchFolder>\bin\nctrl.exe**. In the Script Parameters field, specify **stop**.

After you follow these steps, FS4SP stops automatically in a controlled and graceful manner when Windows shuts down.

Adding and Removing Document Processors

In the list of running processes shown in Figure 5-1, you can see four Document Processor processes. These are the processes that run items through the indexing pipeline, executing every processor for every item that flows through the pipeline. Thus, the number of document processors is one of the factors that limits how fast you can crawl and index items. The "Production Environments" section in Chapter 4 provides in-depth information about how you can distribute the FS4SP components over several servers to achieve optimal performance and avoid bottlenecks.

A default FS4SP single-server installation comes with four document processors, meaning that the solution can process a maximum of four batches of items at one time.

Note Items are not sent one by one through the indexing pipeline, but rather in batches of several items at one time.

It is generally recommended that you enable no more than one document processor per available CPU core. However, depending on your hardware, you might want to increase or decrease this number. If you do, remember to leave some CPU power for the operating system itself and for the rest of the FS4SP processes running on the same server.

Note A dual core CPU with hyper-threading enabled shows up as four CPU cores, so you can enable four document processors.

To dynamically add a new document processor on a server configured with document processors, run the following command.

```
nctrl add procserver
```

After you run the command, the *nctrl status* command should list one additional document processor, for example, "procserver_5." As soon as the process is marked as *Running*, it is live and ready to process incoming documents. Note that it is possible to add document processors to any server within a server installation, but remember that the *nctrl add procserver* command affects only the server that is being run.

Warning If you have developed your own Pipeline Extensibility processors, ensure that all servers on which you intend to run document processors are equipped with a local copy and that the input parameters are correct. Custom code is not distributed automatically. Input parameters that do not exist will make the indexing pipeline skip the item entirely.

You can remove a document processor on a local server with the following command.

```
nctrl remove procserver
```

This command removes the document processor with the highest available number as listed by *nctrl status*. If the document processor is currently running, it will shut down before it is removed.

It is possible to perform these operations during content feeding. However, if you are shutting down a document processor that is currently processing content, you might see warnings in your content source or connector logs. Each currently processed item triggers a callback indicating that it was dropped in the indexing pipeline before it reached the indexer. Both the FAST Content SSA crawlers and the FAST Search specific connectors typically re-feed such items to another document processor as soon as possible after such callbacks occur.

You can also increase the number of document processors by changing the deployment configuration as described in the section "Server Topology Management" later in this chapter, but doing so requires downtime on the servers. In contrast, adding them with *nctrl* is a run-time operation.

A Note on Node Controller Internals

During a full startup or shutdown, the processes are started and stopped in the sequence defined at the top of the Node Controller's configuration file (*<FASTSearchFolder>*\etc\NodeConf.xml). Here you can also see exactly how each internal process is invoked, which binary is called, and what parameters are passed to it.

Even though you can modify which processes run on a particular server by reconfiguring the Node Controller configuration, the supported method to perform deployment reconfiguration is through the deployment configuration templates and the *Set-FASTSearchConfiguration* cmdlet.

More Info For more information about reconfiguring farm deployment, go to *http://technet.microsoft.com/en-us/library/ff381247.aspx.*

Warning Do not modify the Node Controller configuration file unless you know exactly what you are doing. NodeConf.xml is an internal configuration file, so in addition to leaving your system in an unsupported state, you might also end up breaking your installation.

If you do change the Node Controller configuration file, you have to issue the command *nctrl reloadcfg* to force the Node Controller to pick up the changes.

Indexer Administration

FS4SP provides an indexer administration tool called *indexeradmin.exe*. It provides only a few—but invaluable—commands for interacting with the indexer. Additionally, the tool is equipped with a set of parameters that allows you to control all indexers in a multi-server farm, as opposed to just the local indexer.

> **More Info** For more information about *indexeradmin.exe*, go to *http://technet.microsoft.com/en-us/library/ee943517.aspx*.

Suspending and Resuming Indexing Operations

A frequent usage of *indexeradmin* is to instruct it to suspend all indexer processes while feeding FS4SP large volumes of data at once, for example, at a full crawl. When suspending the indexers, FS4SP continues to receive items, run them through the document processors, and generate the intermediate FAST Index Markup Language (FIXML) files used to build the search index, but the indexer(s) will not convert these files into a searchable index. Hence, indexing will be suspended. This suspension reduces the number of simultaneous read and write I/O operations on the disk subsystem, improving the speed at which FS4SP can receive items.

After the large feeding session completes, you can resume indexing operations, at which point the indexer will start processing the FIXML files, making content searchable to the end users.

You suspend indexing operations by issuing the following command.

```
indexeradmin -a suspendindexing
```

The parameter *-a* tells *indexeradmin* to suspend indexing on all indexers in the farm. It is, however, possible to manually go to each server and run the same command without *-a*.

You resume indexing operations on all servers by issuing the following command.

```
indexeradmin -a resumeindexing
```

You can use the tool *indexerinfo.exe* to retrieve information about the FS4SP indexer. To check the status of the indexer(s), issue the following command and examine the XML output, as shown in Figure 5-3.

```
indexerstatus -a status
```

> **More Info** For more information about *indexerinfo.exe*, go to *http://technet.microsoft.com/en-us/library/ee943511.aspx*.

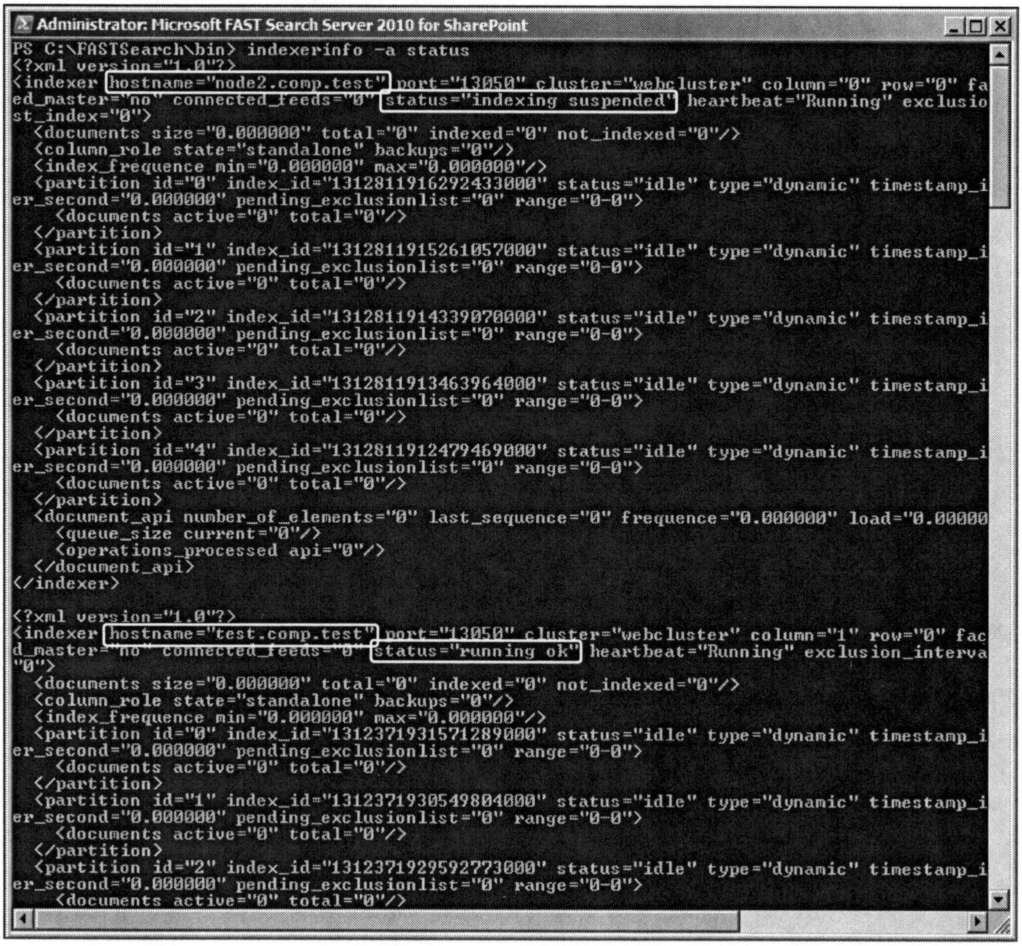

FIGURE 5-3 Status from a two-server deployment, where the server *node2.comp.test* has a suspended indexer while the server *test.comp.test* is "running ok".

Rebuilding a Corrupt Index

You can also use the *indexeradmin.exe* tool to rebuild the binary index from the intermediate FIXML files. If you experience unusual behavior after an index schema configuration change, or notice warnings or even errors in the indexer logs, rebuilding the binary index can often alleviate the problems.

Because you would typically rebuild your index from FIXML only when your solution is malfunctioning, it is considered good practice to stop all current crawls during the process to minimize strain on the solution. Start the process by invoking the following command.

```
indexeradmin -a resetindex
```

This operation is asynchronous, and although you'll see command output that says *SUCCESS* in capital letters, that message indicates only that the indexers have successfully started the procedure.

You can monitor the operation's progress by using the command *indexerinfo -a*. Issue the command repeatedly and observe the attribute *status* of each *<partition>* tag. Each partition will change status from "waiting" to "indexing" until it finally reaches "idle."

> **Note** The *indexeradmin resetindex* command is different from the SharePoint *index reset* procedure. An *indexeradmin resetindex* command rebuilds the binary index on the FS4SP index servers, whereas the FAST Content SSA's *reset index* procedure erases the crawler information in SharePoint, requiring a full crawl of all content sources, and possibly rendering the crawler store and the search index out of sync. For more information about resetting the content index, go to *http://technet.microsoft.com/en-us/library/ff191228.aspx*.

Search Administration

The *indexerinfo* tool previously mentioned has an equivalent for the query matching and query dispatching components in FS4SP. The tool is called *searchinfo.exe*. (For more information about this tool, go to *http://technet.microsoft.com/en-us/library/ee943522.aspx*.)

Running the following command returns an XML report showing the current state of the search and query subsystem of FS4SP.

```
searchinfo -a status
```

As was the case with *indexeradmin* and *indexerinfo*, omitting the parameter *-a* returns only the status from the server that the command is executed from.

The output from *searchinfo* can be extremely large and quite overwhelming. A simple method for making it easier to digest is to use the built-in XML parser in Windows PowerShell. Running the following script in an FS4SP shell rewrites the output from *searchinfo* to a table, as shown in Figure 5-4.

```
[Xml]$xml = (searchinfo status) -Replace '<!DOCTYPE search-stats SYSTEM "search-stats-1.0.dtd">'
$xml."search-stats".fdispatch.datasets.dataset
```

Of particular interest in this report is the uptime of the solution, the total number of searches, and the various search times. You can also inspect the status of each partition by printing the engine property.

```
[Xml]$xml = (searchinfo status) -Replace '<!DOCTYPE search-stats SYSTEM "search-stats-1.0.dtd">'
$xml."search-stats".fdispatch.datasets.dataset.engine
```

The output printed from the previous command gives you a broad view of the status of each index partition across all servers configured as QR Servers. When the status of a partition is listed as "up," the partition is functioning properly, and items stored in the partition are returned for matching queries. When a partition is listed as "down," the particular slice of the index held in the corresponding partition is not searchable.

```
Administrator: Microsoft FAST Search Server 2010 for SharePoint                    _ □ ×
PS C:\FASTSearch\bin> [Xml]$xml = (searchinfo status) -replace '<!DOCTYPE search
-stats SYSTEM "search-stats-1.0.dtd">'
PS C:\FASTSearch\bin> $xml."search-stats".fdispatch.datasets.dataset

id                        : 0
partitions                : 5
first-partition           : 0
max-active-nodes          : 6
active-nodes              : 5
max-active-partitions     : 5
active-partitions         : 5
unit-selection-cost       : 1
total-selection-cost      : 0
up-time                   : 66481.738
total-search-time         : 0.107
total-searches            : 5
avg-sec-per-search        : 0.021
avg-searches-per-sec      : 0.000
avg-uncached-search-time  : 0.021
samples                   : 5
timed-out                 : 0
timed-out-percentage      : 0.000
engine                    : {engine, engine, engine, engine...}


PS C:\FASTSearch\bin>
```

FIGURE 5-4 Search statistics showing five executed searches; the average time per search was 0.021 seconds.

> **More Info** For detailed documentation about the XML report syntax of *searchinfo*, see the TechNet article at *http://technet.microsoft.com/en-us/library/gg471169.aspx*.

Search Click-Through Analysis

If you enabled search click-through analysis during the installation process, you activated the SPRel component of FS4SP. SPRel is a search click-through analysis engine that analyzes which entries users click in search results. SharePoint collects the click-through logs, which are harvested by FS4SP using a timer job. The SPRel component analyzes the logs, flagging the most frequently clicked items as best matches for the terms that were used to retrieve the search result. SPRel uses this information to improve the relevance of future queries, giving the flagged best matches an extra boost in the search results.

Checking the Status of SPRel

You check the status of SPRel with the *spreladmin.exe* command-line tool.

```
spreladmin showstatus
```

Running this command tells you how often SPRel is scheduled to run, lists the overall status, and prints out run-time statistics from previous log analysis sessions.

More Info For more information about *sprelladmin.exe*, go to *http://technet.microsoft.com/en-us/library/ee943519.aspx*.

Reconfiguring SPRel

View the current configuration of SPRel by using the following command.

```
spreladmin showconfig
```

Several aspects of SPRel are configurable, such as the number of CPU cores that will be used during processing and whether old click-through logs are kept or deleted. For example, to change how many days of logs SPRel should consume in each log analysis session, you can reconfigure the *use_clicklogs* parameter.

```
spreladmin setconfig -k use_clicklogs -u 90
```

Note that you can change all other parameters listed from *spreladmin showconfig* in the same manner.

Note Bear in mind that changing how many days of logs SPRel includes in the analysis, as was done in the previous example, is directly related to the ranking of search results. The default setting is 30 days. If it seems that click-through analysis has little to no effect in search results, as is typical in a solution with few users, it makes sense to increase the time span so that more clicks have time to be accumulated.

Be careful when lowering this value from the default, because small amounts of user traffic then would be able to influence the ranking of your search results.

Link Analysis

The Web Analyzer components examine crawled content and scan items for incoming and outgoing links to other items. A link graph is calculated to find highly connected items, which receive a contribution to their rank component. The technique is similar to Google's well-known PageRank algorithm. FS4SP uses this technique not only when crawling external websites, but also when crawling content from SharePoint.

The Web Analyzer, which if necessary can be scaled out to several servers, is made from four logical components:

- **webanalyzer** A single-server process that handles configuration, scheduling, and acts as a master in distributed Web Analyzer configurations.

- **fdmworker** A server that receives tasks from the Web Analyzer master during link processing. Distributed across servers in large-scale solutions.

- ***walinkstorerreceiver***   A server that receives tasks from the Web Analyzer master during link processing. Distributed across servers in large-scale solutions.

- ***walookupdb***   A key-value lookup server that retrieves link processing information. When items are processed, the indexing pipeline talks to this component to find out how well-connected the current item is in the link graph. Distributed across servers in large-scale solutions.

Checking the Status of the Web Analyzer

The *waadmin.exe* tool is the common front end for administrating the Web Analyzer. Check the current status by using the following command.

```
waadmin showstatus
```

The output tells you whether the Web Analyzer is currently processing links, which content collections are being monitored, whether any errors were reported during processing, and other information.

> **More Info** For more information about *waadmin.exe*, go to *http://technet.microsoft.com/en-us/library/ee943529.aspx.*

Forcing the Web Analyzer to Run

You start the Web Analyzer outside of the running schedule with the following command.

```
waadmin forceprocessing
```

Listing the Relevance Data for a Specific Item

The following example shows relevance data for an item with an identifying *<URL>*, assuming the item has been indexed and processed by the Web Analyzer.

```
waadmin -q <URL>
```

> **Tip** The *<URL>* is, confusingly enough, not a standard URL; instead, it's the primary key of the index that FS4SP uses internally. If a particular item has been indexed using any of the FAST Content SSA connectors, the item starts with *ssic*, for example, *ssic://13451*. If a particular item was indexed using any of the FAST Search specific connectors, or by using the *docpush* command-line utility, the *<URL>* is typically a proper URI, such as *http://support.microsoft.com/kb/2592062.*

Find the <URL>—that is, the primary key—for a particular item by using either of the following two methods:

- If the item was indexed through the FAST Content SSA, use Central Administration. Follow these steps:

  1. In Central Administration, click Manage Service Applications, and then click your FAST Content SSA.

  2. Click Crawl Log in the left pane.

  3. Click the Successes number on the content source for your item.

  4. Under Search By, choose URL Or Host Name, and paste it in your document link, for example, **http://test/Docs/workerz/Shared%20Documents/Platform-Test-Framework-1.0.doc**.

  5. Click Search.

  6. Make a note of the internal ID for this document, as shown in Figure 5-5. Prefix this value with **ssic://** to build the item ID expected by the Web Analyzer utilities.

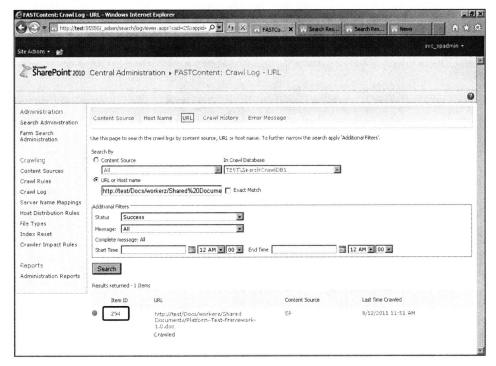

FIGURE 5-5 Inspect a content source for a crawled item and display the item ID. Note that this value will have to be prefixed with *ssic://* to correctly reflect the internal primary key of FS4SP.

- If the item was indexed using the FAST Search specific connectors, use the Search Result Page. Follow these steps:

  1. Navigate to your Search Center result page.

  2. Edit the page, and then edit the Core Results Web Part.

3. Under Display Properties, clear the Use Location Visualization check box, and then add a new column definition to the Fetched Properties list.

```
<Column Name="contentid"/>
```

4. Either edit the XSLT via the XSL Editor... button to include listing the new column, or use the following XSLT to render all data that reaches the Web Part as pure XML without any design elements.

```
<?xml version="1.0" encoding="UTF-8"?>
<xsl:stylesheet version="1.0" xmlns:xsl="http://www.w3.org/1999/XSL/Transform">
<xsl:output method="xml" version="1.0" encoding="UTF-8" indent="yes"/>
  <xsl:template match="/">
    <xmp><xsl:copy-of select="*"/></xmp>
  </xsl:template>
</xsl:stylesheet>
```

5. Save your Web Part, and then reload the Search Center result page.

6. Search for something that will return the item for which you want to find the ID.

7. Make a note of the value listed inside the *<contentid>* tag, as shown in Figure 5-6.

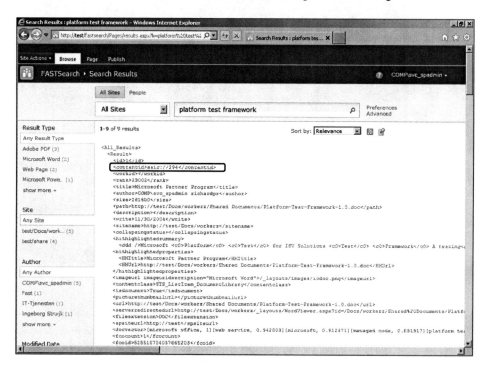

FIGURE 5-6 A search result listed as raw XML, displaying the value that FS4SP uses internally as the primary key of the index.

When you have figured out the exact *<URL>* that the Web Analyzer utility expects, call the *waadmin* tool (shown in the following example command) to show a particular item's link relevance. Example results of running the command are shown in Figure 5-7.

```
waadmin -q ssic://294 ShowURIRelevance
```

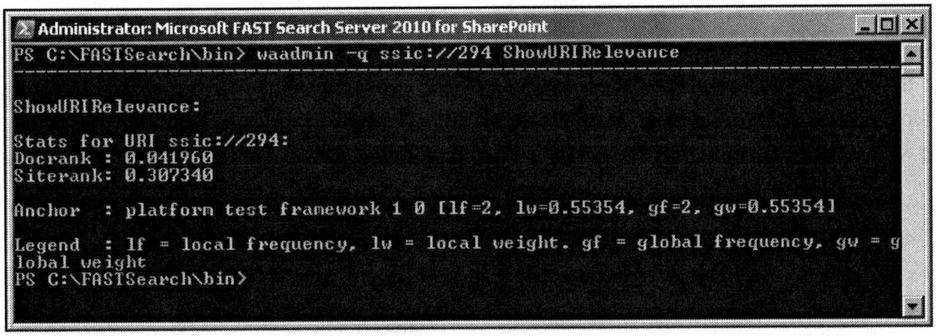

FIGURE 5-7 Retrieving link relevance for the item identified with *ssic://294*.

Server Topology Management

FS4SP was designed from the beginning to scale well. You might, for example, want to increase index volume, get better performance, or add servers for fail-over redundancy. However, because FS4SP is integrated into SharePoint, the different scaling scenarios involve modifying either the FS4SP farm or the SharePoint farm. The following two sections describe which scenarios relate to which farm and outline the steps you need to take.

> **Warning** Modifying the server topology is considered an advanced operation. You should be very careful when doing so, especially in production environments.

Modifying the Topology on the FS4SP Farm

The main scenarios for modifying the topology of your FS4SP farm—that is, adding more machines to your server configuration—are:

- Increasing the index capacity or indexing throughput.

- Increasing the query throughput.

- Adding redundancy to a component.

Important If you add one or more columns to your existing index topology, you need to do a full recrawl of all your content because the index will be deleted. Other topology changes cause downtime, but the index will be left untouched and incremental crawls can be continued.

There is currently no automatic distribution of the existing content from the existing column over to the added one(s), and therefore you must either perform a full crawl of all the content or use the *fixmlfeeder* tool. Because of this limitation, it is recommended that you plan ahead to determine how much content you will need to index in the next one to three years. The more content you have, the longer it will take to run full recrawls.

TechNet provides a step-by-step guide on how to increase the capacity by adding new index columns. Go to *http://technet.microsoft.com/en-us/library/gg482015.aspx*.

Modify the index topology

1. If adding new index columns, stop all crawls and reset the content index.

 More Info For detailed steps about adding index columns, go to *http://technet.microsoft.com/en-us/library/gg482015.aspx*.

2. Edit *<FASTSearchFolder>*\etc\config_data\deployment\deployment.xml on the administration server and make the necessary changes.

3. Stop the FAST Search for SharePoint service and the FAST Search for SharePoint Monitoring service on the administration server.

4. Update the deployment configuration by executing the following command in an FS4SP shell.

   ```
   Set-FASTSearchConfiguration
   ```

5. Start the FAST Search for SharePoint service. This also starts the FAST Search for SharePoint Monitoring service.

6. Repeat steps 2–5 on the other servers in your FS4SP farm.

7. If you added index columns or Query Result (QR) servers, update the FAST Content SSA and FAST Query SSA configuration via Central Administration with the updated values from *<FASTSearchFolder>*\Install_Info.txt.

 More Info For detailed steps about updating FAST Content SSA or FAST Query SSA servers, go to *http://technet.microsoft.com/en-us/library/ ff381247.aspx#BKMK_MakeTheNecessaryChangesOnMOSS*.

8. If you added index columns, start a full crawl on all your content sources.

Adding One or More Index Columns Without Recrawling

As stated previously, a full crawl of all content sources is required when adding index columns to an FS4SP farm deployment. This is because content has to be redistributed to span across all columns, including the new one. Recrawling all content is the easy but time-consuming way to achieve this. Another method, arguably harder but also much faster, involves using the *FIXMLfeeder.exe* tool.

This tool was created for the exact purpose of redistributing content across columns, and is used to refeed the intermediate FIXML files that were generated during the original indexing. Instead of performing a full crawl where all items are processed, the already-processed FIXML files are fed directly to the indexing dispatcher, bypassing the content distributor and indexing pipeline. This direct feeding ensures that content is again distributed correctly across all servers, including the new one.

More Info The steps for using the *FIXMLfeeder.exe* tool to redistribute the index when adding or removing columns are described in detail in the white paper "FAST Search Server 2010 for SharePoint Add or Remove an Index Column," which can be downloaded from *http://www.microsoft.com/download/en/details.aspx?displaylang=en&id=28548*.

More Info For detailed steps about updating FAST Content SSA or FAST Query SSA servers, go to *http://technet.microsoft.com/en-us/library/ff381247.aspx#BKMK_MakeTheNecessaryChangesOnMOSS*.

Modifying the Topology on the SharePoint Farm

Scaling the SharePoint end of your search topology relates mainly to the crawling of content via the FAST Content SSA. It is possible to scale the FAST Query SSA as well, but because all search logic is handled by the FS4SP farm, there is little need for this except to provide failover on the SharePoint farm for search queries. As such, the main scenarios for modifying the topology of your SharePoint farm are:

- Increasing the crawl rate.

- Scaling the crawler database.

The methods used for modifying the topology are as follows:

- **Add crawler impact rules.** You can create crawler impact rules to specify how many items are retrieved in parallel and how long to wait between each request. Before increasing the number of items to retrieve in parallel, make sure the system you are crawling can handle the load and you have enough processing power on the FS4SP farm to handle the increased crawling rate.

More Info For more information about managing crawler impact rules, go to *http://technet.microsoft.com/en-us/library/ff381257.aspx.*

■ **Add crawl components.** If your SharePoint application server is saturated on CPU usage or network bandwidth caused by crawling of content sources, you can distribute the content source crawling by adding crawl components on several SharePoint farm servers. This will distribute the crawl load between the servers.

More Info For more information about adding or removing crawl components, go to *http://technet.microsoft.com/en-us/library/ff599534.aspx.*

■ **Add crawl databases.** When crawling more than 50 million items, you should consider adding additional crawler databases. Doing so avoids crawling as a result of increased time spent updating the SQL server crawl database.

More Info For more information about adding or removing crawl databases, go to *http://technet.microsoft.com/en-us/library/ff599536.aspx.*

■ **Add host distribution rules.** If you have only one crawler database, you do not need to add any host distribution rules. Host distribution rules are used to associate a host with a specific crawl database. By default, hosts are load balanced across crawl databases based on space availability. However, you may want to assign a host to a specific crawl database for availability and performance optimization.

More Info For more information about adding or removing host distribution rules, go to *http://technet.microsoft.com/en-us/library/ff599527.aspx.*

Refer to Chapter 3 for a longer discussion on crawl components and crawl databases.

Changing the Location of Data and Log Files

FS4SP stores data and log files in the *<FASTSearchFolder>*\data and *<FASTSearchFolder>*\var\ log folders. These are predefined locations and not customizable during the installation process. It is possible to change these locations after the installation by editing two internal configuration files, although this is not supported by Microsoft. Service packs or hotfixes might overwrite the configuration files, changing your edits back to the default settings. Creating a junction point from any subfolder below the *<FASTSearchFolder>* folder to other folders and volumes is, however, supported.

> **Note** A junction point is different from a shortcut and is a feature of the NTFS file system. Junction points are transparent to the user; the links appear as normal files or folders and can be acted upon by the user or application in exactly the same manner as if the file or folder were physically present in the location referred to.
>
> You can use the command-line utility *mklink* to create junction points. For information about the *mklink* utility, go to *http://technet.microsoft.com/en-us/library/cc753194(WS.10).aspx*.

Change the location of data and log files

In this scenario, assume the operating system is on the C drive, and FS4SP is installed in the *C:\FAST-Search* folder. Also assume that you want to store the data files on the D drive and the log files on the E drive:

1. Open an FS4SP shell with administrative privileges.

2. Stop the local FS4SP solution by running *nctrl stop*.

3. Move the FS4SP data files to the new volume.

   ```
   move C:\FASTSearch\data c:\newdata
   ```

4. Move the FS4SP log files to the new volume.

   ```
   move C:\FASTSearch\var\log e:\log
   ```

5. Create a junction point from the new volume to the old data location.

   ```
   mklink /j C:\FASTSearch\data d:\data
   ```

6. Create a junction point from the new volume to the old log location.

   ```
   mklink /j C:\FASTSearch\var\log e:\log
   ```

7. Start the local FS4SP solution by running *nctrl start*. Verify that all internal processes are running again by using *nctrl status*.

You need to do this on all your FS4SP servers, and we recommend doing this during initial deployment before you start any indexing to avoid downtime.

Logging

FS4SP can produce log files from almost every aspect of the solution. General-purpose logs are generated during run time, and are a good indicator of the current health of the solution but also useful when something goes wrong. In situations in which something goes wrong, you can typically increase the log-level threshold for the module you suspect is to blame for any problems, and rerun the operation that triggered the error.

Besides generating the general-purpose logs, FS4SP can be configured to emit targeted activity logs regarding document processing and search queries. These are described in the section "Functional Logs" later in this chapter.

In addition to logs, FS4SP publishes a large amount of monitoring data and performance counters that can be consumed by SCOM, the built-in Windows tool Performance Monitor, and custom scripts as well as several third-party monitoring tools. Read more about this in this chapter's section on "Performance Monitoring."

General-Purpose Logs

All FS4SP internal processes log information to files on disk. This topic is covered at the end of this section, in "Internal FS4SP Logs." Depending on the configuration, most information from these file-based logs is also syndicated into the Windows Event Viewer and to the SharePoint Unified Logging Service (ULS) trace logs. However, because the internal FS4SP logs are the source of almost everything else, you should be sure to at least acquire a basic understanding of these.

Windows Event Logs

A good starting point for FS4SP logs is the standard Windows Event Viewer, shown in Figure 5-8. There are two important event log folders: FAST Search and FAST Search Farm. Both of these reside under the *Applications and Services Logs* server.

Logs from all local FS4SP processes are logged into the FAST Search event log folder by the local FS4SP log server. If several servers are involved, the administration server generates aggregated logs from all servers to the FAST Search Farm event log folder. If your solution involves only one FS4SP server, there is still a FAST Search Farm folder, simulating farm-level logs.

Logs that are collected in the Event Viewer are produced from the various FS4SP internal processes. These internal logs are available on disk on each server but are also collected and aggregated on the farm administration server. For troubleshooting, it might be easier to deduce what is wrong from these internal logs, especially when a higher level of detail is required. Note that the log levels in the Windows Event logs and the internal FS4SP logs differ. See Table 5-2 for a comparison, and the section "Internal FS4SP Logs" later in this chapter for more details.

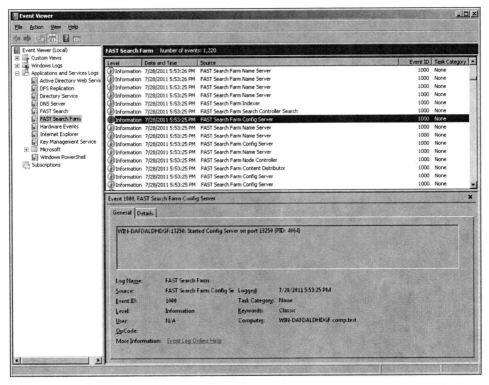

FIGURE 5-8 The Event Viewer showing logs aggregated on the main log server on the FS4SP administration server.

TABLE 5-2 Comparison of log levels used in FS4SP internal logs and the Windows event log

FS4SP logs	Event log	Role
CRITICAL	Error	Critical problems are effectively rendering an important component of FS4SP unusable. Example: indexing, searching, or internal communication in between processes.
ERROR	Error	A specific task failed. May imply bigger problems. Example: FS4SP failed to index a document.
WARNING	Warning	An issue should be looked into, but it is not necessarily crucial to the well-being of the system.
INFO	Information	Standard run-time information is available.
VERBOSE	Information	Verbose run-time information is available. Useful for debugging. Not enabled by default.
DEBUG	Information	Very detailed run-time information is available. Useful for low-level debugging, but sometimes too detailed. Not enabled by default.

SharePoint Unified Logging Service (ULS)

In addition to logging messages to *<FASTSearchFolder>*\var\log, FS4SP is also using the SharePoint Unified Logging Service for logging via the FAST Search for SharePoint Monitoring service. The default log location is %ProgramFiles%\Common Files\Microsoft Shared\ULS\14\Logs on your FS4SP servers.

> **Important** If you install FS4SP on the same machine as a server that has SharePoint installed, the ULS service will not be installed and logs will not be written to the %ProgramFiles%\Common Files\Microsoft Shared\ULS\14\Logs folder.

A good tool for reading and live monitoring of the ULS log files is the free ULS Viewer tool from Microsoft, shown in Figure 5-9.

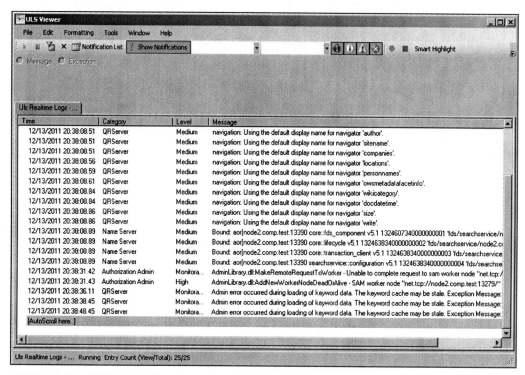

FIGURE 5-9 The ULS Viewer tool.

More Info For more information about the ULS Viewer tool, go to *http://archive.msdn.microsoft.com/ULSViewer.*

Internal FS4SP Logs

All components of FS4SP have their own folder below *<FASTSearchFolder>*\var\log on the server on which they are running. When you experience problems with a component in FS4SP, this is a good place to start looking for errors.

Additionally, the administration server in your deployment stores aggregated logs from all the other servers in the farm in *<FASTSearchFolder>*\var\log\syslog, making it easy to check all the logs using only one server instead of having to check each log on each server.

Functional Logs

Besides the general run-time logs, FS4SP can emit special types of functional logs produced during item processing and when FS4SP receives incoming search queries (query logs).

Item Processing Logging

A couple of tools are at your disposal that make life a lot easier when developing custom Pipeline Extensibility processors or when debugging the indexing pipeline.

Inspect runtime statistics To see statistics about the indexing pipeline and the items that passed through, issue the command *psctrl statistics*. As mentioned in the section "Basic Operations" earlier in this chapter, the *psctrl* tool is used to control all available document processors, regardless of which machine they run on. As such, running *psctrl statistics* gathers run-time data from all relevant servers in the farm.

The output generated from *psctrl statistics* should look similar to Figure 5-10. For each stage, you can inspect time and memory consumption and see how many items have passed through the stage correctly. Note that if a stage drops an item, the item will not continue to be processed in subsequent stages. These statistics are especially important if you added your own external item processing components, because you can examine how much time your custom code consumes, and how many items make it through successfully.

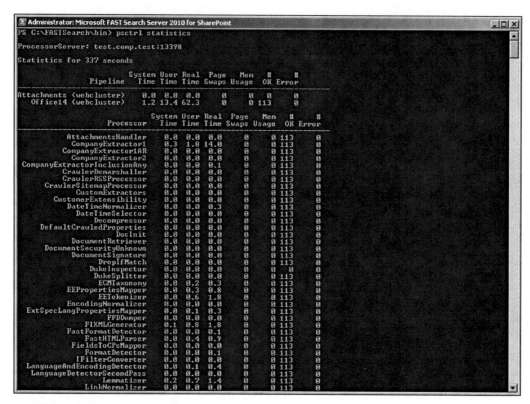

FIGURE 5-10 Statistics per stage in the indexing pipeline.

Even more item processing run-time statistics can be gathered using the resource compiler tool *rc.exe*. Running *rc -r esp/subsystems/processing* shows the minimum, maximum, and average time used per stage in the indexing pipeline.

Note The *rc.exe* tool collects monitoring data from several of the running components of FS4SP, for example, the content distributor, document processors, and indexing dispatcher. For more information about the *rc.exe* tool, go to *http://technet.microsoft.com/en-us/library/ ee943503.aspx*.

Turn on debug and tracing for the running document processors   If you want deep information about what goes on per item in the indexing pipeline, turn on tracing and debug logging using the following commands.

```
psctrl doctrace on
psctrl debug on
```

At the next indexing session, FS4SP will gather trace logs showing items entering and leaving each and every stage in the indexing pipeline, and display all properties that were added, modified, or deleted in any given stage during processing. To inspect these logs, use the tool *doclog.exe*.

> **More Info** For detailed information about the *doclog* tool, go to *http://technet.microsoft.com/en-us/library/ee943514.aspx*.

To display the trace log for every item that passed through the indexing pipeline since tracing was enabled, run the following command.

```
doclog -a
```

However, the output from the preceding command can be a little overwhelming in a large feeding session; the variants *doclog -e* and *doclog -w* show only items that either were dropped in the indexing pipeline or triggered warnings. These two variants are especially useful when debugging a faulty indexing pipeline.

Note that it is possible to run the *doclog* commands just mentioned without turning on *doctrace* and *debug* with *psctrl*, but the information returned lists only logs printed using the INFO log level.

> **Important** After you stop investigating these detailed item processing logs, be sure to disable them with the following commands. The log generation is very expensive and will, if left enabled, put a heavy footprint on your indexing pipeline and also fill up large amounts of disk space.
>
> ```
> psctrl doctrace off
> psctrl debug off
> ```

Inspect crawled properties in the indexing pipeline by using *FFDDumper* *FFDDumper* is a convenient tool for inspecting which crawled properties are actually sent in to the indexing pipeline. This inspection can be particularly useful when mapping crawled properties to managed properties or when you are debugging your own custom processors.

Enable the tool by editing the configuration file for Optional Processing processors residing in *<FASTSearchFolder>*\etc\config_data\DocumentProcessor\optionalprocessing.xml. Change *no* to *yes* in the following line.

```
<processor name="FFDDumper" active="no"/>
```

After editing this file, you must also issue a *psctrl reset* in an FS4SP shell to make the indexing pipeline pick up the changes.

As you probably guessed by now, the *FFDDumper* is nothing more than an item processor. After activation, all crawled properties that are sent into the pipeline, and consequently also through *FFDDumper*, are logged to disk so that they are easily inspected.

The output is put into *<FASTSearchFolder>*\data\ffd\. Start a small test crawl to verify the output. Check the output directory after the test crawl finishes. It should now contain files with the suffix *.ffd*. Open one of these in a text editor. Each line contains the following data:

- A number indicating the length of the crawled property name

- The name of the crawled property

- The character *s*, followed by a number indicating the length of the crawled property

- The content of the crawled property

Be sure to disable the *FFDDumper* by reverting to *active="no"* in *optionalprocessing.xml*.

Note The output files will be stored only on the local server in the FS4SP farm that processes the particular item.

Crawl Logging

Logs from crawling content sources using the built-in FAST Content SSA are easily inspected in Central Admin. On your FAST Content SSA, click Crawling | Crawl Log. Each available content source is listed along with the number of successfully indexed items, the number of items that generated warnings during indexing, and the number of items that could actually not be indexed at all because of an error of some kind. Click any of these numbers to display a list with time stamps and log information detailing what happened and why it happened.

Content crawled and indexed using the FAST Search specific connectors do not have a content source listed on the FAST Content SSA, and as such, this method for inspecting crawler logs is not valid.

Query Logging

FS4SP logs search queries into the *<FASTSearchFolder>*\var\log\querylogs folder on all servers hosting a QR Server component. These logs contain detailed internal timing data and are particularly useful for performance analysis. The logs are stored in plain text.

The log files are named *query_log.[TIMESTAMP]*, for example, *query_log.20110907190001*. Consequently, a log file is created for every hour the local *qrserver* process is running.

Tip It is a good idea to use a competent and fast text editor when inspecting query logs in Notepad. Query logs use a nonstandard suffix, you need to rename the log files to .txt if you want to open them in Notepad. Query logs can grow quite large in high-volume solutions, so it is beneficial to use an editor that performs well even with large files.

Each line in any of the query log files corresponds to a search query and contains information such as originating IP, a UTC time stamp, the internal qrserver request string (into which the user query is converted), an XML representation of the resulting internal query, and some statistics. Quite hidden in the middle of each line, you can find a sequence looking like the one shown in Figure 5-11.

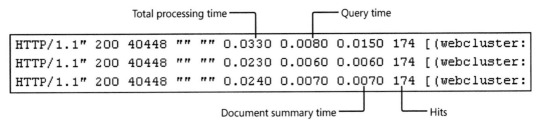

FIGURE 5-11 An excerpt from a query log file.

The numbers depicted in Figure 5-11 reveal some interesting performance data. The last number tells you how many search results were returned for the particular query. The meanings of the time-related parameters are:

- **Total processing time** The total time as seen by the QR Server component—that is, measured from when the query was received until the results were sent back to the service that initiated the search request. The lower boundary of this time is the document summary time plus the query time. However, the time is usually significantly higher because of additional processing in the QR Server and communication overhead between processes in the FS4SP farm.

- **Query time** The time spent locating matching items in the index.

- **Document summary time** Sometimes referred to as the *docsum* time, this number corresponds to the time FS4SP spent actually pulling matching items from the index.

In addition to the query logs located in *<FASTSearchFolder>*\var\log\querylogs, a community tool called *FS4SP Query Logger*, created by one of the authors of this book, can be used to inspect live queries as they arrive. Detailed information about the queries, including a special type of relevance log explaining how rank was calculated, is included. The tool is shown in Figure 5-12.

More Info For more information about this tool, go to *http://fs4splogger.codeplex.com*.

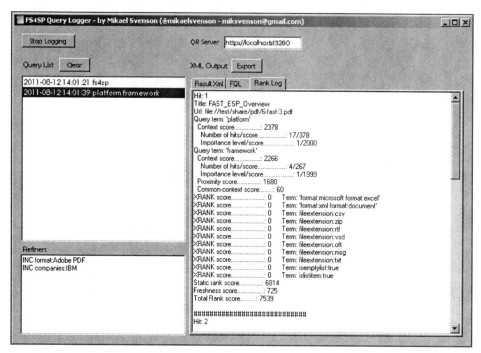

FIGURE 5-12 Live monitoring of queries using the FS4SP Query Logger.

Performance Monitoring

The Windows service FASTSearchMonitoring is automatically installed on all servers in your FS4SP farm with the indexing or search components. The service repeatedly collects statistics, performance counters, and other health information from the FS4SP components and publishes them into performance counters and Windows Management Instrumentation (WMI).

More Info For more information about WMI, go to *http://msdn.microsoft.com/en-us/library/aa394582(VS.85).aspx.*

Monitoring the FS4SP performance counters is one the easiest methods to see how your solution is behaving. Performance counters can be accessed via the Windows Reliability and Performance Monitor (*perfmon.exe*). This tool is preinstalled in the operating system and is shown in Figure 5-13.

More Info For more information about Windows Reliability and Performance Monitor, go to *http://go.microsoft.com/FWLink/?Linkid=188660.*

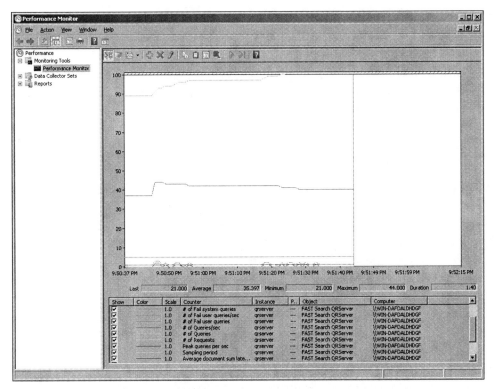

FIGURE 5-13 Viewing FS4SP performance counters by using Windows Reliability and Performance Monitor.

Note Although using *perfmon.exe* is quick and easy, the recommended monitoring solution is Microsoft Systems Center Operations Manager (SCOM). For more information about SCOM, go to *http://technet.microsoft.com/en-us/library/ff383319.aspx*. A preconfigured FS4SP management pack for SCOM is available for download at *http://go.microsoft.com/FWLink/?Linkid=182110*.

Performance counters for FS4SP have 13 different categories, covering areas such as indexing, searching, item processing, link analysis, and the Enterprise Web Crawler. The complete list and explanation of all available performance counters is listed on TechNet at *http://technet.microsoft.com/en-us/library/ff383289.aspx*.)

The sheer amount of performance data can be overwhelming at first. In the following sections, a couple of common and important monitoring scenarios are listed along with their key characteristics.

Identifying Whether an FS4SP Farm Is an Indexing Bottleneck

On the SharePoint server hosting the FAST Content SSA, you can examine the performance counter named *Batches Ready* in the OSS Search FAST Content Plugin category. If this counter reports that zero batches are ready, then FS4SP is processing and indexing content faster than the FAST Content SSA is capable of crawling your content sources. This means that you can further increase your crawling rate. If the number is higher than zero, consider adding more document processors, or see whether you have added an external item processor that slows down the speed of certain items flowing through the indexing pipeline.

If you add more document processors, ensure that the CPU load stays below 90 percent on average. See the next section for more information.

Tip You can increase the crawler speed by adding crawler impact rules, essentially increasing the number of items being crawled in parallel. For more information, go to *http://technet.microsoft.com/en-us/library/ff381257.aspx*.

Identifying Whether the Document Processors Are the Indexing Bottleneck

If the servers hosting the document processors are constantly utilizing 90 percent to 100 percent of the CPU capacity, this is a good indicator that you should add more servers to your FS4SP farm to host additional document processors. In addition to monitoring the CPU load, you can watch the Queue Full State performance counter of the FAST Search Document Processor category. If this counter reports *1* over a long time, it indicates that the queue is full and you are not emptying it quickly enough, in which case you might need to add more document processors. A rule of thumb is to not have more than one document processor per available CPU core in the operation system.

Identifying Whether Your Disk Subsystem Is a Bottleneck

FS4SP is a very disk-intensive system with lots of random disk reads and writes. If you monitor the Avg. Disk Queue Length performance counter in the Physical Disk category, you can see whether your disk is being saturated. If the value stays above *2* for a single disk for longer periods of time, it is an indication of the disk being the bottleneck. The value should stay below *2* for a single disk.

If the volume is built up of six disks in an array and the average disk queue length is 10, the average disk queue length per physical disk is 1.66 (10/6=1.66), which is within the recommended value of *2*.

If your disk is a bottleneck, you can either expand your RAID with more disks or add more columns or rows to your FS4SP farm to spread the load. You need to add an index column if indexing is saturating your disks, and additional search rows if searching is saturating your disks.

Backup and Recovery

Backup and recovery is an important aspect of your disaster recovery plan, and deciding how to implement it depends on several factors, such as how critical the service is for your business and how much downtime is acceptable.

If you require uptime 24 hours a day, seven days a week, you should consider configuring redundancy on the components in FS4SP. This is described in the "Production Environments" section in Chapter 4.

When backing up FS4SP, there are four parts to consider: the FS4SP administration database, the FS4SP configuration files, the FS4SP binary index, and any custom pipeline extensibility modules you have deployed.

FS4SP comes bundled with a Windows PowerShell backup script that backs up all of FS4SP, including any custom pipeline extensibility stages. The backup script uses functions in the *Microsoft .SqlServer.Management.Smo* namespace to perform backup and to restore of the administration database. The tool *robocopy* is used for reliable file copying.

More Info The *Microsoft.SqlServer.Management.Smo* namespace is included with SQL server and is available for download at *http://go.microsoft.com/FWLink/?Linkid=188653*. For more information about robocopy, go to *http://technet.microsoft.com/en-us/library/ cc733145(WS.10).aspx*.

Note Although the backup of the FS4SP files is stored at a specified file area during backup, the administration database is not copied over to this folder. The backup of the FS4SP administration database is located in a folder called *Backup* below the Microsoft SQL Server installation folder on SQL Server. The exact path and host name of the database backup file can be found in the file *SQLServerMetaData.txt* in the backup folder, on the lines that contain *BackupDirectory* and *NetName*. The backup file name can be found in the file *dbbackup.txt* in the backup folder.

With SQL Server 2008 R2, the backup would reside in C:\Program Files\Microsoft SQL Server\ MSSQL10_50.MSSQLSERVER\MSSQL\Backup.

Certificates are not backed up and have to be put in place manually if they expire.

The backup script can be run in two modes: configuration and full. Configuration mode makes copies of the FS4SP internal configuration files, excluding any pipeline extensibility changes, and can be run while the system is up and running. Full mode copies all the folders and data below *<FASTSearchFolder>* and requires suspending indexing while the backup is taking place. Table 5-3 lists what is covered in the different backup modes, including backup of the SharePoint farm.

TABLE 5-3 What is covered by the different backup options in FS4SP

Component	Configuration backup	Full backup	Full backup + SharePoint farm backup
Installer-generated files		Yes	Yes
Config server files	Yes	Yes	Yes
SAM admin configuration	Yes	Yes	Yes
SPRel configuration	Yes	Yes	Yes
Web Analyzer configuration	Yes	Yes	Yes
FAST Enterprise Crawler configuration		Yes	Yes
Binaries and DLLs			
People Search			Yes
Searchable index		Yes*	Yes*
FIXML files		Yes	Yes
Custom folders in <FASTSearchFolder>		Yes	Yes
FAST Search Administration database	Yes	Yes	Yes
FAST Content SSA state			Yes

* Can be disabled with the *-excludeindex* parameter

> **Note** Besides the FAST Search Administration database, FS4SP is also storing content in databases for the FAST Content SSA and the FAST Query SSA. These databases are covered by the backup routines in SharePoint and thus are not covered by the FS4SP backup scripts.

Which backup mode you decide to implement in your backup and recovery strategy is largely dependent on your accepted threshold for downtime. Table 5-4 lists the most common scenarios and recommendations, and the cost related to upfront investments. Lower-cost alternatives might end up costing you more in downtime if, or rather when, disaster strikes.

TABLE 5-4 Downtime considerations

Method	Downtime period	Recommendation	Action Cost
Multiple rows*	No downtime	Add search rows to your deployment in order to provide failover and redundancy for one or more of the FS4SP components.	High You have to add more servers and purchase additional FS4SP server licenses.
Full backup	One or more days	Use the FS4SP backup/restore scripts for full backup or use a third-party backup solution.	Medium The cost is related to storage, and will vary depending on how much data you have indexed.
Configuration backup	Days to several weeks	Reinstall your farm from scratch, use the FS4SP backup/restore scripts for configuration backup/restore, and do a full crawl of all your content sources.	Low Backing up the configuration takes very little space.

* Can also be combined with "Full backup"

> **More Info** You can read more about backup and recovery strategies for SharePoint at TechNet, where business requirements, what parts to backup, and what tools to use are also discussed. Go to *http://technet.microsoft.com/en-us/library/cc261687.aspx*.

Prerequisites

Before you run the backup or restore script in FS4SP, certain prerequisites need to be fulfilled. Table 5-5 lists the prerequisites and can be used as a checklist when preparing your solution for backup.

TABLE 5-5 Prerequisites for running the backup and restore scripts

Prerequisite	Comment	Perform at
The user who runs the backup and restore scripts must be a member of the local FASTSearchAdministrators group.	Commands executed in the scripts are secured by requiring the user to be a member of the FASTSearchAdministrators group.	All FS4SP servers
The user who runs the backup and restore scripts must be a member of the local administrators group.	This is required for Windows PowerShell remoting to work in its default setup.	All FS4SP servers
Windows PowerShell remoting must be enabled on all servers.	To enable remoting, open a Windows PowerShell prompt as an administrator and run the following command. `Enable-PSRemoting -Force`	All FS4SP servers
Windows PowerShell remoting must be set up as a Credential Security Support Provider (CredSSP) server.	To enable the CredSSP server, open a Windows PowerShell prompt as an administrator, and run the following command. `Enable-WSManCredSSP -Role Server -Force`	All FS4SP servers

Prerequisite	Comment	Perform at
Increase the maximum amount of memory allocated to a Windows PowerShell instance to 1 GB.	To increase the memory limit, open a Windows PowerShell prompt as an administrator and run the following command. `Set-Item WSMan:\localhost\Shell\MaxMemoryPerShellMB 1000`	All FS4SP servers
Set up Windows PowerShell remoting as a CredSSP client.	To enable the CredSSP client, open a Windows PowerShell prompt as an administrator and run the following command: `Enable-WSManCredSSP -Role Client -DelegateComputer server1,server2,…,serverN -Force` where *server1,server2,…,server* must be identical to the server names listed in <host name="server"> in <FASTSearchFolder>\etc\config_data\deployment\deployment.xml.	Administration server
The SQL Server Management Objects (SMO) .NET assemblies must be installed.	If SQL server is installed on the same server as the FS4SP administration server, the assemblies are already installed. If not, download Microsoft SQL Server System CLR Types and Microsoft SQL Server 2008 Management Objects. These downloads can be found at *http://technet.microsoft.com/en-us/library/cc261687.aspx* and *http://go.microsoft.com/FWLink/?Linkid=123709*, respectively.	Administration server
The backup store must be available as a UNC path by the user who runs the backup scripts, with read and write permissions.	Ensure that the file share has correct read and write permissions for the user running the backup.	Backup store
The user who runs the backup and restore script must have sysadmin permissions on the FS4SP administration database.	Database permissions can be verified and modified by using SQL Server Management Studio.	SQL Server

Backup and Restore Configuration

The configuration backup option makes a copy of the FS4SP configuration, most importantly the *<FASTSearchFolder>*\etc\config_data folder, and only backs up files that are modified or generated after the initial FS4SP installation. The search index is not a part of this kind of backup. Because the backup contains an incomplete set of files, you have to restore it over an existing FS4SP deployment.

The configuration backup is not deployment-aware and can safely be restored to any system by using the *-action configmigrate* parameter during restore. This means you can restore the configuration from a five-server deployment to, for example, a two-server deployment.

Note A configuration backup is nonintrusive and can be performed without interrupting a live system. It does not require shutting down any FS4SP services.

Be sure to always perform a configuration backup and restore when the set of managed properties changes. If the restored system and the backed-up system have unsynchronized managed properties, your content will not be searchable after the restore and you will have to perform a full crawl to put the system back in a consistent state.

Performing a Configuration Backup

To run a configuration backup, use the Windows PowerShell script *backup.ps1*, located in the *<FASTSearchFolder>*\bin folder. For example:

```
.\backup.ps1 -action config -backuppath <UNC path>
```

> *<UNC path>* is the location of your backup store, for example, *\\storage\fs4spbackup*.

Performing a Configuration Restore

The following procedure can be used to do a configuration restore to a system that uses the same server name(s) and deployment configuration as the backup. This can either be the same system from where you took the backup or an identical mirrored system. The restore process must be performed on a running system, and you do not stop any FS4SP services.

To run a configuration restore, use the Windows PowerShell script *restore.ps1* located in the *<FASTSearchFolder>*\bin folder. For example:

```
.\restore.ps1 -action config -backuppath <UNC path>
```

> *<UNC path>* is the location of your backup store, for example, *\\storage\fs4spbackup*.

If you are restoring the configuration to a system that uses a different deployment configuration, use the *-action configmigrate* parameter as mentioned before. For example:

```
.\restore.ps1 -action configmigrate -backuppath <UNC path>
```

After the restore has completed, restart FS4SP, for example, by executing the following commands on each server in the farm.

```
Stop-Service FASTSearchService
Start-Service FASTSearchService
```

Full Backup and Restore

A full backup makes a complete copy of the FS4SP installation folder and the FS4SP administration database. For each server in your FS4SP farm, the backup stores a copy of the *<FASTSearchFolder>* except for the executable binaries and DLL files. The backup is coupled to the deployment it was generated from and can be restored only on the same set of servers or on exact duplicates of the originating servers.

When performing a full backup, be sure to stop all processes related to item processing and indexing. This ensures that the search will still work during a backup. Doing a full restore, on the other hand, requires you to shut down FS4SP completely on all servers in the farm.

It is important that the data in the crawler database associated with the FAST Content SSA is synchronized with the indexed content in FS4SP to avoid possible duplicates or indexed items not being searchable. Therefore, when setting up your FS4SP backup schedule, be sure to pair it with the backup of your SharePoint farm to ensure consistency.

Avoid Backup Jobs to Conflict with the Spell Tuner

Do not run your backup at around 2 A.M. The default installation of FS4SP uploads spell-tuning dictionaries at 2:05 A.M. and requires the Spell Tuner process to run. The FS4SP backup script will stop the Spell Tuner process during backup, and if a backup is not finished before the scheduled dictionary upload, the dictionary will not be processed.

If you do execute the backup at the same time as the dictionary upload, you have to manually run the spell tuner to update the dictionaries.

On the FS4SP administration server, execute the following command to manually update the dictionaries.

```
spelltuner -f --wordcount-threshold 100000 --spellcheck-threshold 13 --max-wordcount
10000000
```

There is no supported way of changing the time for when the spell tuner is scheduled to run. However, if you open *<FASTSearchFolder>*\etc\nodeconf.xml, you will find the following section, which sets the time to 2:05 A.M.

```
<process name="spelltuner" description="Automatic spellcheck tuning" multi="no">
     <start>
       <executable>$FASTSEARCH/bin/spelltuner</executable>
       <parameters>--download-interval 60 --wordcount-threshold 100000 --spellcheck-
threshold 13 --max-wordcount 10000000 -t 02:05:00</parameters>
     </start>
     <stop>
       <timeout>30</timeout>
       <timeout_action>kill</timeout_action>
     </stop>
   </process>
```

After editing the start time, you need to restart the Spell Tuner with the following command.

```
nctrl restart spelltuner
```

Performing a Full Backup

Before starting the backup, ensure that all crawls are paused by running the following commands in a SharePoint Management Shell.

```
$ssa = Get-SPEnterpriseSearchServiceApplication <FAST Content SSA>
$ssa.Pause()
```

You must also stop all indexing and feeding processes on your FS4SP farm before starting the backup. Do this with the Windows PowerShell script *suspend.ps1* located in *<FASTSearchFolder>*\bin. After the backup has completed, you can resume operations with the *resume.ps1* script.

To run a full backup, run the following commands in an FS4SP shell on the administration server.

```
.\suspend.ps1
.\backup.ps1 -action full -backuppath <UNC path>
.\resume.ps1
```

<UNC path> is the location of your backup store, for example, *\\storage\fs4spbackup*. It is good practice to let the system settle for a few minutes after running suspend.ps1 before starting the backup script to make sure all processes are properly stopped and files have flushed to disk.

When FS4SP is back up and running, you can resume crawling operations by executing the following in a SharePoint Management Shell.

```
$ssa = Get-SPEnterpriseSearchServiceApplication <FAST Content SSA>
$ssa.ForceResume($ssa.IsPaused())
```

Performing a Full Restore

When performing a full restore, it is important that the target system is identical to the source system used for the backup. What this means is that:

- The numbers of servers are the same.

- The roles assigned to each server are the same.

- The names of the servers are the same.

Before restoring FS4SP, be sure that you have done a restore of the SharePoint farm first with the associated SharePoint farm backup.

1. Stop the alternate access mapping job on SharePoint. From a SharePoint Management Shell, run the following commands.

    ```
    $extractorJob = Get-SPTimerJob | where {$_.Name.StartsWith("FAST Search Server 2010 for
        SharePoint Alternate Access Mapping Extractor Job")}
    Disable-SPTimerJob $extractorJob
    ```

2. Perform a restore on the SharePoint Server farm installation. From a SharePoint Management Shell, run the following command.

    ```
    Restore-SPFarm -RestoreMethod overwrite -Directory <path of backup directory>
    -RestoreThreads 1
    ```

3. Resume the alternate access mapping job, and pause all crawls. From a SharePoint Management Shell, run the following commands.

    ```
    $extractorJob = Get-SPTimerJob | where {$_.Name.StartsWith("FAST Search Server 2010
        for SharePoint Alternate Access Mapping Extractor Job")}
    Enable-SPTimerJob $extractorJob
    $ssa = Get-SPEnterpriseSearchServiceApplication <FAST Content SSA>
    $ssa.Pause()
    ```

4. Stop the FS4SP services on all servers, for example, by running the following command.

```
Stop-Service FASTSearchService
Stop-Service FASTSearchMonitoring
```

5. Perform the FS4SP restore. In an FS4SP shell, run the following command.

```
.\restore.ps1 -action full -backuppath <UNC path>
```

6. Start the FS4SP services on all servers, for example, by running the following command.

```
Start-Service FASTSearchService
```

7. Resume crawling operations. From a SharePoint Management Shell, run the following commands.

```
$ssa = Get-SPEnterpriseSearchServiceApplication <FAST Content SSA>
$ssa.ForceResume($ssa.IsPaused())
```

Incremental Backup

You perform incremental backups by adding the *-force* option to the *backup.ps1* script.

```
.\backup.ps1 -action full -backuppath <UNC path> -force
```

You can use the same backup path with this option, and because *robocopy* is run in incremental mode, only modified files are copied, which saves time in subsequent backups.

Speeding Up Backups

You can speed up backups by adding the *-multithreaded* option to the *backup.ps1* script.

```
.\backup.ps1 -action full -backuppath <UNC path> -multithreaded 16
```

This option enables *robocopy* to use multiple threads in parallel during file copying. Though it is configurable, it cannot go outside the range from 1 and 128.

 Warning The multi-thread option of robocopy is not supported on Windows 2008, only on Windows 2008 R2.

Conclusion

A lot of things can happen in a solution as complex as FS4SP. It is important to establish procedures and guidelines in your organization for monitoring the solution and being able to catch indications of problems as they are reported. Knowing the tools that can help identify problems and knowing which logs to examine when something does happen is key to managing the FS4SP farm efficiently, ensuring the best possible search experience for your users.

If you experience server failures or other unexpected problems, you need to have proper routines in place for recovery by using the redundancy capabilities of FS4SP, backing up the FS4SP servers, or using a combination of both. After you choose a backup and recovery strategy, be sure that you perform regular test runs of the procedure so that you are well-prepared when disaster strikes and you have to execute the backup plan in a production environment.

This chapter covered tools and procedures that we think will get you ready for running FS4SP in production. You saw how to monitor an FS4SP deployment and the various areas in which logs related to FS4SP are held and how to effectively monitor them. The chapter also outlined how to effectively and safely modify the FS4SP topology. Finally, the chapter looked at the different methods of backing up an FS4SP deployment and gave several best practices for doing so.

Creating Search Solutions

## CHAPTER 6

Search Configuration

After completing this chapter, you will be able to

- Manage FS4SP functionality in SharePoint, in Windows PowerShell, and through .NET code.

- Manage your index schema and tune relevance.

- Set up full-text indexes, rank profiles, content collections, and search scopes.

- Use the out-of-the-box property extractors.

- Add keywords with synonyms, best bets, visual best bets, and user contexts.

You can manage many features of Microsoft FAST Search Server 2010 for SharePoint (FS4SP) from within Microsoft SharePoint. However, many more feature-control switches and settings are hidden in configuration files on the FS4SP farm. This chapter covers the importance of Windows PowerShell. It also looks into how to manage your search engine on a daily basis and how to tune it to suit your specific business needs. Additionally, the chapter describes the tools available to monitor and analyze the health of the system and explains what you should do to properly back up your solution.

Overview of FS4SP Configuration

FS4SP is a great leap forward compared to pre-Microsoft FAST technology. It combines the convenience of being able to administer the key components from within SharePoint and the power of advanced management with file-level configurations. Although you can change many settings in Central Administration in SharePoint, more-advanced settings are available via the FS4SP configuration files. Beyond that, you can use Windows PowerShell for advanced, yet simple, control of the search system. Finally, Microsoft .NET customization capabilities offer you full control.

Most IT pros who worked with previous versions of FAST technology would agree that FS4SP is an advance in terms of administration. Configuring the solution is more streamlined than before, and there are fewer interaction points and technologies that you need to be concerned about.

However, some aspects of FS4SP can feel unorthodox to a Microsoft professional. For example, the FAST Search specific connectors require a Java run-time environment, and the indexing pipeline is still heavily based on Python. But all in all, FS4SP has come a long way in terms of streamlining the technology to fit into the Microsoft technology stack.

On a high level, FS4SP administration has five main methods, which are described briefly in Table 6-1. The rest of this chapter expands on the administration methods. Where appropriate, this chapter provides examples of how to manage FS4SP through SharePoint Central Administration, by using Windows PowerShell, and by writing .NET code.

> **Note** The sections in this chapter show administration samples that use SharePoint Central Administration, Windows PowerShell, and .NET code. Where SharePoint samples are missing, the capability is missing in SharePoint. For all Windows PowerShell samples, there is a .NET equivalent, but because using Windows PowerShell is very similar to .NET in many cases, some .NET samples have been omitted. Many Windows PowerShell cmdlets return .NET objects, and the methods executed on them are the same.

TABLE 6-1 Operation interaction points

Interaction point	Example of a typical operation
SharePoint	Adding a new content source; for example, setting up a crawl of a SharePoint site collection
Windows PowerShell	Tuning the index schema; for example, changing relevance weights of managed properties
Code	Managing crawled properties from a custom application
Configuration files	Registering a third-party IFilter or configuring the FAST Search specific connectors
Command-line tools	Starting or stopping internal FS4SP processes, retrieving statistics of search nodes, and so on

SharePoint Administration

You perform most basic FS4SP configuration in SharePoint Central Administration, on the FAST Content SSAs and the FAST Query SSAs. This includes setting up and managing new content sources and managing crawled and managed properties. If you are using the FS4SP Web Parts—the Enterprise Search Web Parts—you, of course, also spend time configuring those through SharePoint.

In addition to the administration settings in Central Administration, you can find administration settings on each SharePoint site collection, including administration of keywords for synonyms, best bets, and visual best bets, and administration of document and site promotions.

Windows PowerShell Administration

In addition to the administrative tasks you can manage through Central Administration or Site Collection Administration in SharePoint, you can do even more through Windows PowerShell. Most Windows PowerShell commands that target FS4SP execute in the Microsoft FAST Search Server 2010 for SharePoint shell (FS4SP shell), but a few commands must be run from the SharePoint 2010 Management Shell (SharePoint Management Shell). One example of the latter is when you want to create a new content source. *Content Sources* are a SharePoint Enterprise Search concept used by FS4SP. Therefore, managing content sources from Windows PowerShell is available only from the SharePoint Management Shell.

In general, if a Windows PowerShell cmdlet has the word *FASTSearch* as part of its name, you need to execute the cmdlet in an FS4SP shell on an FS4SP server; otherwise, you should execute it in a SharePoint Management Shell on a SharePoint server.

> **Note** Some of the FS4SP command-line utilities and Windows PowerShell scripts require elevated privileges in order to run. Right-clicking the shell shortcut and choosing Run As Administrator provides the permissions you need. Modifying the shortcut to always run as administrator simplifies management because you then always have the required permissions to execute any FS4SP-related command or script. You can also make sure the logged-in user executing the Windows PowerShell cmdlets is a member of the FASTSearchAdministrators local group on the server, as specified during installation.

Windows PowerShell has more than 80 different FS4SP-related cmdlets. They are roughly divided into these groups:

- Administration
- Index schema
- Installation
- Spell-tuning
- Security

You will read about many of these in this chapter and, where appropriate, throughout the book. A convenient way to list all available cmdlets is to run the following command in an FS4SP shell.

```
Get-Command -Module Microsoft.FASTSearch.PowerShell
```

The cmdlets are all documented according to the Windows PowerShell documentation standard. To see a detailed manual page, you can prefix a cmdlet with *Get-Help,* for example, *Get-Help New-FASTSearchMetadataCategory*). Many cmdlets also show example usages, such as *Get-Help New-FASTSearchMetadataCategory –examples.*

> **Tip** You can list and group all cmdlets by name by using the following Windows PowerShell command.
>
> ```
> gcm -Module Microsoft.FASTSearch.PowerShell | sort noun,verb | group noun | ft -AutoSize
> ```
>
> For a complete list of Windows PowerShell cmdlets, go to *http://technet.microsoft.com/en-us/library/ff393782.aspx.*

Code Administration

If you are building a large search solution, you might find yourself in a situation where you want to modify certain FS4SP features or settings from code running within a custom-built application. The good news is that everything you can do from Windows PowerShell is available using .NET code. The bad news is that it isn't always easy. For a good example, see the "Crawled and Managed Properties" section in this chapter; compare how easy it is to map a crawled property to a managed property in Windows PowerShell versus the number of lines of code required to do the same operation in Microsoft Visual C# or Microsoft Visual Basic.

Using the .NET API is a good option for deployment scenarios: Instead of executing a Windows PowerShell script, you can create crawled and managed properties when a SharePoint feature activates. Depending on your deployment regime, you can choose the option that fits best.

Code Example Assumptions

The code examples in this chapter assume that:

- You are developing in Microsoft Visual Studio 2010 using Microsoft .NET Framework 3.5.

- The application runs locally on the FS4SP administration server.

 More Info For information about setting up an administration server, see Chapter 4, "Deployment."

- The user executing the application is a member of the local FASTSearchAdministrators group on the FS4SP administration server.

When you work with administration via the .NET API, several context classes serve as entry points for different administrative operations, as listed in Table 6-2. Later in this chapter, you see examples that use some of these classes.

 Important If you are developing on a machine that has SharePoint and not FS4SP installed, you will find the DLLs to reference at %CommonProgramFiles%\Microsoft Shared\ Web Server Extensions\14\ISAPI rather than at <FASTSearchFolder>\bin.

TABLE 6-2 Class entry points for working with the .NET administration objects

Class name	Description	MSDN reference
CompiledDictionaryContext	Used when compiling dictionaries added to FS4SP to an internal FS4SP format.	*http://msdn.microsoft.com/en-us/library/ microsoft.sharepoint.search.extended .administration.compileddictionarycontext .aspx*
ContentContext	Used to work with FS4SP content collections. Internally used by (for example) the cmdlet *New-FASTSearchContentCollection*.	*http://msdn.microsoft.com/en-us/library/ microsoft.sharepoint.search.extended .administration.contentcontext.aspx*
DeploymentContext	Used to deploy resources in the FS4SP farm (for example, uploading property extraction or spell-checking lists to FS4SP).	*http://msdn.microsoft.com/en-us/library/ microsoft.sharepoint.search.extended. administration.deploymentcontext.aspx*
EntityExtractorContext	Used for property extraction inclusion and exclusion list functionality.	*http://msdn.microsoft.com/en-us/library/ microsoft.sharepoint.search.extended .administration.entityextractorcontext .aspx*
KeywordContext	Used for search keyword management functionality (for example, search setting groups, best bets, and synonyms).	*http://msdn.microsoft.com/en-us/library/ microsoft.sharepoint.search.extended .administration.keywordcontext.aspx*
LinguisticManagerContext	Used to get access to the Linguistic manager. The Linguistic manager can be used to get the dictionary type.	*http://msdn.microsoft.com/en-us/library/ microsoft.sharepoint.search.extended .administration.linguisticmanagercontext .aspx*
PersistedDictionaryContext	Used for persisting property extractor and spell-checking dictionaries in a *PersistedDictionaryCollection* object.	*http://msdn.microsoft.com/en-us/library/ microsoft.sharepoint.search.extended .administration.persisteddictionarycontext .aspx*
SchemaContext	Used to work with index schema functionality like crawled and managed properties, full-text indexes, and rank profiles.	*http://msdn.microsoft.com/en-us/library/ microsoft.sharepoint.search.extended .administration.schemacontext.aspx*
SpellCheckerContext	Used for the spell-check exclusion list functionality.	*http://msdn.microsoft.com/en-us/library/ microsoft.sharepoint.search.extended .administration.spellcheckercontext.aspx*

If you want to integrate with FS4SP by using code that runs within SharePoint, you need to connect to the FS4SP administration service by using a proxy to the FAST Query SSA. The following code gives an example on how to get a reference to the *SchemaContext* object via the FAST Query SSA proxy.

```
var ssaProxy = (SearchServiceApplicationProxy)SearchServiceApplicationProxy.
GetProxy(SPServiceContext.Current);
if (ssaProxy.FASTAdminProxy != null)
{
    var fastProxy = ssaProxy.FASTAdminProxy;
    SchemaContext schemaContext = fastProxy.SchemaContext;
    // your code here
}
```

Other Means of Administration

In addition to SharePoint Central Administration, Windows PowerShell, and .NET code for FS4SP management, you need to use both configuration files and command-line tools found locally on the FS4SP servers for administration of certain parts of FS4SP.

- **Configuration files**   If you are moving from an older FAST incarnation to FS4SP, you might notice that the number of configuration files has gone down drastically. But many low-level settings are still available only by editing files, whether plain text files or XML. However, you can edit only 16 configuration files without leaving your system in an unsupported state, and these are all XML files; 6 of these files are related to the FAST Search specific connectors. However, there are many other interesting files, which can be tweaked to change functionality. Although these changes are unsupported, you might explore making changes to a few of these because they may be useful in some cases.

> **Important** If you leave your system in an unsupported state and you need to contact Microsoft for support on your FS4SP installation, Microsoft can decline to help you because you have modified files that are not supposed to be changed.

- **Command-line tools**   Many FS4SP operations are run and controlled with command-line tools—that is, the applications that live in the *<FASTSearchFolder>*\bin folder and are available from within the FS4SP shell. All in all, there are 25 of these tools; we touch on the most important of these throughout the book.

  You need to understand the difference between these command-line tools and the Windows PowerShell cmdlets mentioned in the section "Windows PowerShell Administration" earlier in this chapter. Windows PowerShell cmdlets are communicating with FS4SP via the FASTSearchAdminServices Windows Communication Foundation (WCF) service, whereas the command-line tools are talking directly with different FS4SP components via an internal API. Command-line tools can be run both from a command prompt and from an FS4SP shell.

> **More Info** For more information about command-line tools, go to *http://msdn.microsoft.com/en-us/library/ee943520.aspx*.

Index Schema Management

In FS4SP, like in all search engines, the index constitutes the physical and logical core of the solution. Physically, the index is often spread out onto several machines for scale and redundancy. Logically, the index configuration defines how searches should behave and what features are activated.

In this chapter, you learn how to work with the index configuration to tailor the search experience to your business requirements.

> **Note** This chapter focuses on the logical aspect of the index. See the procedure "Modify the index topology" in Chapter 5, "Operations," for information about physical operations, such as how to scale and how to redistribute the index to new servers.

The Index Schema

The very heart of FS4SP is the index configuration, or the index schema. Read Chapter 2, "Search Concepts and Terminology," for a walkthrough of all concepts related to the index schema: how these concepts relate to one another and what their purpose is. This chapter describes how to work with and adapt the index schema to your needs.

In previous incarnations of FAST technology, the index schema is an actual configuration file. Previously, you edited this file by hand and deployed it onto the system to apply the changes. In FS4SP, this procedure has been revamped and is now hidden behind more user-friendly tools. These tools modify the internal configuration file for you, reducing potential configuration errors introduced by manual editing.

As previously mentioned, the index schema is internally stored in a configuration file. If you are curious about how this file looks, it is available at *<FASTSearchFolder>\index-profiles\deployment-ready-index-profile.xml*. Do not change this file directly unless you know exactly what you are doing and are sure you want to make this unsupported change. Your index might become corrupt, and you can render your system unusable. Instead, use the tools described later in this chapter to modify your index. The file is also overwritten if you change behavior of managed properties, full-text indexes, or rank profiles.

Whether you use the SharePoint GUI, the cmdlets, or custom code to modify the index schema, the *Microsoft.SharePoint.Search.Extended.Administration.Schema* namespace is what is used behind the scenes. Using the classes in this namespace modifies and deploys the index schema configuration file mentioned previously.

Figure 6-1 shows the classes available to you via the *SchemaContext* class and how they relate to one another.

Microsoft.SharePoint.Search.Extended.Administration.dll

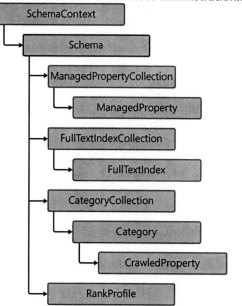

FIGURE 6-1 *SchemaContext* class hierarchy.

Crawled and Managed Properties

As described in Chapter 2, FS4SP has two types of index properties: crawled and managed. Everything you crawl enters the system as crawled properties—either because these properties existed as-is in the particular content source in structured data (for example, database columns, Microsoft Word document titles, or SharePoint columns) or because they were extracted from the document's unstructured data during indexing (for example, webpage headers).

The default setting for most crawled properties is for its contents to be included in the search index without the need for you to take any action in order to search on the data from crawled properties. If you want to create a refiner on it, display it in a particular manner for your search results, sort on it, or use it in a search scope, you have to promote it to a managed property.

> **More Info** The category in which a crawled property belongs determines whether a crawled property is made searchable by default. You can read more about how to change this setting at *http://technet.microsoft.com/en-us/library/ff191246.aspx*.

If you have a crawled property that you want to omit from your search results, you have to change the default settings so that it will not be included. This can be useful for custom SharePoint columns or crawled properties from third-party IFilters that you don't want in your search results.

Crawled properties are grouped in crawled property categories (metadata categories). For example, SharePoint columns go into the SharePoint category, metatags from webpages go into the Web Category, and properties of Word documents go into the Microsoft Office category.

Note A good practice is to create separate categories for crawled properties that you create yourself in order to ease property management. This category separation is similar to grouping site columns in SharePoint.

Content that ends up in a managed property is usable when searching. You can define how queries interact with that data. For example, you can define whether lemmatization should be active, whether wildcard search patterns are allowed, and whether it should be possible to sort a result set on a particular property. All such attributes of a managed property are listed in Table 6-3.

Note The property for turning lemmatization on and off is called *stemming* because the API is shared with SharePoint search.

Note As you will see in the following sections, a managed property is represented internally as a regular object. Therefore, these properties are actual object properties that you get and set in Windows PowerShell and code just as you would for any other class instantiation.

TABLE 6-3 Attributes of a managed property

Attribute	Description	Value
DecimalPlaces	Gets or sets the number of decimal places. Only applicable for decimal-type managed properties.	3 (default) Minimum: −28 Maximum: 28
DeleteDisallowed	Gets a Boolean value that indicates whether the managed property can be deleted. Only applicable for default, internal properties.	True False (default)
Description	Gets or sets a text description for a managed property.	<optional>
IsMapped	Gets or sets a Boolean value that indicates whether the managed property is mapped to support Alternate Access Mapping.	True False (default)
MappingDisallowed	Gets a Boolean value that indicates whether crawled properties can be mapped to the managed property.	True False (default)
MaxIndexSize	Gets or sets the maximum number of kilobytes indexed for a managed property. Only applicable for managed properties of type *text*.	1,024 Maximum: 2,097,151 (2 GB)

Attribute	Description	Value
MaxResultSize	Gets or sets the maximum number of kilobytes that are used for the result of a managed property—that is, how much content can be retrieved from the index for this managed property. This is applicable only for managed properties of type *text*.	*64* Maximum: *2,097,151* (2 GB)
MergeCrawledProperties	Gets or sets a Boolean value that indicates whether to include the contents of all crawled properties mapped to a managed property. If this setting is disabled, the value of the first nonempty crawled property is used as the contents of the managed property. This has to be set to *true* to support multi-value data being assigned to it.	*True* *False* (default)
Name	Gets the name of a managed property. Note that it is not possible to change the name of a managed property without deleting and recreating it.	*<required>*
Queryable	Gets or sets a Boolean value that indicates whether a managed property can be used in query operators and filter terms.	*True* (default) *False*
RefinementEnabled	Gets or sets a Boolean value that indicates whether to enable a refiner for a managed property.	*True* *False* (default)
SortableType	Gets or sets the sortable type for a managed property whether or not sorting is enabled. *LatentSortable* is used to prepare a property for possible sorting in the future. Changing from *LatentSortable* to *SortableEnabled* does not require reindexing.	*SortableDisabled* (default) *SortableEnabled* *LatentSortable*
StemmingEnabled	Gets or sets a Boolean value that indicates whether a managed property is stemmed/lemmatized.	*True* *False* (default)
SubstringEnabled	Gets or sets a Boolean value to indicate whether to enable substring matching for the managed property.	*True* *False* (default)
SummaryType	Gets or sets the summary type for a managed property: *static* or *dynamic*, where the former tells FS4SP to calculate a dynamic teaser in which the search terms are highlighted.	*Disabled* *Static* (default) *Dynamic*
Type	Gets the data type; for example, *Integer* or *Text*. Note that it is not possible to change the type of a managed property without deleting and recreating it.	*<required>* *1* (Text) *2* (Integer) *3* (Boolean) *4* (Float) *5* (Decimal) *6* (Datetime)

Warning Enabling substring matching on a managed property is mainly for supporting Asian languages. The index size greatly increases and search precision is reduced. But there are other uses for it, as you can see in the e-commerce sample in Chapter 10, "Search Scenarios." You can read more about substring matching and Asian languages at *http://technet.microsoft.com/en-us/library/gg130819.aspx*.

In order to search and retrieve results from FS4SP, you need mappings from crawled properties to managed properties. You can, however, just start a crawl of a SharePoint site, a website, or even a file server, and expect to be able to query the index right away. This is because FS4SP comes with a large set of preconfigured crawled and managed properties, and mappings between them, perfectly suitable for most web content and documents. But as soon as you want to change the behavior of a certain property or you want to crawl nonstandard content sources, you very likely will have to tailor both mappings and the configuration of the managed properties.

Both crawled and managed properties have to be created. The FS4SP indexing pipeline contains a crawled property discovery processor called *PropertiesReporter*. This processor looks for structured metadata in the content and creates the corresponding crawled properties. There is also a companion processor called *PropertiesMapper* that makes sure that the mappings you defined are reflected in the internal structures of the index.

 Note If you change a mapping from a crawled to a managed property, you need to recrawl all affected documents for the change to take effect. This is because the PropertiesMapper processor has to resynchronize your new configuration into the index.

Because you typically do not have to create crawled properties yourself, but instead rely on the indexing pipeline to discover and extract them automatically, this chapter focuses on how to create and configure managed properties. When creating deployment scripts, a good recommendation is to create custom crawled and managed properties as part of the script, not relying on crawling to detect and create them. This saves you crawling the content twice only for crawled property discovery, which may take a considerable amount of time for large data volumes.

SharePoint

Working with managed properties via SharePoint Central Administration is a quick way to create, edit, or delete crawled and managed properties. The interface is very similar to that of SharePoint Search.

Create a managed property

1. In Central Administration, click Manage Service Applications, and then click your FAST Query SSA.

2. Under Administration, click FAST Search Administration.

3. Under Property Management, click Managed Properties. You should now see a list of all existing managed properties, as shown in Figure 6-2. For each property, the type, the property's options, and any existing mappings from crawled properties are listed.

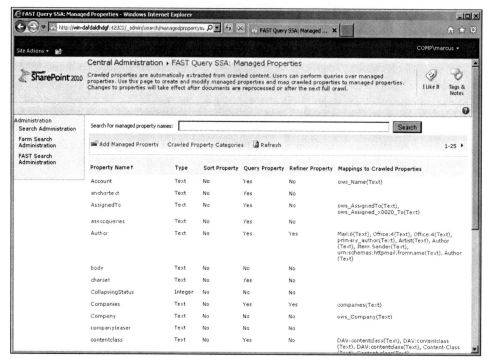

FIGURE 6-2 All existing managed properties, as shown on the FAST Query SSA.

4. Click Add Managed Property, and then fill out the details as needed.

5. At the very least, give the new property a unique name. A good practice is to prefix it with something unique in order to distinguish it from the other managed properties because there is no other way to group a set of managed properties. This makes future management easier.

> **Note** Historically, using lowercase names in FAST has been a good rule of thumb to make sure you do not encounter weird issues. This holds true for FS4SP as well; some cases have been reported on Microsoft forums, where using mixed casing has caused unforeseen trouble.

6. Map one or more existing crawled properties to your new managed property.

7. Indicate whether it should be possible to sort on the new managed property, target a fielded query against it, or refine on it.

8. Decide whether you want to put the property into the default full-text index—that is, whether the content of the property should be searchable as-is. Note that if you omit mapping the property to a full-text index and choose not to check the Query Property, the new property will not be searchable in any way, nor can it be used as a refiner. However, it can still be used for presentation and sorting.

9. Click OK.

Your new managed property should now be available in the list shown in Figure 6-2. If you configured mappings from crawled properties, you will have to recrawl any existing content associated with the crawled properties to make the changes go into effect.

Important When mapping more than one crawled property to a managed property, you have to pay attention to the setting Include Values From A Single Crawled Property Based On The Order Specified, shown in Figure 6-3.

If this option is selected, only the first crawled property to be present in a particular item will be mapped to the managed property according to the order the crawled property mappings are listed.

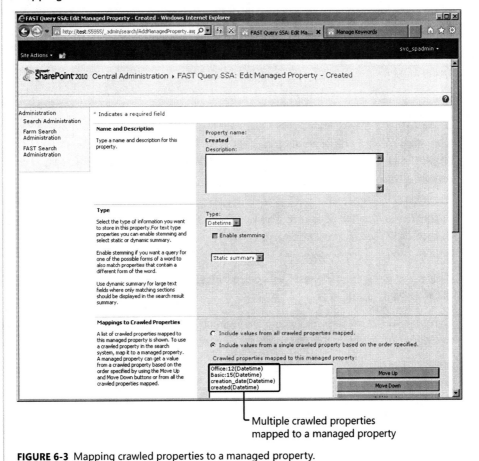

Multiple crawled properties mapped to a managed property

FIGURE 6-3 Mapping crawled properties to a managed property.

Map a crawled property to a managed property

Mappings from crawled properties to a managed property can be added from both "sides" of the mapping. When you create a managed property as previously detailed, you have the option of specifying mappings right away. Also, by clicking an existing managed property in the list shown in Figure 6-2, you can add new mappings after the managed property is created. Both of these methods of creating mappings can be said to be through the perspective of the managed property. It is also possible to add a mapping to a crawled property from the perspective of a crawled property—that is, from the other way around.

There are no differences in creating the mapping from the crawled property or from the managed property perspective. For completeness, the following procedure explains how to do it from the former (because the latter was covered indirectly in the previous section):

1. In Central Administration, click Manage Service Applications, and then click your FAST Query SSA.

2. Under Administration, click FAST Search Administration.

3. Under Property Management, click Crawled Property Categories. You should now see a list of all existing crawled property categories, shown in Figure 6-4. Because the number of crawled properties can be huge, FS4SP sorts the crawled properties into groups, typically according to content source.

 Tip You can create your own crawled properties group with the cmdlet *New-FASTSearchMetadataCategory*.

4. Click any of the groups in which you want to modify a crawled property. In this example, click the SharePoint group.

5. Click the crawled property that you want to modify; alternatively, you can search for it using the Search box at the top. In this example, click the crawled *ows_Company* property.

6. On the Edit Crawled Property page, click the Add Mapping button. This opens a modal dialog box, shown in Figure 6-5.

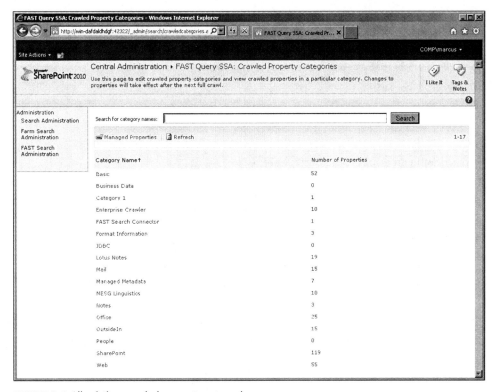

FIGURE 6-4 All existing crawled property categories.

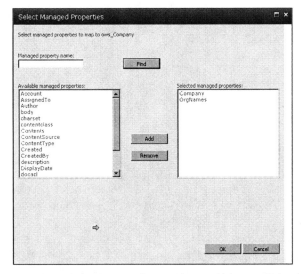

FIGURE 6-5 Select managed properties to which a crawled property should map.

7. Pick one or many managed properties to map the crawled property against.

8. Click OK.

Remember that you have to recrawl your content source to pick up the changes.

Windows PowerShell

The possibilities for working with properties in Windows PowerShell are greater than through the SharePoint GUI but less intuitive. This section contains a brief example of how to inspect and make changes to an existing managed property.

Inspect and modify managed properties

1. Open an FS4SP shell.

2. Run *Get-FASTSearchMetadataManagedProperty* to list each managed property installed in your solution. Run *Get-FASTSearchMetadataManagedProperty | Measure-Object* to find out how many properties there are.

3. Run *Get-FASTSearchMetadataManagedProperty -Name "Keywords"* to inspect each property of the managed *Keywords* property. Your output should look similar to the following.

```
PS C:\FASTSearch\bin> Get-FASTSearchMetadataManagedProperty -Name "Keywords"

Name                   : Keywords
Description            : Keywords for this document
Type                   : Text
Queryable             : True
StemmingEnabled       : True
RefinementEnabled     : False
MergeCrawledProperties : False
SubstringEnabled      : False
DeleteDisallowed      : False
MappingDisallowed     : False
MaxIndexSize          : 1024
MaxResultSize         : 64
DecimalPlaces         : 3
SortableType          : SortableDisabled
SummaryType           : Disabled
```

4. Compare your output to the listing of properties in Table 6-3. From here, you can tell right away that the *Keywords* property is used to hold regular text (*Type*), that it is possible to query using the "keyword: query" syntax (*Queryable*), and that it is neither used for deep refinement (*RefinementEnabled*) nor sorting (*SortableType*). You do not, however, know whether it is included as-is in a free text search because you cannot tell from this output alone whether the property is used in a full-text index. See the following section, "Full-Text Indexes and Rank Profiles," for more information about this.

5. Changing any of the internal properties of a managed property is straightforward and can be done using two methods:

- The simplest method is to use the *Set-FASTSearchMetadataManagedProperty* cmdlet. For example, let's say you need to allocate more internal index space for keywords than the default of 1,024 KB. This is easily achieved using the following.

```
Set-FASTSearchMetadataManagedProperty -Name "Keywords" -MaxIndexSize 2048
```

- Your other option is to change the properties on a managed property object: Store the managed property in an intermediate variable, make a change to an internal property, and issue the property's *Update()* method to update the index schema. Perusing the same example, use the following code.

```
$keywords = Get-FASTSearchMetadataManagedProperty -Name "Keywords"
$keywords.MaxIndexSize = 2048
$keywords.Update()
```

 Note Changes to many of the internal properties of a managed property require that you recrawl your content so that internal index structures reflect your changes; changing the *MaxIndexSize* property is an example of this.

Create a managed property

1. Open an FS4SP shell.

2. Use the *New-FASTSearchMetadataManagedProperty* cmdlet to create a managed property. This cmdlet has two required parameters: *-Name* and *-Type*. The former is simply the desired name of the new managed property. The latter indicates its data type, represented as an integer. Table 6-4 lists all available data types and which integer to use to reference it. For example, to create a managed property called *Salary* that uses the data type *Float*, run the following command.

```
New-FASTSearchMetadataManagedProperty -Name "Salary" -Type 4 -Description "A descriptive text"
```

 Note Make it a habit to always use the *-Description* parameter and give your new managed property a brief explanation. You will thank yourself later.

TABLE 6-4 Data types for managed properties

Integer	Type	Description
1	*Text*	UTF-8 encoded text
2	*Integer*	Signed 64-bit integer
3	*Boolean*	True or False
4	*Float*	Double-precision 64-bit floating point
5	*Decimal*	Integer with up to 28 decimals
6	*DateTime*	Time stamp in the ISO 8601 format

Map a crawled property to a managed property

1. Open an FS4SP shell.

2. Use the *New-FASTSearchMetadataCrawledPropertyMapping* cmdlet to register the mapping. Unfortunately, you cannot reference the managed property and the crawled property by name. Instead, you first retrieve their object references.

```
$mp = Get-FASTSearchMetadataManagedProperty -Name "<ManagedPropertyName>"
$cp = Get-FASTSearchMetadataCrawledProperty -Name "<CrawledPropertyName>"
New-FASTSearchMetadataCrawledPropertyMapping -ManagedProperty $mp -CrawledProperty $cp
```

> **Note** Multiple crawled properties can be mapped to the same managed property. But pay attention; content from the crawled properties are either overwritten or suffixed in the managed property, depending on the value of the managed property's internal property *MergeCrawledProperties*. Also remember that you need to recrawl content before the mapping is effective in the index.

List crawled property categories

1. Open an FS4SP shell.

2. Use the *Get- FASTSearchMetadataCategory* cmdlet to list all available property categories.

3. Use *Get- FASTSearchMetadataCategory* "*<category name>*", where *<category name>* is the name of the category to get a reference to only one category.

Create a crawled property category

When creating custom crawled properties, you may find it useful to store the properties in a separate category for maintenance purposes. The category is identified by a name and a property set in the form of a GUID.

1. Open an FS4SP shell.

2. Use the *New-FASTSearchMetadataCategory* cmdlet to create a crawled property category. Replace *<String>* with the name you want to give your category and *<Guid>* with a GUID of your making. The following sample creates a category named *FS4SP Book* with a random GUID. Be sure to print and make a note of the GUID after creation.

```
$guid = [guid]::NewGuid()
New-FASTSearchMetadataCategory -Name "FS4SP Book" -Propset $guid
```

Configure a category for crawled property discovery and searching

Crawled properties are automatically extracted from crawled content and grouped by category based on the property set of each crawled property. Each category can be configured individually to discover new crawled properties, or not.

1. Open an FS4SP shell.

2. Run the following command to turn off automatic discovery of new crawled properties for the category and to make the crawled properties added to the category searchable by default.

```
$category = Get- FASTSearchMetadataCategory "FS4SP book"
$category.MapToContents = 1
$category.DiscoverNewProperties = 0
$category.Update()
```

.NET

Working with crawled and managed properties via .NET code is very similar to using Windows PowerShell; the only difference is that you need to get a reference to the *Schema* object and property collections before you can start making changes.

Create a managed property

1. Add a reference to the FS4SP administration main assembly by running the following.

```
<FASTSearchFolder>\bin\Microsoft.SharePoint.Search.Extended.Administration.dll
```

2. Add the corresponding namespaces.

```
using Microsoft.SharePoint.Search.Extended.Administration;
using Microsoft.SharePoint.Search.Extended.Administration.Schema;
```

3. Initialize the connection to FS4SP and acquire an object reference to the index schema.

```
SchemaContext schemaContext = new SchemaContext();
Schema indexSchema = schemaContext.Schema;
```

4. Add a new managed property using the following code.

```
indexSchema.AllManagedProperties.Create("MyMP", "A descriptive text", ManagedType.Text);
```

The *AllManagedProperties* property returns a special type of collection that lists all managed properties and exposes the *Create* method that adds new managed properties. The enum *ManagedType* exposes data type values that correspond to those listed in Table 6-4.

> **Note** There are two overloaded *Create* methods; the one not used in this example allows you to directly set several of the internal properties listed in Table 6-3. For more information about these two methods, go to *http://msdn.microsoft.com/en-us/library/ee568851.aspx*.

5. After running the code, run *Get-FASTSearchMetadataManagedProperty -Name "MyMP"* in an FS4SP shell to verify that the managed property was in fact created and deployed.

> **Note** It is also possible to manually configure a connection to FS4SP and acquire the index schema through a proxy. However, *SchemaContext* uses the default endpoint name and configuration file *(<FASTSearchFolder>\etc\Admin.config)* and provides easy access to the index schema as long as you execute your application locally on an FS4SP server. For more information about the *SchemaContext* class, go to *http://msdn.microsoft.com/en-us/library/ee563682.aspx*.

Map a crawled property to a managed property

1. To map a crawled property to a managed property, you first need to obtain the index schema. Perform steps 1–3 from the previous example, "Create a managed property." This leaves you with the *indexSchema* variable.

2. In this example, you map the crawled property *ows_Name* into the managed property *Author*. These are default properties, and unless you manually removed them, this step should work fine.

3. Just like you did when using the Windows PowerShell approach, in order to configure the mapping, you need to get objects for both the managed and the crawled properties. Let's start with the easiest, the managed property.

```
var mp = indexSchema.AllManagedProperties["Author"];
```

4. As you saw in the section on crawled properties, you can use several methods for obtaining an object reference to a crawled property. In this example, you use the *QueryCrawledProperties* method, which lets you query for a crawled property name.

Note that this method returns an *IEnumerable<CrawledProperty>* because several crawled properties might share the same name. In this example, you are giving yourself the liberty of assuming that there is only one property called *ows_Name*, which is the case in a default FS4SP installation. Be sure to put proper safeguards in place in your production environment to avoid null-pointer exceptions.

```
var cp = indexSchema.QueryCrawledProperties("ows_Name", 0, 1).First();
```

 More Info For more information about the *QueryCrawledProperties* method, go to *http://msdn.microsoft.com/en-us/library/microsoft.sharepoint.search.extended .administration.schema.category.querycrawledproperties.aspx.*

The second and third parameters are a query offset and a limit on how many matching crawled properties should be returned. In this example, you want to search the whole set (starting from offset 0), and only care for one specific property (stop after 1 match) using the *First()* method provided by Microsoft Language Integrated Query (LINQ) in the .NET Framework.

5. Next, get a list of all existing mappings from the managed property, add the crawled property to that list, and write the list back to the managed property. Use the following code.

```
var mappings = mp.GetCrawledPropertyMappings();
mappings.Add(cp);
mp.SetCrawledPropertyMappings(mappings);
```

6. After running the code, use the following two lines of Windows PowerShell script, and verify that the crawled property was indeed mapped to the managed property.

```
$mp = Get-FASTSearchMetadataManagedProperty -Name "Author"
Get-FASTSearchMetadataCrawledPropertyMapping -ManagedProperty $mp
```

Full-Text Indexes and Rank Profiles

As previously described in Chapter 2, a full-text index contains a group of managed properties. This makes it possible for search queries to span multiple properties at the same time. Examples of managed properties in the default full-text index are *title*, *body*, and *URL* of an item.

Each managed property in the full-text index is given an importance level from 0 through 7. These levels give input to how FS4SP calculates dynamic rank. On top of this, a rank profile adds the final touches of rank calculation. Full-text indexes and rank profiles are central concepts in FS4SP and are the functionality used behind the scenes when users are doing a normal, "nonfielded" free-text search. When you sort your search results based on relevance, the rank profile is what applies the settings that determine the rank score for each item.

Note Changing a managed property's importance level is an easy way to change user-perceived relevance, but it can also affect index performance, query latency, and disk space requirements. A good guideline to follow is to keep properties that have potentially large amounts of data at one of the lower levels. The top-most levels should be reserved for small and important properties, such as titles.

Each rank profile is associated with at least one full-text index; a one-to-one mapping between a rank profile and a full-text index is the most common scenario, but you can assign multiple full-text indexes to a rank profile as well.

Every FS4SP configuration has at least one full-text index and one rank profile. This is often enough, but if your installation will be used to host completely separate types of data for completely separate purposes, it might be a good idea to set up multiple full-text indexes with separate rank profiles. This lets you tune relevance and index features in each index without worrying about full-text indexes and rank profiles interfering with each other. The recommendation by Microsoft is to have not more than 10 full-text indexes because adding more can have an adverse effect on disk usage and system resources.

More Info For more information about the index schema and its features, go to *http://technet.microsoft.com/en-us/library/gg982954.aspx*.

Multiple Full-Text Indexes Example

You are indexing movie reviews and have one full-text index that contains the managed properties *title*, *abstract*, and *body* of the movie reviews. This could typically be the default full-text index named *content*.

Each movie review also has managed properties for *tag* and *usercomments* that you would like to be able to query. You map these two managed properties to a full-text index named *social*. Both full-text indexes *content* and *social* are mapped to the same rank profile.

You then execute the following query.

```
star wars social:cool
```

You get a result set in which *star wars* is ranked on the movie review and not the tags or user comments, whereas *cool* is ranked only on the social content and not on the review itself.

The default full-text index is called *content*, and the default rank profile is called *default*. Inspect their properties by running the *Get-FASTSearchMetadataFullTextIndex* and *Get-FASTSearchMetadata-RankProfile* cmdlets in an FS4SP shell.

```
PS C:\FASTSearch\bin> Get-FASTSearchMetadataFullTextIndex
Name            : content
Description     : Default FullText Index
StemmingEnabled : True
isDefault       : True
DeleteDisallowed : False

PS C:\FASTSearch\bin> Get-FASTSearchMetadataRankProfile
Name                            : default
isDefault                       : True
RankModelName                   : default
StopWordThreshold               : 2000000
PositionStopWordThreshold       : 20000000
QualityWeight                   : 50
AuthorityWeight                 : 80
QueryAuthorityWeight            : 50
FreshnessWeight                 : 100
FreshnessResolution             : Day
FreshnessManagedPropertyReference : Write

PS C:\FASTSearch\bin> $rp = Get-FASTSearchMetadataRankProfile
PS C:\FASTSearch\bin> $rp.GetFullTextIndexRanks()
FullTextIndexReference : content
ProximityWeight        : 140
ContextWeight          : 50

PS C:\FASTSearch\bin> $rp.GetManagedPropertyBoosts()
ManagedPropertyReference : format
BoostValue               : unknown format,-4000,xml document,-4000,microsoft excel,-4000
```

In this code, you see listed six properties of the rank profile that relate to different weights. The weight numbers are not percentages but are relative weights. Freshness has the highest score in the default rank profile and impacts ranking the most, pushing newly changed content high up on the result list. Table 6-5 explains in more detail the different rank components at play within the rank profile.

> **Important** The value of two rank components with the same weight is not necessarily the same. Changing a weight from 50 to 100 on one component could impact the rank score more than changing a weight from 50 to 100 on another component.
>
> When changing the values of the different weights, you need to use trial and error when you execute sample searches against your data to see how different values change the ranking of your search results. Another, possibly simpler, option to tuning the ranking is to dynamically change the search queries in FAST Query Language (FQL) with the *xrank* operator. This is explained in detail in Chapter 8, "Querying the Index."

TABLE 6-5 Rank components in the rank profile

Rank factor	Description	Rank type
Quality	Quality rank points are derived from the following managed properties: ■ **Urldepthrank** Rank points given to boost shorter URLs ■ **Docrank** Rank points given based on the number of and relative importance of links pointing to an item ■ **Siterank** Rank points given based on the number of and relative importance of links pointing to the items on a site ■ **Hwboost** FS4SP placeholder for generic usage of static/quality rank points You can also add any managed property of type *integer* to the list of static/quality rank components.	Static
Freshness	Rank points based on the age (last modified) of the item compared to the time of the search. The source for the last modified time is the managed property named *Write*. The resolutions used (second/minute/hour/day/year) are important for the ranking; a lower resolution results in smaller time differences that affect the ranking.	Dynamic
Context	Rank points given based on where in the item the search words hit. Context boost is assigned as an overall weight and as a weight for an individual managed property. The different managed properties such as *title* and *body* are mapped into different importance levels. This makes it possible to give more rank points when the search word hits in a title instead of in the body text of the item.	Dynamic
Proximity	Rank points given depending on the distance between the search words and where these words are located in the search item. If two search terms appear close together in the same managed property within the full-text index, the item will get more rank points.	Dynamic
Managed property boost	Rank points given based on a specific value of a managed property. For example, if you want to give additional rank points to items of a specific type, such as Word documents, you would give items that have the value *docx* assigned in the *fileextension* managed property additional rank points.	Dynamic
Authority	Rank points given based on when a search word retrieves hits in the link text (anchor text). This rank boost has two components: ■ **Partial match** When, for example, the link text is *Microsoft Word* and the search is *Microsoft* ■ **Complete match** Additional score if there is an exact match between the search word and the link text	Dynamic
Query authority	Rank points given based on clicked search results (click-through). In the search front end, all of a user's searches and the items that the user clicks that are associated with those searches are stored and processed. For example, if a user searched for *vacation* and clicked the *vacation request template* in the search result (for example, *http://myserver/template/vacation.aspx*), the URL is associated with the search term and receives additional rank points when any new search with the same search word is performed. Processing of the stored queries is run on a daily basis. The last 30 days of clicks are kept for processing, so queries older than that no longer have an effect on the ranking. This rank score also has two components: ■ **Partial match** When, for example, the initial search words that resulted in a click to this item were *Microsoft Word*, and the search word now is *Microsoft* ■ **Complete match** Additional score if there is an exact match between the search word and link text	Dynamic

Any rank profile can be used to sort the search result. Sorting on rank profiles is available both via the SharePoint Search Center and via code.

The full-text index has seven levels of importance, 7 being the highest. You can list the managed properties mapped to each level by running the *GetMappingsForLevel* method of the full-text index object. The following example lists the managed properties mapped to level 7.

```
PS C:\FASTSearch\bin> $fti = Get-FASTSearchMetadataFullTextIndex
PS C:\FASTSearch\bin> $fti.GetMappingsForLevel(7)

Name                    : Title
Description             : The title of the document
Type                    : Text
Queryable               : True
StemmingEnabled         : True
RefinementEnabled       : False
MergeCrawledProperties  : False
SubstringEnabled        : False
DeleteDisallowed        : True
MappingDisallowed       : False
MaxIndexSize            : 1024
MaxResultSize           : 64
DecimalPlaces           : 3
SortableType            : SortableDisabled
SummaryType             : Dynamic

Name                    : DocSubject
Description             :
Type                    : Text
Queryable               : True
StemmingEnabled         : True
RefinementEnabled       : False
MergeCrawledProperties  : False
SubstringEnabled        : False
DeleteDisallowed        : False
MappingDisallowed       : False
MaxIndexSize            : 1024
MaxResultSize           : 64
DecimalPlaces           : 3
SortableType            : SortableDisabled
SummaryType             : Static
```

You can also change the internal weights of each importance level by using the following code in an FS4SP shell.

```
PS C:\FASTSearch\bin> $rankprofile = Get-FASTSearchMetadataRankProfile default
PS C:\FASTSearch\bin> $content = $rankprofile.GetFullTextIndexRanks()|where-Object -filterscript
{$_.FullTextIndexReference.Name -eq "content"}

PS C:\FASTSearch\bin> $content.GetImportanceLevelWeight(1)
30
PS C:\FASTSearch\bin> $content.GetImportanceLevelWeight(2)
10
PS C:\FASTSearch\bin> $content.GetImportanceLevelWeight(3)
20
```

```
PS C:\FASTSearch\bin> $content.GetImportanceLevelWeight(4)
30
PS C:\FASTSearch\bin> $content.GetImportanceLevelWeight(5)
40
PS C:\FASTSearch\bin> $content.GetImportanceLevelWeight(6)
50
PS C:\FASTSearch\bin> $content.GetImportanceLevelWeight(7)
60
```

Important If you examine the importance level weights from the previous output, you notice that level 1 has the same weight as level 4. This is a bug that has yet to be fixed as of the December 2011 cumulative update for FS4SP. You can reset the levels to match their importance by using the following code in an FS4SP shell.

```
PS C:\FASTSearch\bin> $rankprofile = Get-FASTSearchMetadataRankProfile default
PS C:\FASTSearch\bin> $content = $rankprofile.GetFullTextIndexRanks()|where-Object
-filterscript {$_.FullTextIndexReference.Name -eq "content"}
PS C:\FASTSearch\bin> $content.SetImportanceLevelWeight(1,10)
PS C:\FASTSearch\bin> $content.SetImportanceLevelWeight(2,20)
PS C:\FASTSearch\bin> $content.SetImportanceLevelWeight(3,30)
PS C:\FASTSearch\bin> $content.SetImportanceLevelWeight(4,40)
PS C:\FASTSearch\bin> $content.SetImportanceLevelWeight(5,50)
PS C:\FASTSearch\bin> $content.SetImportanceLevelWeight(6,60)
PS C:\FASTSearch\bin> $content.SetImportanceLevelWeight(7,70)
```

If you add more full-text indexes and rank profiles, pay attention to the *isDefault* property, which tells you which full-text indexes and rank profiles are used unless a query is explicitly targeting a specific index.

More Info For details about all the properties of the full-text index and rank profile, see the TechNet documentation for *Set-FASTSearchMetadataRankProfile* at *http://technet .microsoft.com/en-us/library/ff393755.aspx* and for *Set-FASTSearchMetadataFullTextIndex* at *http://technet.microsoft.com/en-us/library/ff393749.aspx*.

SharePoint

Through the SharePoint GUI, the possibilities to tune the full-text index and rank profile parameters are limited. As you will see, the possibilities through Windows PowerShell and code are greater. However, for each managed property, you can assign a full-text index mapping—that is, modify the level of importance used in the rank profile through the GUI. For many FS4SP configurations, this is often enough.

Modify a managed property's full-text index mapping

1. In Central Administration, point to Manage Service Applications, and then click your FAST Query SSA.

2. Under Administration, click FAST Search Administration.

3. Under Property Management, click Managed Properties. You should now see a list of all existing managed properties, as shown in Figure 6-2 earlier.

4. Click a managed property, for example, *body*. This takes you to the Edit Managed Property page.

5. At the very bottom of the page, you can change which importance level, or "priority," should be associated with the managed property by using a drop-down menu. In the same place, you can inspect the default full-text index; see which other managed properties belong to the index and what important levels they have been assigned. Clicking the View Mappings link, directly under the drop-down menu, brings up a modal dialog box with this information, as shown in Figure 6-6.

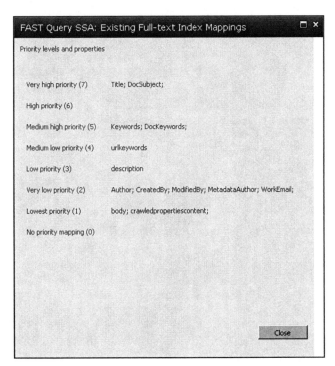

FIGURE 6-6 The modal dialog box showing the default full-text index and which managed properties are part of it.

Windows PowerShell

As you've seen, when you use SharePoint Central Administration, your options are limited to mapping managed properties to the default full-text index and assigning importance levels. Using Windows PowerShell, you can work with any full-text index or rank profile and have full control of your rank tuning.

Create a full-text index with an associated rank profile

1. Open an FS4SP shell.

2. Create a full-text index and rank profile, and then save the object references.

```
$fti = New-FASTSearchMetadataFullTextIndex -Name "myfti" -Description "A short description"
$rp = New-FASTSearchMetadataRankProfile -Name "myrp"
```

The previous command creates the rank profile with default values. Using the *-Template* parameter with *New-FASTSearchMetadataRankProfile*, you can use another existing rank profile to override the defaults. *New-FASTSearchMetadataFullTextIndex* does not support using a template, but you can easily change its default values after creation by modifying the properties of the *$fti* object.

> **Important** Use lowercase names when creating full-text indexes and rank profiles to avoid unexpected errors.

3. Extract the existing rank components from the rank profile, and then add the rank components from the full-text index by using the following code.

```
$rankComponents = $rp.GetFullTextIndexRanks()
$rankComponents.Create($fti)
```

At this point, the new full-text index and rank profile is available and ready for use. However, the full-text index contains no managed properties, and the rank components are left at default values.

4. To start using the new full-text index right away, mark it as default.

```
$fti.MakeDefault()
```

> **Note** You can still use a rank profile for sorting even when the rank profile or the full-text index it is attached to is not set as default.

5. To verify that the procedure worked as expected, either retrieve the list of full-text indexes by using the *Get-FASTSearchMetadataFullTextIndex* cmdlet and look for the *isDefault* property, or go to the Edit Managed Property page in Central Administration and click View Mappings, as shown in Figure 6-6.

Modify the list of full-text index rank components for a rank profile

1. Locate the rank profile you want to modify, and then extract its rank components.

```
$rp = Get-FASTSearchMetadataRankProfile -Name "MyRP"
$rankComponents = $rp.GetFullTextIndexRanks()
```

> **Important** Because each rank profile can be used by many full-text indexes, you have to look up the elements in *$rankComponents* that are associated with your particular full-text index. In other words, modifying the rank components can affect more than one full-text index. Be careful.

2. In this example, you want to increase the relevance boost of important managed properties, which you achieve by doubling the rank importance of the highest importance level (7). Unfortunately, there is no easy way to reference rank components belonging to a certain full-text index, so you have to resort to looping through them until you find the one you are looking for.

```
foreach ($ftiRankComponent in $rankComponents)
{
    if($ftiRankComponent.FullTextIndexReference.Name.Equals("MyFTI"))
    {
        var newFtiRankComponent = 2 * $ftiRankComponent.GetImportanceLevelWeight(7);
        $ftiRankComponent.SetImportanceLevelWeight(7, newFtiRankComponent);
    }
}
```

The changes to importance level weights do not take effect until the next recrawl. This is because the importance levels are part of static rank, which is evaluated at index time and not at query time.

.NET

If you compare the code used in the .NET samples, you see that the code is almost identical to that of Windows PowerShell. Using .NET for full-text indexes and rank profiles provides the same capabilities as Windows PowerShell.

Create a full-text index with an associated rank profile

1. The first step in working with full-text indexes in code is to obtain the index schema. Perform steps 1–3 from the .NET procedure "Create a managed property" in the "Crawled and Managed Properties" section earlier in this chapter. This leaves you with the *indexSchema* variable.

2. When you use the schema's property *AllFullTextIndecies*, creating a new full-text index is straightforward and similar to creating a managed property.

```
var fti = indexSchema.AllFullTextIndecies.Create("MyFTI", "A descriptive text");
```

This creates a full-text index that has default values and is tied against the default rank profile.

3. To verify that the procedure worked as expected, run the *Get-FASTSearchMetadataFullTextIndex* cmdlet and make sure the new full-text index is listed.

4. Because the full-text index uses the default rank profile, if you also want to associate it with a brand new rank profile, add the following lines of code.

```
var rp = indexSchema.AllRankProfiles.Create("newrp");
var rankComponents = rp.GetFullTextIndexRanks();
rankComponents.Create(fti);
```

Just as in the previous Windows PowerShell example, this creates a rank profile and associates the rank components with the full-text index. Note that the *Create* method on *AllRankProfiles* accepts a second parameter that specifies an existing rank profile as a template.

5. To start using the new full-text index right away, mark it as default by using the following code.

```
fti.MakeDefault();
```

6. To verify that the procedure worked as expected, either retrieve the list of full-text indexes by using the *Get-FASTSearchMetadataFullTextIndex* cmdlet and look for the *isDefault* property, or go to the Edit Managed Property page in Central Administration and click View Mappings, as shown in Figure 6-6 earlier.

Modify the list of full-text index rank components for a rank profile

1. The first step in working with full-text indexes in code is to get the index schema. Perform steps 1–3 from the .NET procedure "Create a managed property" in the "Crawled and Managed Properties" section earlier in this chapter. This leaves you with the *indexSchema* variable.

2. Locate the rank profile you want to modify, and then extract its rank components by using the following code.

```
var rp = indexSchema.AllRankProfiles["MyRP"];
```

3. In the same manner as in the previous Windows PowerShell example, you now have to isolate the rank components that are associated with the targeted full-text index. Using LINQ, this is simple.

```
var rankComponents = rp.GetFullTextIndexRanks()
                .Where(rc => rc.FullTextIndexReference.Name.Equals("MyFTI"));
```

4. Now modify each rank component the way you like; in this example, duplicate the scenario from the previous Windows PowerShell version.

```
foreach(var rc in rankComponents) {
    var oldWeight = rc.GetImportanceLevelWeight(FullTextIndexImportanceLevel.
ImportanceLevel7);
    rc.SetImportanceLevelWeight(FullTextIndexImportanceLevel.ImportanceLevel7, 2 *
oldWeight);
}
```

Note You always have to run the *Update* method after editing rank components.

Managed Property Boosts

You can associate one or more managed property boosts with a rank profile. A *property boost* is a rank component that enables you to boost items based on a word match within a given managed property. Managed property boosts are part of the dynamic rank for a results rank score. The value is applied using the *xrank* operator during search.

Note Managed property boosts are global to the rank profile they are added to and will be applied to all search queries.

You can list the managed property boost of the default rank profile by using the *Get-FASTSearch-MetadataRankProfile* cmdlet in an FS4SP shell.

```
PS C:\FASTSearch\bin> $rp = Get-FASTSearchMetadataRankProfile
PS C:\FASTSearch\bin> $rp.GetManagedPropertyBoosts()
ManagedPropertyReference : format
BoostValue               : unknown format,-4000,xml document,-4000,microsoft excel,-4000

ManagedPropertyReference : fileextension
BoostValue               : csv,-4000,txt,-4000,msg,-4000,oft,-4000,zip,-4000,vsd,-4000,rtf,-4000

ManagedPropertyReference : IsEmptyList
BoostValue               : true,-4000

ManagedPropertyReference : IsListItem
BoostValue               : true,-4000
```

Any searchable managed property that has a matching value can be used as input for additional rank points. The boost can be both positive and negative values, either pushing items up or down the result list. With the default rank profile, four property boosts are already in place, as listed in Table 6-6. All of them apply 4,000 negative rank points to push content that is considered noise down the result list.

TABLE 6-6 Property boost from the default rank profile

Managed property	Matching value	Boost applied
Format	unknown format xml document microsoft excel	–4,000
Fileextension	csv txt msg oft zip vsd rtf	–4,000
IsEmptyList	True	–4,000
IsListItem	True	–4,000

Windows PowerShell

For the samples in this section, you work with a boost rule that promotes all items of *format* set to *Web Page* in the default rank profile. This has the effect of ranking these documents higher than, for example, wiki pages.

Create a managed property boost

1. Open an FS4SP shell.

2. Using the following code, obtain a reference to the default rank profile (which also happens to be named *default*).

   ```
   $RankProfile = Get-FASTSearchMetadataRankProfile -Name "default"
   ```

3. Obtain a reference to the managed property *format*.

   ```
   $Property = Get-FASTSearchMetadataManagedProperty -Name "format"
   ```

4. Create the managed property boost for the value *Document* and set the weight.

   ```
   $RankProfile.CreateManagedPropertyBoostComponent($Property, "Web Page, 5000")
   ```

   The property boost should take effect without doing a recrawl, but the boost might take some time to kick in because of caching.

Change a managed property boost

1. Open an FS4SP shell.

2. Obtain a reference to the *default* rank profile.

   ```
   $RankProfile = Get-FASTSearchMetadataRankProfile -Name "default"
   ```

3. Obtain a reference to the managed property you want to update.

   ```
   $Boost = $RankProfile.GetManagedPropertyBoosts()
           | where-object { $_.ManagedPropertyReference.Name -eq "format" -and
                           $_.BoostValue -eq "Web Page, 5000"}
   ```

4. Change the value to promote Word documents instead of webpages.

   ```
   $Boost.BoostValue = "Microsoft Word, 5000"
   ```

5. Update the property boost.

   ```
   $Boost.Update()
   ```

Delete a managed property boost

1. Open an FS4SP shell.

2. Obtain a reference to the *default* rank profile.

   ```
   $RankProfile = Get-FASTSearchMetadataRankProfile -Name "default"
   ```

3. Obtain a reference to the managed property you want to delete.

   ```
   $Boost = $RankProfile.GetManagedPropertyBoosts()
           | where-object { $_.ManagedPropertyReference.Name -eq "format" -and
                           $_.BoostValue -eq "Web Page, 5000"}
   ```

4. Delete the managed property boost.

   ```
   $Boost.Delete()
   ```

.NET

For the samples in this section, you work with a boost rule that promotes all items of *format* set to *Web Page* in the default rank profile. This has the effect of ranking these documents higher than, for example, wiki pages.

Create a managed property boost

1. The first step in working with full-text indexes in code is to get the index schema. Perform steps 1–3 from the .NET procedure "Create a managed property" in the "Crawled and Managed Properties" section earlier in this chapter. This leaves you with the *indexSchema* variable.

2. Using the schema's property *AllRankProfiles*, you obtain a reference to the *default* rank profile.

   ```
   RankProfile rankProfile = indexSchema.AllRankProfiles["default"];
   ```

3. Using the schema's property *AllManagedProperties*, you obtain a reference to the managed property named *format*.

   ```
   ManagedProperty managedProperty = indexSchema.AllManagedProperties["format"];
   ```

4. Obtain the existing managed property boost collection and create a boost for your managed property:

   ```
   var managedPropertyBoosts = rankProfile.GetManagedPropertyBoosts();
   managedPropertyBoosts.Create(managedProperty, "Web Page, 5000");
   ```

Change a managed property boost

The following code sample retrieves the managed property boost created in "Create a managed property boost" and changes the value to *Microsoft Word, 2000*.

```
SchemaContext schemaContext = new SchemaContext();
Schema indexSchema = schemaContext.Schema;

// Fetch the rank profile named 'default', which is the default rank profile.
RankProfile rankProfile = indexSchema.AllRankProfiles["default"];

// Fetch the existing managed property boost for format
ManagedPropertyBoostComponent boostComponent = rankProfile.GetManagedPropertyBoosts()
        .Where(boost => boost.ManagedPropertyReference.Name.ToLower() == "format"
                    && boost.BoostValue == "Web Page, 5000")
        .First();

boostComponent.BoostValue = "Microsoft Word, 2000";
boostComponent.Update();
```

Delete a managed property boost

The following code sample deletes the managed property boost created in "Create a managed property boost."

```
SchemaContext schemaContext = new SchemaContext();
Schema indexSchema = schemaContext.Schema;

// Fetch the rank profile named 'default' which is the default rank profile.
RankProfile rankProfile = indexSchema.AllRankProfiles["default"];

// Fetch the existing managed property boost for format
ManagedPropertyBoostComponent boostComponent = rankProfile.GetManagedPropertyBoosts()
        .Where(boost => boost.ManagedPropertyReference.Name.ToLower() == "format"
                    && boost.BoostValue == "Web Page, 5000")
        .First();

// Delete the property boost
boostComponent.Delete();
```

Static Rank Components

Static rank points, also known as *quality rank points*, are added to items at index time. Static rank boosting is efficient from a search performance point of view because this boosting does not add any complexity to the search evaluation. Static rank points assigned to an indexed item are independent of the search words used. Any managed property of type *integer* can be used as part of the static rank. Table 6-5 earlier in this chapter lists the default managed properties used as static rank components.

The weight assigned to a managed property in the static rank component is a percentage that is used to multiply the number from the managed property. A weight of 100 means the value from the managed property is added to the score, a weight of 200 doubles the value, and a weight of 50 adds half the value. So when assigning the weight multiplier, take into account what number range your managed property will span.

Windows PowerShell

For the sample in this section, you add one-tenth of the items byte size as a static rank component.

 More Info See the e-commerce sample in Chapter 10 for another example of adding static rank components.

Add a static rank component to the default rank profile

1. Open an FS4SP shell.

2. Obtain a reference to the default rank profile (which also happens to be named *default*).

   ```
   $RankProfile = Get-FASTSearchMetadataRankProfile -Name "default"
   ```

3. Obtain a reference to the existing static rank components.

   ```
   $QualityComponents = $RankProfile.GetQualityComponents()
   ```

4. Obtain a reference to the managed property *size*.

   ```
   $Property = Get-FASTSearchMetadataManagedProperty -Name "size"
   ```

5. Add the managed property to the static rank.

   ```
   $QualityComponents.Create($Property, 10)
   ```

Collection Management

A *collection* contains items from one or more content sources, for example, SharePoint sites or web crawls. For crawls based on the FAST Content SSA, the default collection is named *sp*. Because the FAST Search specific connectors do not depend on the FAST Content SSA, these connectors can feed data to any collection.

> **Note** A collection is nothing but a *logical* grouping of indexed items. The index is not physically split to accommodate for different collections. Each item contains an internal property called *meta.collection*. This property tells FS4SP which collection the item belongs to.

You usually do not need to have more than one content collection; the default collection *sp* is enough. In previous FAST technology, having several collections was standard procedure. One could argue that the notion of a collection in FS4SP is redundant and has instead been replaced by the concept of content sources; but in some cases, it is convenient to have more than one content collection, for example when using any of the FAST Search specific connectors and you want to search on or clear all data from one particular FAST Search specific connector. You can read more about the FAST Search specific connectors in Chapter 7, "Content Processing."

Collections are only manageable through the FS4SP shell and the .NET administration API.

Windows PowerShell

Managing collections via Windows PowerShell is done with the following cmdlets:

- *Clear-FASTSearchContentCollection*

- *Get-FASTSearchContentCollection*

- *New-FASTSearchContentCollection*

- *Remove-FASTSearchContentCollection*

To view all currently available collections, run *Get-FASTSearchContentCollection*. Running this also tells you how many items are associated with the collection, which pipeline the collection uses, and when items were last run through the pipeline associated with the collection.

```
PS C:\FASTSearch\bin> Get-FASTSearchContentCollection
Name          : sp
Created       :
Cleared       : 2011-03-14T19:27:32.7753906+01:00
LastInput     : 7/12/2011 5:14:23 PM
DocumentCount : 135
Description   : Default collection for SharePoint content
Pipeline      : Office14 (webcluster)
```

To create or remove collections, run either *New-FASTSearchContentCollection –Name [name]* or *Remove-FASTSearchContentCollection –Name [name]*. Note that the latter also removes all items associated with the collection.

To clear out all items associated with a specific collection without removing the collection itself, run *Clear-FASTSearchContentCollection –Name [name]*. When clearing the content collection, you do not clear the items that are in the corresponding SharePoint crawler database. In order to synchronize the crawler database with clearing a content collection, you have to do an index reset on the FAST Content SSA.

.NET

Managing collections via the .NET API is done using the *ContentContext* class.

Create a content collection

1. Add a reference to the FS4SP administration main assembly.

   `<FASTSearchFolder>\bin\Microsoft.SharePoint.Search.Extended.Administration.dll`

2. Add the corresponding namespaces.

   ```
   using System.Linq;
   using Microsoft.SharePoint.Search.Extended.Administration;
   ```

3. Initialize the connection to FS4SP and acquire an object reference to the *ContentContext* object.

```
ContentContext contentContext = new ContentContext();
```

4. Create a collection. The first parameter is the collection name, the second is the collection description, and the third is the name of the pipeline to use.

```
contentContext.Collections.AddCollection("notes", "Lotus notes", "Office14
(webcluster)");
```

> **Important** The *AddCollection* method in the *ContentCollectionCollection* class has an overloaded method that takes two parameters, the name and the description of the collection. However, there is a bug in this method because it tries to create a collection with a pipeline named *Office14*, but the default pipeline to use is named *Office14 (webcluster)*. Using this method generates an *AdminException* exception.
>
> As of the December 2011 cumulative update, SharePoint 2010 has a bug that points the WCF proxy to a service named *ContentCollection.svc* on the FS4SP administration server, but the correct name is *ContentCollectionService.svc*. In order to use the *ContentContext* within SharePoint, you have to copy *<FASTSearchFolder>\components\admin-services\contentcollectionservice.svc* to a file named *<FASTSearchFolder>\components\admin-services\contentcollection.svc* on the FS4SP administration server.

Delete a content collection

1. Follow steps 1–3 of the previous procedure, "Create a content collection."

2. Get a reference to the collection you want to remove.

```
ContentCollection collection = contentContext.Collections.Where(coll => coll.Name ==
"notes").First();
```

3. Remove the content collection.

```
contentContext.Collections.Remove(collection);
```

Remember that if your collection contains items indexed via the FAST Content SSA, you have to do an index reset on the FAST Content SSA in order to clear the crawler database and keep the FAST Content SSA in sync with the actual index.

Scope Management

A *scope*, or *search scope*, is a filter that users can target queries against. Scopes are a query-time feature and will not affect the underlying index in any way.

 More Info You can read more about scopes in the "Search Scopes" section in Chapter 2, and read more about FQL in Chapter 8.

Although the SharePoint GUI has support for creating simple scopes, the possibilities are not complete. The recommended method is using Windows PowerShell, which allows you to define arbitrary scope expressions by using FQL. Of course, this is also possible through code. Scopes can be created either globally at the search service application level or locally at the site level.

To inspect which scopes exist, either go to your FAST Query SSA and click Scopes under Queries And Results in the navigation pane, as shown in Figure 6-7, or use the following cmdlet *Get-SPEnter-priseSearchQueryScope*. Note that this is a SharePoint Enterprise Search cmdlet and is available only through the SharePoint Management Shell.

```
PS C:\FASTSearch\bin> Get-SPEnterpriseSearchQueryScope -SearchApplication "FAST Query SSA"
Name                    ID   Count  LastCompilationTime    CompilationState
----                    --   -----  -------------------    ----------------
People                  0    0      3/14/2011 6:16:52 PM   Compiled
All Sites               1    0      3/14/2011 6:16:52 PM   Compiled
Global Query Exclusion  2    0      1/1/0001 12:00:00 AM   Empty
Rank Demoted Sites      3    0      1/1/0001 12:00:00 AM   Empty
```

The last two scopes in this code block are internal to the SharePoint search and are not used with FS4SP.

When creating search scopes, you can make them either global—meaning they are accessible for the entire site collection—or you can make them available only for a specific site collection.

SharePoint

Creating scopes via SharePoint Central Administration is similar to that of SharePoint search and allows you to create scopes to limit your search results based on URL matching and managed property values.

Create a global scope

1. In Central Administration, point to Manage Service Applications, and then click your FAST Query SSA.

2. Under Queries And Results, click Scopes. This takes you to the View Scopes page shown in Figure 6-7, where all scopes available to your users are listed.

FIGURE 6-7 The View Scopes page.

3. Click New Scope.

4. Enter a title and description of the new scope.

5. In the Target Results Page section, specify whether you want search results from the scope to be presented in the standard Search Results Page (*Searchresults.aspx*) or in a custom webpage.

6. Click OK to create the scope and return to the View Scopes page. Although the scope is now active, it is not yet of any use because no scope rules are attached to it.

7. On the View Scopes page, click the Add Rules link to the right of the scope name.

8. Specify a rule type. You have the following options:

   • Select the Web Address option if you want the scope to include or exclude content based on a URL—that is, a website, files from a share, and so on.

   • Select the Property Query option if you want the scope to filter results by using a managed property.

Important The managed properties listed in the Add Property Restrictions drop-down are the properties that exist in the index schema of Search Server—that is, the drop-down does not reflect the FS4SP index schema. This is because scopes are functionality from the built-in SharePoint search. If you want to use a managed property from FS4SP in a scope defined using Central Administration, you must also create an identical managed property in the SharePoint search schema. All of the FS4SP default managed properties already have equivalents in Search Server. For a step-by-step guide about creating scopes via Central Administration, go to *http://technet.microsoft.com/en-us/library/ff453895.aspx.*

- Select the All Content option if you want more complex rules scenarios where, for example, you combine a complex rule with an exclusion rule. First include everything, and then exclude something. The All Content rule is used by the built-in search of SharePoint; it has no impact on FS4SP and can be omitted.

9. In the Behavior section, select the Include, the Require, or the Exclude option to specify how this scope rule will affect the overall scope.

10. Click OK to save the new scope rule.

Note If you use more than one scope in a query against FS4SP, *AND* is used; *OR* is not supported.

Windows PowerShell

Using Windows PowerShell for scope management is, in the authors' opinion, the best way to manage scopes in FS4SP unless you only want to limit search results on the default managed properties. With Windows PowerShell, you can take advantage of FQL and create complex rule sets on any queryable managed property.

Create a global scope

1. Search scopes are functionality from SharePoint Enterprise Search; as such, the cmdlets for working with scopes are not available through the FS4SP shell. Instead, use the SharePoint Management Shell.

2. Scopes are created using the *New-SPEnterpriseSearchQueryScope* cmdlet. Because this cmdlet is not FS4SP functionality by itself, you have to specify which Search Service Application (SSA) should be used by using the *-SearchApplication* parameter.

3. In this example, we want to create a scope on a content collection. This scope is particularly useful because there is no other built-in method of querying documents only from a certain collection. We circumvent this limitation by targeting the scope against the internal property *meta.collection*.

> **Note** You typically use multiple content collections with the FAST Search specific connectors, and you cannot filter these using the managed property *ContentSource*.

```
New-SPEnterpriseSearchQueryScope -Name "CollScope" -Description "Scope on collection2"
-SearchApplication "FAST Query SSA" -DisplayInAdminUI 1 -ExtendedSearchFilter "meta.
collection:collection2"
```

4. Give the operation a little while to go into effect because it will be picked up by a SharePoint timer job. When it is fully deployed, you should be able to search for *term scope:CollScope* in your Search Center. This search makes sure results containing *term* also belong to our new search scope.

> **More Info** Even though scopes are not compiled with the end results like they are in the built-in SharePoint search, compilation of the scopes is what makes them available during searching. You can manually start a compilation by opening a SharePoint Management Shell and executing the following commands, where *<FASTQuerySSA>* is the name of your FAST Query SSA.
>
> ```
> $ssa = Get-SPEnterpriseSearchServiceApplication "<FAST Query SSA>"
> $ssa.StartScopesCompilation()
> ```

Modify an existing scope

1. Obtain an object reference to a scope, for example, *CollScope* created in the previous example.

```
$scope = Get-SPEnterpriseSearchQueryScope -Identity "CollScope" -SearchApplication "FAST
Query SSA"
```

> **Note** The name of the scope is specified using the *-Identity* parameter and not with the *-Name*, as was the case with the *New-SPEnterpriseSearchQueryScope* cmdlet.

2. The FQL filter you created in the previous example was specified using the -*ExtendedSearch-Filter* parameter. From the scope object, you can modify the filter by using the *Filter* property. To make changes go into effect, the *Update* method must be called after the scope has been modified.

```
$scope.Filter = "meta.collection:collection3"
$scope.Update()
```

Delete an existing scope

■ Get an object reference to a scope—for example, *CollScope*—and pipe it through the *Remove-SPEnterpriseSearchQueryScope* cmdlet.

```
Get-SPEnterpriseSearchQueryScope -Identity "CollScope" -SearchApplication "FAST Query
SSA" | Remove-SPEnterpriseSearchQueryScope
```

■ Alternatively, you can get a reference to the scope and call the *Delete* method on the object.

```
$scope = Get-SPEnterpriseSearchQueryScope -Identity "CollScope" -SearchApplication "FAST
Query SSA"
$scope.Delete()
```

.NET

Using .NET for scope management offers the same flexibility as using Windows PowerShell. You work with scope management via the *Scopes* object.

Create a global scope

1. Add a reference to the SharePoint search administration main assembly.

```
%CommonProgramFiles%\Microsoft Shared\Web Server Extensions\14\ISAPI\
Microsoft.Office.Server.Search.dll
```

2. Add the corresponding namespace.

```
using Microsoft.Office.Server.Search.Administration;
```

3. While this code runs on SharePoint, you need to first get a reference to the *SearchService-Application* used. You do this via the *SearchServiceApplicationProxy* object from the current SharePoint context.

```
var ssaProxy = (SearchServiceApplicationProxy)SearchServiceApplicationProxy.
GetProxy(SPServiceContext.Current);
var searchApplictionInfo = ssaProxy.GetSearchServiceApplicationInfo();
var searchApplication = SearchService.Service.SearchApplications.GetValue<SearchServiceAp
plication>(searchApplictionInfo.SearchServiceApplicationId);
```

4. Next, you need to get a reference to the *Scopes* object, which is instantiated with the search application object.

```
Scopes scopes = new Scopes(searchApplication);
```

5. Create a global scope that has the same parameters as in the previous Windows PowerShell sample. To create a site-level scope, add the site URL as the third parameter.

```
scopes.AllScopes.Create("CollScope", "Scope on collecion2", null, true, null,
ScopeCompilationType.AlwaysCompile, "meta.collection:collection2");
```

6. Finally, to force the compilation and use of the scope right away, call *StartCompilation* on the object.

```
scopes.StartCompilation();
```

Modify an existing scope

1. Perform steps 1–4 in the previous procedure, "Create a scope," to get a reference to your *scopes* object.

2. Get a reference to the scope you created named *CollScope*.

```
var scope = scopes.GetSharedScope("CollScope");
```

3. Modify the filter property, update the scope, and start a compilation to effectuate the changes right away.

```
scope.Filter = "meta.collection:collection3";
scope.Update();
scopes.StartCompilation();
```

Delete an existing scope

1. Carry out steps 1–4 in the "Create a scope" procedure to get a reference to your *scopes* object.

2. Get a reference to the scope you created named *CollScope*.

```
var scope = scopes.GetSharedScope("CollScope");
```

3. Call the *Delete* method on the scope object.

```
scope.Delete();
```

Scopes That Search Against a Nondefault Full-Text Index

For search scopes, there exists a special keyword named *FullTextIndex* that can be used as part of the scope query. This keyword is not a valid FQL syntax and can be used only as part of a scope—not with other APIs. The *FullTextIndex* keyword can be used to target either a custom full-text index or a specific managed property.

Table 6-7 lists examples for setting the *ExtendedSearchFilter* parameter of the Windows PowerShell cmdlet *New-SPEnterpriseSearchQueryScope*, which is used to create search scopes.

TABLE 6-7 Targeting custom full-text indexes with scope filters

Scope name	Scope *ExtendedSearchFilter*	Sample query	Description
ScopeA	*FullTextIndex=myfulltextindex*	*microsoft Scope:ScopeA*	Searches for the word *microsoft* in the full-text index named *myfulltextindex*.
ScopeB	*title:vista,FullTextIndex= myfulltextindex*	*microsoft Scope:ScopeB*	Filters on results where the managed property *title* contains the word *vista*, and searches for the word *microsoft* in the full-text index named *myfulltextindex*.
ScopeC	*fulltextindex=title*	*vista Scope:ScopeC*	Searches for the word *vista* limited to the managed property *title*. This gives the same result as the user query *title:vista*.

Property Extraction Management

Property extraction can be used to improve the search experience by identifying known properties in your items during indexing. The properties are searched for within all the item text, not just in metadata; you can see this as a way to find structured data in unstructured text. You can read more about property extraction and how to create custom extractors in Chapter 7.

Note Property extraction was known as *entity extraction* in previous FAST versions. Therefore, some of the documentation you find on TechNet and in APIs refer to entity extraction. For all intents and purposes, entities and properties are the same.

Built-in Property Extraction

FS4SP comes with three default property extractors:

- Company names
- Location names
- Person names (not enabled by default)

Each of these lists can be modified by adding entries to *include lists* to make sure the list detects properties not automatically detected out of the box; the same goes for *exclude lists* to ignore entities that it wrongly detects.

The procedure for adding inclusion and exclusion entries is the same for companies, locations, and person names; you use the location list for the samples.

 More Info Custom property extraction is covered in Chapter 7.

SharePoint

Using SharePoint Central Administration for management of the property extraction lists is useful when you want to list the terms added or when you want to add or remove a few of them. Bulk operations are not possible via Central Administration.

Add a term to a property extraction list

1. In Central Administration, point to Manage Service Applications, and then click your FAST Query SSA.

2. Click the FAST Search Administration link in the left column, shown in Figure 6-8.

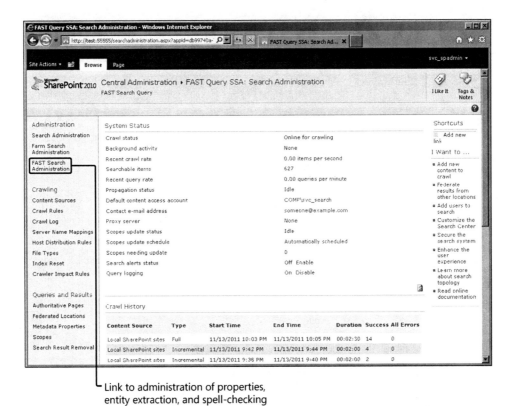

Link to administration of properties,
entity extraction, and spell-checking

FIGURE 6-8 The link to the FAST Search Administration page in the FAST Query SSA.

3. Under Property Extraction, click Manage Property Extraction.

4. Point to Locations, and click the down arrow. Then select Edit Include List, shown in Figure 6-9. Choose Edit Exclude List to add terms that you want to omit from the property extractor.

5. Click Add Item.

6. Enter the term to include a location name extraction, for example, *North Pole*, as shown in Figure 6-10.

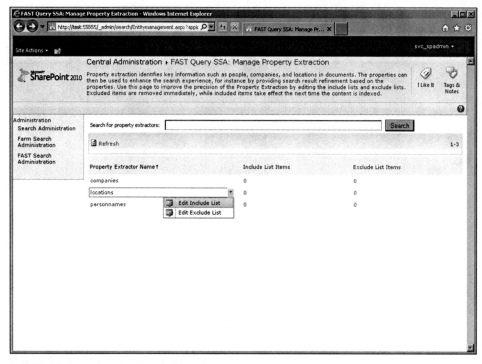

FIGURE 6-9 Property extractor administration.

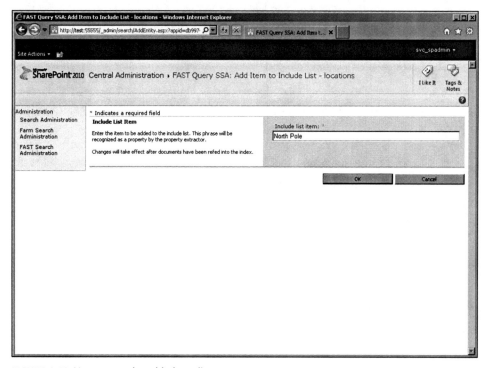

FIGURE 6-10 New term to be added to a list.

Remove a term from a property extraction list

1. Follow steps 1–3 from the previous "Add a term to a property extraction list" procedure.

2. Point to the term you want to remove, and then choose Delete Item, as shown in Figure 6-11.

FIGURE 6-11 Removing a property extraction term.

Windows PowerShell

Using Windows PowerShell is an easy way of bulk-importing terms to the property extraction lists. Windows PowerShell provides functions for reading text files and executing commands that use each line in the file as an input. The following samples can be easily incorporated in such loops.

Add a term to a property extraction list

1. Open an FS4SP shell.

2. No Windows PowerShell cmdlets are included with FS4SP to work with the property extractor lists, but you can use the .NET object in Windows PowerShell to accomplish your task. You can get a reference to the *EntityExtractorContext* object by using the following line of code.

```
$entityExtractorContext = New-Object -TypeName Microsoft.SharePoint.Search.Extended.
Administration.EntityExtractorContext
```

3. Get a reference to the Locations list.

```
$locationEntities = $entityExtractorContext.TermEntityExtractors | where { $_.Name -eq
"locations" }
```

4. Add a new term to the inclusion list.

```
$locationEntities.Inclusions.Add("North Pole")
```

Remove a term from a property extraction list

1. Follow steps 1–3 from the previous "Add a term to a property extraction list" procedure.

2. Remove the term.

```
$locationEntities.Inclusions.Remove("North Pole")
```

.NET

Using .NET, you can maintain your property extraction lists in SharePoint lists that are easily edited by using, for example, Microsoft Excel. Using event receivers on the SharePoint lists, you can automatically trigger the code in the following procedure to batch update the terms.

Add a term to a property extraction list

1. Add a reference to the FS4SP administration main assembly.

```
<FASTSearchFolder>\bin\Microsoft.SharePoint.Search.Extended.Administration.dll
```

2. Add the corresponding namespaces.

```
using System.Linq;
using Microsoft.SharePoint.Search.Extended.Administration;
using Microsoft.SharePoint.Search.Extended.Administration.Linguistics;
```

3. Initialize the connection to FS4SP and acquire an object reference to the *TermEntityExtractor* for locations:

```
EntityExtractorContext entityExtractorContext = new EntityExtractorContext();
TermEntityExtractor locationEntitites = entityExtractorContext.TermEntityExtractors.
Where(t => t.Name == "locations").First();
```

4. Add a term to the inclusion list.

```
locationEntitites.Inclusions.Add("North Pole");
```

1. Follow steps 1–3 in the previous "Add a term to a property extraction list" procedure.

2. Remove the term from the inclusion list.

   ```
   locationEntitites.Inclusions.Remove("North Pole");
   ```

Keyword, Synonym, and Best Bet Management

Using keywords is a great way to enhance your search results. These terms are defined by either an FS4SP administrator or FS4SP keyword administrator on a per-site collection basis. If you have a Search Center on more than one site collection, you have to add the keywords to each site collection where you want them available.

Each keyword can be associated with the following:

- Synonyms

- Best bets

- Visual best bets

- Document promotions

- Document demotions

When a search query is executed via the SharePoint site search box or the Search Center site, the search query is matched against the list of keywords or synonyms, and recommended results from the best bets or visual best bets are displayed above your search results. The same applies to document promotions and document demotions that are matched, but here the actual search result is moved to either the top or bottom of the result list.

Best bets, visual best bets, document promotions, and document demotions can all have a start date and an end date and can be associated with user contexts. A *user context* can be any combination of properties from a user's SharePoint User Profile page. (See the section titled "User Context Management" later in this chapter.) By default, you can base your context on the *Office Location* and *Ask Me About* properties.

> **Important** Keyword terms in search queries must exactly match the defined keyword or one of its synonyms. Partial matches are not matched. If the keyword defined is *car* and the user searches for *red car*, the keyword will not match because it is not an exact match.
>
> Only use synonyms to improve recall for small result sets. If you add synonyms for keywords that already have a large result set, the additional results will be added to the end of the result set and the query performance will be significantly reduced.

More Info Read more about working with keywords via SharePoint Central Admin at *http://office.microsoft.com/en-us/fast-search-server-help/manage-fast-search-keywords-HA010381994.aspx* and via Windows PowerShell at *http://technet.microsoft.com/en-us/library/ff453900.aspx*.

Keywords

Keywords are the base feature for synonyms, best bets, visual best bets, document promotions, and document demotions. You first add a keyword, and then you attach features to it.

Tip Best bets and visual best bets are particularly useful for campaigns and question/answer types of information. For example, if a user on an intranet site searches for *fire extinguisher*, it would be good to show where these are located in the building on an office map, and not necessarily show items containing the words. And if a user on a public-facing insurance company website searches for *car insurance*, you can show this month's good insurance offer as a visual best bet above the other results.

Use visual best bets when you want more control over how you visualize the best bet because regular best bets are text only.

SharePoint

The following samples take you through the steps involved in working with keywords and keyword-related functionality via SharePoint Site Collection Administration.

Display the Manage Keywords page

1. Log on to the home page of your top-level site as a user with site collection administration privileges. Make sure the user is a member of either the local group FASTSearchAdministrators or FASTSearchKeywordAdministrators on the FS4SP administration server.

2. Go to Site Actions | Site Settings | Site Collection Administration.

3. Click FAST Search Keywords, shown in Figure 6-12.

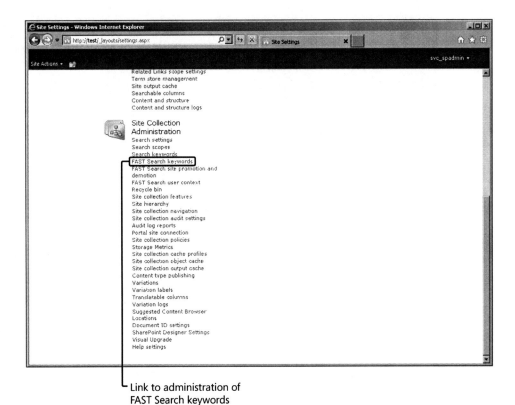

Link to administration of
FAST Search keywords

FIGURE 6-12 A link to FAST Search keywords from Site Collection Administration.

Add a keyword with synonyms

1. Display the Manage Keywords page.

2. Click Add Keyword, shown in Figure 6-13.

3. Fill in the keyword information. The phrase you will match is **fast search for sharepoint**, and you will add two-way synonyms for **fs4sp** and **enterprise search**. This means that when a user searches for *fast search for sharepoint*, he will also search for *fs4sp* and *enterprise search* and vice versa. If you don't want searches to match the synonym, use a one-way synonym instead. Several synonym terms can be added and separated with a semicolon, as shown in Figure 6-14.

4. Click OK.

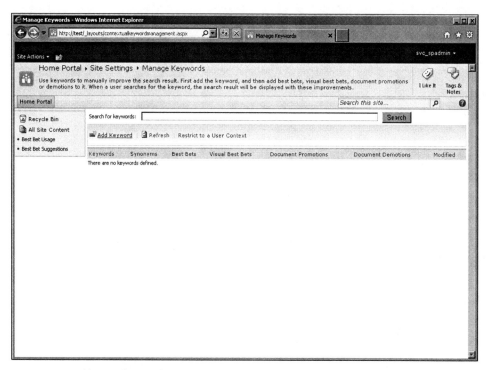

FIGURE 6-13 Add a new keyword.

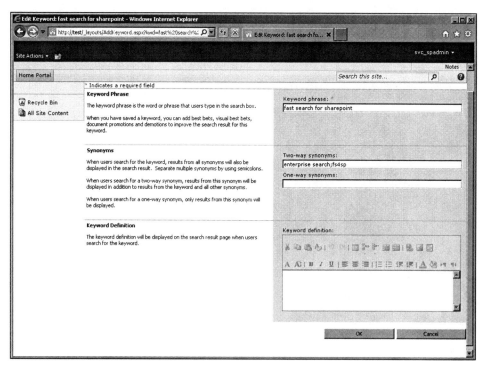

FIGURE 6-14 Add a keyword with synonyms.

Note The actual FQL query being executed when a user searches for *fast search for sharepoint* is shown in the following code. Pay attention to the *filter()* operator around the synonyms that turn off any stemming (or actually, lemmatization) for the synonym terms.

```
or(
    string(
        "fast search for sharepoint",
        annotation_class="user",
        mode="simpleall"
    ),
    filter(
        or(
            "\"enterprise search\"",
            "\"FS4SP\""
        )
    )
)
```

Add a best bet

1. Display the Manage Keywords page.

2. Point to your keyword, click the down arrow, and choose Add Best Bet from the displayed menu, as shown in Figure 6-15.

3. Fill in the Title, Description, and URL boxes for your best bet, as shown in Figure 6-16. This information will be shown above the other results on your search page in the Best Bets Web Part. You can also fill in a start date and an end date for when the best bet is to be shown, and associate one or more user contexts.

4. Click OK.

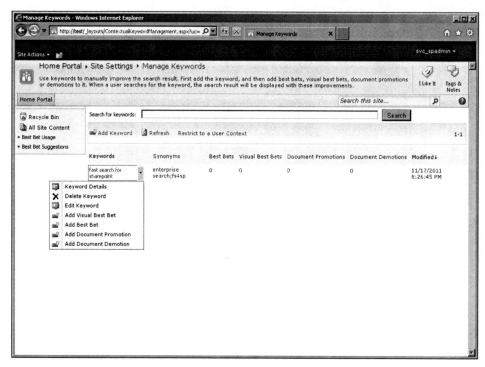

FIGURE 6-15 Add best bets and document boosts to a keyword.

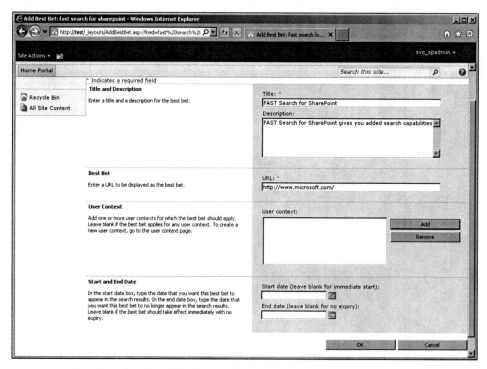

FIGURE 6-16 Associate a best bet with a keyword.

Remove a best bet

1. Display the Manage Keywords page.

2. Point to the best bet count for your keyword, and then click the down arrow.

3. Move your pointer over Delete Best Bets, and pick the best bet you want to delete, as shown in Figure 6-17.

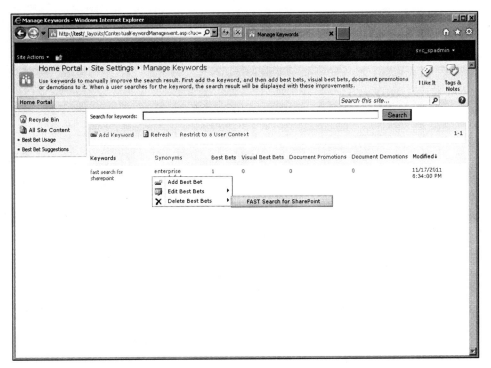

FIGURE 6-17 Remove a best bet association from a keyword.

Add a visual best bet

1. Display the Manage Keywords page.

2. Move the mouse over your keyword, click the down arrow, and choose Add Visual Best Bet from the displayed menu, as shown in Figure 6-15.

3. Fill in the Title and URL boxes for the visual best bet, as shown in Figure 6-18. You can also fill in a start date and an end date for when the visual best bet is to be shown, and associate one or more user contexts.

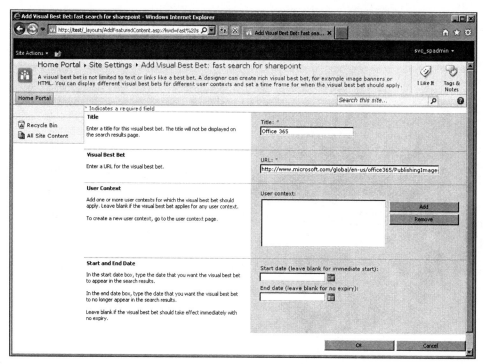

FIGURE 6-18 Associate a visual best bet with a keyword.

 Note The URL of a visual best bet can point to either an image or a webpage. The visual best bet is loaded into an iframe, so make sure the content fits inside the dimensions specified in the Visual Best Bet Web Part. For more information about iframes, go to *http://en.wikipedia.org/wiki/Iframe#Frames*.

 Tip If you are going to display a SharePoint page as a visual best bet, you can try to append *IsDlg=1* at the end of the URL. This removes most of the default SharePoint chrome and is the same parameter used when SharePoint displays pages as dialog boxes internally.

Remove a visual best bet

1. Display the Manage Keywords page.

2. Point to the visual best bet count for your keyword, and then click the down arrow.

3. Move your pointer over Delete Visual Best Bets, and then pick the visual best bet you want deleted, as shown previously in Figure 6-17.

Add a document promotion

1. Display the Manage Keywords page.

2. Point to your keyword, click the down arrow, and then choose Add Document Promotion from the displayed menu shown in Figure 6-15 earlier.

3. Fill in the Title and URL boxes for your document promotion as shown in Figure 6-19. The promoted item will be moved to the top of a search query matching the associated keyword. You can also fill in a start date and an end date for when the document promotion should be active, and you can associate one or more user contexts.

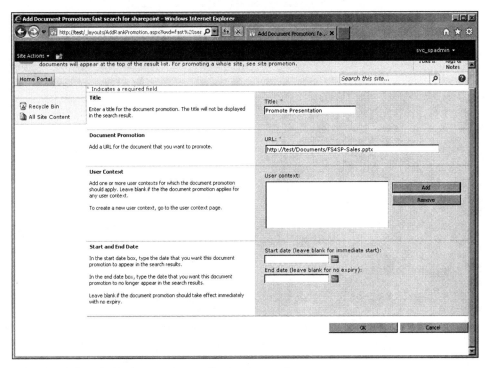

FIGURE 6-19 Associate a document promotion to a keyword.

Note When you examine the FQL generated for a document boost, you see that the promoted item is given 1,000,000 extra rank points, effectively moving it to the top of the result list.

```
xrank(
    string(
        "fast search for sharepoint",
        annotation_class="user",
        mode="simpleall"
    ),
     meta.contentid:equals(
        string(
            "http://test//Documents/FS4SP-Sales.pptx",
            linguistics="off",
            wildcards="off"
        )
    ),
     boost=1000000
)
```

Remove a document promotion

1. Display the Manage Keywords page.

2. Point to the document promotion count for your keyword, and then click the down arrow.

3. Point to Delete Document Promotion, and then pick the promotion you want to delete.

Add a document demotion

1. Display the Manage Keywords page.

2. Point to your keyword, click the down arrow, and then choose Add Document Demotion from the displayed menu shown earlier in Figure 6-15.

3. Fill in the Title and URL boxes for your document demotion. The promoted item will be moved to the bottom of a search query matching the associated keyword. You can also fill in a start date and an end date for when the document demotion is to be active, and you can associate one or more user contexts.

Note The generated FQL is similar to the one for document promotions, but the demoted item is given –1,000,000 rank points, moving it to the bottom of the result list.

Remove a document demotion

1. Display the Manage Keywords page.

2. Point to the document demotion count for your keyword, and then click the down arrow.

3. Point to Delete Document Demotion, and then pick the promotion you want to delete.

Windows PowerShell

The following samples take you through the steps involved in working with keywords and keyword-related functionality via Windows PowerShell.

Add a keyword with synonyms

1. Open an FS4SP shell.

2. You need to get a reference to a search settings group. If you added a keyword for a site collection by using SharePoint Site Collection Administration, this group is already created for you. If not, you need to create it yourself. If you have only one site collection, you have one search settings group and can omit the *Name* parameter. You can also execute *Get-FASTSearchSearchSettingsGroup* by itself to list all groups already created. The name of the search settings group is the ID of the site collection it belongs to.

   ```
   $searchSettingGroup = Get-FASTSearchSearchSettingGroup -Name "<GUID>"
   ```

3. Add the keyword, and get a reference to it.

   ```
   $keyword = $searchSettingGroup.Keywords.AddKeyword("fast search for sharepoint")
   ```

4. Now you need to add the synonyms either by using one-way or two-way expansion:

   - Add the synonyms by using two-way expansion.

     ```
     $keyword.AddSynonym("fs4sp")
     $keyword.AddSynonym("enterprise search")
     ```

   - Add the synonyms by using one-way expansion.

     ```
     $keyword.AddSynonym("fs4sp", "OneWay")
     $keyword.AddSynonym("enterprise search", "OneWay")
     ```

More Info The search settings group name is in the form of a GUID and is a reference to the site collection for which your keywords should be added. From a SharePoint Management Shell, execute the following command to get the correct GUID.

```
(Get-SPSite -Identity "http://test").ID
```

Then in an FS4SP shell, create the new search settings group by using the following command. Use the GUID from the previous command as the name parameter if it is not already created for you.

```
New-FASTSearchSearchSettingGroup -Name "<GUID>"
```

Add a best bet

1. Open an FS4SP shell.

2. Get a reference to the keyword on the site collection where you want to add the best bet.

   ```
   $searchSettingGroup = Get-FASTSearchSearchSettingGroup -Name "<GUID>"
   $keyword = $searchSettingGroup.Keywords.GetKeyword("fast search for sharepoint")
   ```

3. Create a URI object that points to the location of the best bet, where *<URL>* is the URL, for example, *http://www.contoso.com*.

   ```
   $uri = New-Object -TypeName System.Uri -ArgumentList "<URL>"
   ```

4. Add the best bet location to the keyword, where *<BestBetName>* is the title of the best bet and *<HTMLTeaser>* is the teaser linked to the best bet in HTML. The teaser is neither used nor displayed in the Best Bet Web Part.

   ```
   $keyword.AddBestBet("<BestBetName>", "<HTMLTeaser>", $uri)
   ```

Remove a best bet

1. Follow steps 1–2 of the previous "Add a best bet" procedure.

2. Remove the best bet.

   ```
   $keyword.RemoveBestBet("<BestBetName>")
   ```

Add a visual best bet

1. Follow steps 1–3 of the "Add a best bet" procedure.

2. Add the visual best bet link to the keyword, where *<VisualBestBetName>* is the title of the visual best bet and the URL points to the visual best bet content.

```
$visualBestBet = $keyword.AddFeaturedContent("<VisualBestBetName>")
$visualBestBet.Uri = $uri
```

Remove a visual best bet

1. Follow steps 1–2 of the "Add a best bet" procedure.

2. Remove the visual best bet.

```
$keyword.RemoveFeaturedContent("<VisualBestBetName >")
```

Add a document promotion/demotion

1. Follow steps 1–2 of the "Add a best bet" procedure.

2. Add the document promotion, where *<PromotionName>* is the title of the document promotion, *<DocumentId>* is the URL of the item you want promoted, and *<BoostValue>* is the value you want to boost the item with. Negative values demote the item instead of promoting it. The value used via Central Administration is 1,000,000 to ensure the item is put at the top of the result list, but you can reduce the value to create a softer boost.

```
$promotion = $keyword.AddPromotion("<PromotionName>")
$promotion.BoostValue = "<BoostValue>"
$promotion.PromotedItems.AddPromotedDocument("<DocumentId>")
```

Remove a document promotion/demotion

1. Follow steps 1–2 of the "Add a best bet" procedure.

2. Remove the document promotion, where *<PromotionName>* is the title of the document promotion and *<DocumentId>* is the URL of the item you promoted.

```
$promotedItems = $keyword.Promotions["<PromotionName>"].PromotedItems
foreach ($promotedDocument in @($promotedItems.GetPromotedDocumentEnumerator()))
{
    if ($promotedDocument.DocumentId -eq "<DocumentId>")
    {$promotedItems.Remove($promotedDocument)}
}
```

Create a global best bet/visual best bet

Using Windows PowerShell, you can create best bets or visual best bets that always appear for any query and do not match a specific keyword search term. Remember that *global* means within one site collection.

1. Open an FS4SP shell.

2. Get a reference to the search settings group on the site collection where you want to add the global best bet.

    ```
    $searchSettingGroup = Get-FASTSearchSearchSettingGroup -Name "<GUID>"
    ```

3. Create a URI object that points to the location of the best bet, where *<URL>* is the URL, for example, *http://www.contoso.com*.

    ```
    $uri = New-Object -TypeName System.Uri -ArgumentList "<URL>"
    ```

4. Add the global best bet or visual best bet.

    ```
    // Add a global best bet
    $searchSettingGroup.BestBetsWithoutKeyword.AddBestBet("<GlobalBestBetName>", $uri)

    // Add a global visual best bet
    $searchSettingGroup.FeaturedContentWithoutKeyword.AddFeaturedContent("<GlobalVisualBestB
    etName>", $uri)
    ```

Create a global document promotion/demotion

Using Windows PowerShell, you can create a document promotion or demotion that applies for any query and does not match a specific keyword search term.

1. Follow steps 1–2 of the "Add a best bet" procedure.

2. Add the document promotion, where *<GlobalPromotionName>* is the title of the document promotion, *<DocumentId>* is the URL of the document you want promoted, and *<BoostValue>* is the value you want to boost the document with. Negative values demote the document instead of promoting it.

    ```
    $globalPromotions = $searchSettingGroup.PromotionsWithoutKeyword
    $globalPromotion = $globalPromotions.AddPromotion("<GlobalPromotionName>")
    $globalPromotion.BoostValue = "<BoostValue>"
    $globalPromotion.PromotedItems.AddPromotedDocument("<DocumentId>")
    ```

.NET

Working with keywords in .NET code is achieved via the *KeywordContext* class. This class resides in the *Microsoft.SharePoint.Search.Extended.Administration.Keywords* namespace.

The following code sample walks you through the steps needed to work with keywords in .NET. The sample consists of a main function called *KeywordWalkthrough,* where all the keyword operations are shown; and a helper function called *GetSearchSettingGroup,* which retrieves the correct search settings group for the site collection you are working with. If the group does not exist, it will be created.

```
using System;
using System.IO;
using System.Linq;
using Microsoft.SharePoint;
using Microsoft.SharePoint.Search.Extended.Administration;
using Microsoft.SharePoint.Search.Extended.Administration.Keywords;
using Microsoft.SharePoint.Search.Extended.Administration.ResourceStorage;
using Microsoft.SharePoint.Search.Extended.Administration.Schema;

public class FS4SPKeywordsSample
{
    private void KeywordWalkthrough()
    {
        using (SPSite siteCollection = new SPSite("http://test/"))
        {
            SearchSettingGroup searchSettingGroup = GetSearchSettingGroup(siteCollection);
            // Add keyword
            var keyword = searchSettingGroup.Keywords.AddKeyword("fast search for sharepoint");

            // Add synonym with two-way expansion
            keyword.AddSynonym("fs4sp", SynonymExpansionType.TwoWay);

            // Add synonym with one-way expansion
            keyword.AddSynonym("enterprise search", SynonymExpansionType.OneWay);

            // Remove a synonym
            keyword.RemoveSynonym("enterprise search");

            // Add a Best Bet to the keyword
            keyword.AddBestBet("Microsoft", new Uri("http://www.microsoft.com"));

            // Remove a Best Bet from the keyword
            keyword.RemoveBestBet("Microsoft");

            // Add a Visual Best Bet to the keyword with start date and end date
            var featuredContent = keyword.AddFeaturedContent("Microsoft Logo");
            featuredContent.Uri = new Uri("http://site/microsoft_logo.png");
            featuredContent.StartDate = DateTime.UtcNow;
            featuredContent.EndDate = DateTime.UtcNow.AddMonths(1);
```

```csharp
    // Remove a Visual Best Bet from the keyword
    keyword.RemoveFeaturedContent("Microsoft Logo");

    // Add two document promotions to the keyword
    var promotion = keyword.AddPromotion("Top promotions");
    promotion.BoostValue = 1000000;
    promotion.PromotedItems.AddPromotedDocument("http://site/Docs/Mydoc.docx");
    promotion.PromotedItems.AddPromotedDocument("http://site/Docs/Myotherdoc.docx");

    // Remove a document promotion from the keyword
    var documentEnumerator = promotion.PromotedItems.GetPromotedDocumentEnumerator();
    string removeId = "http://site/Documents/Mydocument.docx";
    while (documentEnumerator.MoveNext())
    {
        if (documentEnumerator.Current.DocumentId != removeId) continue;
        promotion.PromotedItems.Remove(documentEnumerator.Current);
        break;
    }

    // Add a soft demotion of the home page to the keyword
    var demotion = keyword.AddPromotion("Soft demotion");
    demotion.BoostValue = -1000;
    demotion.PromotedItems.AddPromotedDocument("http://site/default.aspx");

    // Add a site promotion to the keyword
    var sitepromotion = keyword.AddPromotion("Site promotion");
    sitepromotion.BoostValue = 1000;
    Uri promoUri = new Uri("http://www.microsoft.com");
    sitepromotion.PromotedItems.AddPromotedLocation(promoUri);

    // Add a global site promotion
    var sitepromo = searchSettingGroup.PromotionsWithoutKeyword.AddPromotion("Site");
    sitepromo.BoostValue = 1000;
    sitepromo.PromotedItems.AddPromotedLocation(new Uri("http://www.microsoft.com"));

    // Remove a global site promotion URL
    var siteEnumerator = keywordsitepromotion.PromotedItems.GetPromotedLocationEnumerator();
    Uri removeLocation = new Uri("http://www.microsoft.com");
    while (siteEnumerator.MoveNext())
    {
        if (siteEnumerator.Current.Uri != removeLocation) continue;
        keywordsitepromotion.PromotedItems.Remove(siteEnumerator.Current);
        break;
    }

    // Remove a global site promotion
    searchSettingGroup.PromotionsWithoutKeyword.RemovePromotion("Site");

    // Remove the keyword
    searchSettingGroup.Keywords.RemoveKeyword("fast search for sharepoint");
    }
}
```

```
// Helper method to get the correct search setting group
private SearchSettingGroup GetSearchSettingGroup(SPSite siteCollection)
{
  KeywordContext keywordContext = new KeywordContext();
  SearchSettingGroupCollection ssg = keywordContext.SearchSettingGroups;
  SearchSettingGroup group = ssg
          .Where(searchSettingGroup => searchSettingGroup.Name.ToLower() ==
                                siteCollection.ID.ToString().ToLower())
          .FirstOrDefault();
  // Create the group if it does not exist
  if( group == null)
  {
      group = ssg.AddSearchSettingGroup(siteCollection.ID.ToString());
  }
  return group;
  }
}
```

Site Promotions and Demotions

Items that belong to highly relevant sites can be given a soft site promotion that causes the items to appear somewhat higher on the result list. When the user types a query that matches an item within the promoted site, the item will appear higher up in the search result list than what the normal ranking would imply. Similarly, you can apply soft site demotions to items from sites that are less important.

SharePoint

The following samples take you through the steps involved in working with site promotions and demotions via SharePoint Site Collection Administration.

Add a site promotion

1. Log on to the home page of your top-level site as a user with site collection administration privileges. Make sure the user is a member of either the local group FASTSearchAdministrators or FASTSearchKeywordAdministrators on the FS4SP administration server.

2. Go to Site Actions | Site Settings | Site Collection Administration.

3. Under Site Collection Administration, click FAST Search Site Promotion And Demotion.

4. Click Add Site Promotion.

5. Give the site promotion a title, and then click the Add button in the Promoted Sites category to add a new site to promote.

6. Enter the URL of the site you want to promote, and then click Add. You can add several URLs by repeating this step. Example: *http://www.contoso.com/*.

Note The URLs of the result items will match if they start with the URL entered in the site promotion and they are given a soft promotion of 1,000 rank points. If a user searches for *microsoft* and you have a site promotion for *http://www.contoso.com*, the final FQL that is executed will look like the following.

```
xrank(
    string(
        "microsoft", annotation_class="user", mode="simpleall"
    ),
    urls:starts-with(
        string(
            "http://www.contoso.com/",
             linguistics="off", wildcards="off", tokenization="generic"
        )
    ),
    boost=1000
)
```

Add a site demotion

1. Log on to the home page of your top-level site as a user with site collection administration privileges.

2. Navigate to Site Actions | Site Settings | Site Collection Administration.

3. Under Site Collection Administration, click FAST Search Site Promotion And Demotion.

4. Click Manage Site Demotion.

5. Click Add Site Demotion.

6. Give the site demotion a title, and then click the Add button in the Demoted Sites category to add a new site to demote.

7. Enter the URL of the site you want to demote, and then click Add. You can add several URLs by repeating this step. Example: *http://www.contoso.com/*.

More Info For more information about working with site promotion and demotion using SharePoint administration, go to *http://office.microsoft.com/en-us/fast-search-server-help/ promoting-or-demoting-sites-HA010381927.aspx*.

Windows PowerShell

The following samples take you through the steps involved in working with site promotions and demotions via Windows PowerShell.

Add a site promotion to a keyword

1. Open an FS4SP shell.

2. Get a reference to the keyword on the site collection where you want to add the best bet.

```
$searchSettingGroup = Get-FASTSearchSearchSettingGroup -Name "<GUID>"
$keyword = $searchSettingGroup.Keywords.GetKeyword("fast search for sharepoint")
```

3. Add the document promotion, where *<PromotionName>* is the title of the site promotion, *<URL>* is the URL of the site you want promoted, and *<BoostValue>* is the value you want to boost the site with. Negative values demote the site instead of promoting it.

```
$promotion = $keyword.AddPromotion("<PromotionName>")
$promotion.BoostValue = <BoostValue>
$uri = New-Object -TypeName System.Uri -ArgumentList "<URL>"
$promotion.PromotedItems.AddPromotedLocation($uri)
```

Add a global site promotion

Remember that *global* means within one site collection.

1. Follow steps 1–2 of the previous "Add a site promotion to a keyword" procedure.

2. Add the site promotion, where *<GlobalPromotionName>* is the title of the site promotion, *<URL>* is the URL of the site you want promoted, and *<BoostValue>* is the value you want to boost the site with. Negative values demote the site instead of promoting it.

```
$globalPromotions = $searchSettingGroup.PromotionsWithoutKeyword
$globalPromotion = $globalPromotions.AddPromotion("<GlobalPromotionName>")
$globalPromotion.BoostValue = "<BoostValue>"
$uri = New-Object -TypeName System.Uri -ArgumentList <URL>
$globalPromotion.PromotedItems.AddPromotedLocation($uri)
```

More Info For more information about working with site promotion and demotion using SharePoint administration, go to *http://technet.microsoft.com/en-us/library/ff191225.aspx*.

.NET

See the .NET sample in the "Keywords" section earlier in this chapter for information about how to add site promotions and demotions with code.

FQL-Based Promotions

Earlier in this chapter, you learned about promoting and demoting items and sites based on URLs. Another option, which is not available via the SharePoint administration page, is creating promotions based on FAST query language (FQL).

In its simplest form, FQL-based promotions can be used in a fashion similar to managed property boosts, by boosting items where a managed property has a specific value. The main difference with FQL-based promotions and managed property boosts is that a managed property boost is applied to all search queries run against the rank profile it is attached to, whereas a promotion is scoped to queries from one site collection. In addition, FQL-based promotions can be attached to a keyword and user contexts. All in all, FQL-based promotions are more flexible than managed property boosts.

Windows PowerShell

The following Windows PowerShell script achieves the same results as the sample for managed property boosts, where you wanted to promote all items that have *format* set to *Web Page* with 5,000 rank points. Run the Windows PowerShell script in an FS4SP shell.

```
$searchSettingGroup = Get-FASTSearchSearchSettingGroup -Name "<GUID>"
$globalPromotions = $searchSettingGroup.PromotionsWithoutKeyword
$globalPromotion = $globalPromotions.AddPromotion("FQL Promo")
$globalPromotion.BoostValue = "5000"
$fql = 'format:"Web Page"'
$globalPromotion.PromotedItems.AddPromotedExpression($fql)
```

Taking this a bit further, you can create a global demotion that demotes all items that are larger than 3 MB and from a file server that has –4,000 rank points.

```
$searchSettingGroup = Get-FASTSearchSearchSettingGroup -Name "<GUID>"
$globalPromotions = $searchSettingGroup.PromotionsWithoutKeyword
$globalPromotion = $globalPromotions.AddPromotion("FQL size and file")
$globalPromotion.BoostValue = "-4000"
$fql = 'and(size:range(int("3145728"),max,from="gt",to="le"),url:starts-with("file://"))'
$globalPromotion.PromotedItems.AddPromotedExpression($fql)
```

User Context Management

In the previous section, you learned about how you can add keywords with features such as synonyms, best bets, and document promotions. All of these features can be attached to one or more user contexts. As you learned earlier in the chapter, user contexts enable you to promote documents differently depending on the person doing the search. In addition, user contexts show different best bets above the search results. This is a good start to personalizing the search experience for your users. In order to create user contexts, you have to configure the User Profile Service Application.

After you create your user contexts, they are available for use with the FAST Search Keywords and FAST Search Site Promotion And Demotion links.

More Info For detailed information about how to set up the User Profile Service Application in SharePoint, go to *http://technet.microsoft.com/en-us/library/ee721049.aspx.*

SharePoint

The following sample takes you through the steps involved in setting up a user context via SharePoint Site Collection Administration.

Create a user context

1. Go to Site Actions | Site Settings | Site Collection Administration.

2. Click FAST Search User Context, shown in Figure 6-20.

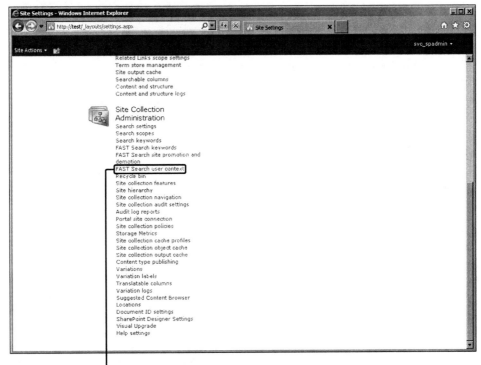

Link to administration of
FAST Search user context

FIGURE 6-20 Link to FAST Search User Context from Site Collection Administration.

3. Click Add User Context.

4. Give the user context a name in the User Context Name box.

5. Pick values for the Office Location box and/or values for the Ask Me About box, shown in Figure 6-21.

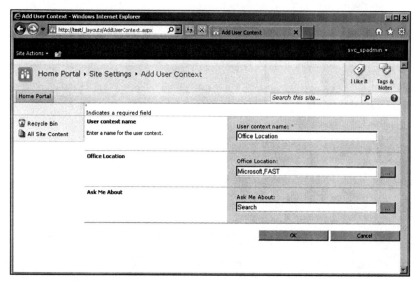

FIGURE 6-21 Create a user context.

6. Click OK.

Windows PowerShell

The following sample takes you through the steps involved in setting up a user context via Windows PowerShell.

 More Info For detailed tutorials about how to use Windows PowerShell with user contexts, go to *http://technet.microsoft.com/en-us/library/ff191223.aspx*.

Create a user context

1. Open an FS4SP shell.

2. Get a reference to the search settings group for your site collection, where *<GUID>* is the ID of your site collection. See the "Add a keyword with synonyms" procedure earlier in this chapter for information about how to obtain a reference to your site collection ID.

    ```
    $searchSettingGroup = Get-FASTSearchSearchSettingGroup -Name "<GUID>"
    ```

3. Add a new search context, where *<ContextName>* is the name you give your user context.

```
$context = $searchSettingGroup.Contexts.AddContext("<ContextName>")
```

4. Add user profile properties to your newly created context. You build a context expression by using *AND*, *OR*, and *NOT* operators, as in the following example.

```
$andExpression = $context.AddAndExpression()
$orExpression = $andExpression.AddOrExpression()
$orExpression.AddMatchExpression("<PropertyName0>","<PropertyValue0>")
$orExpression.AddMatchExpression("<PropertyName1>","<PropertyValue1>")
$notExpression = $andExpression.AddNotExpression()
$notExpression.AddMatchExpression("<PropertyName2>","<PropertyValue2>")
```

Where *<PropertyName>* items are names of user properties and *<PropertyValue>* items are the values you want to check against for the given property. The preceding sample yields the following expression after it is computed.

```
(<PropertyName0>:<PropertyValue0> OR <PropertyName1>:<PropertyValue1>)
AND
(NOT (<PropertyName2>:<PropertyName2>))
```

> **Note** The Boolean operator object used when creating the user context is not to be confused with keyword syntax or FQL used during searching. This is a domain-specific syntax for user contexts.

Adding More Properties to User Contexts

As seen in the previous example, by default, you can choose from only two properties when creating a user context, namely *Office Location* and *Ask Me About*. Using other properties from a person's profile page to create user contexts could also be useful.

Add a user profile property to be used in user contexts

1. In Central Administration, point to Manage Service Applications, and then click User Profile Service Application.

2. Under the People section, click Manage User Properties.

3. Pick the property you would like to use in your user context (for example *Department*), and then click Edit.

4. Record the name of the property shown in the Name box. It is important to use the internal name of the property and not the display name; these differ for some properties.

5. Open a SharePoint Management Shell.

6. Execute the following commands to retrieve the existing properties of *SPS-Location* and *SPS-Responsibility*, and then add Department to the list.

```
$contextprops = Get-SPEnterpriseSearchExtendedQueryProperty -SearchApplication "FAST
Query SSA" -Identity "FASTSearchContextProperties"

$newprops = $contextprops.Value + ",Department"
Set-SPEnterpriseSearchExtendedQueryProperty -SearchApplication "FAST Query SSA" -Identity
"FASTSearchContextProperties" -Value $newprops
```

7. The new field should appear after a short time, or you can force it by recycling the SharePoint web application pool.

8. Follow the previous procedure, "Create a user context," and you can now use your added property.

Conclusion

Out of the box, FS4SP has many features that you can take advantage of by simply using the administrative interfaces in SharePoint. This is a powerful offering because search administrators or power users can modify and tune the search solution without the involvement of technical personnel.

But, as you saw from the samples that use Windows PowerShell or .NET code, these two options give you even more flexibility and functionality. Windows PowerShell is also a good option for larger deployments because you can script everything when moving between environments. Or you can program the setup in .NET and run the code, for example, on feature activation in SharePoint. Both approaches make it easier to set up new servers and environments, and also to upgrade them, as you adapt your search solution.

Some of the changes you do to your full-text indexes and rank profiles can have a severe impact on your search solution and might require you to recrawl all the content, whereas others can be added and tested right away. Keywords and scopes are both easy to configure and have low system impact. Editing the managed properties and creating good user contexts require more understanding of your content, your users, and how FS4SP works internally in order to get it right.

By testing the different options available and understanding how they work, you will gain valuable insight into FS4SP and learn to create powerful search solutions. In the end, it is up to you to familiarize yourself with the differences between the tools and pick the one most suited for your particular need.

## CHAPTER 7

Content Processing

After completing this chapter, you will be able to

■ Connect to a source system and crawl its content.

■ Use SharePoint built-in connectors.

■ Use FAST Search specific connectors.

■ Manipulate and enrich content before it is indexed by using the FS4SP framework for item processing.

■ Understand the indexing pipeline.

■ Configure and use the optional item processing components.

■ Develop, integrate, and use your own External Item Processing component.

Content Processing in Microsoft FAST Search Server 2010 for SharePoint (FS4SP) can be defined as connecting to a source system, sending the data extracted from the system through the indexing pipeline, and finally, merging the output from the indexing pipeline into the searchable index. This chapter covers the two most important phases: connecting to a source system and processing the data that was from extracted from the system.

Introduction

Connecting to a source system can be difficult by itself. Luckily, FS4SP contains several prebuilt connectors that require only a few configuration steps before it can index your designated source system. In addition, FS4SP supports Business Connectivity Services (BCS), making it easy to build custom connectors that target more esoteric source systems or source systems with specialized requirements. Of course, you can build your own custom connectors from scratch (although doing so is probably more difficult than you might think). You can also purchase additional connectors from third-party vendors. In one way or another, FS4SP is able to index data from the vast majority of source systems.

Unfortunately, after you've tapped into a source system and looked at what data it contains, it is often painfully obvious that the data quality in the source system is low. Even in large organizations with strict routines and large budgets for information management, the data quality is—more often than not—very low.

Notes About Content Processing Vocabulary

As already mentioned, FS4SP is the result of Microsoft merging technology acquired from FAST Search & Transfer into the world of Microsoft SharePoint. Although the technology from the merge has come a long way, understanding how things fit together can be daunting and frustrating because two different technology paradigms are running behind the scene. As such, a distinct and unambiguous vocabulary is of utmost importance when talking about the components of FS4SP.

The following list summarizes the terms used in this chapter and how they relate to each other. Note that the official Microsoft documentation is not always coherent and might deviate from this—and its own—vocabulary from time to time. The terms are also summarized in the schematic overview in Figure 7-1.

- **Content processing** As explained in the previous section, content processing is the umbrella term for everything that goes on before items are indexed and made available through searches.

- **Connector** This is the module that is responsible for connecting to a source system and extracting its content. A connector is sometimes ambiguously referred to as a "crawler" (which is better described as a certain type of connector).

- **Crawling** This is the act of having a connector extract data from a source system, for example, executing a *SELECT*-statement on a database, traversing a file share, or spidering the web. Note that in layman's terms, *crawling* typically refers to "crawling the web"—that is, using a special type of connector to follow links on websites and send the website content to the index.

- **Indexing pipeline** A connector sends content to the indexing pipeline, in which the data is refined and manipulated and eventually sent to the indexer that makes the data searchable. The indexing pipeline is an ordered set of small tools that each work on each item flowing through it.

- **Item processing** This is the act of sending items through the indexing pipeline.

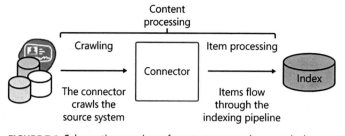

FIGURE 7-1 Schematic overview of content processing vocabulary.

Because relevance is of utmost importance in any search engine, you need a systematic, configurable, and extendable framework for manipulating the content pulled from a source system before that content reaches the index. In other words, the framework should enrich or straighten out the content so that it corresponds to what's required of the search index. The whole point of such an exercise is, of course, to make sure users' queries return the most relevant possible search results. The FS4SP framework for such content manipulation is referred to as the *indexing pipeline*. Each item extracted from the source system by using any of the connectors is sent through the indexing pipeline. In this pipeline, a large set of small tools work on the item's content in sequence until the item comes out on the other side of the pipeline fully processed and ready to be placed in the index.

This whole chain of events, starting from reaching into the source system and ending by sending items to the indexer process, is called *content processing*. The key point to understand here is that relevance, as perceived by the end user, is immensely important. Consequently, being able to systematically enrich and manipulate content before it reaches the index is truly the foundation of building a great search solution.

Crawling Source Systems

FS4SP has two types of connectors: those that are available and integrated in SharePoint and listed as Content Sources on your FAST Content Search Service Applications (SSA), and the so-called FAST Search specific connectors. The latter type is available only in FS4SP and not in the built-in SharePoint Search.

FAST Search specific connectors are different from the SharePoint built-in connectors in that they are not hosted or configured in SharePoint. As such, they function and scale much differently than the SharePoint built-in connectors. Figure 7-2 shows the differences between the content flow of these two types of connectors.

Note People Search is handled by SharePoint, and the FS4SP index is not used for user profile content in a default solution. To complicate matters, People Search crawls are managed from the FAST Query SSA. Read more about this in Chapter 2, "Search Concepts and Terminology." A technical reference can be found at *http://technet.microsoft.com/en-us/library/hh582311.aspx*.

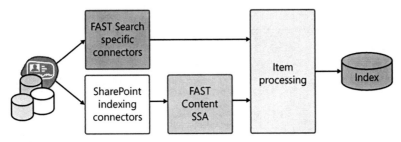

FIGURE 7-2 Schematic overview of the content flows of the two types of connectors.

Both types of connectors emit content that ultimately finds its way into the FS4SP index. However, because the FAST Content SSA is bypassed when you use the FAST Search specific connectors, the SSA is, for all intents and purposes, completely unaware of any external crawling going on through those connectors. Consequently, there is no way of inspecting crawl logs and crawl history in the SSA, as is the case with the SharePoint built-in connectors.

> **Note** Even though the FAST Search specific connectors bypass the FAST Content SSA, content that is indexed using these connectors is still subject to the same mappings between crawled and managed properties as all other content. The reason for this is two-fold: Managed properties are defined in the other SSA—that is, the FAST Query SSA—and the actual mappings are made in the indexing pipeline, which all content passes on its way toward the index.

There is an overlap between the two connector groups. For example, SharePoint has a built-in web crawler, but FAST Search specific connectors also have a web crawler among them. Both connector groups serve their purposes and should be chosen depending on your scenario and requirements. Table 7-1 and Table 7-2 list all available connectors in each group, and the sections that follow expand on each of the connectors. Additionally, a decision tree that showcases each connector's advantages and disadvantages is presented in the section "Choosing a Connector" later in this chapter.

TABLE 7-1 The SharePoint built-in connectors

Connector	Targeted source system
SharePoint indexing connector	Sites and content stored inside SharePoint
Web site indexing connector	Intranets and the Internet
File share indexing connector	Content in local or remote file shares
Exchange indexing connector	Email messages and attachments in Microsoft Exchange Server public folders
Line of business (LOB) Data indexing connector	Content fed from BCS
Documentum indexing connector	Content stored in EMC Documentum*
Lotus Notes indexing connector	Content stored in Lotus Notes**

* For information about EMC Documentum, go to *http://www.emc.com/domains/documentum/index.htm*.

** For information about Lotus Notes, go to *http://www-01.ibm.com/software/lotus/products/notes/*.

TABLE 7-2 The FAST Search specific connectors

Connector	Targeted source system
FAST Search Web crawler	Intranets and the Internet
FAST Search database connector	Any type of database that can be accessed via the Java Database Connectivity (JDBC) data access API
FAST Search Lotus Notes connector	Content stored in Lotus Notes

More Info The Documentum indexing connector and Lotus Notes indexing connector require separate installation. For more information, see the section "Content Source Types" later in this chapter.

Note Besides the built-in SharePoint connectors and the FAST Search specific connectors, there are third-party connectors. The market has no shortage of different source systems, and odds are that FS4SP must be able to connect to a more unusual source system if deployed in a large organization. Purchasing a third-party connector can be a good idea to limit implementation time and project risk.

Crawling Content by Using the SharePoint Built-in Connectors

The SharePoint built-in connectors have a Content Sources concept. Each content source is linked to one of the connectors and targets a certain source system, whether it's the local SharePoint farm or a remote source system like Lotus Notes or EMC Documentum.

In FS4SP, you manage content sources by using the FAST Content SSA in Central Administration. To create or modify existing content sources, navigate to the FAST Content SSA, and then click Content Sources in the left panel. Figure 7-3 shows how this page looks before you configure any content sources.

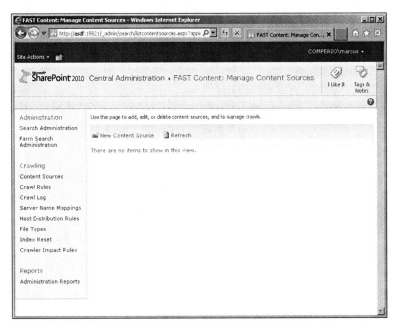

FIGURE 7-3 The Manage Content Sources page in the FAST Content SSA, without any previously defined content sources.

Warning Both the FAST Content SSA and the FAST Query SSA share the same structure. This is unfortunate because some functionality seemingly is shared between the two. For example, the FAST Query SSA also has a Crawling section. This is where People Search crawls are managed. Read more about the reasons and side effects of sharing the same structure in Chapter 3, "FS4SP Architecture."

To add a content source, click New Content Source at the top of the page shown in Figure 7-3. On the returned page, you can configure details of your new content source. Most importantly, this is where you specify which SharePoint connector to use—that is, which Content Source Type you want to use. The Add Content Source page is shown in Figure 7-4.

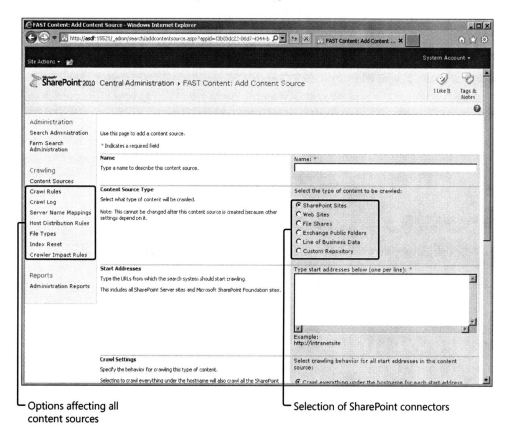

Options affecting all content sources

Selection of SharePoint connectors

FIGURE 7-4 The Add Content Source page in a default installation without any additional SharePoint connectors installed.

 Note It is not possible to change the type of the content source after it has been created. If you want to change it, you must first delete your existing one and create a new one.

Content sources that use BCS are sorted under the label *Line of Business Data*. Also note that not all SharePoint connectors are listed in a default installation. The Documentum and Lotus Notes indexing connectors must be installed manually, after which they show up under the label *Custom Repository*.

All SharePoint connectors are configured similarly. You first give the new content source a unique name and select which connector to use. Then you define where the connector should start crawling—for example, a SharePoint site or a particular URL—and how often the content source should be scheduled for crawling. However, each connector brings a set of unique options that you need to decide on. In the following sections, you will explore each of the SharePoint connectors, using the Add New Content Source page as a starting point. The exact sequence of mouse clicks is left as an exercise for the reader.

One thing to point out in particular before delving into the different SharePoint built-in connectors is that modifying options underneath the Crawling panel to the left in the FAST Content SSA affects all content sources defined in the SSA. This means that, for example, crawl rules and file type configuration are global to all SharePoint connectors.

 Note If you have experience working with other Enterprise Search solutions, for example, legacy FAST technology, you might find it confusing that all SharePoint connectors share some global options, such as crawl rules. If you do, think of the SharePoint connectors as just one connector with the same back end—but with various source system adapters.

Content Source Types

When creating a new content source, you specify its content source type. This is the equivalent of deciding which of the SharePoint built-in connectors shown in Table 7-1 to use. The following sections describe the different content source types.

SharePoint sites Indexing content stored in the local SharePoint farm is arguably one of the most common use-cases in FS4SP. You can index both the local SharePoint farm that lives alongside the FS4SP installation, as well as a remote farm. All SharePoint Server and SharePoint foundation sites are supported. You can also index earlier versions such as Microsoft Office SharePoint Server (MOSS) 2007 and MOSS 2003.

Before running your first crawl, make sure that your content access account has sufficient permissions to read all the content you want crawled. This is done either by modifying the rights of the default content access account or by implementing a crawl rule that specifies which account to use for a particular location. If you're indexing a remote farm, the crawl rule approach is often recommended. Of course, in those cases you can also opt to set up a web application policy for the account on the remote farm.

When configuring the SharePoint indexing connector, you specify a list of start addresses where the connector should begin to look for content, and determine which strategy the connector should use to fetch it: either by indexing everything underneath each start address or by indexing the site collection of each start address. Figure 7-5 shows these settings as they are listed on the Add Content Source page.

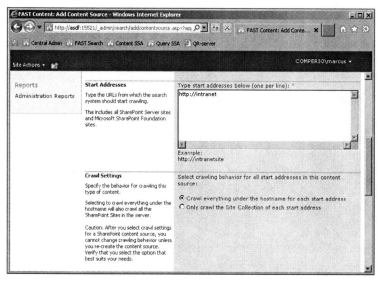

FIGURE 7-5 The crawl settings of the SharePoint indexing connector.

Web Sites   The settings of the Web site indexing connector are similar to those of the SharePoint indexing connector: You create a list of start addresses where crawling should begin, and then specify which of the following three crawling strategies should be used:

- **Only crawl within the server of each start address**   The crawler indexes only pages on the same server as the start address. This could be particularly useful if you are, for example, tasked with indexing the external website of the company that owns the FS4SP solution but does not use SharePoint for powering that website. Using this option means that the crawler won't follow links pointing outside of the company's web server.

- **Only crawl the first page of each address**   The crawler indexes only the exact pages that are listed in the start addresses text area. This is useful when you know exactly what you want to crawl and can trust that those pages won't disappear anytime soon.

- **Custom-specify page depth and server hops**   By choosing this strategy, you can explicitly specify how many consecutive links away from each start address the crawler will follow. Unless you're using aggressive crawl rules, specifying a high number can make the size of your index grow exponentially.

 Note Instead of using the Web site indexing connector, you can also opt to use the FAST Search Web crawler, which provides more fine-grained control over the crawl settings, with the trade-off that it's harder to configure and maintain. See the section "Crawling Content by Using the FAST Search Specific Connectors" later in this chapter for more information.

File Shares The File share indexing connector is useful for indexing files and documents stored in shared folders or on a network share. Top-level folders are specified as start addresses, and the connector either indexes only the exact folder as specified by the start address or all subfolders below it depending on which crawl settings you specify.

You can index content from any file share that implements the Server Message Block (SMB) standard, which is what all standard Microsoft file shares use. In the Linux/UNIX world, you can configure a Samba file share to allow FS4SP to fetch its content, but this would also require you to implement your own mapping of user accounts and groups because these are not natively bound to Active Directory accounts. Note that indexing remote file shares can be very taxing on the network connection between the file share and the FS4SP server hosting the crawl component.

> **Tip** If you want to index files on the server hosting the crawler component, configure a file share containing the particular directory to make it accessible to the connector. Do this by right-clicking your target folder, selecting the Sharing tab in the My Documents Properties dialog box, and then clicking the Share button shown in Figure 7-6. Make it available either to the solution's default content access account or set up a crawl rule that has a specific content access count for the file share.

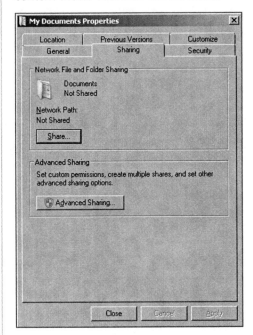

FIGURE 7-6 Sharing a local folder, thus making it available to the File share indexing connector.

Exchange Public Folders   The Exchange public folders indexing connector is used to index email messages and their attachments, discussions, and other collaborative content that is stored in Exchange Server. This connector is very similar to the File share indexing connector in that it also can be set up to either index everything under each start address, or just the exact location of each start address.

BCS   The content source type Line Of Business Data in Figure 7-4 is the bridge into BCS with which you can tap into external systems and bring their content into SharePoint, and hence also into FS4SP.

> **More Info**   BCS is a broad topic well worth exploring. A good starting point can be found online at *http://msdn.microsoft.com/en-us/library/ee556826.aspx*.

Using BCS to bring content into FS4SP boils down to the following three key steps:

1.   **Create an external content type in BCS**   A core concept in a BCS connection is an *external content type*, which is essentially a representation of an entity in the source system that you're targeting. This content type can be as simple as a row in a database or something much more advanced, for example, an aggregated representation of certain properties existing across several source systems. It all depends on how you choose to define the external content type in BCS. Each column from a database connection or property in the entity becomes a column of the external content type (ECT).

2.   **Configure a BCS profile page**   The entity represented via the external content can provide a "landing page"—that is, something to show to users when they click the item in the search results. Again, this might be straightforward (the source system you target might already have a view for this very purpose), or perhaps you need BCS to generate one for you.

> **Note**   The creation of profile pages for items in BCS is one advantage over using the FAST Search database connector because profile pages make it easier to have clickable results from a database.

3.   **Add a content source that uses the Line Of Business Data content type**   The external content type you created in BCS is shown after selecting the Line Of Business Data content source type. You can choose to crawl all of them or just a select few, as shown in Figure 7-7.

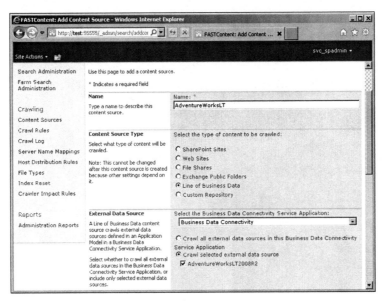

FIGURE 7-7 Adding an external content type from BCS as a content source.

Custom Repository The custom repository content source type makes it possible to develop your own custom indexing connectors. How to do this is out of the scope of this book. However, you can go to *http://msdn.microsoft.com/en-us/library/ff625806.aspx* for documentation and an implementation example.

Note Writing a custom indexing connector is recommended only if the targeted source system is not supported by BCS or if the data model of the source system is extremely dynamic, makes use of domain-specific data types impossible to handle in BCS, or is so large or complex that the crawling implementation needs very fine-grained control. Although creating a custom connector is not that difficult and the example solution given on MSDN can be compiled and used relatively easily, figuring out how your source system can communicate with that connector successfully is more difficult. You should write custom indexing connectors only as a last resort solution.

After the connector is registered in SharePoint, it should appear when you select Custom Repository on the Add Content Source page. Figure 7-8 shows how this looks without any custom indexing connectors registered.

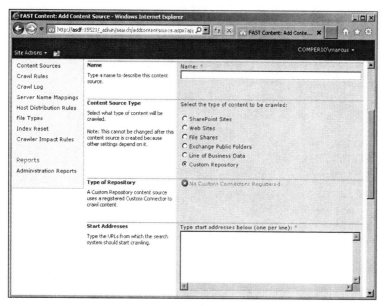

FIGURE 7-8 The Add Content Source page without having any custom indexing connectors registered in SharePoint.

Note Custom indexing connectors were previously referred to as *protocol handlers*. This is because, when you registered the connector, you actually defined a new protocol in Windows, in addition to the standard ones, such as *http://* or *ftp://*. URIs using this protocol are then used for defining the start addresses of the custom repositories. Protocol handlers needed to be written in C++ and could be complicated and difficult to build. Although they are still supported in this version of SharePoint, the new connector framework and BCS offer an easier development experience and more flexibility.

Documentum The Documentum indexing connector enables SharePoint to crawl content stored in EMC Documentum. This functionality is not enabled by default and requires you to download and install a separate package. For a detailed description of the installation and configuration process, go to *http://technet.microsoft.com/en-us/library/ff721975.aspx*. Note that after installation, the Documentum indexing connector shows up as a Custom Repository.

Lotus Notes The Lotus Notes indexing connector enables SharePoint to crawl content stored in Lotus Notes. Just like the Documentum indexing connector, it is not enabled by default and, after configuration, shows up as a Custom Repository. Although it is not necessary to download a separate installation package, you need to go through some steps of manual configuration in order to use the Lotus Notes indexing connector. For detailed instructions about configuring and using the Lotus Notes connector, go to *http://technet.microsoft.com/en-us/library/ff463593.aspx*.

> **Note** You can also use the FAST Search Lotus Notes connector (one of the FAST Search specific connectors) to crawl content stored in Lotus Notes. Consider this when you need to synchronize complex security mappings or when you want to index items such as attachments to email messages.

Crawl Rules Management

Every time any of the SharePoint indexing connectors crawls a content item, the system looks for an applicable crawl rule. The crawl rule tells SharePoint whether the particular item should be included or excluded from the crawl and whether a particular authentication account and method should be used to retrieve the item. The Add Crawl Rule page is shown in Figure 7-9.

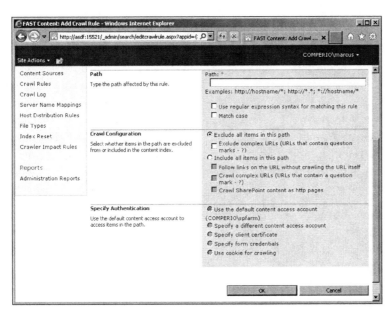

FIGURE 7-9 The Add Crawl Rule page is used for inclusion/exclusion of content in addition to specifying authentication methods other than the default content access account.

It's a good idea to keep your index as slim as possible. Content you don't ever want to be included in search results should be excluded using the appropriate set of crawl rules. Failing to do so leads to longer crawl times, larger disk consumption, and to some extent, slower search queries. However, depending on the complexity of your content source, it's not always possible to set up crawl rules to match your needs. In those situations, consider using search scopes to stop your queries from returning unwanted search results.

If you experience problems with a particular content item, odds are that a crawl rule is interfering by either erroneously including or excluding the content item. The crawl rule test functionality, directly available when clicking the Crawl Rules link in the SSA, can be of great help when troubleshooting this.

Crawl rules are managed from the SSA on which the content sources are defined. For your content crawls, this means the FAST Content SSA. For People Search, crawl rules are defined in the FAST Query SSA.

Warning The crawl rules are global to all content sources defined in the particular SSA. This can be problematic if you have two overlapping content sources that are using the same protocol, for example, two web crawls with similar start addresses. Unless care is taken, your crawl rules could affect both content sources and possibly produce results you did not expect.

Crawler Impact Rules Management

When using a pull-based approach for getting data into FS4SP, such as when using the connectors described in this chapter, you should always consider the performance footprint you're making in the source system. There is a trade-off between getting new content into the index and how much strain you want to put on the source system by continuously crawling it. Additionally, crawling is, by nature, a resource-intensive activity. Although you can improve performance by adding servers that have a crawl component, you might also want to set limits on how fast SharePoint is allowed to request data from your content sources. IT administrators are commonly surprised by the impact the crawler has, not only on hardware dedicated to the search engine but also on the systems from which it is collecting information—systems that are often old, slow, and already under strain by users.

You use crawler impact rules to configure the number of simultaneous requests and the interval to use in between requests. These rules are defined in the FAST Content SSA. The Add Crawler Impact Rule page, shown in Figure 7-10, is reachable from the Crawling section on the panel to the left on the FAST Content SSA page. Although there are no standard metrics for crawler impact because of the fact that no two source systems are the same, administrators should be able to estimate a reasonable request rate for the system. A simple solution is to have the crawler access a mirror of the actual source system if such a thing is available.

Tip Before experimenting with crawler impact rules, make sure you have an optimal crawler schedule for your content sources. Some sources might handle a single-threaded incremental crawl every five minutes, whereas others can handle multiple threads during off hours. Combining both with a well-configured FS4SP farm yields the best indexing performance but requires some testing to get right.

Note Crawler impact rules apply on a per crawl–component basis. Take this into account if you have multiple crawl components in your farm. However, the need for multiple crawl components is limited with FS4SP because item processing is handled by the FS4SP farm. Read more about crawl components in Chapter 3.

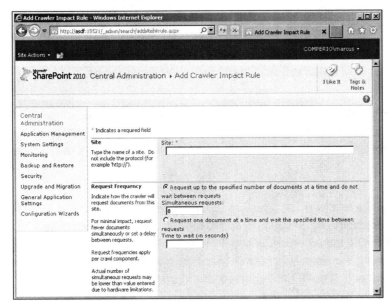

FIGURE 7-10 The Add Crawler Impact Rule page.

Warning Take special care when crawling external websites beyond your control. You can very well bring down a web server simply by requesting pages too quickly.

Crawling Content by Using the FAST Search Specific Connectors

For the majority of crawling scenarios, the crawlers directly available through SharePoint or indirectly using BCS are more than enough to cover your needs. However, FS4SP also includes three additional connectors: the FAST Search specific connectors known as the *FAST Search Web crawler*, the *FAST Search database connector*, and the *FAST Search Lotus Notes connector*.

These three connectors and some others were available in the products that existed before Microsoft acquired FAST. However, because the SharePoint built-in connectors and BCS eliminated the need for most, if not all such connectors, they were not brought into FS4SP. One can only speculate why just these three were included, but they all provide great configuration flexibility and could also serve well those organizations that are migrating from earlier FAST technology. It is, however, not unreasonable to believe they will be removed in future releases because they don't follow the standard methodology of how crawling works in SharePoint. This should tell you to use some caution if you dedicate resources to work with these connectors when a SharePoint alternative will do.

Important The FAST Search Web crawler is particularly different because it can be configured to scale to several machines on the farm—which is also completely unnoticeable from SharePoint's point of view.

Even though all three FAST Search specific connectors are available in a standard FS4SP installation, they are not used unless you specifically configure them yourself.

Each of the FAST Search specific connectors are described in the following sections. As you will see, they all share the same technical foundation: They are all configured using a single XML configuration file and they feed content straight to the FS4SP content distributor component, thus bypassing SharePoint.

Note It is recommended to always use a custom content collection when indexing content with the FAST Search specific connectors, and to *not* use the default collection *sp*. This makes it easier to maintain the collection, especially to remove it, without interfering with content crawled by using the SharePoint built-in connectors. See the section "Collection Management" in Chapter 6, "Search Configuration," for information about how to create content collections.

Other FAST Search Specific Functionality for Indexing Content

Before going into details about the three FAST Search specific connectors, it should also be mentioned that there are two other FAST Search specific means of pushing content directly to the index. These two techniques communicate with FS4SP in the same way as the FAST Search specific connectors but are not proper connectors in themselves.

The Content API You can build your own connectors from scratch by using the Content API for FS4SP. This library communicates with FS4SP in the same manner as the FAST Search specific connectors—that is, without going through the FAST Content SSA. This API is provided as-is and is released to cater to some very specialized use cases, for example, providing backward compatibility with custom connectors built for older FAST platforms, or implementing a custom connector where full control of all aspects of feeding items into FS4SP is required. One advantage of this API is that you can create push-based or event-based indexing, which means you don't have to schedule full and incremental crawls. This API can be downloaded from *http://www.microsoft.com/download/en/details.aspx?id=5210*.

The *docpush* command-line tool   Yet another FAST Search specific connector–like functionality in FS4SP is the command-line tool *docpush*. You can use this command to index individual files on the local server. Although this is far from a "connector" as such, it implements the same methodology for communicating with FS4SP as the FAST Search specific connectors, and it is useful for testing purposes. Open an FS4SP shell and execute **docpush --help** if you are curious about the details. To index a test file, issue the following command.

```
docpush -c [collection] [file path]
```

> **Note** All FAST Search specific connectors, as well as the Content API and the *docpush* tool, are capable of not only indexing items but also of removing items from the index. The *-d* parameter activates this feature when using *docpush*.

FAST Search Web Crawler

The FAST Search Web crawler is the most prominent of the three connectors that are specific to FS4SP. It was originally developed for large-scale public web crawls, and as such, can be configured to crawl the whole Internet—if scaled accordingly. If you have experience working with legacy FAST technology, you might know the connector as the *Enterprise Crawler*.

SharePoint also has a web crawler, namely the Web site indexing connector available in the FAST Content SSA. If you are crawling a large set of external websites or need to have fine-grained control of crawl rules and performance, the FAST Search Web crawler provides superior scaling and configurability over the Web site indexing connector. Additionally, if you're migrating to FS4SP from legacy FAST technology, it is easy to also migrate your FAST Search Web crawler configuration.

The FAST Search Web crawler is included by default in a standard FS4SP installation, but as long as you don't configure and run it explicitly, it stays inactive. Surprisingly, the crawler's internal processes are always running—disregarding whether you're using the crawler. Figure 7-11 shows the output of the **nctrl status** command on a single-server FS4SP farm. All processes related to the FAST Search Web crawler have boxes around them.

> **Note** Part of the reason the FAST Search Web crawler is included in the Node Controller (shown in Figure 7-11) is that it contains its own internal scheduler. As soon as you configure and start a crawl, the webpages included in the crawl are automatically monitored for as long as the FAST Search Web crawler is running. This is different than both the other FAST Search specific connectors, which run only when you explicitly tell them to do so. Hence, they are not included in the Node Controller.

```
Administrator: Microsoft FAST Search Server 2010 for SharePoint                    _□×
PS C:\FASTSearch\bin> nctrl status
Connecting to Node Controller at localhost:13260..
Issuing 'status' request to Node Controller..

Status for node : asdf

FAST Search       : C:\FASTSE~1
Disk status       : 49% used - 31.03 GB free - 28.97 GB used - 60.00 GB total

Module Name                              Process Name              PID    Status
─────────────                            ─────────────             ───    ──────
Browser Engine                           browserengine                    Running
Config Server                            configserver              3432   Running
Content Distributor                      contentdistributor        3664   Running
Enterprise Crawler                       crawler                   6896   Running
FDMWorker                                fdmworker                 5980   Running
RTS Indexer                              indexer                   3936   Running
Indexing Dispatcher                      indexingdispatcher        5280   Running
Name Service                             nameservice               3248   Running
Document Processor                       procserver_1              8880   Running
Document Processor                       procserver_2              7128   Running
Document Processor                       procserver_3              7156   Running
Document Processor                       procserver_4              1296   Running
QRProxy Service                          qrproxy                          Running
QRServer                                 qrserver                  360    Running
SAM Admin                                samadmin                         Running
SAM Worker                               samworker                        Running
RTS Search                               search-1                  4300   Running
Automatic spellcheck tuning              spelltuner                6804   Running
SPRel                                    sprel                     6728   Running
RTS Top Dispatcher                       topfdispatch              4884   Running
WALinkStorerReceiver                     walinkstorerreceiver      6564   Running
WALookupDB                               walookupdb0               6184   Running
WebAnalyzer                              webanalyzer               6636   Running

PS C:\FASTSearch\bin> _
```

FIGURE 7-11 The internal FS4SP processes that relate to the FAST Search Web crawler.

If you're not actively using the crawler, you can stop these processes with a few commands in the form of **nctrl stop [process name]**. Although you can shave off something like 50–200 MB of RAM usage by stopping these processes, this is not recommended for the average user. The three processes at the bottom of Figure 7-11 belong to the Web Analyzer, which—although tightly integrated with the FAST Search Web crawler—is also used for calculating relevance data when crawling SharePoint intranets. See Table 3-1 in Chapter 3 if you're curious about what each process does.

> **More Info** Read more about how the FAST Search Web crawler works internally at *http://technet.microsoft.com/en-us/library/ff383271.aspx*.

Basic operations The main configuration concept in the FAST Search Web crawler is a "collection," which is not to be confused with the index's notion of a content collection. Each crawl collection contains the configuration applicable to the particular collection, such as which start addresses and crawl rules to apply. A typical solution might have crawl collections such as *Extranet* or *Blogs*.

> **Note** Even though a *crawl collection* and a *content collection* are distinctly different concepts, it is the name of the crawl collection that stipulates in which content collection crawled data ends up. As such, there must be an equally named content collection for each of your crawl collections.

To see which crawl collections are defined in your solution, open up an FS4SP shell and peruse the main crawler command-line tool *crawleradmin*. An example invocation is shown in Figure 7-12. As with most FS4SP command-line tools, you can inspect its parameters by using the *--help* switch.

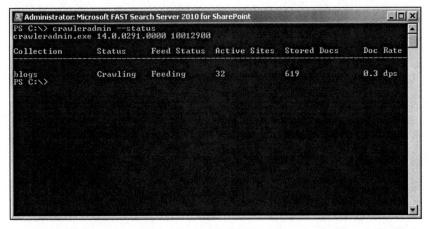

FIGURE 7-12 Output of the command **crawleradmin --status**, showing the crawl collection *blogs*.

From the output in Figure 7-12, you can deduce that the FAST Search Web crawler is currently occupied with the following:

- **Spidering the web**   The collection's Status is *Crawling*. In fact, the crawler is currently active on 32 individual sites.

- **Feeding data into the index**   The collection's Feed Status is *Feeding*.

- **Storing documents**   As indicated under Stored Docs, 619 webpages have been persisted to disk. Note that this does not necessarily mean that 619 pages have been indexed, merely that the crawler has pulled them from the web and put them in what is called the *crawler store* and marked them as due for indexing.

- **Retrieving documents from the Internet**   The speed at which webpages are fetched from the Internet is 0.3 documents per second (DPS). This number should not be confused with how fast FS4SP indexes documents.

You can choose to temporarily disable either *Crawling* or *Feeding*. This can be useful for performance and testing purposes and is also achieved using the *crawleradmin* tool. To disable crawling—that is, to stop the FAST Search Web crawler from spidering the web—use the *--suspendcollection* switch.

```
PS C:\> crawleradmin --suspendcollection blogs
crawleradmin.exe 14.0.0291.0000 10012900

Crawling of 'blogs' suspended

PS C:\> crawleradmin --status
crawleradmin.exe 14.0.0291.0000 10012900
```

Collection	Status	Feed Status	Active Sites	Stored Docs	Doc Rate
blogs	Suspended	Feeding	0	1,156	N/A

Notice how *Status* went from *Crawling* to *Suspended* in the same way *Active Sites* went down to *0*. Issue the following command to start crawling again.

```
crawleradmin --resumecollection blogs
```

Correspondingly, to temporarily disable indexing of the fetched webpages, use the *--suspendfeed* switch.

```
PS C:\> crawleradmin --suspendfeed blogs
crawleradmin.exe 14.0.0291.0000 10012900

Feeding of 'blogs' suspended

PS C:\> crawleradmin --status
crawleradmin.exe 14.0.0291.0000 10012900
```

Collection	Status	Feed Status	Active Sites	Stored Docs	Doc Rate
blogs	Crawling	Queueing	32	1,178	0.0 dps

This time, *Feed Status* was changed into *Queueing*, which means that crawled documents are stacked up in the crawler store but not sent down the indexing chain. Issue the following command to start feeding to the index again.

```
crawleradmin --resumefeed blogs
```

Besides using the *crawleradmin* tool to start and stop individual crawl collections from being crawled and/or sent to the indexer, you can also operate the whole FAST Search Web crawler via the **nctrl** command, for example, by using **nctrl stop crawler** to halt all activity.

 More Info Read more about how to operate the FAST Search Web crawler at *http:// technet.microsoft.com/en-us/library/ff383317.aspx*.

Crawl configuration   The configuration of each crawl collection is defined using an XML configuration file. This file is then loaded into the crawler by using yet another **crawleradmin** command.

```
PS C:\> crawleradmin -f .\crawlerconfig-blogs.xml
crawleradmin.exe 14.0.0291.0000 10012900

Added collection config(s): Scheduled collection for crawling
```

As soon as you run this command, a crawl collection is either created or updated if it already existed. If the XML configuration file defined a new crawl collection, the FAST Search Web crawler immediately starts spidering the web according to the configuration.

Note It is not significant where this XML configuration file is stored on disk. The only thing that matters is that it has been loaded into the crawler. But to save you from maintenance headaches, it is recommended to store these files in a convenient location, for example, in *<FASTSearchFolder>*\etc. However, if you end up losing any such file, you can always get it back using the *G* parameter as shown in the following code, given that it has previously has been loaded into the crawler.

```
PS C:\> crawleradmin -G blogs >> .\crawlerconfig-blogs.xml
```

In the XML configuration file, certain options *must* be defined, for example, the start addresses where the crawler should start looking for content (and links to follow). But most of the configuration options are optional. If you omit any such configuration option, the FAST Search Web crawler will revert to whatever is default for that particular option. All default configuration parameters are listed in the file *<FASTSearchFolder>*\etc\CrawlerGlobalDefaults.xml. This file follows the same structure as any of the XML files you'll define by yourself when configuring your crawl collections. As such, you can refer to this file to understand which options you can work with. Even better, of course, is to refer to the FAST Search Web crawler XML configuration reference at *http://technet.microsoft.com/en-us/library/ff354932.aspx*.

Additionally, Microsoft has included three sample XML configuration files in your FS4SP installation. These files are well documented and include a minimal configuration for each use case. Use them as both references and for templates when configuring your crawl collections:

- **<FASTSearchFolder>\etc\CrawlerConfigTemplate-Simple.xml** Contains an example of a simple web crawl configuration without any advanced settings.

- **<FASTSearchFolder>\etc\CrawlerConfigTemplate-Advanced.xml** Advanced example, where many fine-grained crawler settings are exposed. This configuration also enables very detailed logging of each step in the crawling process. By default, such log files are stored at *<FASTSearchFolder>*\var\log\crawler\[crawl collection].

- **<FASTSearchFolder>\etc\CrawlerConfigTemplate-RSS.xml** Demonstrates how to use one or many RSS feeds to find start addresses where crawling should begin. This can be very useful for keeping crawl times short when targeting pages with aggregated data, such as blogs and news sites.

Use any of these files, in addition to the XML configuration reference, to build your own crawler configuration. Store it wherever you like and then load it into the crawler by using the following command.

```
crawleradmin f [filename]
```

Remember that you must specify a unique name for the crawl collection and match it against an identically named content collection in the index.

The name of the crawl collection is specified in the XML configuration file, as shown in Figure 7-13. Use the *New-FASTSearchContentCollection* cmdlet to create a new content collection that matches the name you choose. If you will define only one crawl collection ever, you can, of course, stick to using the default content collection *sp*.

> **Note** It is recommended that you always keep content indexing with the FAST Search specific connectors in a separate collection. This simplifies maintainability significantly because management of such content would never interfere with the content crawled using the SharePoint built-in connectors.

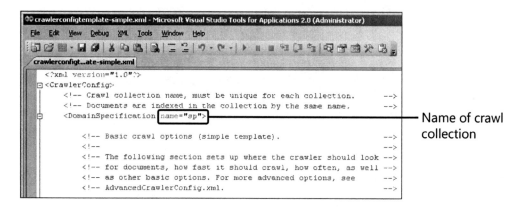

FIGURE 7-13 The name of the crawl collection as defined in the crawl collection's XML configuration file.

> **More Info** Read more about all the configuration options and different functionality of the FAST Search Web crawler at *http://technet.microsoft.com/en-us/library/ff381266.aspx*.

Crawled properties Given the unstructured nature of webpages, the FAST Search Web crawler can make very few assumptions about which crawled properties to emit from each content crawl. All content derived from a webpage is instead populated into the internal crawled property *data*. This property is then analyzed for structure and metadata in the indexing pipeline by the various document processors. The most notable one is the FastHTMLParser processor, which makes sure that basic HTML elements such as the *<title>* tag are extracted and stored in corresponding crawled properties, later to be mapped to managed properties.

You can also write your own Pipeline Extensibility stage that further analyzes the crawled property *data* for content. There is, however, a set of five predefined crawled properties that the FAST Search Web crawler always emits for each crawled webpage. These crawled properties are grouped in the enterprise crawler crawled property category and are listed in Table 7-3.

TABLE 7-3 The FAST Search Web crawler predefined crawled properties

Crawled property	Type	Mapped to managed property	Description
Links	Text	-	All hyperlinks on the webpage.
Crawltime	Datetime	docdatetime, write	Time stamp of when the page was most recently crawled. Only updated if the content of the page was updated since it was last crawled.
Mime	Text	contenttype	The MIME type of the webpage.
http_lastmodified	Text	write	The Last-Modified HTTP header.
Size	Integer	size	The size in bytes of the webpage.

When RSS feeds are crawled, the list of predefined crawled properties becomes a bit longer. This is because RSS feeds, by definition, are more structured than regular webpages. The complete listing is available at *http://technet.microsoft.com/en-us/library/ff383266.aspx*.

FAST Search Database Connector

The FAST Search database connector is built for indexing arbitrary database content. People with experience in earlier versions of FAST technology know it as the *JDBC Connector*, which indicates that the connector can crawl any source database as long as it can expose its content by using a Java Database Connectivity (JDBC) interface. This is supported by the vast majority of databases, including Microsoft SQL Server, MySQL, Oracle, and PostgreSQL.

Note Because the FAST Search database connector is using the JDBC standard to communicate with databases, a Java Runtime Environment (JRE) is required to run the connector. The connector itself is preinstalled with FS4SP, but you must manually install a 32-bit JRE with at least version 1.6 in order to run it. See the installation notes at *http://technet.microsoft.com/en-us/library/ff381259.aspx*.

Just like the other FAST Search specific connectors, the FAST Search database connector is configured using XML files and managed from the command line. But unlike the FAST Search Web crawler, there is no built-in scheduler in the FAST Search database connector. This means that whenever you want to crawl a database, you must invoke the connector yourself, either manually or by having an external scheduler—for example, the Task Scheduler built into Windows—do it for you.

The most central concept of the FAST Search database connector is the SQL statement you define for fetching content from the database. In addition to this statement, you can define other statements to be executed before and after the crawling. This means that you can actually modify and work with the data in the database, as well as fetch the content you like. The connector can also calculate hash sums over database rows, which is useful for doing automatic incremental crawling.

More Info Read more about the FAST Search database connector at *http://technet.microsoft.com/en-us/library/ff383279.aspx.*

Basic operations As mentioned earlier, there is no built-in scheduler in the FAST Search database connector. Instead, it's invoked by running the following script along with the appropriate set of parameters and—most importantly—an XML configuration file.

```
<FASTSearchFolder>\bin\jdbcconnector.bat
```

Given that you already have an XML configuration file, you initiate a database crawl by running the following command in an FS4SP shell.

```
jdbcconnector.bat start -f <XML configuration file>
```

As opposed to the FAST Search Web crawler, there is no such thing as loading the configuration into the connector. The configuration file is used merely for the particular invocation it is currently running.

Crawl configuration A typical configuration tells the FAST Search database connector to connect to a database, run a simple *SELECT* statement, and convert each database row into a content item that is sent to the indexer for further processing. There are, however, more advanced possibilities.

Microsoft has included the XML configuration template file *<FASTSearchFolder>\etc\jdbctemplate.xml*. It is well documented and describes most of the available configuration possibilities. Use this file as a template when defining your own configurations. Make sure that you do not overwrite it! The complete XML configuration reference is available at *http://technet.microsoft.com/en-us/library/ff354942.aspx.*

An important configuration parameter is the *JDBCURL*, which defines how the FAST Search database connector connects to your database. Exactly what this connection string looks like depends on the database you're connecting to. To verify that the connection string works as intended, you can use the *testconnections* parameter to tell the connector to try to initiate a connection to both the source system (your database) and the destination (the local FS4SP installation).

```
jdbcconnector.bat testconnections -f <XML configuration file>
```

When you use this command, nothing is fetched from the database and, consequently, nothing is sent to the FS4SP indexer.

 Note Depending on which database you're connecting to, you might need to download the correct JDBC driver from the database vendor's webpage. Such drivers come in the Java Archive format (.jar), and you place them in the *<FASTSearchFolder>\lib* folder.

Crawled properties   Databases can contain arbitrary content, and the FAST Search database connector makes no assumptions about their content. Instead, each column returned from the *SELECT* statement used for content fetching is made available to FS4SP as a crawled property. All crawled properties extracted from the database are stored in the crawled property group *jdbc*.

You can choose to specify a statement on the form *SELECT* * to return all columns from the particular statement as crawled properties. You can also hardcode which columns you want to have returned, and you can rename columns in the *SELECT* statement to best fit your index. How you do this depends on which database you're crawling but typically takes the following form.

```
SELECT column_name AS new_column_name
```

> **Note**   When renaming columns, remember that FS4SP is case sensitive. It is recommended to use all lowercase names to avoid potential problems.

FAST Search Lotus Notes Connector

The FAST Search Lotus Notes connector makes it possible to index data stored in Lotus Notes content sources. The entire Lotus Notes security model is supported, including roles. Additionally, the connector can index Lotus Notes databases as attachments. These two features alone make the FAST Search Lotus Notes connector superior to the SharePoint built-in Lotus Notes indexing connector described earlier in this chapter in the section "Crawling Content by Using the SharePoint Built-in Connectors."

The FAST Search Lotus Notes connector has two connectors inside of it: a user directory connector and a content connector. Just as with the two other FAST Search specific connectors, XML configuration files are used to configure the FAST Search Lotus Notes connector.

> **Note**   Although the connector is installed and available in a plain FS4SP installation, you have to manually install a 32-bit JRE with at least version 1.6 in order to run it. In addition, you must install Lotus Notes Client 6.5.6. You also need to configure a special user in the Domino domain that the connector will use for content access. See *http://technet.microsoft.com/en-us/library/ff381256.aspx* for instructions on this.

Basic operations   The FAST Search Lotus Notes connector is operated in a very similar manner as the FAST Search database connector. The exception is that you'll need to run and potentially schedule two tools. Both of these tools have their own XML configuration file and are executed as shown in the following code.

```
# Run the content connector
lotusnotesconnector.bat start -f <content connector XML configuration file>

# Run the user directory connector
lotusnotessecurity.bat start -f <user directory connector XML configuration file>
```

As with the FAST Search database connector, these two scripts also have a *testconnections* option. For example, run the following to test connectivity by using the content connector.

```
lotusnotesconnector.bat testconnections -f <content connector XML configuration file>
```

> **More Info** Read more about how to operate the Lotus Notes content connector at *http://technet.microsoft.com/en-us/library/ff383312.aspx* and how to operate the Lotus Notes user directory connector at *http://technet.microsoft.com/en-us/library/ff383285.aspx*.

Crawl configuration Microsoft has included two template files to be used when creating XML configuration files for the FAST Search Lotus Notes connector. These are:

- ***<FASTSearchFolder>\etc\lotusnotestemplate.xml*** Contains a boilerplate configuration for the content connector part of the FAST Search Lotus Notes connector. The full XML reference is located at *http://technet.microsoft.com/en-us/library/ff383273.aspx*.

- ***<FASTSearchFolder>\etc\lotusnotessecuritytemplate.xml*** Contains a boilerplate configuration for the user directory connector part of the FAST Search Lotus Notes connector. The full XML reference is located at *http://technet.microsoft.com/en-us/library/ff381268.aspx*.

In addition to these template files, you can go to the following two websites for guidance about how to configure each part of the FAST Search Lotus Notes connector: *http://technet.microsoft.com/en-us/library/ff383273.aspx* and *http://technet.microsoft.com/en-us/library/ff381268.aspx*.

Crawled properties Each content item emitted from the FAST Search Lotus Notes connector—more specifically, the content connector part of it—is populated with a fairly large set of crawled properties. These are all listed in the crawled property category called *Lotus Notes* and described in detail at *http://technet.microsoft.com/en-us/library/ff383270.aspx*.

Choosing a Connector

Many indexing connectors are available in FS4SP, and it is often not immediately obvious which one to use. The choice of indexing connector is influenced by such things as what kind of content you want to crawl, the complexity of your particular source system deployment, and various preferences or particular requirements in your organization.

Most content can be crawled using the indexing connectors available in SharePoint through the FAST Content SSA. Given that these connectors are flexible, scalable, and easy to administer through the SharePoint Central Administration, it is recommended to always consider using these connectors before venturing into other options. However, you can use the flowchart shown in Figure 7-14 as guidance when deciding which connector to choose. Understand that the decision points identified in the flowchart do not necessarily paint the full picture but should merely be used as indications of their use cases.

In addition to using the flowchart, go to *http://technet.microsoft.com/en-us/library/ff383278.aspx* for additional best practices.

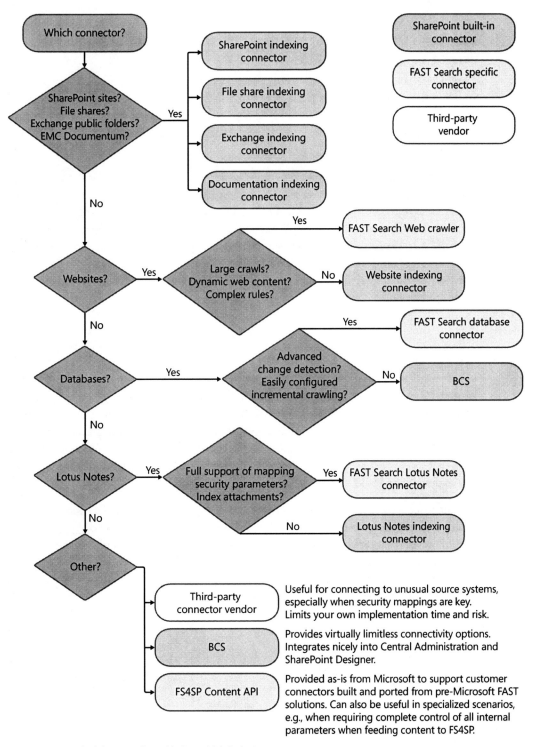

FIGURE 7-14 A decision tree for selecting which indexing connector to use.

Developing a Custom Connector vs. Purchasing from a Connector Vendor

If your FS4SP solution grows in your organization, you might encounter specialized source systems that FS4SP can't index out of the box. If so, the first thing to consider is whether you can use BCS to connect to the source system. It might also be possible to use another crawler, such as any of the web crawlers or the FAST Search database connector, to get hold of the source system's content.

But it might also be tempting to develop your own connector, either by writing a custom indexing connector for SharePoint or even by writing a custom connector that uses the Content API for FS4SP. But before doing so, think long and hard about purchasing a prebuilt connector from a third-party connector vendor. Writing connectors is a lot harder than it sounds. Just mapping security users, security roles, and security groups can be a tremendous challenge. The time and cost of your own implementation might very well go above and beyond the license cost of a prebuilt connector. In addition, you would also benefit from a support agreement and future updates to the connector.

Item Processing

A schematic overview of the content flow from the source system all the way to when content is indexed and made searchable is outlined in Figure 7-1. The section "Crawling Source Systems" earlier in this chapter addressed the far-left part of this content flow; the section explained which connectors are available in FS4SP and how they connect with the different source systems. This section starts where the earlier section left off—that is, when a connector has extracted an item from a source system and is ready to send it into FS4SP.

For an individual content item, the connector's job is done when the item has been extracted from the source system and has been sent off to the FS4SP process content distributor. This process is the gateway for an item into the indexing pipeline. It is responsible for routing items to machines in your farm where document processors are running. In turn, these modules are responsible for pumping items through the indexing pipeline, executing each processor stage on the item's data as the item progresses through the pipeline. The whole process is outlined in Figure 7-15.

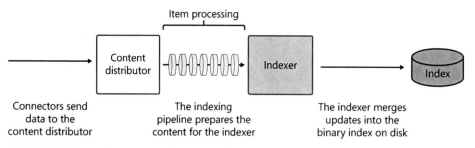

FIGURE 7-15 Schematic overview of item processing.

Note When you first installed your FAST Content SSA, you manually added the service location to the content distributor. Without that reference, the SSA wouldn't be able to send data into the index. In the same way, all FAST Search specific connectors contain an internal reference to the service location(s) of the content distributor. If your farm contains multiple content distributors, you add a semicolon-separated list with all the service locations, as exemplified in Figure 7-16. Multiple content distributors are used to achieve fault tolerance. Having multiple content distributors on the farm can also increase indexing performance, although the content distributor rarely becomes a bottleneck; its job is merely to forward items to the indexing pipeline without doing any additional computing.

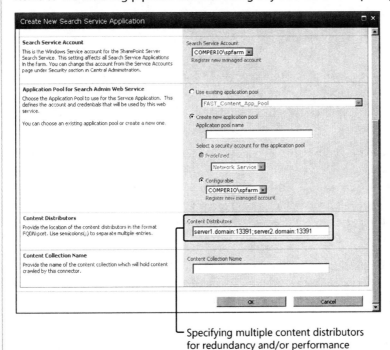

Specifying multiple content distributors
for redundancy and/or performance

FIGURE 7-16 The FAST Content SSA is configured with references to the content distributor(s) during installation.

Understanding the Indexing Pipeline

In FS4SP, the indexing pipeline is the very bricks and mortar of item processing. Each item that a connector submits for indexing passes through the indexing pipeline, in which a predefined set of modules manipulates the items one by one. At the end of this, the FIXML needed for indexing has been produced and is handed over to the indexer.

More Info Read more about FIXML in Chapter 2 in the section "Crawling and Indexing." All FIXML produced by the indexing pipeline is stored on the local server it was created on, in the folder *<FASTSearchFolder>*\data\data_fixml. For debugging purposes, it might be useful to inspect these files. Because it's not obvious which FIXML file corresponds to a certain item, Microsoft has published a helpful tool for finding the FIXML for a certain item on the TechNet Script Repository at *http://gallery.technet.microsoft.com/scriptcenter/14105abb-29da-43fd-90f4-ac12f1a0233a*.

Typical data manipulation happening in the indexing pipeline is property extraction, data mapping, language and format detection, linguistic processing (for example, lemmatization and synonym expansion), and content filtering.

More Info Read more about these item processing concepts in Chapter 1, "Introduction to FAST Search Server 2010 for SharePoint," in the section "Item Processing." See Chapter 5, "Operations," for specifics about how to monitor and debug the indexing pipeline.

The modules in the indexing pipeline that handle all this processing are called *processors* or *stages*. These modules are defined in the XML configuration file *<FASTSearchFolder>*\etc\PipelineConfig.xml. This file must never be edited except for testing or debugging purposes, but it is helpful to know about its existence. It starts off with a long list of *<processor>* elements, in which each processor, or *stage*, is defined. The actual indexing pipeline—that is, the ordered sequence of processors—is defined at the bottom of this file.

A screenshot of how the indexing pipeline definition looks is shown in Figure 7-17. The *Office14 (webcluster)* pipeline is the default and is used for all content that is indexed in FS4SP. Note that not all processors are shown in the figure—there are about 80 processors in total.

The FS4SP processes that run items through the indexing pipeline are the document processors. These processes are responsible for loading the indexing pipeline and its individual processors into memory and then routing content items through them. As described in Chapter 5, you can add more processing power by multiplying and distributing them to different servers in your farm.

Note As with anyone who has experience with the FAST-technology that was available pre-Microsoft can tell you, the processors defined in *PipelineConfig.xml* are written in Python. As such, the compiled code for all modules reside in *<FASTSearchFolder>*\lib\python2.5\processors. It is absolutely possible to inject your own Python code, put the code in this location, and update *PipelineConfig.xml* to include this code during item processing. If you're in the process of migrating your solution to FS4SP from, for example, FAST ESP, it might even be worth considering to port over any custom Python pipeline code you've previously invested heavily in. But know that this is unsupported and that these changes might break with future updates of FS4SP.

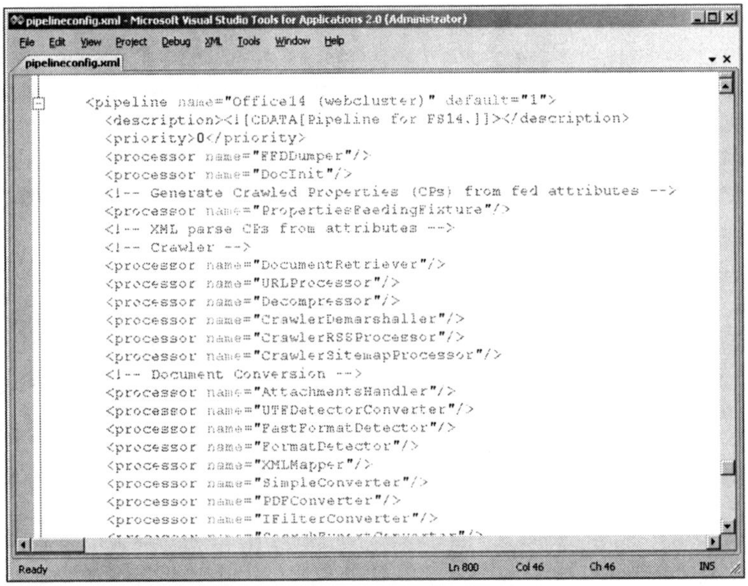

FIGURE 7-17 Definition of the default Office14 (webcluster) indexing pipeline in *<FASTSearchFolder>\etc\ PipelineConfig.xml*.

Without deviating from the supported methodologies, item processing can be customized either by using the Optional Item Processing stages or by developing and integrating your own External Item Processing components. The combined forces of these two concepts provide great flexibility and extensibility of your solution's item processing. The following two sections explore these two concepts.

Optional Item Processing

The Optional Item Processing stages represent distinct functionality that has shown to be useful in Enterprise Search solutions but not worthy to be included by default. By leaving these stages as optional while allowing you to modify their behavior if you choose to enable them, FS4SP gives you a flexible platform for implementing a search solution that fits your organization's requirements.

The components of the Optional Item Processing toolbox contain functionality for:

- Working with property extraction, either using the built-in extractors or by building upon your own custom-built extractors.

- Mapping XML content into managed properties.

- Preventing pornographic content from showing up in the search results.

- Enabling additional item processing debugging.

- Enabling extended metadata extraction on Microsoft Word and Microsoft PowerPoint documents.

- Enabling additional document conversion.

All these components are enabled (or disabled) by editing the main configuration file *Optional-Processing.xml*, although some components need additional configuration. They all share one requirement: All items in the index that relate to the perceived result of the component must be reindexed. If this comes as a surprise, remember that the very purpose of Optional Item Processing is to modify how items are processed as they make their way into the index. As such, all relevant items need to run through the indexing pipeline after every change to the Optional Item Processing components.

Note All Optional Item Processing stages defined in *OptionalProcessing.xml* translate into low-level processors defined in the indexing pipeline's internal configuration file (*PipelineConfig.xml*). As such, it's possible to achieve similar results by modifying *PipelineConfig.xml* instead of *OptionalProcessing.xml*. Doing so is not supported and will make your solution susceptible to risk when applying service packs and cumulative updates to FS4SP.

The following sections go into depth on each of the Optional Item Processing components. The sections are ordered so that they mimic how each component is presented in *OptionalProcessing.xml* as well as in the reference literature on TechNet, hopefully making this somewhat hard-to-navigate area easy to understand. But before diving into each component, a brief explanation of how to edit *OptionalProcessing.xml* is in order.

More Info Make sure to also read the official reference material about how to configure Optional Item Processing at *http://msdn.microsoft.com/en-us/library/ff795826.aspx*.

The *OptionalProcessing.xml* Configuration File

The Optional Item Processing components are enabled or disabled in the configuration file *<FASTSearchFolder>\etc\config_data\DocumentProcessor\OptionalProcessing.xml*. In a multi-server farm, this file exists on the FS4SP administration server. There's no need to manually distribute this file onto other servers in the farm.

Note Files that are stored underneath *<FASTSearchFolder>*\etc\config_data are loaded into the *configserver* process and don't need to be distributed manually to other servers in your farm. FS4SP processes needing any of these files will make internal service calls to the *configserver* asking for the appropriate files.

The syntax of *OptionalProcessing.xml*, which is very straight forward, is shown in the following code. A *<processor>* tag represents functionality in the indexing pipeline, which can be turned on and off by setting the attribute *active* to either *yes* or *no*. Note that it is not supported to add or delete any lines from this file unless documentation from Microsoft explicitly tells you to do so.

```
<optionalprocessing>
  <processor name="personnameextraction" active="yes" />
  <processor name="XMLMapper" active="no" />
  <processor name="OffensiveContentFilter" active="yes" />
  ...
</optionalprocessing>
```

After editing this file, you'll have to do two things in order for your changes to go into effect:

1. In an FS4SP shell, issue the command **psctrl reset**. This tells the indexing pipeline to reload its configuration, which is necessary to have future item processing reflect your changes. Running this command should produce output similar to what's shown in Figure 7-18.

FIGURE 7-18 Running **psctrl reset**—that is, reinitializing each document processor in your farm.

In detail, running this command tells each document processor in your farm to reinitialize each processor in the indexing pipeline, hence picking up the changes you just made to *OptionalProcessing.xml*. The same effect could be achieved by manually restarting each document processor by using *nctrl restart procserver_1 etc.*

 More Info The **psctrl** command is used to control your document processors. The tool can be run from any server in your FS4SP farm, even those without any document processors. Read more about what you can do with **psctrl** in Chapter 5 or at *http://technet.microsoft.com/en-us/library/ee943506.aspx*.

2. Reindex all content that is relevant for the component you just activated. For example, say you activated Offensive Content Filtering and you know that a certain content source is especially prone to contain content unsuitable for minors. Then you should be sure to recrawl that content source. Of course, to be 100 percent certain your index is now free of inappropriate content, you need to recrawl the whole index.

What Happens If Your Edit Is Invalid?

If you happen to introduce an error to *OptionalProcessing.xml*, you would typically not notice it until you start indexing content, and perhaps not even at that point. The document processors in your farm simply skip the Optional Item Processing stages and let your item pass through the pipeline without being affected. This might lead to a lot of wasted time, especially if your index is large and you immediately start a full recrawl of all your content after issuing the **psctrl reset** command.

To avoid such problems, it's a good idea to verify in the document processors' log files that your new configuration was picked up correctly. The log file for each document processor is located at *<FASTSearchFolder>*\var\log\procserver. If something went wrong, you would see log errors indicating that the XML parsing of the file failed, as shown in Figure 7-19.

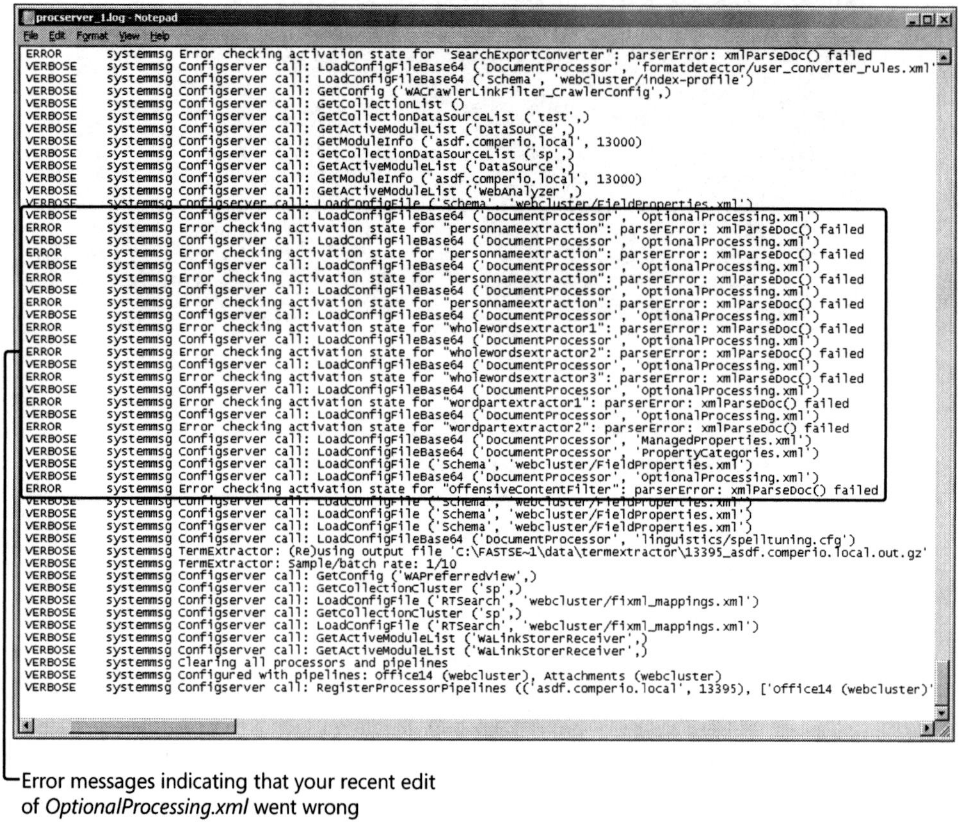

Error messages indicating that your recent edit
of *OptionalProcessing.xml* went wrong

FIGURE 7-19 Error messages in the document processor logs, indicating that *OptionalProcessing.xml* is invalid.

Built-in Property Extraction

Property extraction, or what's sometimes referred to as *entity extraction*, is one of the most important and potentially useful features of item processing in FS4SP. It allows the textual content of your source documents to be analyzed for specific entities or concepts. These entities are pulled out from unstructured content (typically, but structured data works just as well) and put into structured properties that FS4SP later can use to enrich the search user experience. Examples of such enrichments could be building a refiner for the extracted property, allowing users to sort the result set on the property, or incorporating the property's value in a relevance model.

The FS4SP indexing pipeline has three built-in property extractors: a person name extractor, a location extractor, and a company name extractor. These are based on generic dictionaries shipped with FS4SP and designed to work with FS4SP supported languages. In a default FAST Search Center, after crawling the local SharePoint farm, these property extractors show up as refiners, as shown in Figure 7-20. However, note that not all refiners are because of property extraction. Many refiners are also put together right away from structured content, for example, by using what is in the Managed Metadata Service.

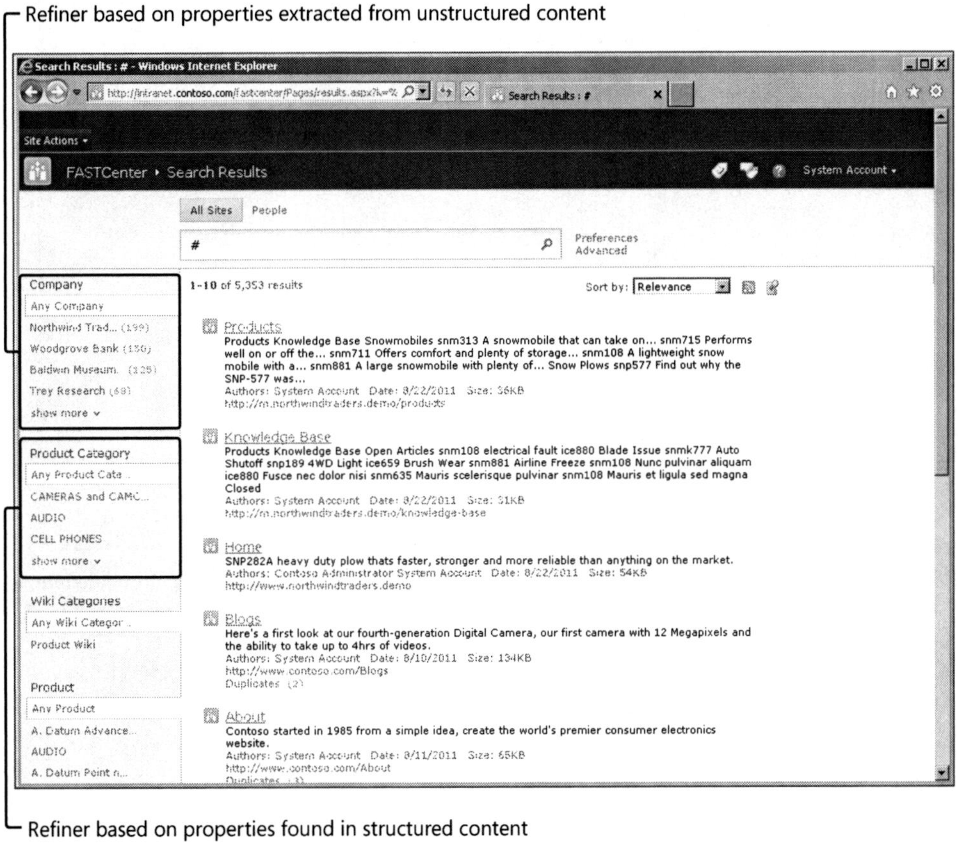

Refiner based on properties extracted from unstructured content

Refiner based on properties found in structured content

FIGURE 7-20 A company name refiner, which, by default, is using data from the built-in company name extractor.

More Info For a list of supported languages for the three built-in extractors, visit *http://msdn.microsoft.com/en-us/library/ff795826.aspx#optional-item-proc-property.*

You can add your own inclusion or exclusion list to each of the three built-in extractors. If you're working with a small set of custom entries, which is easy to maintain manually, Central Administration supports doing this on a term-by-term basis, as shown in Figure 7-21. To find this page in SharePoint, go to your FAST Query SSA, click FAST Search Administration, and then click Managed Property Extraction. Be sure to reindex any content that you want to reflect the new white or blacklisted term when you're finished.

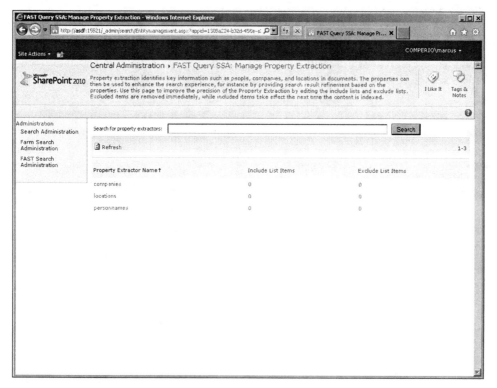

FIGURE 7-21 Working with inclusion and exclusion lists for the built-in property extractors through Central Administration.

If you're working with larger quantities of terms, perhaps person names extracted from your organization's customer relationship management (CRM) system, you can also use Windows PowerShell to import this data into the inclusion or exclusion lists. There is, unfortunately, no prebuilt FS4SP cmdlet to do this, so the process is fairly involved. Use the following steps as guidance:

1. Open an FS4P shell.

2. Acquire a reference to the *EntityExtractor* namespace.

```
$context = New-Object
        -TypeName Microsoft.SharePoint.Search.Extended.Administration.
                EntityExtractorContext
```

The *$context variable* contains the property *TermEntityExtractors*. Inspecting this variable shows a preview of which terms are included and/or excluded in each built-in property extractor so far.

```
PS C:\FASTSearch\bin> $context.TermEntityExtractors
```

Name	Exclusions	Inclusions	Language
companies	{}	{Microsoft, Comp...	ANY
locations	{Siberia}	{}	ANY
personnames	{}	{}	ANY

3. Acquire a reference to one of the extractors. Either loop over the *$context.TermEntityExtractors* collection or isolate one of the extractors by using the following code.

```
$extractor = $context.TermEntityExtractors | Where-Object -FilterScript {$_.Name -eq
"companies"}
```

4. Add or remove terms from either the inclusion or the exclusion by working on the properties of the *$extractor* variable.

```
PS C:\FASTSearch\bin> $extractor.Inclusions.Add("term1")
PS C:\FASTSearch\bin> $extractor.Exclusions.Remove("term2")
```

Updates to these variables immediately go into effect. There's no need to reinitialize the indexing pipeline or do anything in particular. Of course, you will need to reindex any related content that you want to reflect the changes you just made.

> **More Info** For additional reference material about how to work with the built-in property extractors' inclusion and exclusion lists, go to *http://technet.microsoft.com/en-us/library/ff191250.aspx*.

If Windows PowerShell scripting is not enough, you can, of course, go even further and work on the *EntityExtractorContext* namespace through Microsoft .NET code. This could be particularly useful if you need to push content from a different system into the property extractors right after the content is updated in the source system, or if you want to call out to, say, BCS for fetching the terms. Such code would mimic the previous Windows PowerShell scripting very closely, but be sure to read the *EntityExtractorContext* namespace reference at *http://msdn.microsoft.com/en-us/library/microsoft.sharepoint.search.extended.administration.entityextractorcontext.aspx*.

The following three subsections explore each built-in extractor. The next section, "Custom Property Extraction," goes into detail about how to build your own extractor to fully take advantage of your organization's domain knowledge.

Person names   The person name extractor as defined in *OptionalProcessing.xml* is *not* enabled by default. This might seem surprising because a standard FS4SP Search Center returns an author refiner when showing result sets with SharePoint documents. This data is instead based on the author metadata in the documents stored in SharePoint and do not reflect which person names are mentioned in the actual content of those documents.

To enable the extraction of person names from the textual content of items, edit *OptionalProcessing.xml* so that it matches the following snippet shown. Remember to then run **psctrl reset** in an FS4SP shell and reindex all content sources that need to reflect this change.

```
<optionalprocessing>
  ...
  <processor name="personnameextraction" active="yes" />
  ...
</optionalprocessing>
```

After doing so, and after having reindexed some content, the crawled property *personname (31)* will contain any matching person names. Map this crawled property to a managed property in order to use it for refinement or sorting, or as a component in a relevance model.

Locations   The location extractor looks for geographical locations in the textual content of items passing through the indexing pipeline. This stage is enabled by default and is also not possible to disable through *OptionalProcessing.xml*. As such, it could be argued that this processor is not "optional" at all. Although it's possible to disable it by modifying *PipelineConfig.xml*, the only supported method for not using the extracted geographical locations is to simply not map the crawled property *locations (Text)* to any managed property.

> **Note** Remember to reindex your content if you remove a mapping from a crawled property to a managed property.

Companies   The company name extractor, just like the location extractor, is enabled by default and also not possible to deactivate through *OptionalProcessing.xml*. If company extraction from textual content of your index's item is not relevant for your use case, simply do not map the crawled property *companies (31)* to any managed property.

> **Note** Remember to reindex your content if you remove a mapping from a crawled property to a managed property.

Custom Property Extraction

In addition to the built-in property extractors, you can create custom dictionaries to extract known entities or concepts from the text of an item and map these values to managed properties. In turn, you can use the properties as refiners in your queries to narrow the result set, for building custom sorting, or as components in a relevance model—just as with the output from the built-in property extractors. Custom property extraction is often part of an Enterprise Search solution, which makes the implementation go beyond the standard capabilities and fit your organization better.

Examples of custom dictionaries are product groups, vendor names, project names, office locations, colors, and production facilities. Basically, any entity that has meaning to your organization and can be found within the text of your items (documents, presentations, spreadsheets, and so on) is a candidate for custom property extraction.

 Important The format of the custom property extraction dictionaries changed with Service Pack 1 (SP1). This chapter covers the new format. The previous implementation was limited to five custom dictionaries, but this limitation was removed as of SP1.

Custom property extraction dictionaries are registered in the configuration file *<FASTSearchFolder>\ etc\config_data\DocumentProcessor\CustomPropertyExtractors.xml*. The format of this file is shown in the following code.

```xml
<?xml version="1.0" encoding="UTF-8"?>
<extractors>
  <extractor name="<extractorName>" type="<extractorType>" property="<propertyName>">
    <dictionary name="<dictionaryName>" yield-values="yes|no"/>
  </extractor>
</extractors>
```

In the code, *<extractorName>* is the name you decide for the extractor, *<extractorType>* is the type of extractor as listed in Table 7-4, *<propertyName>* is the name of the crawled property to hold the extracted entity during indexing, and *<dictionaryName>* is the name of your dictionary file excluding file path and file extension.

The *yield-values* option is used to decide whether you want to return the key (matched term) in your crawled property or you want to return another value defined in your dictionary file, typically used for normalizing data. For example, you can match the terms *Microsoft Word* and *Apple Pages*, and receive the output value of *Word Processor* for both of them. For each new custom extractor, you add an *<extractor>* section to the file.

TABLE 7-4 Extractor types

Value	Matching performed by property extractor
WholeWords	Case-sensitive whole word matching
WordParts	Case-sensitive word part matching
Verbatim	Case-insensitive whole word matching
Substring	Case-insensitive word part matching

Note You must create the crawled property before you use the property extractor. The crawled property must have variant type *31 (string)* and property set value *"48385c54-cd-fc-4e84-8117-c95b3cf8911c" (MESG Linguistics)*. You must also map it to a managed property of type *string (type 1)*. How to do this is shown in step 5 of the following procedure "Create a custom property extractor by using Windows PowerShell."

For this example, you create a property extractor to match pure-bred dog names and map the breed name to the size of the dog, which can be used as a refiner.

Note You cannot add custom property extraction dictionaries via SharePoint Central Administration.

Create a custom property extractor by using Windows PowerShell

1. Create an XML file called **dogsize.xml** that contains the following content, and be sure to save it as UTF-8 without a byte-order mark (BOM). You can use most advanced text editors and IDEs to do this, but it's not possible in Notepad.

```
<dictionary>
  <entry key="westie" value="Small" />
  <entry key="german shepherd" value="Big" />
  <entry key="great dane" value="Humongous" />
  <entry key="rotweiler" value="Big" />
  <entry key="chihuahua" value="Small" />
</dictionary>
```

2. On the FS4SP administration server, edit the file *<FASTSearchFolder>\etc\config_data\DocumentProcessor\CustomPropertyExtractors.xml* to register in your custom dictionary by using the following entry. If this is your first custom property extractor, you must create the file first. Use a case-insensitive extractor, and map the value for the matching term by setting *yield-values* to *yes*.

```
<?xml version="1.0" encoding="UTF-8"?>
<extractors>
  <extractor name="dogsize" type="Verbatim" property="mydogsize">
    <dictionary name="dogsize" yield-values="yes"/>
  </extractor>
</extractors>
```

3. Because you used a verbatim matcher that is case-insensitive by design, it is recommended that you make sure the dictionary is normalized. FS4SP includes a handy utility for this very purpose: the *<FASTSearchFolder>\bin\lowercase.exe* command-line tool.

    ```
    lowercase dogsize.xml dogsize_normalized.xml
    ```

4. Upload the custom property extraction dictionary to the FS4SP resource store by using the Windows PowerShell cmdlet *Add-FASTSearchResource*, where *x:\path* is where you created your dictionary file.

    ```
    Add-FASTSearchResource -FilePath x:\path\dogsize_normalized.xml -Path dictionaries\
    matching\dogsize.xml
    ```

5. In order to use the extracted data, you must create a crawled property and map it to a managed property within the index schema, as shown in the following code.

    ```
    $cp = New-FASTSearchMetadataCrawledProperty -Name mydogsize -Propset 48385c54-cdfc-4e84-
    8117-c95b3cf8911c -VariantType 31
    $mp = New-FASTSearchMetadataManagedProperty -Name dogsize -type 1
    $mp.StemmingEnabled=0
    $mp.RefinementEnabled=1
    $mp.MergeCrawledProperties=1
    $mp.Update()
    New-FASTSearchMetadataCrawledPropertyMapping -ManagedProperty $mp -CrawledProperty $cp
    ```

6. Reindex your content and add the *dogsize* refiner to the Refinement Panel in your FAST Search Center.

7. A good way to test your custom property extraction is to use the command-line utility *docpush* (previously described in the section "The docpush command-line tool") to manually send a simple test document for indexing. Verify in your FAST Search Center that the *dogsize* refiner reflects the new custom property extractor.

1. Add a reference to the FS4SP administration resource storage assembly to your project.

   ```
   <FASTSearchFolder>\bin\Microsoft.SharePoint.Search.Extended.Administration.
   ResourceStorage.dll
   ```

 More Info For more information, go to *http://msdn.microsoft.com/en-us/library/ ee572018.aspx.*

2. Add the corresponding namespace.

   ```
   using Microsoft.SharePoint.Search.Extended.Administration.ResourceStorage;
   ```

3. Initialize the connection to FS4SP, and acquire an object reference to the resource store.

   ```
   ResourceStorageContext resourceContext = new ResourceStorageContext();
   ResourceStore resourceStore = resourceContext.ResourceStore;
   ```

4. The upload method of the resource store takes a stream that contains the dictionary in XML format, as shown in step 1 of the previous Windows PowerShell sample. For simplicity, read the file from disk, but see the section "Creating a Custom Property Extractor Dictionary Based on a SharePoint List" in Chapter 9, "Useful Tips and Tricks," for a more extensive sample.

   ```
   using (Stream stream = File.OpenRead(@"C:\temp\dogsize_normalized.xml"))
   {
       resourceContext.ResourceStore.Upload(@"dictionaries\matching\dogsize.xml", stream);
   }
   ```

5. Create the crawled and managed property as described in step 5 of the Windows PowerShell example, or create them via .NET code as explained in Chapter 5 in the procedure "Modify the index topology."

Custom XML Item Processing

A common task for Enterprise Search solutions is to consume data stored in XML, either as files on disk or as returned from a service. If you just crawl the XML without doing any special configuration, you will find that the XML is treated as ordinary text. This is shown in Figure 7-22, in which the configuration file *PipelineConfig.xml* has been crawled.

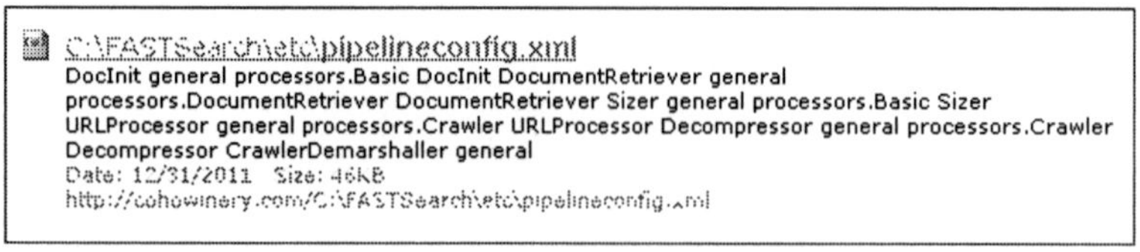

C:\FASTSearch\etc\pipelineconfig.xml
DocInit general processors.Basic DocInit DocumentRetriever general
processors.DocumentRetriever DocumentRetriever Sizer general processors.Basic Sizer
URLProcessor general processors.Crawler URLProcessor Decompressor general processors.Crawler
Decompressor CrawlerDemarshaller general
Date: 12/31/2011 Size: 46kB
http://cohowinery.com/C:\FASTSearch\etc\pipelineconfig.xml

FIGURE 7-22 A crawled XML file without any special configuration for handling the XML structure.

As you see, all XML literals have been stripped off and only attribute and node values are left behind. This makes sense because FS4SP cannot make assumptions about the content of your XML, for example, know how to display it or otherwise use it so that it fits your use case. However, the XML files are probably structured for a reason. Using the Optional Processing component XMLMapper, it's possible to use this structure and make individual nodes and attributes in the XML show up as managed properties in the index. You can then use these properties any way you want, for example, in FQL queries or for customizing the result views in the search result.

To use this functionality, you first have to make sure the indexing pipeline knows it has received XML. If you're using the SharePoint built-in connectors, this generally works without any special functionality. But if you're using the FAST Search database connector or a custom BCS interface, you need to make sure the XML contents of the item ends up in the crawled property *data*.

> **Note** Most, if not all, databases support dynamically renaming columns in the result sets, typically using a statement similar to the following.

```
SELECT some_column_containing_xml AS data FROM the_table
```

The first stop to activate Custom XML item processing is to edit *OptionalProcessing.xml* so that it matches the following snippet shown. You also have to run **psctrl reset** in an FS4SP shell to reinitialize the document processors in your farm. Although there's no harm in doing that right away, you also need to add an additional configuration file containing the actual XML mapping directives, which also require **psctrl reset** before it's picked up.

```
<optionalprocessing>
  ...
  <processor name="XMLMapper" active="yes" />
  ...
</optionalprocessing>
```

You define the file with the XML mapping directives yourself—there's no such file available out of the box. On the FS4SP administration server, create the file (or update it if you've used the functionality before) *<FASTSearchFolder>\etc\config_data\DocumentProcessor\XMLMapper.xml*. Be sure to save this file in UTF-8 without a BOM. (You'll need to use an advanced text editor or an IDE to do this.)

Which parts of the XML content to map to crawled properties is specified in XPath 1.0 syntax, although the XMLMapper component also provides some additional string manipulation functionality. The full reference is available at *http://msdn.microsoft.com/en-us/library/ff795809.aspx*. Also see the example at *http://msdn.microsoft.com/en-us/library/ff795813.aspx#custom-xml-example*.

After you've created the file with your mappings, be sure to run **psctrl reset** in an FS4SP shell and create mappings from the new crawled properties (where the XML data will end up) to managed properties. If you don't create the crawled properties manually using Windows PowerShell, you'll also need to run a single item through the indexing pipeline to make the crawled properties appear.

Warning After you enable the XMLMapper component, FS4SP will try to map all items believed to be XML according to your mapping directives. Unless care is taken to avoid this, items in your index might get associated with erroneous metadata because the configuration may unintentionally match crawled XML items of no interest.

Using the XMLMapper has some shortcomings. You have to store one item per XML file, mapping multiple XML schemas is not easy, and all XML files are parsed, regardless of whether they are of the correct schema. Also, IFilter tries to convert each XML file even though the files are being parsed with the XMLMapper.

If your XML files are stored on a file share, a better solution than using the XMLMapper is to use the Custom XML Indexing Connector sample developed by the SharePoint team, described at *http://blogs.msdn.com/b/sharepointdev/archive/2012/01/25/creating-a-custom-xml-indexing-connector-for-fast-search-server-2010-for-sharepoint.aspx* and downloadable from *http://code.msdn.microsoft.com/windowsdesktop/Create-custom-XML-indexing-8e057de6*.

Offensive Content Filtering

When you enable the Offensive Content Filtering component, the textual content of each item is matched against a set of predefined dictionaries for pornographic terms. The crawled property *Score* in the category *OCF*, is populated with a number that indicates how likely the item is to be offensive. If this number goes beyond the fixed threshold of 30, the item is deemed offensive and is dropped from the indexing process.

Note The Offensive Content Filter inspects only the crawled properties *title*, *body*, and *ocfcontribution*. The first two are typically populated by the connectors running the crawl, whereas *ocfcontribution* is empty by default. As its name indicates, the purpose of *ocfcontribution* is so that you can add additional content for inspection. For information about how to populate *ocfcontribution*, see the section "Preventing an Item from Being Indexed" in Chapter 9.

If an item is dropped because it exceeds the offensive content threshold, the connector in use is informed about this. If you're using any of the SharePoint built-in connectors, this information shows up as an error in the crawl logs in the FAST Content SSA, as shown in Figure 7-23.

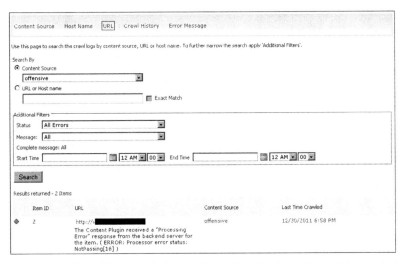

FIGURE 7-23 A crawl log entry indicating that an item has been dropped from indexing because of offensive content.

To enable Offensive Content Filtering, edit *OptionalProcessing.xml* so that it matches the following snippet. Remember to then run **psctrl reset** in an FS4SP shell and reindex all content sources that need to reflect this change.

```
<optionalprocessing>
  ...
  <processor name="OffensiveContentFilter" active="yes" />
  ...
</optionalprocessing>
```

More Info For more details on Offensive Content Filtering, as well as a list of all supported languages, go to *http://msdn.microsoft.com/en-us/library/ff795826.aspx#optional-item-proc-offensive*.

Note There is also one additional use case for the Offensive Content Filtering component: You can use it to prevent certain items from being indexed. See Chapter 9 for an example of how to achieve this. This can be generalized so that you can implement your own business rules for dropping arbitrary documents from the indexing pipeline.

Debugging Item Processing

One of the Optional Item Processing components is the FFDDumper processing stage. This component is different from the others in that it does not produce anything that is useful for improving the search experience. Its sole purpose is show which crawled properties have been collected for a specific item by the connector. This can be particularly useful when setting up new content sources, especially when targeting source systems with dynamic content.

To enable the FFDDumper stage, edit *OptionalProcessing.xml* so that it matches the following snippet. Remember to then run **psctrl reset** in an FS4SP shell. For every item that is indexed after doing so, there will be a log file available in *<FASTSearchFolder>*\data\ffd\ (on the server where the item was processed) describing which crawled properties are associated with the item.

```
<optionalprocessing>
  ...
  <processor name="FFDDumper" active="yes" />
  ...
</optionalprocessing>
```

> **Warning** Don't keep the FFDDumper enabled on a production system where lots of content is being indexed! The produced log files will consume a lot of disk space and also negatively affect indexing latency.

> **More Info** For more details on the FFDDumper stage and item processing logging in general, see the "Item Processing Logging" section in Chapter 5. Also read the FFDDumper reference at *http://msdn.microsoft.com/en-us/library/hh285835.aspx#debug_ffd*.

Extended Metadata Extraction of Word and PowerPoint Documents

The Extended Metadata Extraction component, which is available only in SP1, enables more advanced metadata generation of Word and PowerPoint documents.

Without this component, the properties representing the title and date of such files are based on what's written in the Word or PowerPoint internal metadata. In a perfect world, that metadata would always be correct, but it's not unusual to find that it's instead completely incorrect and doesn't at all reflect what's written on, for example, the title page of the document. This component tries to alleviate this problem by inspecting the actual content of the documents for an alternative title and date.

After deployment of SP1, the Extended Metadata Extraction component is active by default. The managed properties *Title* and *Write* (containing the date) on each processed Word or PowerPoint document then reflect whatever the component could extract from the content of the documents. If the extraction fails, FS4SP falls back on using the document metadata as if the Extended Metadata Extraction component was disabled.

To *disable* the component, edit *OptionalProcessing.xml* so that it matches the following snippet. Remember to then run **psctrl reset** in an FS4SP shell and reindex all content sources that need to reflect this change. However, there should be very little reason to disable this component; disabling it could cause the quality of the metadata in your index to go down.

```
<optionalprocessing>
  ...
  <processor name="MetadataExtraction" active="no" />
  ...
</optionalprocessing>
```

> **More Info** For more details on the extended Metadata Extraction of Word and PowerPoint documents, see *http://msdn.microsoft.com/en-us/library/ff795826.aspx#optional-item-proc-metadata*.

Document Conversion

The very bottom of the *OptionalProcessing.xml* file contains a reference to a processing stage called *SearchExportConverter*. This is the name of the item processor that carries out the additional document conversions made available by enabling the Advanced Filter Pack.

Although it is possible to enable or disable the Advanced Filter Pack by reconfiguring *Optional-Processing.xml*, Microsoft has stipulated that users instead should follow the methodology outlined in Chapter 9; that method involves running a prebuilt installation script containing safeguards that prevent things from going wrong.

> **Note** There's literally no downside to enabling the Advanced Filter Pack; it only adds to the number of supported document formats. Note that document conversion for the standard formats is based on IFilters, and the Advanced Filter Pack uses a special library called upon from the item processing stage.

Integrating an External Item Processing Component

In an advanced Enterprise Solution, you might encounter scenarios in which the built-in features of the indexing pipeline or the additional possibilities of the Optional Item Processing components are not enough to satisfy your business requirements. Perhaps you need to manipulate items in a very specialized manner or there's a need to enrich items by using content from another source system. With FS4SP, you can solve this problem by integrating your own custom code into the indexing pipeline through the concept of External Item Processing components.

An External Item Processing component is essentially a filter—an executable that takes as input a set of crawled properties from the item and emits a new set of crawled properties that reflect whatever business logic was implemented in the component. Besides this code being referred to as an *External Item Processing component*, it is also called *Pipeline Extensibility* and sometimes *Customer Extensibility*. Either way, it's a method for enriching the FS4SP indexing pipeline with additional functionality.

The default indexing pipeline contains a special processor called *CustomerExtensibility*. This processor is responsible for invoking any potential External Item Processing components defined in your solution. During configuration, you specify which crawled properties should be sent into the component and which crawled properties are returned from it. For each item flowing through the pipeline, the CustomerExtensibility processor extracts the subset of crawled properties you defined and serializes them to an XML document that is then passed into the custom component. Output from the component is handled in the same manner. As such, your custom components will all read as input in an XML file and are expected to produce an XML file as output.

A schematic overview of the content flow through the indexing pipeline when External Item Processing components are in use is shown in Figure 7-24. The figure also shows the PropertiesMapper processor, which, although not directly related to the External Item Processor, is a very important step in the process. This is where crawled properties are mapped into proper managed properties and your custom-crawled properties are of no value unless you make them available as managed properties.

Custom code is executed in an internal sandbox, which enforces limits on processing time, memory consumption, and the number of CPU threads. Additionally, the custom code has only read/write access to publicly available files—more specifically, to the %USERPROFILE%\AppData\LocalLow folder. These limitations are put in place in order to guarantee the safety and sanity of the FS4SP server that the code runs on. The custom code should be concerned only with modifying the item that is passing through it.

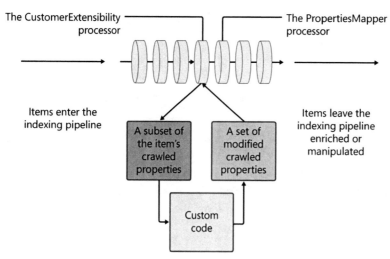

FIGURE 7-24 The content flow through the indexing pipeline when an External Item Processing component is in use.

The following sections describe how to configure the indexing pipeline to route items through your own External Item Processing component, give you guidelines on writing the code itself, and show you how to debug a component in a test FS4SP deployment.

> **More Info** See the technical reference about how to integrate an External Item Processing component at *http://msdn.microsoft.com/en-us/library/ff795801.aspx*.

Configuration

You define any External Item Processing components in the file named *<FASTSearchFolder>\etc\PipelineExtensibility.xml* file on the server running the document processor component. In other words, if you have distributed document processors across an FS4SP farm, you have to manually synchronize this file over the corresponding servers. A good rule of thumb is to have this file on all FS4SP servers at all times.

> **Warning** Because this file is not required by FS4SP, it is not included in the backup scripts that come with FS4SP. You must backup/restore this file manually! See the section "Backup and Recovery" in Chapter 5 for general backup instructions.

A template for *PipelineExtensibility.xml* comes with your FS4SP installation. You might want to consider keeping this section around as a reference and just add your own segments below it. This default content is shown in the following excerpt. Each *<Run>...</Run>* section defines a single External Item Processing component; you can define as many components as you like. They are executed in sequence, from top to bottom.

```
<PipelineExtensibility>
    <!--
    <Run command="binary.exe %(input)s %(output)s">
        <Input>
            <CrawledProperty propertySet="" varType="" propertyId=""/>
            <CrawledProperty propertySet="" varType="" propertyName=""/>
            <CrawledProperty propertySet="" varType="" propertyName=""/>
        </Input>
        <Output>
            <CrawledProperty propertySet="" varType="" propertyName=""/>
            <CrawledProperty propertySet="" varType="" propertyName="" defaultValue=""/>
        </Output>
    </Run>
    -->
</PipelineExtensibility>
```

In this configuration excerpt, *binary.exe* is your External Item Processing component. You can call it whatever you like and put it wherever you like. Just make sure the file is executable and in a path accessible by FS4SP. Also note that this file, just like *PipelineExtensibility.xml* itself, must be put on each server hosting the document processor component.

Note Because the External Item Processing component is nothing else than an ordinary executable file, there are no restrictions on which programming languages you can use to build it. You can, of course, also reuse any existing tool as long as the tool's input and output interfaces allow this.

The somewhat-cryptic strings *%(input)s* and *%(output)s* are placeholders for the temporary files that will contain the input and output XML—that is, the actual data of the crawled properties.

Tip An external item processor does not have to have both an input and output parameter. Using only an input can be useful if you are sending data to an external system for each item processed, and using only an output parameter is useful if you want to assign certain metadata to all items being processed. Omitting both input and output is allowed but not very useful.

Crawled properties are defined using a property set, a variant type, and a property ID (or a property name if available for the particular crawled property), just as when you're referencing crawled properties by using the Windows PowerShell cmdlets. Note that you can also specify a default value for the output crawled properties. This value is used as fallback if your custom component does not emit the crawled property itself. The full reference for *PipelineExtensibilty.xml* is available at *http://msdn.microsoft.com/en-us/library/ff795825.aspx*.

After editing the *PipelineExtensibilty.xml* file, you must issue **psctrl reset** in order for the indexing pipeline to pick up the new configuration. Make sure that your executable is available at this point—the indexing pipeline starts to use it as soon as the next item passes through the system.

Developing an External Item Processing Component

As previously mentioned, you can choose to implement an External Item Processing component in your preferred programming language as long as it can generate an executable file and run on your FS4SP servers.

FS4SP requires that the input file that your component reads and the output file it emits must follow the XML standard outlined at *http://msdn.microsoft.com/en-us/library/ff795804.aspx*. Because both files are syntactically identical, it's possible to chain together several External Item Processing components as mentioned in the previous section.

Warning If you do end up writing several External Item Processing components and are chaining them together in *PipelineConfig.xml*, you may consider instead putting all code in one component. This saves time by avoiding launching additional processes and when reading and writing the input and output XML files. Even a small performance overhead can drastically increase the total indexing time if your solution is crawling many items. You may also want to consider calling out to a web service in your custom component and putting any heavy operations running on a completely different machine. This is especially useful if launching your executable is slow because of loading large binaries at startup. Either way, you don't want your custom component to become a bottleneck in an otherwise properly scaled FS4SP solution.

The syntax of the input and output XML files are exemplified in the following code. In this example, an input file with a crawled property *full name* is sent in to the custom component, which then splits this component into a *surname* and a *family name*, and finally emits these two entities as distinct crawled properties.

```
Input XML:

<Document>
  <CrawledProperty propertySet="f29f85e0-4ff9-1068-ab91-08002b27b3d9" varType="31"
propertyId="6">
    McCormack, Michael
  </CrawledProperty>
</Document>

Output XML:

<Document>
  <CrawledProperty propertySet="f29f85e0-4ff9-1068-ab91-08002b27b3d9" varType="31"
propertyId="7">
    Michael
  </CrawledProperty>
  <CrawledProperty propertySet="f29f85e0-4ff9-1068-ab91-08002b27b3d9" varType="31"
propertyId="8">
    McCormack
  </CrawledProperty>
</Document>
```

The following code contains boilerplate code for building an External Item Processing component in Microsoft Visual C#. Refer to this code only as an example of what you need to do—that is, reading the input XML file, working on the content that the crawled properties contained, and, finally, serializing these crawled properties (or new ones) to the output XML file.

```csharp
using System;
using System.Collections.Generic;
using System.Linq;
using System.Xml.Linq;
using System.Text;

namespace PipelineExtensibility
{
    class ProcessorTemplate
    {
        static void Main(string[] args)
        {
            // Read the input XML file that was provided by FS4SP through %(input)s
            XDocument input = XDocument.Load(args[0]);

            // Fetch the crawled properties from the input file, e.g., using
            var inputCPs = input.Descendants("CrawledProperty");

            //
            // Insert code for working on the crawled properties data here
            //

            // Create an output XML file, the file must _at least_ contain
            // <Document></Document>
            XElement output = new XElement("Document");

            // Add crawled properties to the output file
            // The template below adds a crawled property with mock values to
            // the output document
            output.Add(
                new XElement("CrawledProperty",
                    new XAttribute("propertySet", new Guid("<GUID for the property set>")),
                    new XAttribute("propertyName", "<Name of the property>"),
                    new XAttribute("varType", <The property's variant type, e.g. 31>),
                        "Some contents")
            );


            // Save the output XML where FS4SP designated through %(output)s
            output.Save(args[1]);
        }
    }
}
```

Remember to test your code properly before you deploy it to your FS4SP solution. Using unit tests is, of course, advisable, but you should also test the component on the servers in your farm by invoking the component manually from a command line. Be sure to use real-world content for the crawled properties to reflect a live item processing session as closely as possible.

> **More Info** See Chapter 9 for instructions about how to debug an External Item Processing component that is running in a live FS4SP deployment.

Logging Problems

If your custom component emits a status code other than 0, the indexing pipeline will send whatever has been printed to either Standard Output or Standard Error to the crawl log in the FAST Content SSA. This is useful when trapping exceptions. An example of how to do this is shown in the following code.

```
try
{
// Insert custom code here, throwing exception if something goes wrong
}
catch (Exception e)
{
    // This will end up in the crawl log, since exit code != 0
    Console.WriteLine("Failed: " + e.Message + "/" + e.StackTrace);
    return 1;
}
return 0;
```

The Mythical PEWS Framework

Microsoft Consulting Services (MCS) has developed a framework for item processing called *Pipeline Extensibility Web Services* (PEWS). If you're working on an FS4SP solution that was initially set up by MCS, you might encounter this framework. It is provided as-is by the MCS department and is not generally available, nor do any problems encountered from using this framework qualify for support through standard support agreements.

The PEWS framework is targeted for FS4SP customers with advanced item processing requirements and who are limited by the possibilities in FS4SP. More specifically, PEWS makes it possible to avoid the sandbox that custom components otherwise are executed in. It does this by using the standard External Item Processing framework, in which a special component calls out to a web service hosted by PEWS. Behind the curtains of this web service, you can define additional indexing pipelines and use another set of processing stages that come with PEWS. You can also write your own custom components and put those into the PEWS framework.

Conclusion

FS4SP uses connector functionality from two separate worlds: the connector framework available through SharePoint and the more-complex FAST Search specific connectors. In the vast majority of use cases, you're well off with the SharePoint built-in connectors, but a few specialized scenarios warrant looking into the FAST Search specific connectors instead. Either way, in FS4SP, you're armed with a large set of connectors and should rarely have to resort to implementing your own connector code—which is, of course, entirely possible.

It's impossible to build a good search user experience without high-quality content, which is why being able to systematically manipulate and improve the content that is pulled from a source system is considered core functionality in an Enterprise Search solution. Quality of source data is often low, but by using property extraction, normalization techniques, and perhaps also by adding additional metadata that makes sense in your organization, you can improve the source material and be able to build truly unique search user experiences. As such, the concept of item processing is most relevant for anyone aspiring to understand FS4SP and its possibilities.

## CHAPTER 8

Querying the Index

After completing this chapter, you will be able to

- Configure the FAST Search Center.

- Create queries by using both Keyword Query Syntax and FQL.

- Understand the different query APIs available and how to use them.

- Go beyond the FAST Search Center and build truly flexible search applications.

Chapter 7, "Content Processing," focused on how to get data into the search index. This chapter covers the different ways to get the data back out—in other words, how to query the index.

Included in Microsoft SharePoint are four different APIs that can be used when querying the search index, all catering to different usage scenarios. You can also use two different query languages: the Keyword Query Syntax is shared with SharePoint search, and the FAST Query Language is unique to Microsoft FAST Search Server 2010 for SharePoint (FS4SP). The latter is covered more in depth in this chapter.

Introduction

Your first encounter with querying the search index usually happens when you execute a search query—either from the upper-right search box shown in Figure 8-1 or from the FAST Search Center shown in Figure 8-2.

FIGURE 8-1 The search box located in the SharePoint site templates.

FIGURE 8-2 The FAST Search Center search box.

The result page of the Search Center is composed of several Web Parts, which use APIs from the Federated Search Object Model to execute the search queries. Although it might seem likely that one of the search box Web Parts passes the query to the object model, the Search Core Results Web Part is actually what submits the query and displays the result set. The object model allows the result page to display results from both FS4SP and from People Search, in addition to other results such as news articles from the Internet—all from the same query. This process is called *Federated Search* and is explained in more detail in Chapter 2, "Search Concepts and Terminology." It is essential that the query use this method because the People results come from a different search index.

In addition to searching with the Search Center, you can create custom Web Parts that take advantage of the APIs from the object model, or you can use the *KeywordQuery* class from the Query Object Model.

Note When the Federated Search Object Model returns results, it uses the Query Object Model internally to return results from FS4SP and People Search.

When developing applications hosted outside of SharePoint, you can take advantage of the Query Web Service, which makes it easy to execute searches against FS4SP from any application capable of communicating with a web service.

The query APIs are not unique to FS4SP—in fact, they're the same as those used with SharePoint search. Having a common platform and common APIs for both FS4SP and SharePoint Server search makes it possible for developers to create search-based applications that work with both technologies. What is unique, however, are API features that let you take advantage of the more advanced query features available with FS4SP, such as dynamic ranking, sort by formula, deep refiners, and contextual search.

Another notable distinction with FS4SP is the support of the FAST Query Language (FQL). This is a powerful and rich query language, similar to T-SQL in many ways. In most cases, FQL is not suitable for end users, but you can take advantage of it in search-driven applications and use it in conjunction with your Search Center via search scopes.

This chapter discusses the different APIs available to developers, reviews the API capabilities, and provides typical use cases in which you might want to choose one API over the other.

Query Languages

Query languages are required to describe and pass the details of a user's search to the search engine. Even when a user searches for only a single term, many additional parameters are usually added that add meaning and context to that search term and help to return a more relevant set of results. For example, if a user searches for *invoice* from the finance site in a SharePoint portal, the original search query will be appended with the user's identity, a scope limiting results to items within the finance site, and any predefined search scopes that are set for the Search Center the user is searching from.

FS4SP uses two search query languages to describe and communicate search parameters: the *Keyword Query Syntax* built into SharePoint and the FAST Search specific FQL. Both query languages pass search terms (tokens) and operators (AND, OR, and so on). The terms are usually the text that a user has entered; operators are usually added to delimit or expand the relationships of those terms. Tokens can be free text query terms or specified properties.

Keyword Query Syntax

The Keyword Query Syntax, sometimes referred to as the *Keyword Query Language* (KQL), is a query syntax that works with both SharePoint search and FS4SP. KQL was originally built for SharePoint. Support for FS4SP was added later, so there are some limitations to using KQL compared with the FAST-native FQL. However, for most search interfaces, KQL is a simple and effective query syntax.

KQL supports a number of search query operators, such as Boolean *AND* keyword queries that can consist of any term or terms, phrase queries, prefix matching (also known as *wildcard search*), and property queries. Wildcard search is supported only for prefix matching or "trailing wildcards," where an asterisk (*) character may be placed at the end of several characters to match terms that start with the specified characters. KQL also supports Boolean operators and property operators such as equals (=) and contains (:). For more information about Boolean search logic, see Chapter 2.

Property operators can be applied to mapped properties. These operators take the form *<property name><property operator><property value>*. Table 8-1 outlines the available operators in KQL. You can apply a property query with or without a keyword query. However, if applied together without another operator, the property query will be added as a Boolean *AND*, thus returning a result set with items that contain all the keyword terms and only those for which the property query matches. Table 8-1 shows the keyword operators and Table 8-2 shows property query operators.

 Note Keyword property operators (such as *wildcard*) are not available in property queries and vice versa.

TABLE 8-1 Keyword Query Syntax keyword operators

Operator	Description	Usage	Example
"TermA termB"	Double quotation marks	Placing double quotation marks around a multiple-term query makes the query a phrase search— only items that match the terms together in an exact phrase are returned.	Searching for *Swedish meatballs* returns only items with *swedish* and *meatballs* together.
AND/+	Boolean *AND* operator (the + character can also be used)	This is the default operator and need not be specified. It sets the query to return only items with *termA* and *TermB* in them.	A search for *Swedish meatballs* returns only items that have *swedish* and *meatballs* somewhere in them but not necessarily together. *Swedish AND meatballs* and *Swedish +meatballs* are essentially the same query.
OR	Boolean *OR* operator	This is the disjunct operator and specifies that matching either of the terms on either side of this operator will satisfy the query. That is, items with either *termA* or *TermB* are returned.	Searching for *Swedish OR meatballs* returns any item with the term *swedish* in it and any item with the term *meatballs* in it.
NOT/-	*NOT* operator (the - character can also be used)	This is the negation operator; it sets a trailing term to be an exclusion query. That is, any item that contains this term is excluded from the result set.	Searching for *Swedish NOT meatballs* returns items that match *Swedish* but no items with the term *meatballs* in them are returned. *Swedish -Meatballs* is essentially the same query.
*	Prefix matching wildcard	The wildcard operator can be added to the end of partial words to match terms with 0 or more trailing characters. Essentially, all terms starting with the entered characters up to the wildcard are matched.	Searching for *Swed* Meat** matches *Swedish meatballs*, *Sweden meatballs*, *Sweden Meatloaf*, *Swedish Meat*, and so on. These terms are not necessarily together. Phrase search is not supported with wildcards in KQL.
NEAR	Proximity operator	The proximity operator matches terms that are within a specific proximity of each other. The trailing term is considered a match to the preceding term if it falls within eight terms of it. The order of the terms is respected; therefore, the trailing term is not looked for before the preceding term. The proximity operator does not work with property queries.	Searching for *Swedish NEAR meatballs* returns items with the term *meatballs* coming after *Swedish* within eight terms after the term *Swedish*. So items with the phrase "Swedish people love meatballs" is returned but "Meatballs invade Swedish town" is not.

Operator	Description	Usage	Example
WORDS(termA,termB) or ANY(termA termB)	Synonym operator	The synonym operator allows you to specify terms that should be considered synonyms of each other in the query. *TermA* and *TermB* should be considered to have the same meaning and, therefore, be searched for. This is equivalent to using the *OR* operator between *termA* and *termB*. This operator cannot be used with property queries.	Searching for *WORDS(Swedish, Svensk)* returns all items with the term *Swedish* and all items with the term *Svensk*.
ALL(termA termB)	Boolean *AND* operator	Enclosing terms with the *ALL* operator is the same as writing the terms with a Boolean *AND* between them.	Searching for *ALL(Swedish meatballs)* returns only items with *Swedish* and *meatballs* together.
()	Parenthesis	Parentheses are used to enclose and isolate a specific part of a complex query. If an opening parenthesis is used, a closing parenthesis must be provided.	*Meatballs NOT (Danish OR Norwegian)* represents a query where all items with the term *meatballs* returns as long as the terms *Danish* or *Norwegian* are not also present.

TABLE 8-2 Keyword Query Syntax property operators

Property Operators	Description	Supported Property types	Example
=	Equals	*Text, DateTime, Integer, Decimal*	*Filetype=docx*
:	Contains	*Text, Datetime, Integer, Decimal, Binary, YesNo*	*Author:Mikael*
<	Less than	*DateTime, Integer, Decimal*	*>03/05/2007*
>	Greater than	*DateTime, Integer, Decimal*	*<06/24/2011*
<=	Less than or equal	*DateTime, Integer, Decimal*	*<=06/24/2011*
>=	Greater than or equal	*DateTime, Integer, Decimal*	*>=03/05/2007*
<>	Does not equal	*DateTime, Integer, Decimal*	*<>06/24/2011*
..	Range	*DateTime, Integer, Decimal*	*03/05/2007..06/24/2011*

FQL

Fast Query Language (FQL) is a more powerful option for passing search queries to the FS4SP engine because it is the native query language of the FAST engine. (KQL queries are eventually translated to FQL when you run them.) FQL provides extended support for more complex queries than KQL, but mastering FQL takes more time, particularly to master more specialized queries. The *XRANK* operator is especially worth mentioning because you can use it to dynamically influence the ranking of search results. This provides a powerful and flexible way to change the ranking of your search results.

Important When using FQL as the query language, you cannot use the FS4SP keyword management features, such as synonyms, promotions/demotions, and best bets. When you use FQL in search scope definitions, this limitation does not apply.

Note FQL can be used only when integrating via the Query Object Model and the Query XML Web service. It is not exposed in the SharePoint search Web Parts.

Overview

FQL can be used with the Query Object Model and the Query Web Service to execute complex search queries. This may be desirable when KQL does not offer sufficient flexibility. A good example is when you request result sets that have custom ranking sequences. These sequences can be set by boosting term or property values in the query. These boost values are usually context-aware and hidden from the end user. This way, users do not realize their specific search would rank differently; they simply experience a more relevant result.

Usage

Although SharePoint search Web Parts do not support FQL, they can be modified to do so, and you can create new Web Parts that can use FQL. FQL is the native language for querying the FAST index and has several capabilities beyond KQL:

- *RANK* and *XRANK* operators can be applied at query time to manipulate the ranking order of the result set based on term weighting or property weighting.

- *SORT* and *SORTFORMULA* operators can be used to apply sorting to the result set.

- The *NEAR* operator can be used to apply proximity search to the result set.

- Complex queries based on a combination of the operators named in this list and a variety of other possible operators can be used (see Table 8-4).

More Info Modified Web Parts that support FQL are available on CodePlex, courtesy of the SPSearchParts project team, at *http://spsearchparts.codeplex.com*.

FQL takes the query and splits it into operators and query strings. It isolates query strings rather than individual terms. These strings, whether text or some other value, are tokenized and special characters are removed. This is because not all characters are eligible to be tokenized and searched for.

Note Some characters are eligible for escaping but are not covered here.

More Info FQL conforms to Augmented Backus-Naur Form (ABNF) syntax. Go to *http:// msdn.microsoft.com/en-us/library/ff394661.aspx* for more details.

The identified operator takes a set of values enclosed in parentheses and can be limited by a scope specification. For example, the query *title:string("Swedish meatballs", mode="and")* passes a Boolean *AND* for *Swedish meatballs* in the title of the items. The specification *title:* limits the scope of the query to the title of the items in the search index; the string operator takes the values in parentheses and passes them with the limitation. In this case, *Swedish AND meatballs* is passed by the string operator. Simpler queries can be passed (such as *title:"Swedish meatballs"*), but you should be as specific as possible to avoid any reserved terms in the query language.

Tip Although you don't have to use quotation marks with the query strings in FQL, it is recommended that you do so to avoid FQL parsing errors with the reserved words. If you want to search for the reserved words *any*, *and*, or *or*, you should write your query like this: *or("any", "and", "rank")*. A similar query without quotation marks and that is nonreserved would be *or(apple, banana, orange)*, which is legal syntax. With quotation marks, it would be *or("apple", "banana", "orange")*.

FQL can support nested sub-expressions and queries that consist of search tokens (keywords), properties, and operators. As in KQL, queries are limited to 2,048 characters, and queries are not case sensitive.

Warning When you create complex FQL statements or include item URLs in your FQL statement, the 2,048-character barrier might be a limitation. Unfortunately, there is currently no way to change this, even if FAST can handle larger queries internally.

Field/Scope specification A scope specification limits a query to a particular field of indexed content. That field can be a managed property like *body* and *title* or a full-text index field that contains a set of managed properties. The scope specification prefixes the query specification with the *In* operator, which is set using a colon, for example, *body:"Swedish meatballs"*. If you do not define a scope specification, the default specification is used, which would be the default full-text index in the index profile definition. The default composite field or full-text index in FS4SP is named *content*.

Wildcard expressions FQL uses the asterisk character (*) or the question mark character (?) as wildcard characters for substitution expressions. Matches in any managed property or the full-text index may be matched by the wildcard character, where the asterisk matches zero or more character substitutions and the question mark matches only a single character. A wildcard expression matches only terms as they appear in the items *before* lemmatization and works at the token level on tokenized content. Therefore, wildcards will not match white space, characters treated as white space, or reserved characters. See Table 8-4 for examples. Also see Chapter 9, "Useful Tips and Tricks," for an example of wildcard usage.

Reserved words and characters A number of words and characters are used in FQL itself, so those terms and characters are reserved. This does not mean you have to exclude the use of these terms in query strings, but you should take care to put these reserved words in double quotation marks to specify them as part of the query string so that they won't function as operators. Although FQL accepts unquoted strings, you should always enclose search terms and phrases in double quotation marks anyhow because doing so avoids any possibility of conflict with reserved terms. The reserved terms are *and, or, any, andnot, count, decimal, rank, near, onear, int, int32, int64, float, double, datetime, max, min, range, phrase, scope, filter, not, string, starts-with, ends-with, equals,* and *count*.

Reserved characters are always removed, regardless of quotation encapsulation. Therefore, the queries *title:(Swedish meatballs), title:("[Swedish] <meatballs>"),* and *title:("Swedish Meatballs")* are considered identical. Table 8-3 shows the reserved characters.

TABLE 8-3 Reserved characters used in non-quoted strings and for escaping

Reserved character	Usage
Newline	Escape character \n
Carriage return	Escape character \r
Tab	Escape character \t
Backspace	Escape character \b
Form feed	Escape character \f
Double quote	Escape character "
Single quote	Escape character '
Backslash	Escape character \
Tab	Can be used only within double quotation marks
Newline	Can be used only within double quotation marks
Carriage return	Can be used only within double quotation marks
Space	Can be used only within double quotation marks
(	Can be used only within double quotation marks
)	Can be used only within double quotation marks
,	Can be used only within double quotation marks
/	Can be used only within double quotation marks
:	Can be used only within double quotation marks
=	Can be used only within double quotation marks
]	Can be used only within double quotation marks
;	Can be used only within double quotation marks
[	Cannot be used as the first character outside of quoted text
"	Cannot be used as the first character outside of quoted text
<	Cannot be used as the first character outside of quoted text
>	Cannot be used as the first character outside of quoted text

Simple Query Language   Many users will be familiar with common query syntax from global search engines on the World Wide Web. They may also be familiar with KQL and even with the use of the *AND*, *OR*, and *NOT* operators + and -. If Simple Query Language is enabled as part of an FQL query, you can pass simple query expressions by using + or -. The format uses the string operator with a mode parameter of *simpleany* or *simpleall*, which indicates a Boolean *OR* or Boolean *AND* search, respectively. Simple Query Language expressions that use quotation marks to specify a phrase must be escaped with a backslash (\), for example, *string("\"Swedish meatballs\" +recipe", mode="simpleall")*.

XRANK   A lot of attention is given to the *XRANK* operator and the ability to control ranking in the result set. FQL has *RANK* and *XRANK* operators, but *XRANK* is more powerful and performs better, so it is a natural choice. *XRANK* can also add dynamic rank to property queries, whereas *RANK* works only on the full-text index. *XRANK* takes two or more operands, which can be terms or sub-expressions in valid FQL. *XRANK* performs well in queries that return large result sets and can add dynamic rank, even to items that do not already have a rank by using the *boostall=yes* parameter. The ranking can be increased using the *boost* parameter to add ranking weight to specific terms or properties that may appear on items in the result set. The values added by *XRANK* are constant, whereas *RANK* adds value based on specific operands.

> **Important** Although *RANK* is supported, using *XRANK* is much more flexible because you can control the *boost* value and use it against all managed properties and not just full-text indexes, which RANK is limited to.

The first operand of the *XRANK* operator is always the main query expression. This expression is matched in the index. All subsequent operands modify that result set by adjusting the rank values of its items. *XRANK* has an additional *boost* parameter that has a default value of 100. Using *boost* increases the rank of items that match a specific operand. The *boost* value can be set higher or lower. For example, the following expression boosts all items that contain *meatballs* by 200 if they also contain *Swedish*, as well as boosting those with the term *Norwegian* by 500.

```
xrank(xrank("meatballs","Swedish",boost=200),"Norwegian",boost=500, boostall=yes)
```

Adding *boostall=yes* to the outermost *xrank* of the preceding query ensures that items containing *meatball*, *Swedish*, and *Norwegian* are guaranteed to get a boost of 500—even if the items previously did not have any rank. With the default rank profile in FS4SP, all items will most likely have dynamic rank and setting the *boostall* parameter has no effect.

> **Note** Document and site promotion/demotion in FS4SP uses *XRANK* to change how items appear in the final result set without the use of the *boostall* parameter.

Examples

Table 8-4 lists the available operators in FQL and gives a brief explanation of their usage and syntax, and provides some examples. More information and examples are available from Microsoft at *http://msdn.microsoft.com/en-us/library/ff394462.aspx*.

TABLE 8-4 List of FQL operators and examples of usage

Operator	Description	Usage	Example
:	*IN* operator	For property queries, the property name precedes the *IN* operator. With other queries, the scope specification or operator precedes it, and parentheses containing the operands follow.	*Title:"Recipe" Body:"Swedish meatballs"* finds all items where *Recipe* is in the *Title* field and *Swedish meatballs* are in the *Body* field.
* or ?	Wildcard	Use * for matching zero or more characters in a word or phrase. Use *?* For matching a single character. White space is not matched with a wildcard. The number of matching characters for a * wildcard can be set using the string operator operands *minexpansion* and *maxexpansion*—that is, *string(S, minexpansion=<n1>, maxexpansion=<n2>)*, where *S* is the string with wildcards and *n* can be any value between zero or more.	Adding a wildcard to match zero or more trailing characters: *meatba**
			Adding a wildcard to match zero or more preceding characters: **ish*
			Adding a wildcard to match zero or more characters within a term or phrase: *m*balls*
			Adding a wildcard to match a single character: *mea?balls*
		Warning: Even though starting a search term with a wildcard is syntactically supported, it expands to more than 10,000 terms and generates a "1012 – resource limit exceeded" error in most cases. Wildcards can, however, be used directly against a managed property if the property contains fewer than 10,000 unique terms.	Using a wildcard with the string operator: *string:("Swedi?h me*lls")*
string	STRING	The *string* parameter can be used to easily pass a text string from the query box in FQL. The *string* operator takes the following syntax. *string("<text string>" [, mode=<mode>] [, n=<near>] [, weight=<n>] [, linguistics=<on|off>] [, fuzzy=<on|off>] [, fuzzythreshold=<threshold>] [, fuzzycutoff=<cutoff>] [, wildcard=<off|basic|ext>]) where mode="PHRASE"|"AND"|"OR"| "ANY"|"NEAR"|"ONEAR"| "SIMPLEANY"|"SIMPLEALL"*	*string("Swedish meatballs", mode="AND")*
and	*AND* operator	The *AND* operator matches items that contain all operands. Operands can be terms or nested valid FQL sub-expressions. The syntax is as follows. *and(operand, operand [, operand]*)*	*and(Swedish, meatballs)* returns only items with both the terms *Swedish* and *meatballs* in them.
or	OR operator	The *OR* operator matches items that satisfy any of the operands. Operands can be terms or nested valid FQL sub-expressions.	*or(Swedish, meatballs)* returns all items with either the term *Swedish* or *meatballs* in them.
not	Negation operator	The negation operator returns only items that do not match the operand. *not(operand)*	*not(Norwegian)* returns items that satisfy any other part of a larger query and do not contain *Norwegian*.

Operator	Description	Usage	Example
any	OR operator	Similar to the OR operator except that the dynamic rank (the relevance score in the result set) is affected by neither the number of operands that match nor the distance between the terms in the item. The operands may be a single term or any valid FQL sub-expression.	or(Swedish, meatballs) returns all items with either Swedish or meatballs in them. Items with both words are not ranked higher than those with just one of the words.
andnot	ANDNOT operator	The andnot operator matches all items that contain the first operand and do not match all subsequent operands. So, if all operands are terms, the result set will contain items that contain the first term but do not contain all remaining terms. Operands can, however, be nested expressions and sub-expressions as long as they are valid FQL. andnot(operand, operand [,operand]*)	andnot(meatballs, Danish, Norwegian) returns all items with the term meatballs in them but not items with Danish or Norwegian.
equals	Property equality operator	The equals operator applies to properties for matching exact terms or phrases to content in a specific property. equals(<term or phrase>)	author:equals("Marcus Johansson") returns all items with the exact phrase Marcus Johansson in the author property.
near	NEAR operator	Specifies that terms in the query must appear within a specific distance or tokens where the operator takes two or more terms and a numeric value to specify the distance N. The default numeric value is 4. near(arg, arg [, arg]* [, N=<numeric value>])	near(Swedish, meatballs, recipe, N=10) returns items that have the terms within 10 tokens of each term.
onear	Ordered NEAR	Ordered variant of the NEAR operator, where the terms must appear in the specified order.	onear(Swedish, meatballs, recipe) returns items with the terms Swedish, meatballs, and recipe, and only in that order.
count	COUNT operator	The count operator specifies a range of hits that must appear on an item for it to be returned. A minimum or maximum alone may be defined. count(term [,from=<numeric value>, to=<numeric value>])	count(meatballs, from=10, to=50) returns items that had at least 10 but not more than 50 occurrences of the term meatballs.
rank	RANK modifying operator	RANK boosts the dynamic rank of matching items in a result set without changing the composition of the result set. The first operand is used for creating the result set and the following operands are used for modifying the dynamic rank. rank(operand, rank-operand [, rank-operand]*)	and(recipe, rank(meatballs, Swedish)) returns all items that contain both recipe and meatballs but ranks higher those that contain Swedish.
xrank	XRANK rank modifying operator	XRANK allows for modification of the ranking values in the result set based on an expression and a boost value. XRANK can be applied against both the full-text index and managed properties. The queries take the following format. xrank(operand, rank-operand [, rank-operand]* [,boost=n].[,boostall=yes])	xrank(and(Swedish, meatballs), spicy, boost=200, boostall=yes) returns all items with Swedish and meatballs and boosts any item by 200 with the term spicy in it.

Operator	Description	Usage	Example
range	*RANGE* operator	This operator enables range matching expressions on numeric and date/time managed properties. The format of the operator is as follows. *range(start, end [,from="GE"|"GT"] [,to="LE"|"LT"])* Default value for *from* is *GE* and default value for *to* is *LT*. GE = Greater than or Equal GT = Greater than LE = Less than or Equal LT = Less than You can use the values of *min* and *max* in the *from* and *to* parameters to specify an absolute boundary in that range direction.	*write:range(min, 2012-03-01T00:00:00)* matches items older than and not including 2012-03-01T00:00:00 *write:range(2012-01-01T00:00:00, max, from=GT)* matches items modified after and not including 2012-01-01T00:00:00 *write:range(2012-01-01T00:00:00, 2012-03-01T00:00:00, from=GT, to=LT)* matches items newer than 2012-01-01T00:00:00 and up to but not including 2012-03-01T00:00:00 *and(size:range(15000, max), description:starts-with("fs4sp"))* matches items where the descriptions starts with *fs4sp* and the item size is at least 15,000 bytes.
phrase	*PHRASE*	Returns only items that have the query string in a phrase. *phrase(term [, term]*)*	*phrase(Swedish, meatballs)* returns items with the phrase *Swedish meatballs* in them.
filter	*FILTER*	The *filter* operator is used for filtering result sets based on metadata property matches. The *filter* operator cannot be used with linguistics and it will be set to *off*. This operator is often nested in a broader query expression to delimit that expression based on available property matches. *filter(<any valid FQL operator expression>)* Refiners in FS4SP use the *filter* operator internally when matching values.	*and(body:"Swedish meatballs", title:recipes, filter(doctype:equals("pdf")))* returns items with *Swedish meatballs* in the body text, *recipes* in the title, and of item type *pdf*.
starts-with	*STARTS-WITH* property operator	Specifies that items in the result set must start with the specified term or phrase in the specified property. *starts-with(<term or phrase>)* Only applies to properties.	The query *author:starts-with("Marcus")* matches all items that have an author property that starts with *Marcus*.
ends-with	*END-WITH* property operator	Specifies that items in the result set must end with the specified term or phrase in the specified property. *ends-with(<term or phrase>)*	The query *author:ends-with("Johansson")* matches all items that have an author property that ends with *Johansson*.
int	*INTEGER*	32-bit signed integer for matching numeric term expressions. Mainly used for performance improvements because the FQL query parser is skipped and the values are sent directly to the query matching component.	*and(string("fs4sp"), filter(id:int("1 20 49 124 453 985 3473", mode="or")))* matches items with the word *fs4sp* and one of the numbers specified for the *id* managed property.

Operator	Description	Usage	Example
float	*FLOAT*	Float or double for matching numeric term expressions. Usually not needed because the type of the query term is detected according to the type of the target numeric managed property.	*float(42)* treats the number as a floating point
formula	Sort Formula	A formula set for sorting the result set *formula:<sort-formula>*. You can use multiple methods for sorting. *	*formula:abs(20-height)*
datetime	*DATETIME*	Operator for matching Date-time expressions. Supported formats are as follows: *YYYY-MM-DD,* *YYYY-MM-DDThh:mm:ss,* *YYYY-MM-DDThh:mm:ssZ* where *YYYY* is a four-digit year, *MM* is a two-digit month, and *DD* is a two-digit day. The letter *T* specifies an expected time, *hh* is a two-digit hour in the 24-hour clock, *mm* is a two-digit minute, and *ss* is a two-digit second. The letter *Z* stands for Zulu time or Coordinated Universal Time (UTC).	*datetime("2011-12-25T12:00:00Z:)* returns items tagged with the *datetime* property for exactly noon on December 25th, 2011 UTC.

* For more information about ranking and sorting, go to *http://msdn.microsoft.com/en-us/library/ff394654.aspx*.

Search Center and RSS URL Syntax

When you execute searches in a Search Center in SharePoint, you will notice that the query string changes and that your query parameters get turned into URL parameters. For example, if you search for the term *meatball*, the URL will look like the following after the query is executed.

```
http://intranet.contoso.com/search/Pages/results.aspx?k=meatball
```

The search term is added after the *k* query string parameter in the URL. The URL syntax can be used both against the *Result.aspx* page of your Search Center and against the *srchrss.aspx* page for retrieving the results as an RSS feed. Table 8-5 lists the available parameters to use when constructing a URL, and Table 8-6 lists RSS feed–only parameters.

TABLE 8-5 URL query string parameters for Search Center and the RSS search page use

URL parameter	Description	Example
k	Specifies the keywords.	*results.aspx?k=swedish%20meatballs* Note that special characters such as the space are URL-encoded.
v	Specifies the result view that is to be used for the query. This parameter must be either: ■ The name of a sortable managed property. ■ The name of a rank profile.	*results.aspx?v=write* (sorts on last modified date) *results.aspx?v=default* (sorts on default relevance)

URL parameter	Description	Example
start	Specifies which results page number to show.	*results.aspx?start=11* (skips the first 10 results)
s	Specifies the search scope. This parameter can contain multiple values, separated by *%2c*, as shown in the second example to the right.	*results.aspx?s=SDKContent* *results.aspx?s=SDKContent%2cTechnicalArticles*
a	Appends text to your query but is not shown in the search box.	*results.aspx?k=fs4sp&a=author%3Amikael* This adds *"author:mikael"* to the query and is the equivalent of *sharepoint author:Mikael*.
u	Limits items to a certain URL or site.	*results.aspx?k=fs4sp&u=http://contoso.com* This is equivalent to *fs4sp site:"http://contoso.com"*.
r	Specifies refiners in an encoded format.	See Chapter 9 for an example of how to build the *r=* parameter.
similarto *simlartype*	Used when enabling "Find similar" functionality. The value of *similarto* is retrieved from the *docvector* managed property. The value of *similartype* is as follows: ■ *Find* ■ *Exclude* ■ *Refine*	*results.aspx?k=red&similarto=[adventure works, 1][aspx,* *0.707107]&similartype=find*

TABLE 8-6 RSS feed–specific URL parameters

URL parameter	Description	Example
provider	Used to specify the search provider when running against *srchrss.aspx* (RSS feed)	Required and must be set to *FASTSearch*. *srchrss.aspx?k=fs4sp&provider=FASTSearch*
count	Used to specify the page size	*srchrss.aspx?k=fs4sp&provider=FASTSearch&count=5* Returns five items in the search result.
lang	Used to set the query language	*srchrss.aspx?k=fs4sp&provider=FASTSearch&lang=en* Will execute the query with English as the query language.
es	Used to specify whether lemmatization is on or off for the query	By default, lemmatization is turned off. *es=1* enables lemmatization

Tip If your search results page contains multiple queries, you can specify which query the parameter applies to by appending a number from 1 through 5, indicating the Search Query Results ID between the parameter and the "=" character in the URL. However, this is not possible for the *k* parameter, so you have to use the same search terms for all queries on the page.

Search APIs

Three groups of APIs are available for executing search queries against FS4SP:

- Federated Search Object Model

- Query Object Model

- Query Web Service

The first two are used when developing applications that are hosted inside of SharePoint, and the last one is primarily used when an external application wants to query against FS4SP. For example, this can be a web portal created in PHP or a plug-in in Microsoft Outlook.

In addition to the Query Web Service, you can use a second option when querying FS4SP from outside of SharePoint. The Search Center in SharePoint allows results to be returned as an RSS feed. Crafting search queries that you run against the Search Center URL to return RSS is an easy way to get results back.

> **Note** RSS is a standardized format of XML that is used to publish frequently updated works such as blog entries, news headlines, audio, and video. An RSS document includes full or summarized text in addition to metadata such as publishing dates and authorship. Go to *http://en.wikipedia.org/wiki/Rss* for more information about RSS.

An overview of how the different query options tie into each other is shown in Figure 8-3.

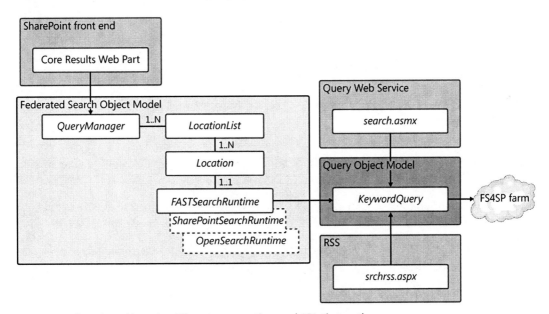

FIGURE 8-3 Overview of how the different query options and APIs tie together.

As you see from the diagram in Figure 8-3, all the query APIs end up using the *KeywordQuery* class for the actual query execution. This chapter examines each of the query APIs that are available in SharePoint and shows example usage.

Tip To return all available search results for a user with FS4SP, you can use the search term #. You can use the hash sign to return all results for all available query APIs.

The API classes available for querying the search index are listed in Table 8-7.

TABLE 8-7 Query API classes available when developing SharePoint applications with FS4SP

URL parameter	Namespace	Example
SharedQueryManager	*Microsoft.Office.Server.Search.WebControls*	*Microsoft.Office.Server.Search* in *Microsoft.Office.Server.Search.dll*
RefinementManager	*Microsoft.Office.Server.Search.WebControls*	*Microsoft.Office.Server.Search* in *Microsoft.Office.Server.Search.dll*
QueryManager	*Microsoft.Office.Server.Search.Query*	*Microsoft.Office.Server.Search* in *Microsoft.Office.Server.Search.dll*
Location	*Microsoft.Office.Server.Search.Query*	*Microsoft.Office.Server.Search* in *Microsoft.Office.Server.Search.dll*
LocationList	*Microsoft.Office.Server.Search.Query*	*Microsoft.Office.Server.Search* in *Microsoft.Office.Server.Search.dll*
FASTSearchRuntime	*Microsoft.Office.Server.Search.Query*	*Microsoft.Office.Server.Search* in *Microsoft.Office.Server.Search.dll*
KeywordQuery	*Microsoft.Office.Server.Search.Query*	*Microsoft.Office.Server.Search* in *Microsoft.Office.Server.Search.dll*

Querying a QR Server Directly

In addition to using the search APIs via SharePoint, you have the option to query a QR Server directly. This works only when logged onto an FS4SP server that has the QR role because you have to access it with *localhost*.

More Info You can read more about the QR Server in Chapter 3, "FS4SP Architecture."

If you installed FS4SP and used 13,000 as the base port, you can access the QR Server at *http://localhost:13280 (http://localhost:13280/)* via a web browser, as shown in Figure 8-4.

When you access the QR Server webpage, the page opens by default on the search page tab, and you can execute queries in FQL. The page can be used for testing and debugging purposes in order to see if you get any results back.

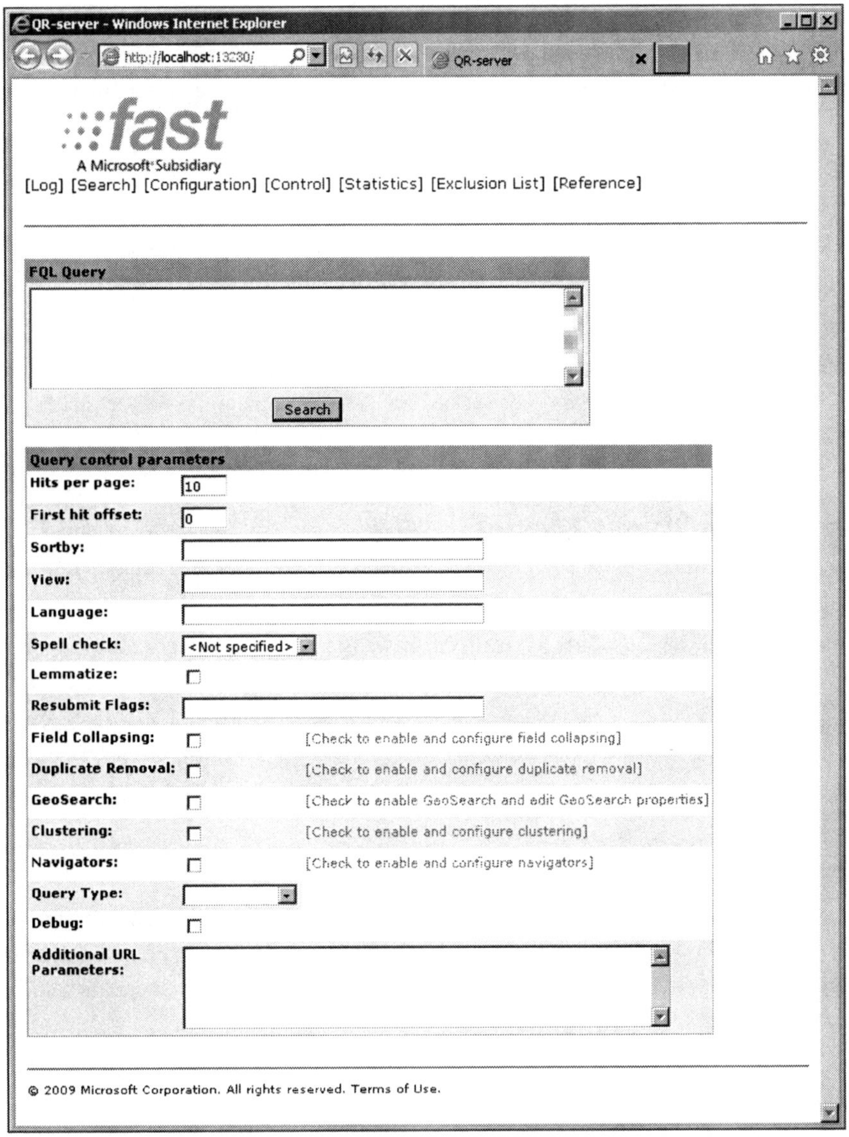

FIGURE 8-4 Query webpage of the QR Server.

Keep in mind that the queries you execute are not passing user credentials; therefore, you get back only results that are publicly available unless you modify *<FASTSearchFolder>\etc\qrserver\qtf-config.xml* and comment out the line.

```
<instance-ref name="securityfql"    critical="1" />
```

This effectively disables all security trimming for your search results, including those executed via SharePoint. Remember to restart the QR Server process in order for the change to be effective.

Most of the options seen in Figure 8-4 are equal to those used in the available SharePoint query APIs, but some of the features listed are not available via the normal query APIs. This is because the page has been carried over from FAST ESP without being modified to fit the available query APIs in SharePoint.

One example is *GeoSearch*, which is a prebuilt version of geographical search where you search for items within a radius from a latitude and longitude coordinate. This is typically used to find, for example, hotels close to a specific address. The built-in geo search feature is not available via the query APIs; instead, you have to apply a sort formula in which you calculate the radius yourself.

The QR Server contains several pages with useful information. The Configuration page lists a lot of statistics on search queries, what steps a search query goes through in the query pipeline, and information about the different managed properties set up. The Reference page has a short guide about how to write FQL queries.

Federated Search Object Model

With the Federated Search Object Model, you can bring results together from multiple search engines or repositories at the same time. The Federated Search Object Model allows you to query against SharePoint Server search, FS4SP, OpenSearch locations, and custom-developed *Location* run times.

> **Note** An example usage scenario for a custom run time is to implement a run time that executes search queries against a Microsoft SQL Server database. This allows you to use the search Web Parts in SharePoint to query against your database without the need to create a custom search page.

The search result Web Parts in SharePoint are built using the Federated Search Object Model. An example of this is the default result page that shows results from FS4SP in the middle and people results in the right column. Results from two different search engines are returned via the same object model, in this case, the page's *SharedQueryManager*.

SharedQueryManager and *QueryManager*

The search Web Parts included in SharePoint use the *SharedQueryManager* class to get a reference to the current page's *QueryManager*. All search Web Parts displaying information from the same result set share this *QueryManager*.

When you use *QueryManager* to search, results are returned as XML. The returned XML is formatted to work with the XSLT transformation included in the search Web Parts that turn the XML into the HTML displayed to the end user.

An example of two Web Parts sharing a *QueryManager* is the core results Web Part and the refinement Web Part. During search execution, they each register which parts of the search result they want returned and only one query is sent over to FS4SP. This returns both refiner results and the search hits at the same time. The refiners are retrieved via the *RefinementManager* class, which is the refiner equivalent to the *SharedQueryManager*. *RefinementManager* in turn uses the *QueryManager* internally.

> **Tip** The primary use for the *QueryManager* and *RefinementManager* is when you create a Web Part that inherits from *CoreResultsWebPart* or *RefinementWebPart*, or when you create a custom Web Part that is to be placed on a page together with one of the aforementioned Web Parts.

The *QueryManager* is implemented as a *List<LocationList>*, as shown in Figure 8-3, and has very few options that you can set. These options are described in Table 8-8.

TABLE 8-8 Properties of the *QueryManager* class

Property	Description
DefaultFASTSearchSort	Gets or sets the *sort* property used with FS4SP.
	This can be a sortable managed property, the name of a rank profile, or the name of a full-text index. Prepend the name with + for descending sort and - for ascending sort.
	Default value: +*default*
	(*default* is the name of the default rank profile)
Timeout	Gets or sets the query timeout value for the federated search location.
	Default value: 90,000 milliseconds (ms)
TrimDuplicates	Gets or sets a Boolean value that specifies whether duplicate items should be removed from the search results.
	Default value: *true*
UserQuery	Gets or sets the search query to send to the federated location.

> **More Info** Find the *QueryManager* class in the *Microsoft.Office.Server.Search.Query* namespace. MSDN documentation about this class can be found at *http://msdn.microsoft.com/en-us/library/microsoft.office.server.search.query.querymanager.aspx*.

LocationList

The *LocationList* class contains a list of federated locations and is implemented as a *List<Location>*. As you move down the class hierarchy, you can see that the class options get more specific toward the search being executed, as shown in Table 8-9.

TABLE 8-9 Properties of the *LocationList* class

Property	Description
ItemsPerPage	Gets or sets the number of search results to display per page. Default value: *10* (Core Results Web Part)
ReturnedResults	Gets the number of search results returned for the query. The count is an aggregate of the number of returned results per *Location*.
StartItem	Gets or sets the number of the first item returned in the search results. Default value: *1*
TotalResults	Gets the total number of search results returned for the query. The count is an aggregate of the total number of returned results per *Location*, excluding duplicate entries if duplicate removal has been enabled for the query.
TotalResultsIncludingDuplicates	Gets the total number of search results returned for the query, including duplicate results. The count is an aggregate of the total number of returned results per *Location*, including duplicate entries.

More Info The *LocationList* class can be found in the *Microsoft.Office.Server.Search.Query* namespace. MSDN documentation about this class can be found at *http://msdn.microsoft.com/en-us/library/microsoft.office.server.search.query.locationlist.aspx*.

Location

The *Location* class represents a federated location. A *federated location* is any search location listed under Federated Locations on your FAST Query SSA in SharePoint Central Administration. For FS4SP, the *Location* is named *Local FAST Search Results*, or *FASTSearch*, which is the internal name you have to use when referring to it, as shown in Table 8-10.

TABLE 8-10 The display names and internal names of preinstalled search locations in SharePoint

Display name	Internal name
Internet Search Results	*InternetSearchResults*
Internet Search Suggestions	*InternetSearchSuggestions*
Local Search Results	*LocalSearchIndex*
Local People Search Results	*LocalPeopleSearchIndex*
Local FAST Search Results	*FASTSearch*

More Info If you want to query additional Internet sources from within SharePoint, you can download several federated search connectors from TechNet at the Federated Search Connector Gallery for Enterprise Search. Go to *http://technet.microsoft.com/en-us/enterprisesearch/ff727944.aspx*. The files contain OpenSearch 1.1 definition files and include XSLT, both of which work with the search Web Parts in SharePoint.

The *Location* class has 21 properties that work with FS4SP; these classes are listed in Table 8-11. The other properties available are SharePoint Search specific.

TABLE 8-11 Properties of the *Location* class available for use with FS4SP

Property	Description
CurrentUserProfile	Gets or sets the user profile to use for the search query.
	Used when you enable contextual search scopes as described in the section "User Context Management" in Chapter 6, "Search Configuration."
DefaultOperator	Gets or sets the default operator.
	Used to specify whether the keywords used in the query should have *AND* or *OR* between them as default.
	Default value: *AllKeywords (AND)*
EnableStemming	Gets or sets a Boolean value specifying whether stemming is enabled.
	For FS4SP, this property enables lemmatization and not stemming. See Chapter 2 for an explanation of the difference between stemming and lemmatization.
Exception	Gets the exception returned from the federated location.
HitHighLightProperties	Gets the list of hit-highlighted properties for the current result set.
ItemsPerPage	Gets or sets the number of search results to display per page.
QueryInfo	Gets the query log data for a single click-through for the search query.
QueryModification	Gets or sets the modified query. The *QueryModification* property is used with the Did You Mean search feature.
RefinementFilters	Gets or sets the set of refinement filters used when issuing a refinement query.
RequestedLanguage	Gets or sets the language for the query.
RequestedProperties	Gets or sets the list of properties that should be included for each item in the search results.
Result	Gets the search result set for the federated location.
	Make sure the query has been executed before accessing this property. If you don't, the property returns *null*.
ReturnedResults	Gets the number of search results returned for the query.
SpellingSuggestion	Gets or sets an alternate spelling for a search term that is not recognized.
StartItem	Gets or sets the number of the first item returned in the search results.
SupplementaryQueries	Gets or sets additional terms to append to the search query.
TimeZone	Gets or sets the time zone for the search query.
TotalResults	Gets the total number of search results returned from the federated location for the query.
TotalResultsIncludingDuplicates	Gets the total number of search results returned for the query, including duplicate results.
TrimDuplicates	Gets or sets a Boolean value that specifies whether duplicate items should be removed from the search results.
UserQuery	Gets or sets the query to send to the federated location.

> **More Info** The *Location* class can be found in the *Microsoft.Office.Server.Search.Query* namespace. MSDN documentation for this class can be found at *http://msdn.microsoft.com/en-us/library/microsoft.office.server.search.query.location.aspx*.

FASTSearchRuntime

The *FASTSearchRuntime* is what ties together the *Location* definition with the *KeywordQuery* class and runs the query via the FAST Query SSA over to the FS4SP farm, as shown in Figure 8-3. Together with the *KeywordQuery* class, the *FASTSearchRuntime* class is the only class that you can use to enable FQR for a search query and specify how you want the results sorted. In addition, several properties control how the result should be performed and formatted, and there are properties for controlling the refiners. All available properties are listed in Table 8-12.

TABLE 8-12 Properties of the *FASTSearchRuntime* class

Property	Description
Config	Sets the configuration information for the FS4SP farm location.
	The configuration for *FASTSearchRuntime* is viewable when looking at Local FAST Search Results below Federated Locations on your FAST Query SSA in SharePoint Central Administration.
EnableFQL	Gets or sets a Boolean value that specifies whether the query string is written in FQL syntax.
	If set to *false*, the query string is interpreted using the Keyword Query syntax.
EnableSpellcheck	Gets or sets the flag for how spelling corrections and suggestions are handled for a query.
	Values are:
	■ **On** Apply spell corrections to the query text prior to evaluating the query.
	■ **Off** Do not apply spell correction to the query text.
	■ **Suggest** Suggest spelling corrections on the query in the result, but do not apply spell checking to the actual query performed. This enables did-you-mean functionality in the result pages.
Location	Gets or sets the FS4SP location.
MaxShallowRefinementHits	Gets or sets the number of results to use to calculate shallow refinement results.
MaxSummaryLength	Gets or sets the maximum character length of the hit highlighted summary. This value is not a hard limit but a hint to the dynamic summary generator to try to limit the summary length to this value.
	Default value: *185*
	Maximum value: ~400 with current FS4SP internal settings
MaxUrlLength	Gets or sets the maximum character length of the hit highlighted *url (hhurl)* element. The hit highlighted *url* element is truncated if it is longer than this value. Default value: *2048*
RefinementManager	Gets or sets an object representing the refinement manager that configures the query refinement filters.

Property	Description
Refiners	Gets or sets a comma-separated list of refiners to return in the search result.
	No refiners are returned with the query result if the *Refiners* property is empty.
ResubmitFlags	Gets or sets the flag specifying the criteria for automatically resubmitting a query that yielded no results.
SimilarTo	Contains a string that represents the similarity reference when searching for similar items.
SimilarType	Specifies the type of Find Similar query to be performed.
	Values are:
	■ **None** No Find Similar query performed.
	■ **Find** The similarity vectors are added to the query by using an OR operator.
	■ **Refine** The query matches if the original query conditions and the similarity vector conditions are met.
	■ **Exclude** The query matches if the original query conditions are met but not the similarity conditions.
SortList	Gets or sets the list of properties by which the search results are ordered.
SortSimilar	A Boolean value that specifies that query results based on similarity shall be sorted by similarity. If set to *false*, the result is sorted by relevance.
SupportsAsync	Gets a Boolean value that specifies whether the FS4SP run time supports asynchronous query requests.
	Default value: Always returns *false*.
TrimDuplicatesIncludeId	Specifies the value associated with a collapse group, typically used when a user clicks the Duplicates (n) link of an item with duplicates. This value corresponds to the value of the *fcoid* managed property that is returned in query results.
	Go to *http://msdn.microsoft.com/en-us/library/ff521593.aspx* for more information about duplicate removal and hit collapsing with FS4SP.
TrimDuplicatesKeepCount	An attribute that specifies how many items to keep for each set of duplicates. Default value: *1*
TrimDuplicatesOnProperty	Indicates the name of a nondefault managed property to use as the basis for duplicate removal.
UserContextGroupID	Gets or sets the identifier for getting the correct keyword settings, such as synonyms, best bets, and visual best bets. The ID is the Site Collection ID for the site collection where these keyword features have been configured.
	Important: This property has to be assigned in order for Keyword functionality like synonyms, best-bets, and promotions to work.
VisualBestBets	Gets a list of *VisualBestBetHelper* objects that hold visual vest bet information for the query result.
XmlHighConfDoc	Gets an XML representation of the best bets.

 More Info Find the *FASTSearchRuntime* class in the *Microsoft.Office.Server.Search.Query* namespace. MSDN documentation for this class can be found at *http://msdn.microsoft.com/en-us/library/microsoft.office.server.search.query.fastsearchruntime.aspx*.

> **Note** In addition to *the FASTSearchRuntime*, the Federated Search Object Model includes two more run times: the *SharePointSearchRuntime* and the *OpenSearchRuntime*. With FS4SP, the *SharePointSearchRuntime* is used for People Search, and the *OpenSearchRuntime* is used for any external search location, such as Bing News. You can also create your own search *Location* classes using a custom search run time.

Executing a Query by Using *QueryManager*, *LocationList*, and *Location*

When using the *QueryManager* class to execute a search query, you have to use both *LocationList* and *Location*. The following sample illustrates the use of the *SharedQueryManager* to execute two different queries against FS4SP inside of a Web Part on a SharePoint page.

```
// Get a reference to the Query SSA Proxy
var searchProxy = (SearchServiceApplicationProxy) SearchServiceApplicationProxy.
GetProxy(SPServiceContext.Current);

// Get a reference to the SharePoint page's query manager
var qm = SharedQueryManager.GetInstance(Page).QueryManager;

// Create a new LocationList object
var locationList = new LocationList();

// Create a Location object for query #1 and add to the list
var fastLocationOne = new Location("FASTSearch", searchProxy);
fastLocationOne.UserQuery = "FAST Search for SharePoint";
fastLocationOne.ItemsPerPage = 2;
locationList.Add(fastLocationOne);

// Create a Location object for query #2 and add to the list
var fastLocationTwo = new Location("FASTSearch", searchProxy);
fastLocationTwo.UserQuery = "Microsoft";
fastLocationTwo.ItemsPerPage = 2;
locationList.Add(fastLocationTwo);

// Add and trigger the federated locations
qm.Add(locationList);
qm.IsTriggered(locationList);
// Execute the query and get merged XML
XmlDocument resultXml = qm.GetResults();
// Number of results returned - 4 in total (2+2)
int returnedResults = locationList.ReturnedResults;
// Total number of results aggregated for both queries
int totalResults = locationList.TotalResults;
```

> **More Info** You can see another detailed example of querying with the Federated Object Model at *http://msdn.microsoft.com/en-us/library/ff407955.aspx*.

The following example shows the XML output returned from the previous code. The sample has been shortened for readability. The interesting part is that the XML for each location is merely appended after each other. First are two results for the query *FAST Search for SharePoint* with *id 1* and *2*, followed by the number of results and total results for that query. Next are the two results from the query *Microsoft*, also with *id 1* and *2*, and the number of results and total results. Appending result sets in this manner makes parsing the XML more complicated. The use of *GetResults()* from the *QueryManager* might not be the best way to get the result XML when you query more than one federated location at a time.

```
<All_Results>
  <Result>
    <id>1</id>
    <rank>18890</rank>
    <title>FS4SP Book Project</title>
    <size>3793511</size>
    <path>http://test/Shared Documents/FS4SP book Project.pptx</path>
    <write>5/16/2011</write>
    <contentclass>STS_ListItem_DocumentLibrary</contentclass>
    <isdocument>True</isdocument>
    <url>http://test/Shared Documents/FS4SP book Project.pptx</url>
    <fileextension>PPTX</fileextension>
  </Result>
  <Result>
    <id>2</id>
    <rank>18862</rank>
    <title>FS4SP Workshops</title>
    <size>2092916</size>
    <path>http://test/Shared Documents/FS4SP presentation.pptx</path>
    <write>5/27/2011</write>
    <contentclass>STS_ListItem_DocumentLibrary</contentclass>
    <isdocument>True</isdocument>
    <url>http://test/Shared Documents/FS4SP presentation.pptx</url>
    <fileextension>PPTX</fileextension>
  </Result>
  <TotalResults>3</TotalResults>
  <NumberOfResults>2</NumberOfResults>
  <Result>
    <id>1</id>
    <rank>1921</rank>
    <title>Microsoft Partner Program</title>
    <size>281600</size>
    <path>http://test/Shared Documents/Platform-Test-Framework-1.0.doc</path>
    <write>11/30/2004</write>
    <contentclass>STS_ListItem_DocumentLibrary</contentclass>
    <isdocument>True</isdocument>
    <url>http://test/Shared Documents/Platform-Test-Framework-1.0.doc</url>
    <fileextension>DOC</fileextension>
  </Result>
  <Result>
    <id>2</id>
    <rank>1582</rank>
    <title>Processing components.docx</title>
    <size>239493</size>
    <path>http://test/Shared Documents/Processing components.docx</path>
    <write>6/23/2011</write>
    <contentclass>STS_ListItem_DocumentLibrary</contentclass>
    <isdocument>True</isdocument>
```

```
  <url>http://test/Shared Documents/Processing components.docx</url>
  <fileextension>DOCX</fileextension>
</Result>
<TotalResults>18</TotalResults>
<NumberOfResults>2</NumberOfResults>
</All_Results>
```

In order to avoid the appending of XML, you can remove the following line.

```
XmlDocument resultXml = qm.GetResults(locationList);
```

Replace it with the following two lines.

```
XmlDocument locationOneXml = fastLocationOne.GetResults(qm);
XmlDocument locationTwoXml = fastLocationTwo.GetResults(qm);
```

This way, you get one XML document per result set, which is easier to work with.

> **Important** If you query two different locations, for example, *FASTSearch* and
> *InternetSearchResults*, *FASTSeach* will return XML as just shown, but *InternetSearchResults*
> will return XML in RSS format. Merging two completely different XML formats is not a good
> idea and emphasizes that using *GetResults()* on the *Location* object is a better approach.

Getting the Correct Total When Using Duplicate Trimming

The previous code sample has duplicate trimming turned on by default, but both *TotalResults* and
TotalResultsIncludingDuplicates return the same total even if there are duplicates being removed from
the result set.

In order to get the exact number of results when *TrimDuplicates* is enabled, you have to enable
refiners for your search query. Because duplicate trimming is applied only to search results and not
to refiner results, the total count of a refiner can be higher than that of the search result if there are
duplicates within the result set.

Internally, the *TotalResultsIncludingDuplicates* property is assigned from the refiner values if there
is a refiner with a higher value than that of the *TotalResults* property. The refiner property has to
cover all returned items in order to get the correct count. Examples of managed properties that you
can use are *write* and *size*, which both contain values for all items. When using the default configuration of the *RefinementManager*, *write* is included.

If you modify the code sample shown in the "Executing a Query by Using *QueryManager*,
LocationList, and *Location*" section earlier in this chapter with refiner settings added, you get the correct count in *TotalResultsIncludingDuplicates*. Look at the code that follows.

```
var searchProxy = (SearchServiceApplicationProxy)SearchServiceApplicationProxy.
GetProxy(SPServiceContext.Current);
var qm = SharedQueryManager.GetInstance(Page).QueryManager;
var locationList = new LocationList();
var fastLocationOne = new Location("FASTSearch", searchProxy);
fastLocationOne.UserQuery = "FAST Search for SharePoint";
fastLocationOne.ItemsPerPage = 2;
locationList.Add(fastLocationOne);

qm.Add(locationList);
qm.IsTriggered(locationList);

// Get a reference to the SharePoint page's refinement manager
RefinementManager refinementManager = RefinementManager.GetInstance(this.Page);
// Use the default refiner configuration for FAST
refinementManager.UseDefaultConfiguration = true;

// Initialize the use of refiners on the query
refinementManager.Initialize(fastLocationOne);

XmlDocument resultXml = qm.GetResults();
int returnedResults = locationList.ReturnedResults;
int totalResults = locationList.TotalResults;
int totalResultsIncludingDuplicates = locationList.TotalResultsIncludingDuplicates;
```

```
RefinementManager refinementManager = RefinementManager.GetInstance(this.Page);
XmlDocument refinementXml = refinementManager.GetRefinementXml();
```

Executing a Query by Using *FASTSearchRuntime*

Querying with *FASTSearchRuntime* requires an instance of a *Location* object that points to *FASTSearch* and a reference to the Query SSA Proxy. The following code sample executes a search for *microsoft* by using FQL and sorts the results with the newest items on top using *FASTSearchRuntime*.

```
// Get a reference to the Query SSA Proxy
var searchProxy = (SearchServiceApplicationProxy)SearchServiceApplicationProxy.
GetProxy(SPServiceContext.Current);
FASTSearchRuntime runtime = new FASTSearchRuntime(searchProxy);
// Create a Location object for FASTSearch
runtime.Location = new Location("FASTSearch", searchProxy);
```

```
// Enable queries written in FQL
runtime.EnableFQL = true;
// Set sort order
runtime.SortList.Add("write", SortDirection.Descending);
// Execute query
XmlDocument resultXml = runtime.SendRequest("string(\"microsoft\")");
```

Query Object Model

The Query Object Model in SharePoint consists of the *FullTextSqlQuery* class and the *KeywordQuery* class. The *FullTextSqlQuery* class is not available for use with FS4SP; however, in addition to Keyword Query Syntax, the *KeywordQuery* class supports the use of the FQL, which removes the need for an additional query class.

Although the Federated Search Object Model allows you to query any search engine defined under Federated Locations on your FAST Query SSA in SharePoint Central Administration, the *KeywordQuery* class can be used only to query SharePoint Search or FS4SP.

Keyword Query

When developing custom search applications that are not based around the search Web Parts included in SharePoint, the *KeywordQuery* class offers the most flexibility compared to the APIs in the Federated Search Object Model in terms of the parameters available when specifying a search query, as listed in Table 8-13. When using *KeywordQuery*, the search results are returned as a *ResultTableCollection* and not as XML like the Federated Search Object Model APIs.

TABLE 8-13 Properties of the *KeywordQuery* class

Property	Description
AuthenticationType	Gets or sets the authentication type for the query. Values are: ■ *NtAuthenticatedQuery* ■ *PluggableAuthenticatedQuery*
Culture	Gets or sets the locale for the query.
CustomRefinementIntervals	Gets or sets the refinement intervals that should be imposed on the refinements.
DirectServiceEndpointUri	Gets or sets the address that the Search service application proxy should use instead of the URL specified in the constructor for the Search service application proxy.
EnableFQL	Gets or sets a Boolean value that specifies whether the query string is according to the FQL syntax.
EnablePhonetic	Gets or sets a Boolean value that specifies whether the phonetic forms of the query terms are used to find matches. Only applicable for People Search.

Property	Description
EnableSpellcheck	Gets or sets the flag for how spelling corrections and suggestions are handled for a query. Values are: ■ **On** Apply spell corrections to the query text prior to evaluating the query. ■ **Off** Do not apply spell correction to the query text. ■ **Suggest** Suggest spelling corrections on the query in the result, but do not apply spell check to the actual query performed. This enables did-you-mean type search tip in the result pages.
EnableStemming	Gets or sets a Boolean value that specifies whether stemming is enabled. For FS4SP, this property enables lemmatization and not stemming. See Chapter 2 for an explanation of the difference between stemming and lemmatization.
HitHighlightedProperties	Gets the collection of hit-highlighted properties for the query.
KeywordInclusion	Gets or sets a value that specifies whether the query returns results that contain all or any of the specified search terms. This property is only applicable to queries using the Keyword Query Syntax.
MaxShallowRefinementHits	Gets or sets the number of results to be used to calculate shallow refinement results. In most cases, you use deep refinement with FS4SP and can ignore this property.
MaxSummaryLength	Gets or sets the maximum length of the search result summary. This value is not a hard limit but a hint to the dynamic summary generator to try to limit the summary length to this value.
MaxUrlLength	Default value: *185*
QueryInfo	Maximum value: ~400 with current FS4SP internal settings
QueryText	Gets or sets the text for the search query.
RefinementFilters	Gets or sets the set of refinement filters used when issuing a refinement query. A string containing a set of refinement tokens separated by space. Refinement tokens are returned as part of the *RefinementResults* table for the previous query.
Refiners	Gets or sets the set of refiners to be returned in a search result. The value for each refiner is a comma-separated format string that specifies the name of the managed property to use as a refiner and, optionally, a set of refinement options for this refiner. No refiners are returned with the query result if the property is empty, which it is by default. When specifying refiners, you can add parameters such as sorting and return intervals. See *http://msdn.microsoft.com/en-us/library/gg984547.aspx* for reference on how you can customize refiner configuration.
ResubmitFlags	Gets or sets the criteria for automatically resubmitting a search query that yielded no results. Values are: ■ *NoResubmit* ■ *EnableSpellcheckOnResubmit* ■ *EnableSpellcheckSuggestOnResubmit* ■ *EnableStemmingOnResubmit* ■ *AddSynonymsAutomatically* See *http://msdn.microsoft.com/en-us/library/microsoft.office.server.search.query .resubmitflag.aspx* for reference on these options.

Property	Description
ResultsProvider	Gets or sets the search provider used for the search query. Values are: ■ *Default* (uses the default SSA set in the application proxy group) ■ *SharePointSearch* ■ *FASTSearch*
ResultTypes	Gets or sets a value that specifies the search result type. Values are: ■ **None** No result type is specified. ■ **RelevantResults** Specifies the result set containing the main search results from the content index. ■ **SpecialTermResults** Specifies the result set containing best bets. ■ **HighConfidenceResults** Specifies the result set containing high-confidence results. (Same as SpecialTermResults but for People Search only.) ■ **DefinitionResults** Specifies the result set containing definitions for keywords. ■ **VisualBestBetsResults** Specifies the result set containing visual best bets. ■ **RefinementResults** Specifies the result set containing the refiners.
RowLimit	Gets or sets the maximum number of items returned in the search results. This is the page size you want returned. Used in conjunction with *StartRow*. Maximum value is *10,000*.
RowsPerPage	Not used with FS4SP.
SearchTerms	Gets the terms used for the search query.
SelectProperties	Gets a list of the properties to return in the search results.
SimilarTo	Gets or sets the similarity reference when performing a Find Similar query.
SimilarType	Gets or sets the type of Find Similar query to perform. Values are: ■ **None** No Find Similar query performed. ■ **Find** The similarity vectors are added to the query by using an *OR* operator. ■ **Refine** The query matches if the original query conditions and the similarity vector conditions are met. ■ **Exclude** The query matches if the original query conditions are met but not the similarity conditions.
Site	Gets the site the search query is executed from.
SiteContext	Gets or sets the site URL for the search query.
SortList	Gets the collection of properties by which the search results are ordered. You use the *Add()* method of the collection to add more properties.
SortSimilar	Gets or sets a Boolean value that specifies whether query results based on similarity shall be sorted by similarity.
StartRow	Gets or sets what is the first row included in the search results—that is, how many results to skip.
TimeZone	Gets or sets the time zone for the search user.

Property	Description
TrimDuplicates	Gets or sets a Boolean value that specifies whether duplicate items should be removed from the search results. This property can also be used to collapse hits in the result set. Collapsing means to group items, whereas removing duplicates keeps one.
TrimDuplicatesIncludeId	Specifies the value associated with a collapse group, typically used when a user clicks the Duplicates (n) link of an item with duplicates. This value corresponds to the value of the *fcoid* managed property that is returned in query results. See *http://msdn.microsoft.com/en-us/library/ff521593.aspx* for more information about duplicate removal and hit collapsing with FS4SP.
TrimDuplicatesKeepCount	Gets or sets the number of duplicates to keep if duplicates are returned in the search results. Default value: *1*
TrimDuplicatesOnProperty	Gets or sets the property that the duplicates trimming is based on. Default value: *documentsignature*
UrlZone	Gets the originating URL zone for the query request.
UserContextData	Gets or sets the user context data associated with the FS4SP search settings.
UserContextGroupID	Gets or sets the identifier for getting the correct keyword settings, such as synonyms, best bets, and visual best bets. The ID is the Site Collection ID for the site collection where these keyword features have been configured. **Important:** This property has to be assigned in order for Keyword functionality like synonyms, best-bets and promotions to work.

More Info Find the *KeywordQuery* class in the *Microsoft.Office.Server.Search.Query* namespace. MSDN documentation about this class can be found at *http://msdn.microsoft.com/en-us/library/microsoft.office.server.search.query.keywordquery.aspx*.

Executing a Query by Using the *KeywordQuery* Class

Many properties are available with *KeywordQuery*, and it takes time to get to know them all. The following sample queries for *FAST Search for SharePoint* sorts the results with the newest items on top, and, if the dates are equal, sorts on rank. The sample includes best bets and visual best bets and includes refiners for last modified date and the format of the items. The sample also shows a second query, refining on Microsoft PowerPoint files, where the refiner is picked from the first query.

For the third query, you execute a Find Similar query by using the first result hit as the source for the query.

```
// Get a reference to the Query SSA Proxy
var searchProxy = (SearchServiceApplicationProxy)SearchServiceApplicationProxy.
GetProxy(SPServiceContext.Current);
KeywordQuery kq = new KeywordQuery(searchProxy);
kq.QueryText = "FAST Search for SharePoint";
kq.ResultsProvider = SearchProvider.FASTSearch;
```

```
// Return search results, refiners and best bets
kq.ResultTypes = ResultType.RelevantResults | ResultType.RefinementResults | ResultType.
SpecialTermResults;

// Add refiner for last modified date and file format
// "write" is needed for exact TotalRowsIncludingDuplicates count
kq.Refiners = "write,format";
// Set sorting to newest items on top
kq.SortList.Add("write", SortDirection.Descending);
// If dates are the same, sort on rank
kq.SortList.Add("default", SortDirection.Descending);

// Set the user context group in order to get Synonyms, Promotions,
// Best Bets and Visual Best Bets
kq.UserContextGroupID = SPContext.Current.Site.ID.ToString();

// Execute query
ResultTableCollection resultTableCollection = kq.Execute();

// Get a reference to the search results
ResultTable resultTable = resultTableCollection[ResultType.RelevantResults];

// Get the total count with and without duplicates from the search result table
int totalRows = resultTable.TotalRows;
int totalRowsIncludingDuplicates = resultTable.TotalRowsIncludingDuplicates;

// Get the visual best bets
ResultTable visualBestBetsTable = resultTableCollection[ResultType.VisualBestBetsResults];

// Pulls out and discards the values to show the retrieval process
foreach (DataRow row in visualBestBetsTable.Table.Rows)
{
    string name = (string)row["Name"];
    string uri = (string)row["Uri"];
    string description = (string)row["Description"];
    string keyword = (string)row["Keyword"];
    string teaser = (string)row["Teaser"];
    string contentType = (string)row["TeaserContentType"];
}

// Get a reference to the refiners
ResultTable refinementTable = resultTableCollection[ResultType.RefinementResults];

// Find the PowerPoint refiner
string powerPointRefinerToken = null;
foreach (DataRow row in refinementTable.Table.Rows)
{
    if ((string)row["RefinerName"] == "format"
                && (string)row["RefinementName"] == "Microsoft PowerPoint")
    {
        // Save the token for the PowerPoint refiner
        powerPointRefinerToken = (string)row["RefinementToken"];
        break;
    }
}
```

```
// Add the PowerPoint refinement token to the query object
if (!string.IsNullOrEmpty(powerPointRefinerToken))
    kq.RefinementFilters.Add(powerPointRefinerToken);

// Add docvector to be used in the subsequent find similar query
kq.SelectProperties.Add("docvector");

// Execute the search one more time with refinement on "PowerPoint" files
resultTableCollection = kq.Execute();

// Prepare a find similar query for the first hit
resultTable = resultTableCollection[ResultType.RelevantResults];
string docvector = (string)resultTable.Table.Rows[0]["docvector"];

kq.SimilarType = SimilarType.Find;
kq.SimilarTo = docvector;

// Remove refinement for "PowerPoint" files
kq.RefinementFilters.Clear();

// Execute the search one more time using find similar
resultTableCollection = kq.Execute();
```

Important Make sure you set *UserContextGroupID* to the ID of your Search Settings Group when using the *KeywordQuery* class to return best bets and visual best bets. If you don't, they will always be empty. See the section "Keyword, Synonym, and Best Bet Management" in Chapter 6 for more information about keywords and the Search Settings Group. In most cases, this property corresponds to the GUID of your site collection.

More Info You can see other examples of querying with the Query Object Model at *http://msdn.microsoft.com/en-us/library/ms551453.aspx* and in Chapter 9.

Executing a Query by Using FQL with the *KeywordQuery* Class

The following sample code searches for the term *FAST Search for SharePoint* and gives 1,000 extra rank points to items created by the author *Mikael*. If the items also contain the names *Marcus* and *Robert*, an additional 2,000 rank points are given.

FQL formatted for readability

```
xrank(
    xrank(
        string(
            "FAST Search for SharePoint",
            mode="simpleall"
        ),
        author:string(
            "mikael"
        ),
        boost=1000
```

```
    ),
     or(
        string(
            "marcus"
        ),
         string(
            "robert"
        )
    ),
     boost=2000
)
```

KeywordQuery class executing an FQL query

```
// Get a reference to the Query SSA Proxy
var searchProxy =
    (SearchServiceApplicationProxy)SearchServiceApplicationProxy.
GetProxy(SPServiceContext.Current);
KeywordQuery kq = new KeywordQuery(searchProxy);

// Enable FQL
kq.EnableFQL = true;
// Add the FQL query
kq.QueryText = "xrank(xrank(string(\"FAST Search for SharePoint\", mode=\"simpleall\"), author:s
tring(\"mikael\"),boost=1000), or(string(\"marcus\"), string(\"robert\")), boost=2000)";
kq.ResultsProvider = SearchProvider.FASTSearch;

// Return search results
kq.ResultTypes = ResultType.RelevantResults;

// Execute search
ResultTableCollection resultTableCollection = kq.Execute();
```

Query Web Service

When you create applications that are hosted outside of SharePoint but you want the applications to be searchable within SharePoint, you use the Query Web Service. This service can be consumed by any programming language that can talk to a web service.

To access the Query Web Service and its methods, add a web service reference to the following URL, where *server* is your SharePoint web application URL and *[site collection]* is the root folder of your site collection.

```
http://server/[site collection/]_vti_bin/search.asmx
```

 Tip You can get the WSDL for the search Web Service by using the URL *http://server/_vti_bin/search.asmx?wsdl*.

The Query Web Service contains eight methods, listed in Table 8-14. The most important methods are *Query*, *QueryEx*, and *GetSearchMetadata*.

TABLE 8-14 Public methods available via the Query Web Service with FS4SP relevant settings

Method	Description
GetPortalSearchInfo	Returns a list of scopes for the SharePoint Server search. This method is deprecated and should not be used in new applications.
GetQuerySuggestions	Returns suggested queries from the query history or from manually added entries. It is meant for assisting the user with suggested queries as he/she is typing into the search box and is typically invoked using JavaScript.
GetSearchMetadata	Returns a list of all the managed properties and scopes in an ADO.NET DataSet. Table names: ■ *FASTSearchProperties* ■ *Scopes*
Query	Returns an XML document containing the search results set for the specified query. This method cannot be used to return refiners, best bets, or visual best bets.
QueryEx	Returns an ADO.NET DataSet containing a DataTable for each search results set returned for the specified query. Table names: ■ *RelevantResults* ■ *SpecialTermResults* ■ *RefinementResults* ■ *VisualBestBetsResults*
RecordClick	This member is reserved for internal use and is not intended to be used directly from your code.
Registration	Returns the name and provider registration information for the search Shared Service Provider.
Status	Returns availability of the search service. Returns a status of *ONLINE* or *OFFLINE* to indicate the availability of the search service.

More Info The schema for writing search queries by using the Query Web Service is described at *http://msdn.microsoft.com/en-us/library/ms563775.aspx*. The WSDL for the Query XML can be found at *http://msdn.microsoft.com/en-us/library/dd955992(office.12).aspx*.

Executing a Query by Using the Query Web Service

The following sample builds a console application that uses the executing user's domain credentials for authentication. The Query Web Service is added as a Web Service reference created with *wsdl.exe* (Microsoft Web Services Description Language Utility).

The sample queries for *FAST Search for SharePoint* sort the results with the newest items on top, includes best bets and visual best bets, and includes refiners for last modified date and the format of the items. The sample also shows a second query, refining on PowerPoint files, where the refiner is picked from the first query.

Important Note that if anonymous access is disabled for the Query Web Service's web application, you have to provide user credentials on calls to the Query Web Service. The results returned from the Query Web Service are filtered according to what the executing user has rights to, similar to how search works inside of SharePoint.

```
using System;
using System.Data;
using System.Net;

namespace FS4SP.ConsoleSamples
{
    internal class Program
    {
        private static void Main(string[] args)
        {
            // The Query Packet XML template for our query
            string templateXml =@"
<QueryPacket xmlns=""urn:Microsoft.Search.Query"">
   <Query>
      <Context>
         <QueryText language=""en-US"" type=""STRING"">FAST Search for SharePoint</QueryText>
      </Context>
      <SupportedFormats>
         <Format revision=""1"">urn:Microsoft.Search.Response.Document:Document</Format>
      </SupportedFormats>
      <ResultProvider>FASTSearch</ResultProvider>
      <Range>
         <StartAt>1</StartAt>
         <Count>10</Count>
      </Range>
      <EnableStemming>true</EnableStemming>
      <EnableSpellCheck>Off</EnableSpellCheck>
      <IncludeSpecialTermResults>true</IncludeSpecialTermResults>
      <IncludeRelevantResults>true</IncludeRelevantResults>
      <ImplicitAndBehavior>true</ImplicitAndBehavior>
      <TrimDuplicates>true</TrimDuplicates>
      <SortByProperties>
         <SortByProperty name=""write"" direction=""Descending"" />
      </SortByProperties>
      <IncludeRefinementResults>
         <Refiners>
            <Refiner>format</Refiner>
            <Refiner>write</Refiner>
         </Refiners>
      </IncludeRefinementResults>
      {0}
      <Properties>
         <Property name=""Rank"" />
         <Property name=""Title"" />
         <Property name=""Author"" />
         <Property name=""Size"" />
```

```
            <Property name=""Path"" />
            <Property name=""Write"" />
            <Property name=""SiteName"" />
            <Property name=""ContentClass"" />
            <Property name=""IsDocument"" />
            <Property name=""Url"" />
            <Property name=""FileExtension"" />
            <Property name=""SpSiteUrl"" />
            <Property name=""docvector"" />
        </Properties>
    </Query>
</QueryPacket>";

            // Accept all certificates - should only be used against sites you trust!
            ServicePointManager.ServerCertificateValidationCallback +=
                (sender, certificate, chain, sslPolicyErrors) => true;

            // Get an instance to the Web Service proxy
            // Generated with "wsdl.exe http://<server>/_vti_bin/search.asmx
            QueryService service = new QueryService();

            // Set the SharePoint server URL
            service.Url = "http://test/_vti_bin/search.asmx";

            // Set credentials for the executing user
            service.PreAuthenticate = true;
            service.UseDefaultCredentials = false;
            service.Credentials = CredentialCache.DefaultNetworkCredentials;

            // Create the Query Packet and execute the query
            string queryXml = string.Format(templateXml, string.Empty);
            DataSet resultSet = service.QueryEx(queryXml);

            // Get a reference to visual best bets and display the results
            DataTable visualBestBetsTable = resultSet.Tables["VisualBestBetsResults"];
            if (visualBestBetsTable != null)
            {
                foreach (DataRow row in visualBestBetsTable.Rows)
                {
                    Console.WriteLine(row["Name"]);
                    Console.WriteLine(row["Uri"]);
                    Console.WriteLine(row["Description"]);
                    Console.WriteLine(row["Keyword"]);
                    Console.WriteLine(row["Teaser"]);
                    Console.WriteLine(row["TeaserContentType"]);
                }
            }

            // Get a reference to results and print properties and values
            DataTable resultTable = resultSet.Tables["RelevantResults"];
            for (int i = 0; i < resultTable.Rows.Count; i++)
            {
                Console.WriteLine("RESULT #" + (i + 1));
                DataRow row = resultTable.Rows[i];
                for (int colIdx = 0; colIdx < row.ItemArray.Length; colIdx++)
```

```
        {
            Console.WriteLine(resultTable.Columns[colIdx].ColumnName
                + ":" + row.ItemArray[colIdx]);
        }
        Console.WriteLine("------------------------");
    }

    // Get a reference to the refiners
    DataTable refinementTable = resultSet.Tables["RefinementResults"];

    // Find the PowerPoint refiner
    string powerPointRefinerToken = null;
    foreach (DataRow row in refinementTable.Rows)
    {
        if ((string)row["RefinerName"] == "format"
            && (string)row["RefinementName"] == "Microsoft PowerPoint")
        {
            // Save the token for the PowerPoint refiner
            powerPointRefinerToken = (string)row["RefinementToken"];
            break;
        }
    }

    // Create the refinement filter for the query and add it to the Query Packet XML
    string refinementXml = "<RefinementFilters><RefinementFilter>" +
                           powerPointRefinerToken +
                           "</RefinementFilter></RefinementFilters>";
    queryXml = string.Format(templateXml, refinementXml);

    // Execute the search one more time with refinement on "PowerPoint" files
    resultSet = service.QueryEx(queryXml);
        }
    }
}
```

If you want to execute the query by using FQL instead of Keyword Query Syntax, replace the following line.

```
<QueryText language="en-US" type="STRING">FAST Search for SharePoint</QueryText>
```

Use the following line as the replacement.

```
<QueryText language="en-US" type="FQL">string("fast for sharepoint", Mode="AND")</QueryText>
```

Query via RSS

SharePoint includes a search page that returns the result as RSS. This page accepts the same URL syntax as the Search Center in addition to unique parameters listed earlier in Table 8-6.

To access the RSS feed for a search result, use the following URL.

```
http://server/[site collection/]_layouts/srchrss.aspx
```

Executing a search for *FAST Search for SharePoint* on all sites against a site collection at the URL *http://test (http://test/)* would look like the following.

```
http://test/_layouts/srchrss.aspx?k=fast%20search%20for%20sharepoint&s=All%20Sites&start=1&prov
ider=FASTSearch
```

Using RSS can be a good option for many programming languages because the format is standardized and most languages have libraries that make it easy to read and parse RSS feeds. The RSS feed viewed in Windows Internet Explorer 9 looks similar to that of Figure 8-5.

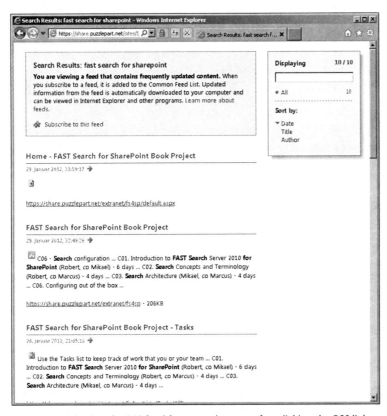

FIGURE 8-5 Viewing the RSS feed for a search query after clicking the RSS link on a Search Center.

Choosing Which API to Use

This chapter covered four different search APIs, all with different characteristics and each one useful for different scenarios. Table 8-15 summarizes the different APIs and the usage areas for each one.

TABLE 8-15 Feature set and usage area for the different query APIs

API	Search Center Web Part	Custom Web Part	Applications outside of SharePoint	FQL support	Refiners	Best bets and visual best bets
Federated Search Object Model	X	X		X*	X**	X***
Query Object Model		X		X	X	X
Query Web Service			X	X	X	X
Query via RSS			X			

* Available using reflection to get access to the *FASTSearchRuntime*. See Chapter 9 for an example on extending the Core Results Web Part to support FQL.

** Via *RefinementManager*

*** Via *FASTSearchRuntime*

Conclusion

As you see in this chapter, several APIs and two different query languages—KQL and FQL—can be used for searching against FS4SP. Knowing the strengths and limitations of each one is important when setting out to create your next search-driven application.

Whether you choose to customize the existing Search Center and its Web Parts or do a fully custom search application is up to you. Although the Search Center option makes it easy to get up and running, it limits how you can sort and rank results on multiple levels and limits you to only using KQL. Extending the Web Parts to support this functionality is often more work compared to using the *KeywordQuery* class directly. On the other hand, using the *KeywordQuery* class gives you full flexibility in terms of how you query the index by using FQL but leaves it up to you to create the user experience. You also lose the keyword functionality with synonyms and best bets unless you develop it yourself. Both options are valuable and cater to different needs and different skill sets when it comes to building the UI.

You have been given samples about how to query with the APIs using the Federated Search Object Model or the Query Object Model when developing applications hosted inside of SharePoint and using either the Query Web Service or query via RSS for applications hosted outside of SharePoint.

The goal of this chapter has been to give you an overview of the different query options available to you in FS4SP, and to explain how these options all tie together behind the scenes. The options available are almost similar to that of the built-in SharePoint search, but with provided extensions for FS4SP-specific features. Mastering the new feature set available with FS4SP when it comes to querying the search index takes time, but hopefully you have gained a better understanding of what is available and how you can tap into their potential.

## CHAPTER 9

Useful Tips and Tricks

After completing this chapter, you will be able to

- Perform a variety of technical tasks with FS4SP and know what business case they solve.

- Use FS4SP and its feature set to build better search-based solutions.

As earlier chapters have shown, Microsoft FAST Search Server 2010 for SharePoint (FS4SP) is a powerful Enterprise Search platform. You can solve many information retrieval problems with it. However, figuring out how to use the vast feature set of FS4SP to solve many of these problems and create an optimal solution is often not that straightforward. Therefore, along with the other FS4SP information outlined in this book, we have added this chapter, which aims to explain how you can accomplish typical tasks needed for search-based solutions and the business value behind tasks.

By reading over these various tips and tricks, you should gain both technical and business insight into what search can do when you're designing solutions in Microsoft SharePoint. Additionally, you should be able to quickly identify recipes for the most common setup scenarios in FS4SP by jumping to the relevant sections in this chapter. Each section is clearly labeled with the goal and is followed by the steps to achieve the goal.

Searching Inside Nondefault File Formats

Many organizations have used a large variety of software programs over the last few decades. Some companies adopted information technology earlier than others when little standardization existed, some have only recently adopted a Microsoft platform, and others have document formats that are specific to a business need, for example, computer-aided design (CAD). Thus, you may need to search inside documents besides Microsoft Office formats, Adobe PDF files, or plain-text file formats. Luckily, FS4SP can, with little effort, support many of these special or legacy document formats. All you need to do is enable what is known as the *Advanced Filter Pack*.

The default installation of FS4SP indexes all the normal file formats you would expect, but by enabling the Advanced Filter Pack, you get access to file converters for several hundred formats. See Chapter 4, "Deployment," for a list of all the supported default file formats.

Enable the Advanced Filter Pack

1. Open an FS4SP shell on the FS4SP administration server.

2. Browse to the *<FASTSearchFolder>*\installer\scripts folder.

3. Execute the following command.

   ```
   .\AdvancedFilterPack.ps1 –enable
   ```

4. Type **y** to answer *yes* to the question shown in Figure 9-1.

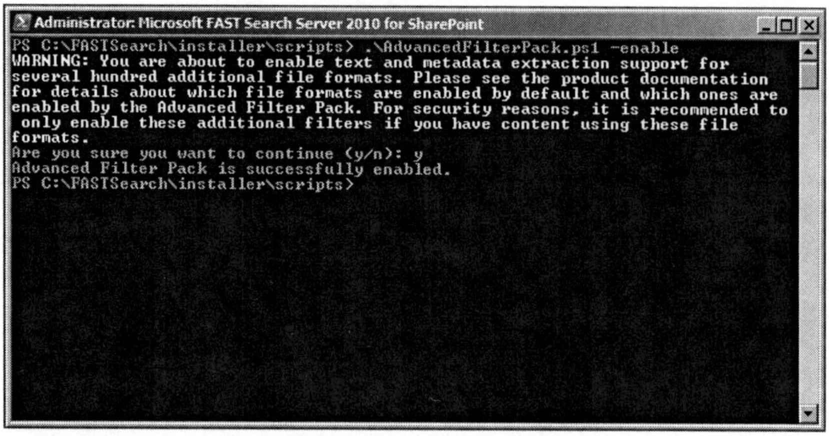

FIGURE 9-1 Enabling the Advanced Filter Pack.

Disable the Advanced Filter Pack

1. Open an FS4SP shell on the FS4SP administration server.

2. Browse to <FASTSearchFolder>\installer\scripts.

3. Execute the following command

   ```
   .\AdvancedFilterPack.ps1 –disable
   ```

Installing Third-Party IFilters

If the standard IFilters or the Advanced Filter Pack is unable to convert your files, you can look to third-party vendors who offer IFilters for numerous file formats. An online search for *purchase ifilter* provides a list of IFilter vendors.

When using a third-party IFilter, you have to register the IFilter with Windows Search, configure the user converter rules configuration file to process the item correctly, and make sure that the file type is not excluded by the FAST Content SSA.

1. Install the custom IFilter on all FS4SP servers running the document processor component.

2. Open the following file on the FS4SP administration server.

   <FASTSearchFolder>\etc\config_data\DocumentProcessor\formatdetector
   user_converter_rules.xml

3. Update the extension, MIME type, and format description that the third-party IFilter supports by using code such as the following.

```
<ConverterRules>
  <IFilter>
    <trust>
      <ext name=".zip" mimetype="application/zip" />
    </trust>
  </IFilter>
  <MimeMapping>
    <mime type="application/zip">Zip Archive</mime>
  </MimeMapping>
</ConverterRules>
```

> **Important** Changes made to *user_converter_rules.xml* are overwritten and lost when installing a FS4SP cumulative update or service pack. See the section "Installation Guidelines" in Chapter 4 for a list of configuration files that need to be backed up manually before applying updates.

4. On the FS4SP administration server, run the **psctrl reset** command to reset all currently running item processors in the system and reload the updated user converter rules configuration file.

5. In Central Administration, click Manage Service Applications, and then click your FAST Content SSA.

6. Click File Types in the left pane.

7. Make sure your added file extension is *not* in the list displayed. If it is, remove it.

Extending the Expiration Date of the FS4SP Self-Signed Certificate

When installing FS4SP, a certificate with a one-year expiration date is generated and used for communication between the SharePoint farm and the FS4SP farm. This means that after one year, the installed certificate expires and you have to generate a new certificate in order for the communication between the farms to work. This needs to be done annually.

Alternatively, if you want to skip management of certificates after the initial deployment, you can generate a certificate that expires far into the future.

 Note The difference between self-signed certificates and certificates issued by a common certification authority is explained in the section "Certificates and Security" in Chapter 4.

Extending the default expiration date for the self-signed certificate created by FS4SP requires that you edit one of the script files that ships with the FS4SP installation. Alternatively, you can create a new script based on its contents.

Your edits can be overwritten with a service pack or cumulative update, but that should not matter if you extend the validity of the certificate so far into the future that you don't need to run the script ever again.

 Important This procedure works only on Windows Server 2008 R2, not on Windows Server 2008 SP2.

Create a long-lasting self-signed certificate

1. Open the following file in a text editor.

   <FASTSearchFolder>\installer\scripts\include\certificatesetup.ps1

2. Scroll down to line number 246, which reads as follows.

   ```
   Add-Content -Path $infFile -Value "SuppressDefaults=true"
   ```

3. Insert the following lines beneath line number 246 to extend the expiration date of the certificate to 100 years from the time you generate the certificate.

   ```
   Add-Content -Path $infFile -Value "ValidityPeriod=Years"
   Add-Content -Path $infFile -Value "ValidityPeriodUnits=100"
   ```

4. Save the file, which should look similar to Figure 9-2.

5. Regenerate and install the new self-signed certificate by using *replacedefaultcertificate.ps1*, as described at *http://technet.microsoft.com/en-us/library/ff381244.aspx#BKMK_ReplaceTheSelf SignedCertificateWithANewSelfsignedCertificate*.

```
233   #Create inf file
234   LogVerbose $LogHeading "Creating $infFile file."
235   $unwanted = New-Item -ItemType "file" -Path $infFile
236
237   Add-Content -Path $infFile -Value "[NewRequest]"
238   Add-Content -Path $infFile -Value "RequestType=Cert"
239   Add-Content -Path $infFile -Value "Exportable=TRUE"
240   Add-Content -Path $infFile -Value "HashAlgorithm=md5"
241   Add-Content -Path $infFile -Value "Subject='CN=$certificateName'"
242   Add-Content -Path $infFile -Value "ProviderName='Microsoft Strong Cryptographic Provider'"
243   Add-Content -Path $infFile -Value "HashAlgorithm=md5"
244   Add-Content -Path $infFile -Value "KeySpec=AT_KEYEXCHANGE"
245   Add-Content -Path $infFile -Value "SMIME=false"
246   Add-Content -Path $infFile -Value "SuppressDefaults=true"
247   Add-Content -Path $infFile -Value "ValidityPeriod=Years"
248   Add-Content -Path $infFile -Value "ValidityPeriodUnits=100"
249   $infFileQuoted = QuoteArgument $infFile
250   $reqFileQuoted = QuoteArgument $reqFile
```

└─ Added lines to extend validity period to 100 years

FIGURE 9-2 Extending the self-signed certificate validation period.

Replacing the Default FS4SP Certificate with a Windows Server CA Certificate

Instead of using the default certificate installed with FS4SP, you can use a certificate issued by a certification authority (CA) in order to achieve a higher level of security in a production environment. Your organization may have an existing public key infrastructure (PKI) that can issue these certificates.

The following procedure assumes you have access to a Windows CA server with an account that has permissions to create certificate templates, and that you are using FS4SP and SharePoint servers under the same parent domain. The account must have Enterprise Administrator privileges in order to duplicate a template that is used in the procedure.

More Info See Chapter 4, "Deployment," for more information regarding certificates and security in FS4SP. See *http://technet.microsoft.com/en-us/library/ff381244.aspx* for information about how to replace the default certificate with one issued by a CA.

Note The procedure for generating a new CA certificate has been provided courtesy of John Lenker of Discover Technologies.

Create a template

1. Log on to your CA server with an account that has appropriate permissions to create certificate templates.

2. Open Certification Authority, right-click Certificate Templates, and select Manage.

3. Right-click Web Server and select Duplicate Template. Choose Windows Server 2003 Enterprise, and then click OK.

4. Select the General tab in the Properties window.

5. Set the template display name to **FAST Search Server**, the template name to **FASTSearch Server**, and the validity period to, for example, 100 Years to create a long lasting certificate.

6. Select the Request Handling tab.

7. Set the purpose to Signature And Encryption and the minimum key size to 2048. Select Allow Private Key To Be Exported, and set Requests Must Use One Of The Following CSPs to Microsoft DH SChannel Cryptographic Provider and Microsoft RSA SChannel Cryptographic Provider.

8. Select the Subject Name tab.

9. Select Build From This Active Directory Information, set the subject name format to Common Name, and select the DNS Name check box for Include This Information In Alternate Subject Name.

10. Select the Server tab and select both options.

11. Select the Issuance Requirements tab and clear all options.

12. Select the Superseded Templates tab and remove any template listed.

13. Select the Extensions tab.

14. Edit Application Policies and add all possible policies.

15. Edit Basic Constraints and clear the Enable This Extension check box.

16. Edit Issuance Policies and remove all possible policies. Clear the Make This Extension Critical check box.

17. Edit Key Usage, select the Digital Signature and Signature Is Proof Of Origin check boxes, select Allow Key Exchange Without Key Encryption, and select the Make This Extension Critical check box.

18. Click OK to save the template.

Request a certificate

You need to generate a certificate for each of your FS4SP servers and SharePoint servers that has a FAST Content SSA.

1. Log in to the server for which you want to generate a certificate.

2. Follow the guide at *http://technet.microsoft.com/en-us/library/ff625722(WS.10).aspx* to start the Certificate Enrollment wizard with an enterprise CA.

3. Choose Active Directory Enrollment Policy on the enrollment screen.

4. Select the Subject tab.

5. Choose the FAST Search Server template you created in the previous procedure.

6. Click the edit link to configure settings before you enroll the certificate.

7. Set the subject name type to Common Name and enter the FQDN of your server as the value. Then click the Add button.

8. Set the alternative name type to DNS and enter the FQDN of your server as the value. Then click the Add button.

9. Select the General tab.

10. Enter a friendly name and description for your certificate.

11. Select the Extensions tab.

12. For key usage, add the following:

    - Data Encipherment

    - Digital Signature

    - Key Certificate Signing

    - Key Encipherment

13. For extended key usage, add all available options.

14. Select the Private Key tab.

15. Under Cryptographic Service Provider, choose RSA Provider. The DH check box can be cleared. Under the Key options, your key length should be 2048 and it must be exportable. Key type can remain the default of Exchange. For an FS4SP server, Key Permissions must give the FS4SP service account full access to the certificate's private key. For a SharePoint server with the FAST Content SSA, give the service account for the FAST Content SSA full access to the certificate's private key.

16. Click OK to save your settings.

17. Click Enroll.

    The certificate should now appear in the Personal folder under the Local Computer's hierarchy.

After you have generated certificates for each server, follow the TechNet procedure at *http:// technet.microsoft.com/en-us/library/ff381244.aspx#Replace_Default* about how to properly install the certificate for your FS4SP server and your SharePoint servers.

To test that the certificates are properly installed, from a SharePoint Management Shell on the FAST Content SSA servers, issue the following Windows PowerShell cmdlet, where *fs4spserver.mydomain.com* is the FS4SP server to test the connection against. The value for your newly installed certificate should read *true* in the *ConnectionSuccess* column, and you should now be able to start crawling content with the new certificates installed.

```
Ping-SPEnterpriseSearchContentService <fs4spserver.mydomain.com>
```

Removing the FAST Search Web Crawler

FS4SP comes with several FAST Search specific connectors; one of these is the FAST Search Web crawler. It is typically used for crawling pages that the SharePoint built-in web crawler has trouble with and for crawling RSS feeds. The FAST Search Web crawler is vastly more configurable than its Share-Point counterpart; however, in many cases, web content will not be part of your search solution or the SharePoint crawler's feature set will suffice for your web crawling needs. You can read more about the FAST Search Web crawler in Chapter 7, "Content Processing."

If you are not planning to use the FAST Search Web crawler, you can edit your deployment configuration file to remove the crawler option; there is no reason to install unneeded software. If you need the FAST Search Web crawler at a later time, you can re-enable it using the same procedures that remove it.

Remove the FAST Search Web crawler before initial configuration

1. Create a copy of *<FASTSearchFolder>\etc\deployment.sample.single.xml* on the FS4SP administration server.

2. Open the file in a text editor, and then remove the line *<crawler role="single" />*.

3. Edit the database connection string *<connector-databaseconnectionstring />*.

4. Insert the server host name **<host name="single01.search.microsoft.com">**.

5. Save the file.

6. Select the Use An Existing Deployment File check box (see Figure 4-7 in Chapter 4), and browse to your newly created deployment file.

7. Continue the configuration process.

Remove the FAST Search Web crawler after initial configuration

1. Open *<FASTSearchFolder>\etc\config_data\deployment\deployment.xml* in a text editor on the FS4SP administration server.

2. Remove the line *<crawler role="single" />*.

3. Save the file.

4. Stop the FAST Search for SharePoint Monitoring service.

5. Stop the FAST Search for SharePoint service.

6. Open an FS4SP shell on the FS4SP administration server.

7. Re-create configuration files by typing the command **Set-FASTSearchConfiguration**.

8. Start the FAST Search for SharePoint service.

 Note This also starts the FAST Search for SharePoint Monitoring service.

9. Verify that all required processes are running by typing the command **nctrl status**.

Upgrading from SharePoint Search to FS4SP

It is common for organizations to mature into needing a more configurable and powerful search engine. That need may be a result of a growing number of documents, a more demanding user base, or the realization that SharePoint search is just not effectively delivering the results users need. Therefore, migrating from standard SharePoint search to FS4SP is a common scenario when installing FS4SP. Although the migration is straightforward, the obvious method creates some undesirable downtime.

Migrating an existing solution that uses SharePoint Search over to FS4SP involves creating two Search Service Applications (SSAs), reindexing your content, and then, at some point, switching out the Standard SSA with the FAST Query SSA in your application proxy group, as shown in Figure 9-3.

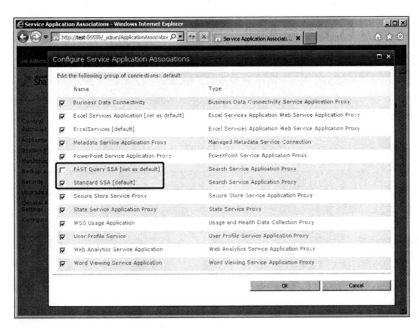

FIGURE 9-3 Default service application associations.

In addition, you have to create a Search Center for your FS4SP results in order to verify that you actually get results back and verify that they look the way you expect. Unless you have a complete replica of the search installation, this can be done only in the production environment. When testing your new search solution against FS4SP, you must switch the default SSA in the application proxy group from the SharePoint one to the FS4SP one. This puts the built-in search in a nonworking state while you test FS4SP. After you switch back, the FAST Search Center will not work.

Another option is to create a web application, site collection, and search site in your production environment to carry out the tests. Because you have one application proxy group per site collection, this option does not affect your running environment. When you are finished setting it up and have completed testing, you can either direct searches to the new web application or reconfigure your existing search and proxy group to use the FAST Query SSA.

 More Info You can use the SharePoint Enterprise Search Migration Tool for SharePoint Server 2010 to migrate keyword settings, search scopes, and Search Center URL settings. You can download the tool from *http://archive.msdn.microsoft.com/odcsp2010searchmigra*.

Reducing the Downtime When Migrating from SharePoint Search to FS4SP

If you look at the architecture behind the SSAs, you discover that the FAST Query SSA is actually a regular SSA with some extra parameters. To reduce the downtime when switching from SharePoint Search to FS4SP, you can upgrade your existing SSA to take the role of the FAST Query SSA. You still have to reindex all your content (except for People Search) and most likely need to customize a new Search Center, but you can do these things without touching the proxy application group or creating new web applications or site collections. In effect, you can do the preparation and switch without any downtime for your search solutions.

Upgrading is done using Windows PowerShell in order to set some extended properties on the current SSA, turning it into a FAST Query SSA. Before the upgrade, make sure the Search Location of your old Search Center is set to Local Search Results in order for it to retrieve results from the old index. Your new Search Center based on the FAST Enterprise Search site template should point to Local FAST Search Results, which returns results from your FS4SP farm.

 Note If you are using the *KeywordQuery* class in parts of your solution and the property *ResultsProvider* is set to *Default* but you want results from the SharePoint index and not from FS4SP, you need to change the property to *SharePointSearch* because the default provider is pointing to FS4SP.

The following Windows PowerShell upgrade script is executed from a SharePoint 2010 Management Shell. You must modify the script to match the settings found in *<FASTSearchFolder>\Install_Info.txt*.

After the upgrade of the SSA completes, you can continue to index content into both the SharePoint Search and the FS4SP index side by side until you are ready to make the switch. The FAST Query SSA now acts as both the SharePoint standard SSA and the FAST Query SSA, depending on the search location specified in the queries.

```
# upgrade_ssa.ps1
#
# The below script is based on a script found in
# "Microsoft® SharePoint® 2010 Administrator's Companion", and fixed for bugs.
# The port numbers used assume you are using 13000 as the FS4SP base port,
# and use http and not https for the query traffic.
# Edit $SrvName, $ResLoctV and $ssa to match your system

Function Set-FASTProp {
param ($SSA, [string] $Cmd, [string] $Prop, [string] $PropValue)
# Initialise $obj to Extended property object
$obj = "SPEnterpriseSearchExtended" + $cmd + "Property"
$GetProp = &("Get-" + $obj) -Sea $ssa -id $Prop -ErrorAction SilentlyContinue

  if ($GetProp)
  {
    # Property exists
    &("Set-" + $obj) -SearchApplication $ssa -ID $Prop -Value $PropValue
  } else {
    # Property does not exist
    &("New-" + $obj) -SearchApplication $ssa -Name $Prop -Value $PropValue
  }
} # End of Function Set-FASTProp

$ssa = "Standard Search SSA"
$SrvName = "://fs4sp.contoso.com:"
$AdminUserV = "contoso\svc_spadmin"
$QueryLoc = "FASTSearchQueryServiceLocation"
$QueryLocV = "http" + $SrvName +"13287"
$AdminLoc = "FASTSearchAdminServiceLocation"
$AdminLocV = "http" + $SrvName + "13257"
$AdminUser = "FASTSearchAdminServiceAuthenticationUser"
$ResLoc = "FASTSearchResourceStoreLocation"
$ResLoctV = "http" + $SrvName + "13255"

Set-SPEnterpriseSearchServiceApplication $ssa -DefaultSearchProvider "FASTSearch"

Set-FASTProp $ssa "Query" $QueryLoc $QueryLocV
Set-FASTProp $ssa "Query" $AdminLoc $AdminLocV
Set-FASTProp $ssa "Query" $AdminUser $AdminUserV
Set-FASTProp $ssa "Query" $ResLoc $ResLoctV
```

Improving the Built-in Duplicate Removal Feature

The built-in duplicate detection in FS4SP uses the title of a document and the first 1,024 characters of the indexed item in order to check whether a document is a duplicate of another. If you have many documents created from the same template, you run the risk of treating them as duplicates because the first 1,024 characters might be the same. This can be solved by using more than the first 1,024 characters of the text or by using metadata such as a document number instead to identify duplicates.

Using checksums is a common way to compare data. Comparing two numbers instead of comparing large text strings is a lot quicker, and FS4SP lets you use any managed property of type *integer* for detecting duplicate documents.

If you want to improve the logic used for the default duplicate detection, you can create a managed property that has the special name *documentsignaturecontribution*. Any text that you map to *documentsignaturecontribution* is considered when creating a checksum for the item.

After the checksum is computed in the item processing pipeline, it is stored as an integer in the managed property *DocumentSignature*. This managed property is used by default when you turn on duplicate removal on search queries.

Important FS4SP uses a 32-bit checksum for duplicate checking. Checksum algorithms are usually built in such a way as to avoid collisions. A *collision* appears when two different byte sequences yield the same checksum. Theoretically, this gives us more than 4 billion unique values (2^32), but in real life, there is a 50 percent probability that you will get a collision after just 77,000 items and a 99 percent probability that you will get a collision when you reach 200,000 indexed items. (See the birthday paradox at *http://en.wikipedia.org/wiki/Birthday_paradox* for more information.) Thus, when indexing more than 200,000 items and using the duplicate removal function in FS4SP, you are bound to get erroneous duplicates.

Create a duplicate checksum based on all text in an item

1. Open an FS4SP shell.

2. Create a crawled property, a managed property, and the mapping between them. The following code adds the crawled property to the MESG Linguistics metadata category (property set), but you can use a custom metadata category as well.

    ```
    $mp = New-FASTSearchMetadataManagedProperty -Name documentsignaturecontribution -Type 1

    $cp = New-FASTSearchMetadataCrawledProperty -Name documentsignaturecontribution -Propset
    48385c54-cdfc-4e84-8117-c95b3cf8911c -VariantType 31

    New-FASTSearchMetadataCrawledPropertyMapping -ManagedProperty $mp -CrawledProperty $cp
    ```

3. Create an External Item Processing component that adds the text of the *body* crawled property to the *documentcontribution* property. The following sample is a Windows PowerShell script that can be saved as *C:\FASTSearch\bin\duplicatecontribution.ps1*.

Important Remember to copy the script to all FS4SP servers configured to run the document processor component.

Warning The use of Windows PowerShell in the sample is used to illustrate the logic of the item processor. Using Windows PowerShell for item processors should be used only for testing purposes because it will have an adverse impact on performance.

```
# <FASTSearchFolder>\bin\duplicatecontribution.ps1
function DoWork()
{
    param ([string]$inputFile, [string]$outputFile)
    $template = @"
<?xml version="1.0" encoding="utf-8"?>
<Document>
  <CrawledProperty propertySet="{0}" propertyName="{1}" varType="{2}">{3}</
CrawledProperty>
</Document>
"@
    $groupIn = "11280615-f653-448f-8ed8-2915008789f2" # FAST internal group
    $nameIn = "body" # property name
    $typeIn = 31 # text

    $groupOut = "48385c54-cdfc-4e84-8117-c95b3cf8911c" # MESG Linguistics
    $nameOut = "documentsignaturecontribution" # property name
    $typeOut = 31 # text

    $xmldata = [xml](Get-Content $inputFile -Encoding UTF8) # read file
    $node = $xmldata.Document.CrawledProperty | Where-Object {
        $_.propertySet -eq $groupIn -and
        $_.propertyName -eq $nameIn -and
        $_.varType -eq $typeIn }
    $data = $node.innerText

    $resultXml = [string]::Format( $template, $groupOut, $nameOut, $typeOut, $data)
    $resultXml | Out-File $outputFile -Encoding UTF8 # write file
}
DoWork $args[0] $args[1]
```

4. Open *<FASTSearchFolder>\etc\pipelineextensibility.xml* and register *duplicatecontribution. ps1* as shown here, where you add the *<Run>* node below the existing *<PipelineExtensibility>* node.

```
<PipelineExtensibility>
    <Run command="C:\Windows\System32\WindowsPowerShell\v1.0\PowerShell.exe
      C:\FASTSearch\bin\duplicatecontribution.ps1 %(input)s %(output)s">
        <Input>
            <CrawledProperty propertySet="11280615-f653-448f-8ed8-2915008789f2"
                propertyName="body" varType="31"/>
        </Input>
        <Output>
            <CrawledProperty propertySet="48385c54-cdfc-4e84-8117-c95b3cf8911c"
                propertyName="documentsignaturecontribution" varType="31"/>
        </Output>
    </Run>
</PipelineExtensibility>
```

5. Issue **psctrl reset** to reload the document processor configuration files.

6. Recrawl your content.

You can create custom managed properties for duplicate removal instead of using the built-in one, but using a custom managed property for duplicate removal is supported only via the Query Object Model and the Query Web Service, not via the default Core Results Web Part in the Search Center. If you want to use a custom managed property in your Search Center, you must create a custom Core Results Web Part as well.

Create a duplicate removal checksum based on file size and file type

1. Open an FS4SP shell.

2. Create a crawled property, a managed property, and the mapping between them. The following code adds the crawled property to the MESG Linguistics metadata category (property set), but you can use a custom metadata category as well.

```
$mp = New-FASTSearchMetadataManagedProperty -Name customcrc -Type 2
$mp.SortableType = "SortableEnabled"
$mp.Update()
$cp = New-FASTSearchMetadataCrawledProperty -Name customcrc -Propset 48385c54-cdfc-4e84-
8117-c95b3cf8911c -VariantType 20
New-FASTSearchMetadataCrawledPropertyMapping -ManagedProperty $mp -CrawledProperty $cp
```

3. Create an External Item Processing component that uses the file size and file type of the item to calculate a new checksum to be used for duplicate removal.

   The following sample is a Windows PowerShell script that can be saved as *C:\FASTSearch\bin\customcrc.ps1*.

> **Important** Remember to copy the script to all FS4SP servers configured to run the document processor component.

> **Warning** The use of Windows PowerShell in the sample is used to illustrate the logic of the item processor. Using Windows PowerShell for item processors should be used only for testing purposes because it will have an adverse impact on performance.

```
# <FASTSearchFolder>\bin\customcrc.ps1
function DoWork()
{
    param ([string]$inputFile, [string]$outputFile)

    $template = @"
<?xml version="1.0" encoding="utf-8"?>
```

```
<Document>
  <CrawledProperty propertySet="{0}" propertyName="{1}" varType="{2}">{3}</
CrawledProperty>
</Document>
"@
    $groupIn = "11280615-f653-448f-8ed8-2915008789f2" # FAST internal group
    $nameIn = "data" # property name
    $typeIn = 31 # text

    $groupIn2 = "7262A2F9-30D0-488F-A34A-126584180F74" # Format Information group
    $nameIn2 = "mime" # property name
    $typeIn = 31 # text

    $groupOut = "48385c54-cdfc-4e84-8117-c95b3cf8911c" # MESG Linguistics
    $nameOut = "customcrc" # property name
    $typeOut = 20 # integer

    $xmldata = [xml](Get-Content $inputFile -Encoding UTF8) # read file
    $node = $xmldata.Document.CrawledProperty | Where-Object {
        $_.propertySet -eq $groupIn -and
        $_.propertyName -eq $nameIn -and
        $_.varType -eq $typeIn }
    $size = $node.innerText.length

    $node = $xmldata.Document.CrawledProperty | Where-Object {
        $_.propertySet -eq $groupIn2 -and
        $_.propertyName -eq $nameIn2 -and
        $_.varType -eq $typeIn }

    $mime = $node.innerText

    $crc = "$mime $size".GetHashCode() # Get CRC32

    $resultXml = [string]::Format( $template, $groupOut, $nameOut, $typeOut, $crc)
    $resultXml | Out-File $outputFile -Encoding UTF8 # write file
}
DoWork $args[0] $args[1]
```

4. Open *<FASTSearchFolder>\etc\pipelineextensibility.xml* and register *customcrc.ps1* as shown
   here, where you add the *<Run>* node below the existing *<PipelineExtensibility>* node.

```
<PipelineExtensibility>
    <Run command="C:\Windows\System32\WindowsPowerShell\v1.0\PowerShell.exe C:\FASTSearch\
bin\customcrc.ps1 %(input)s %(output)s">
        <Input>
            <CrawledProperty propertySet="11280615-f653-448f-8ed8-2915008789f2"
propertyName="data" varType="31"/>
            <CrawledProperty propertySet="7262A2F9-30D0-488F-A34A-126584180F74"
propertyName="mime" varType="31"/>
        </Input>
        <Output>
            <CrawledProperty propertySet="48385c54-cdfc-4e84-8117-c95b3cf8911c"
propertyName="customcrc" varType="20"/>
        </Output>
    </Run>
</PipelineExtensibility>
```

5. Issue **psctrl reset** to reload the document processor configuration files.

6. Recrawl your content in order to make the new managed property *customcrc* available for use in duplicate removal.

To use your new property for duplicate trimming by using the *KeywordQuery* class, you assign the name of the managed property to the *TrimDuplicatesOnProperty* property of the *KeywordQuery* class as shown in the following code. When this property is not set, it defaults to using *DocumentSignature*.

```
KeywordQuery kq = new KeywordQuery(...);
kq.TrimDuplicatesOnProperty = "customcrc";
```

Returning All Text for an Indexed Item

By default, FS4SP only returns metadata, a hit-highlighted title, and hit-highlighted summaries to the user interface. However, for some scenarios, you might want to return the full text of an item and not just metadata or hit-highlighted summaries. It could be that you want the text as input for an external component such as a clustering engine or want to create custom hit highlighting.

The text of an item is actually stored in a managed property named *body*. When looking at the settings for this managed property, you see that the *SummaryType* is set to *Dynamic*. In order to retrieve all the text, you need the *SummaryType* to be set to *Static*.

Instead of modifying the *body* property, which is used by FS4SP internally, you should create a new one and copy the contents of *body* over to the new property. The steps involved to accomplish this are as follows:

1. Create a crawled property to hold a copy of the item text.

2. Create a managed property with *SummaryType* set to *Dynamic*.

3. Map the crawled property to the managed property.

4. Create a custom extensibility stage to copy the data from *body*.

You can follow the same procedure listed earlier in "Create a duplicate checksum based on all text in an item," or you could reuse the *documentsignaturecontribution* managed property. This property has *SummaryType* set to *Static* by default.

When executing search queries, you have to add the property to your query in order to return it. The following is an example that uses the *KeywordQuery* class in Microsoft .NET and includes *documentsignaturecontribution* in the search result.

Important By default, a managed property stores up to 1,024 KB of raw text and returns up to 64 KB of text in a search result. If your items contain more text or you want more returned per search result, you have to increase the *MaxIndexSize* and *MaxResultSize* properties of the managed property. You should at least match them to the default for the *body* managed property, which is 16,384 KB for maximum size and 512 KB returned in a search result. You can set these values by using the *Set-FASTSearchMetadataManagedProperty* Windows PowerShell cmdlet.

Executing Wildcard Queries Supported by FQL

Using wildcard characters when searching is a way of increasing the recall for a search query. When you use wildcards, the entered term is expanded into more terms, and thus it is able to match more items. Wildcards can be a useful way of not missing out on potentially good hits that were omitted because of plural forms of a term, concatenated words, or common misspellings.

 More Info See Chapter 2, "Search Concepts and Terminology," for an explanation about recall and precision.

The Keyword Query Language (KQL) supports only the asterisk (*) wildcard character—and only at the end of a term. FAST Query Language (FQL) supports two wildcard characters:

- **Question mark (?)** Matches one arbitrary letter or number
- **Asterisk (*)** Matches zero or more arbitrary letters or numbers

 Important Wildcards will not match white space or special characters such as punctuation marks, commas, quotation marks, and apostrophes.

The wildcard characters can be used anywhere in a term, but if the returned expansion set of the term is greater than 10,000, you receive the query error "There are too many results for this search. Please try your search again with more specific keywords." If you craft wildcard queries and receive this error, try to limit searching to specific fields (managed properties) instead, where the total amount of unique expansion terms would be fewer than 10,000. Table 9-1 provides examples of using wildcard characters in search terms when writing FQL.

TABLE-9-1 Wildcard use in search terms

Query	Matches
wild*	Both *wild* and *wildcard*
*ild	Both *wild* and *child*
?ar	Both *car* and *far*, but not *calendar*
*eet???	*Meetings*, but not *meet* or *meeting*
co*ing	Both *connecting* and *collaborating*

Note that some cases in which you could use wildcards are better solved using lemmatization or stemming. For example, *car* and *cars* would both be returned as matches when querying for *car* with lemmatization turned on for the query. Using wildcards at the beginning of a term fails in most cases because it expands to more than 10,000 terms. However, it does work when targeting managed properties with fewer than 10,000 unique terms.

> **More Info** See Chapter 2 for an explanation about the difference between stemming and lemmatization.

When using an asterisk as the wildcard character, you can state the minimum and maximum number of characters it should expand to. The following two FQL statements yield the same results, matching words starting with *prefix* and followed by zero to four characters.

```
any("prefix","prefix?","prefix??","prefix???","prefix????")
```

```
string("prefix*",maxexpansion=4)
```

If you want to match terms at the beginning or end of data in a specific managed property, you can take advantage of the two FQL operators *starts-with* and *ends-with*. These operators are useful when querying specific fields, such as the author or title fields. Table 9-2 lists examples of the equivalent queries using wildcards and *starts-with/ends-with*.

TABLE 9-2 Queries using *starts-with/ends-with* against the managed property *author*

Query	Matches
title:starts-with("fast search for sharepoint")	*Fast search for sharepoint* but not *sharepoint has fast search for everyone*
author:ends-with("svenson")	*Mikael Svenson* and *Svenson*, but not *Mikael Svenson II*

> **Note** If the wildcard characters ? and * are part of your query, you can turn off wildcards for your FQL queries to treat those as regular characters instead. This causes them to be replaced by white space during tokenization instead of being expanded. For example, the following code will not match the title "What is bit?"
>
> ```
> title:string("What is BI?", mode="PHRASE", wildcard="off")
> ```

Getting Relevancy with Wildcards

The sorting or ranking of search results is an important factor when it comes to search. However, if you use wildcard characters on all the search terms, the linguistic part of the ranking algorithm in FS4SP counts next to nothing when sorting the result set. This is because only full terms (words) or their lemmatized versions are used to build the rank score for an item. There are no perfect solutions to this, but you can reduce the problem and influence ranking by expanding your FQL queries.

> **More Info** See Chapter 2 and the section "Full-Text Indexes and Rank Profiles" in Chapter 6, "Search Configuration," for information about the different parts of the rank profile and how to tune them.

If a user searches for *collab* proj**—meaning *collaboration project*—and you are using the abbreviations in your items, you can get a higher ranking by including the stemmed forms as *OR* parts of a query.

Original query
```
string("collab* proj*", mode="simpleall")
```

Expanded query using stems
```
or(
    string(
        "collab* proj*",
        mode="simpleall"
    ),
    string(
        "collab proj",
        mode="simpleall"
    )
)
```

If the terms are commonly used abbreviations, you could also expand the search by using proper synonyms. Synonyms could either be pulled out from the Keywords list via code or you could maintain a custom list in SharePoint where you look up the synonyms.

> **More Info** See the section "Keyword, Synonym, and Best Bet Management" in Chapter 6 for more information about the Keywords list.

Expanded query using stems and known synonyms
```
or(
    string(
        "collab* proj*",
        mode="simpleall"
    ),
    string(
        "collab proj",
mode="simpleall"
```

```
    ),
    string(
"collaboration project",
        mode="simpleall"
    )
)
```

An alternative to using *OR* to expand the query as shown in the previous two examples is to use the *xrank* operator to boost queries that contain either the stemmed form of the term or the synonyms. Using this operator ensures that your manual expansions will not increase the recall of the original query but rather will merely boost items that contain your known term forms.

Expanded query using *XRANK*

```
xrank(
    string(
        "collab* proj*",
        mode="simpleall"
    ),
    string(
        "collab proj collaboration project",
        mode="simpleany"
    ),
    boost=4000
)
```

The preceding sample uses *simpleany* for the *XRANK* query in order to give boost to any item containing one of the four known forms. You can, of course, modify the query to require that both words are present and even give more boost to items that contain both the abbreviated and the full form of the terms.

Debugging an External Item Processing Component

You should always test your External Item Processing components thoroughly before deploying them to your FS4SP production environment. In the best of worlds, this includes using unit tests for development but also manual tests from the command-line on each server that will execute the component during live item processing. However, it's not always easy to test a processing component without running it in a real FS4SP deployment. The following two sections give you guidance on how to inspect what's going on in your processor during live item processing.

Inspecting Crawled Properties by Using the Spy Processor

The *Spy processor* is a useful item processing stage that is available in FS4SP. The whole purpose of the processor is to dump all crawled properties of the item—with the values they contain at that very position in the pipeline—to a file. To make this happen, you add the Spy processor at the place in the indexing pipeline configuration where you want to examine the state of the crawled properties.

When you debug an External Item Processing component, it can be useful to know *exactly* what was sent in to the component and what came out on the other side. This is very easy to find out by using the Spy processor.

As described in the section "Understanding the Indexing Pipeline" in Chapter 7, the principal configuration file for the indexing pipeline and all the default processors is *<FASTSearchFolder>\etc\pipelineconfig.xml*. Figure 9-4 shows the portion in which the Spy processor is defined.

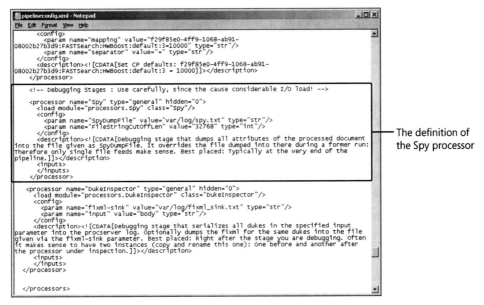

The definition of the Spy processor

FIGURE 9-4 The configuration of the default Spy processor in *pipelineconfig.xml*.

As you see from Figure 9-4, the name of the processor is simply *Spy*. You can use this name to add the processor to any location within the indexing pipeline. In order to do this, and thus be able to inspect all crawled properties of the item at the specific place in the indexing pipeline, do the following:

1. On your FS4SP administration server, open *<FASTSearchFolder>\etc\pipelineconfig.xml*, where you find the definition of the actual pipeline. The first lines of that segment are shown in the following XML configuration section.

    ```
    <pipeline name="Office14 (webcluster)" default="1">
      <description><![CDATA[Pipeline for FS14.]]></description>
      <priority>0</priority>
      <processor name="FFDDumper"/>
      <processor name="DocInit"/>
      <!-- Generate Crawled Properties (CPs) from fed attributes -->
      <processor name="PropertiesFeedingFixture"/>
      <!-- XML parse CPs from attributes -->
      <!-- Crawler -->
      <processor name="DocumentRetriever"/>
      <processor name="URLProcessor"/>
      <processor name="Decompressor"/>
      ...
      ...
    ```

2. Add the Spy processor in the place you think is appropriate. For example, let's say you're wondering why a certain item was dropped in the pipeline by the Offensive Content Filtering

processor. It might be of interest to inspect the item right before it reaches this stage. In that case, add the Spy processor right before the OffensiveEntityFilter processor:

```
<processor name="Spy"/>
<processor name="OffensiveEntityFilter"/>
```

3. Save and close the file.

4. Reset the document processors by running **psctrl reset** in an FS4SP shell. This makes the indexing pipeline pick up the new directives from *pipelineconfig.xml*.

From this point forward, for every item that is sent through the indexing pipeline, a file called *<FASTSearchFolder>\var\log\spy.txt* is created on the server that processed the item. The location is configurable and determined by the *SpyDumpFile* value in the *pipelineconfig.xml* file, as shown in Figure 9-4. Note that the same file is overwritten for each item processed, so make sure only a single document is being indexed or you will get only the output from the last file that was processed.

Warning Don't leave this stage enabled in the pipeline in a production system. It may have a negative effect on indexing latency and will leave your installation in an unsupported state.

The content of *spy.txt* follows an internal syntax, in which all crawled properties are represented by a line in the following format. Each line starting with #### *ATTRIBUTE* is followed by the name of the crawled property, then its type, and then its current value.

```
#### ATTRIBUTE size <type 'int'>: 446
```

A real-world example of a *spy.txt* file is shown in Figure 9-5. Note that the first two lines are internal attributes used for, among other things, deciding in which content collection the item should end up. As shown in this example, using the Spy processor can be very convenient when debugging item processing. What is even more convenient? Using it twice.

When debugging an External Item Processing component, you want to know both what entered the component and what came out on the other side. Sure, you can do this by implementing custom logging in the component, but the Spy processor can help you out as well. In order to do this, you need to have two Spy processors, but a default configuration has only one. If you were to reuse the Spy processor, both before and after the External Item Processing component, the *spy.txt file* would always be overwritten by the last invocation.

More Info For inspiration about implementing code that logs input for all items and not just the last one to your External Item Processing component, go to *http://blogs.msdn.com/b/ thomsven/archive/2010/09/23/debugging-and-tracing-fast-search-pipeline-extensibility- stages.aspx*.

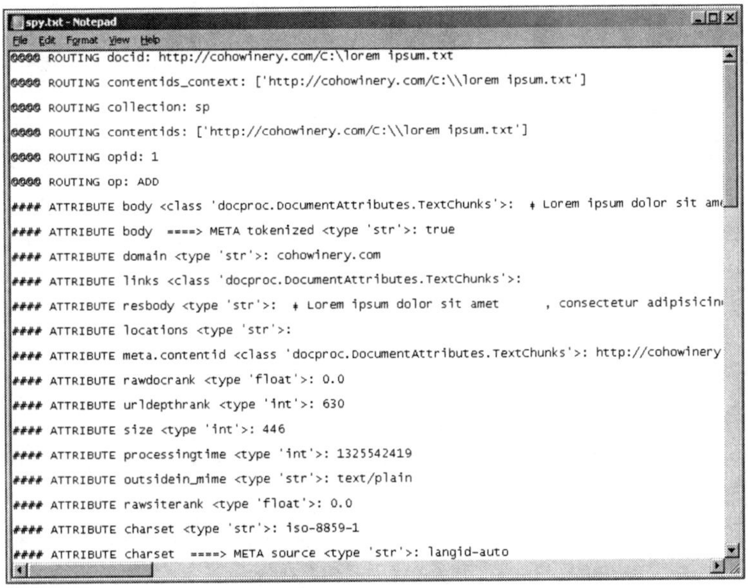

FIGURE 9-5 Example of a *spy.txt* file.

The following steps outline how to add an additional Spy processor and wrap the External Item Processing component by using Spy processors on both sides.

1. On your FS4SP configuration server, open *<FASTSearchFolder>\etc\pipelineconfig.xml*. Scroll down to the definition of the Spy processor, which was shown in Figure 9-4. Replace it with the following code.

```
<processor name="SpyBefore" type="general" hidden="0">
  <load module="processors.Spy" class="Spy"/>
  <config>
    <param name="SpyDumpFile" value="var/log/spyBefore.txt" type="str"/>
    <param name="FileStringCutOffLen" value="32768" type="int"/>
  </config>
  <description><![CDATA[Debugging stage that dumps all attributes of the processed
document into the file given as SpyDumpFile. It overrides the file dumped into there
during a former run: Therefore only single file feeds make sense. Best placed: Typically
at the very end of the pipeline.]]></description>
  <inputs>
  </inputs>
</processor>

<processor name="SpyAfter" type="general" hidden="0">
  <load module="processors.Spy" class="Spy"/>
  <config>
    <param name="SpyDumpFile" value="var/log/spyAfter.txt" type="str"/>
    <param name="FileStringCutOffLen" value="32768" type="int"/>
  </config>
  <description><![CDATA[Debugging stage that dumps all attributes of the processed
document into the file given as SpyDumpFile. It overrides the file dumped into there
during a former run: Therefore only single file feeds make sense. Best placed: Typically
at the very end of the pipeline.]]></description>
```

```
      <inputs>
      </inputs>
    </processor>
```

Instead of having just one Spy processor, you now have two: *SpyBefore* and *SpyAfter*. Notice that the *SpyDumpFile* value has been changed to point to different files.

2. The standard processor that executes the custom code in your External Item Processing component is the CustomerExtensibility processor. Add the two new Spy processors around it by using the following lines of XML.

```
<processor name="SpyBefore"/>
<processor name="CustomerExtensibility"/>
<processor name="SpyAfter"/>
```

3. Save and close the file. Then reset the document processors by running **psctrl reset** in an FS4SP shell. Running this command makes the indexing pipeline pick up the new directives from *pipelineconfig.xml*.

The next time you index an item, the two Spy files will be generated in the <FASTSearchFolder>\var\log folder.

Using the Visual Studio Debugger to Debug a Live External Item Processing Component

When you debug complex External Item Processing components, it may be practical to be able to step through your custom code by using a proper debugger. If you've written your code by using .NET and have access to a test FS4SP farm with Microsoft Visual Studio installed, you can attach the Visual Studio debugger to the processor deployed in your solution.

As an example, let's assume that you've written a very simple Pipeline Extensibility processor with one simple goal: to make lowercase all textual crawled properties you send into it. This example uses the following code. Note that there is no error handling and that the code puts some requirements onto the *PipelineExtensibility.xml* configuration file. See the comments in the code for more information about this.

```
using System;
using System.Collections.Generic;
using System.Linq;
using System.Xml.Linq;
using System.Text;
using System.Threading;

namespace PipelineExtensibility
{
    class Program
    {
        static int Main(string[] args)
        {
            #if DEBUG
            Thread.Sleep(1000 * 30);
            #endif
```

```
try
{
    // Read the input XML file that was provided by FS4SP through %(input)s
    XDocument input = XDocument.Load(args[0]);

    // Fetch all crawled properties
    var inputCPs = input.Descendants("CrawledProperty");

    // Lowercase all crawled properties of type String, i.e. VariantType == 31
    foreach (var inputCP in inputCPs)
    {
        if (inputCP.Attribute("varType").Value == "31")
        {
            inputCP.Value = inputCP.Value.ToLower();
        }
    }

    // Create an output XML file
    XElement output = new XElement("Document");

    // Add all crawled properties to the output field
    // Note that this requires that the <input> and <output> segment of this
    // component's definition in PipelineExtensibility.xml is identical
    foreach (var inputCP in inputCPs)
    {
        output.Add(
            new XElement("CrawledProperty",
                new XAttribute("propertySet",
                    new Guid(inputCP.Attribute("propertySet").Value)),
                new XAttribute("propertyName",
                    inputCP.Attribute("propertyName").Value),
                new XAttribute("varType", inputCP.Attribute("varType").Value),
                inputCP.Value)
        );
    }

    // Save the output XML where FS4SP designated through %(output)s
    output.Save(args[1]);
}
catch (Exception e)
{
    // This will end up in the crawl log, since exit code != 0
    Console.WriteLine("Failed: " + e.Message + "/" + e.StackTrace);
    return 1;
}

return 0;
    }
  }
}
```

Most of the code is not very relevant for the purpose of this example, but here is a quick walk-through anyhow: The input XML is read, all crawled properties with the variant type *31 (text)* are lowercased, and the output XML is created and saved in the designated location. See the section "Integrating an External Item Processing Component" in Chapter 7 for more information about how to develop one of these components.

However, three lines of code are of special interest: the compiler directives at the very start of the main method.

```
#if DEBUG
Thread.Sleep(1000 * 30);
#endif
```

If the solution has been built in debug mode and deployed into FS4SP as such, all items passing through the component will sleep here for 30 seconds. This should give you enough time to attach the Visual Studio debugger to the running process. The following is an example of how to do this using the simple Pipeline Extensibility processor code just shown.

1. In Visual Studio, create a C# Console Application, and then paste the previous code into *Program.cs*. Call the solution **PipelineExtensibility**.

2. Build the solution in debug mode. This is required for the compiler directives to activate the sleep statement. Keep Visual Studio open, and have the solution loaded. Be sure to have a breakpoint set up, for example, at the line loading the XML input document as follows.

   ```
   XDocument input = XDocument.Load(args[0]);
   ```

3. Copy the executable *PipelineExecutable.exe* to a path where the indexing pipeline is allowed to execute it, for example, *<FASTSearchFolder>\PipelineExtensibility.exe*.

4. Configure *<FASTSearchFolder>\etc\PipelineExtentisibility.xml* so that your newly built solution is used. In this example, use the *docpush* command-line tool to index a single text file. When doing so, a crawled property called *ext* will contain the file suffix in uppercase. We want to make this value lowercase.

   ```
   <PipelineExtensibility>
       <Run command="C:\FASTSearch\PipelineExtensibility.exe %(input)s %(output)s">
           <Input>
               <CrawledProperty propertySet="7262a2f9-30d0-488f-a34a-126584180f74"
   varType="31" propertyName="ext"/>
           </Input>
           <Output>
               <CrawledProperty propertySet="7262a2f9-30d0-488f-a34a-126584180f74"
   varType="31" propertyName="ext"/>
           </Output>
       </Run>
   </PipelineExtensibility>
   ```

5. Issue the command **psctrl reset** in an FS4SP shell to reload the indexing pipeline.

6. Create a text file **C:\test.txt** containing some dummy content of your choice. Index the text file using *docpush* by executing the following in an FS4SP shell.

   ```
   docpush -c sp C:\test.txt
   ```

7. Quickly, go back to Visual Studio, expand the Debug menu on the toolbar, and choose Attach To Process, as shown in Figure 9-6.

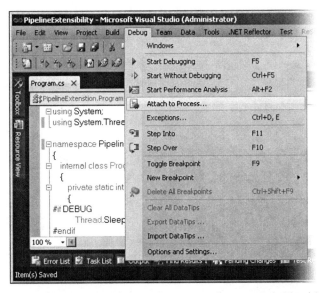

FIGURE 9-6 Attach a debug session to a running process in Visual Studio.

8. In the Attach To Process dialog box that appears (see Figure 9-7), select the process *PipelineExtensibility.exe*, and then click Attach. Note that you might have to select the Show Processes From All Users check box to be able to select it.

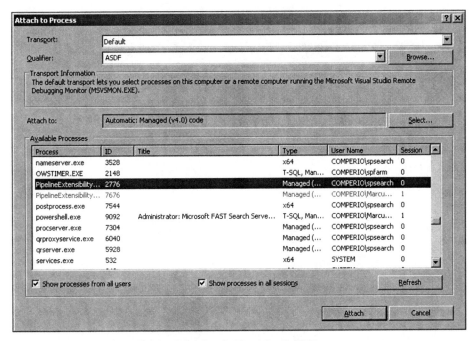

FIGURE 9-7 The Attach To Process dialog box in Visual Studio 2010.

After the sleep cycle has ended, the code hits your breakpoint. You can now freely step through the code and inspect it as usual.

Using the Content of an Item in an External Item Processing Component

A special property set with the id *11280615-f653-448f-8ed8-2915008789f2* and a variant type of *31* contains crawled properties that are created inside the item processing pipeline. Three read-only properties are available in this property set:

- **url**   The URL that is displayed when the item occurs in the query results.

- **data**   The binary content of the source document encoded in base64.

- **body**   The text extracted from the item by parsing the data property. The body is extracted by using an IFilter or other document parser.

Because the properties are read-only, you cannot modify the data in the properties and overwrite with new values.

Configuration for an external item processing component accessing the *body* and *data* properties may look like the following sample.

```
<PipelineExtensibility>
    <Run command="C:\FASTSearch\bin\module.exe %(input)s %(output)s">
        <Input>
            <CrawledProperty propertySet="11280615-f653-448f-8ed8-2915008789f2" propertyName="body"
varType="31"/>
            <CrawledProperty propertySet="11280615-f653-448f-8ed8-2915008789f2" propertyName="data"
varType="31"/>
        </Input>
        <Output>
            <CrawledProperty propertySet="48385c54-cdfc-4e84-8117-c95b3cf8911c"
propertyName="someproperty" varType="31"/>
        </Output>
    </Run>
</PipelineExtensibility>
```

Creating an FQL-Enabled Core Results Web Part

Basing custom Web Parts on the Core Result Web Part is an easy way of getting search results and showing them inside your search applications; this Web Part has a lot of settings you can tune via properties and a ready XSLT to show the results. Building on something that already works saves you time compared to writing a Web Part from scratch.

As mentioned in Chapter 8, "Querying the Index," the Core Results Web Part uses the Federated Search Object Model API via the *QueryManager* when executing search queries. This API does not support FQL directly and you are left using the Keyword Query Syntax instead.

In order to execute FQL-based queries, you have to get access to the *FASTSearchRuntime* instance used in the query as well as using the *FixedQuery* property of the *CoreResultsWebPart*.

When traversing the object hierarchy shown in Figure 9-8, there is no public access to *FASTSearchRuntime* from the *Location* class, but you can access it via reflection. Why this property is internal to SharePoint and not accessible for programmers via public methods that can be overridden in the call stack is unknown, but it could very well be something that was not thought of at the time of implementation.

You have to inherit the following three classes before being able to enable FQL via an instance of *FASTSearchRuntime*.

- *CoreResultsWebPart*
- *CoreResultsDatasource*
- *CoreResultsDatasoureView*

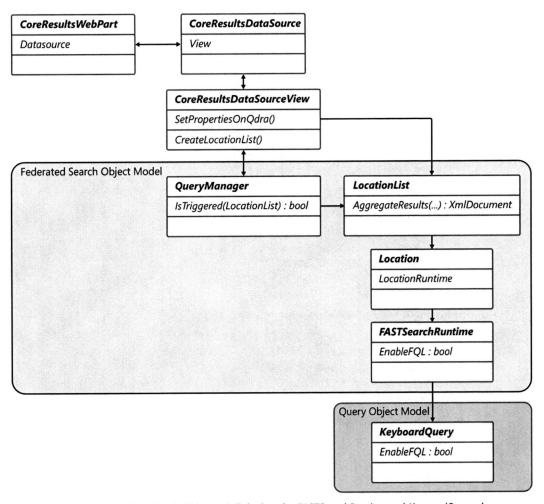

FIGURE 9-8 The way the Core Result Web Part is linked to the *FASTSearchRuntime* and *KeywordQuery* classes.

The following code sample shows how to implement a custom Web Part that inherits from the *CoreResultsWebPart* and enables FQL support. The search terms entered in the search box or via the *k* URL parameter are executed as an FQL *simple-all* query, and then all items written by an author whose name starts with *Mikael, Marcus,* or *Robert* are promoted upwards in the result list.

Custom Core Results Web Part

```
using System.ComponentModel;
using System.Web;
using Microsoft.Office.Server.Search.WebControls;

[ToolboxItem(false)]
public class Ch9FQLEnabledCoreResults : CoreResultsWebPart
{
    protected override void ConfigureDataSourceProperties()
    {
        FixedQuery = GetQuery();
        base.ConfigureDataSourceProperties();
    }

    /// <summary>
    /// Executes a query where the entered keywords are evaluated as
    /// a simple-all query, and results which have the author being either
    /// mikael, marcus or robert will be promoted in the result
    /// </summary>
    /// <returns>FQL query</returns>
    private string GetQuery()
    {
        // Get the query terms from the search box
        string query = HttpUtility.UrlDecode(HttpContext.Current.Request["k"]);
        if (string.IsNullOrEmpty(query)) return null;
        string template =
            @"xrank(
                string(""{0}"", mode=""simpleall""),
                or(
                    author:starts-with(""mikael""),
                    author:starts-with(""marcus""),
                    author:starts-with(""robert"")
                ),
                boost=5000
            )";
        string fql = string.Format(template, query);
        return fql;
    }

    protected override void CreateDataSource()
    {
        // Create a custom DataSource and suppress calling
        // the base class method.
        DataSource = new CoreFqlResultsDataSource(this);
    }
}
```

Custom Core Results Data Source

```
using Microsoft.Office.Server.Search.WebControls;
```

```csharp
public class CoreFqlResultsDataSource : CoreResultsDatasource
{
    private const string CoreFqlResultsViewName = "CoreFqlResults";

    public CoreFqlResultsDataSource(CoreResultsWebPart parentWebPart)
        : base(parentWebPart)
    {
        // Create a custom DataSourceView and suppress calling
        // the base class method.
        base.View = new CoreFqlResultsDataSourceView(this, CoreFqlResultsViewName);
    }
}
```

Custom Core Results Data Source View

```csharp
using System;
using System.Linq;
using System.Reflection;
using System.Reflection.Emit;
using Microsoft.Office.Server.Search.Query;
using Microsoft.Office.Server.Search.WebControls;

internal class CoreFqlResultsDataSourceView : CoreResultsDatasourceView
{
    private static readonly ReflectionHelper<Location>.GetPropertyDelegate<ILocationRuntime>
        _internalGetHelper =
            ReflectionHelper<Location>.GetProperty<ILocationRuntime>("LocationRuntime");

    public CoreFqlResultsDataSourceView(SearchResultsBaseDatasource dataSourceOwner, string
viewName)
        : base(dataSourceOwner, viewName)
    {
        // Verify that we work with the custom DataSource class
        CoreFqlResultsDataSource fqlDataSourceOwner = base.DataSourceOwner as
CoreFqlResultsDataSource;
        if (fqlDataSourceOwner == null)
        {
            throw new ArgumentOutOfRangeException("dataSourceOwner", "Only CoreFqlResultsDataSource
is supported");
        }
    }

    /// <summary>
    /// Set properties on QueryManager
    /// </summary>
    public override void SetPropertiesOnQdra()
    {
        base.SetPropertiesOnQdra();
        // At this point the query has not yet been dispatched to a search
        // location and we can modify the properties on that location, which will
        // let it understand the FQL syntax.
        UpdateFastSearchLocation();
    }

    private void UpdateFastSearchLocation()
    {
        if (base.LocationList == null) return;
```

```
            // Iterate the Location objects and enable FQL on the FASTSearchRuntime
            foreach (var runtime in
                base.LocationList.Select(location => _internalGetHelper.Invoke(location))
                    .OfType<FASTSearchRuntime>())
            {
                // Enable FQL on the FASTSearchRuntime instance
                runtime.EnableFQL = true;
                return;
            }
        }
    }

    /// <summary>
    /// Helper class to get access to the internal LocationRuntime
    /// property of the Location object
    /// </summary>
    /// <typeparam name="TSource"></typeparam>
    internal class ReflectionHelper<TSource>
    {
        public delegate TProperty GetPropertyDelegate<TProperty>(TSource obj);

        public static GetPropertyDelegate<TProperty> GetProperty<TProperty>(string memberName)
        {
            Type v = typeof(TSource);
            PropertyInfo pi = v.GetProperty(memberName, BindingFlags.Public | BindingFlags.NonPublic |
    BindingFlags.Instance);
            if (pi == null)
                throw new NullReferenceException("No Property or Field");

            DynamicMethod dm = new DynamicMethod("GetPropertyorField_" + memberName,
    typeof(TProperty), new[] { v }, v.Module);
            ILGenerator il = dm.GetILGenerator();

            il.Emit(OpCodes.Ldarg_0); // loaded c, c is the return value
            il.EmitCall(OpCodes.Call, pi.GetGetMethod(true), null);
            il.Emit(OpCodes.Ret);
            return (GetPropertyDelegate<TProperty>)dm.CreateDelegate(typeof(GetPropertyDelegate<TProp
    erty>));
        }
    }
```

Creating a Refinement Parameter by Using Code

When you click a refiner in the FAST Search Center, an additional parameter is added to the URL: the *r*= parameter. This parameter includes the refinement settings in a binary format that is base64-encoded.

There is no public API available for constructing such URLs, but constructing Search Center URLs from other SharePoint pages can be very useful—for example, if you have a page with some keywords attached to it, you want to include a link that uses the keywords as search terms, and you want to refine on the current user without adding the filter to the search box query.

Warning For many cases, you can achieve the same effect by using the *a=* parameter, which appends terms to the query, but this will prevent synonyms and other keyword functionality from working for the query.

The following is an example refinement URL parameter.

```
r=advcategory%3D%22AQpIYW5kbGViYXJzC2FkdmNhdGVnb3J5AQFeASQ%3D%22%20advlang%3D%22AQJlbgdhZHZsYW5
nAQFeASQ%3D%22
```

If you URL-decode the parameter and remove the *r=* part, it looks as follows.

```
advcategory="AQpIYW5kbGViYXJzC2FkdmNhdGVnb3J5AQFeASQ="
advlang="AQJlbgdhZHZsYW5nAQFeASQ="
```

When this is decoded, it refines on *advcategory=Handlebars* and *advland=en*. The managed property you are refining on is followed by a base64-encoded token enclosed in quotation marks. Multiple parameters are separated by a space. The hard part is constructing the token values. The following code shows how to deserialize and serialize a refinement token.

Note The code is based off of the FS4SP internal code for constructing refiner parameters.

```csharp
using System;
using System.Diagnostics;
using System.IO;
using System.Text;

namespace FS4SP.Samples
{
    internal class Test
    {
        public static void DeserializeSerialize()
        {
            // Original token - advcategory=Handlebars
            string token = "AQpIYW5kbGViYXJzC2FkdmNhdGVnb3J5AQFeASQ=";
            Trace.WriteLine("Deserializing Token: {0}", token);

            // Deserialize the token
            Refinement refinement = RefinementTokenEncoder.Deserialize(token);

            Trace.WriteLine("Refiner: {0}", refinement.ManagedPropertyName);
            Trace.WriteLine("RefinementName: {0}", refinement.RefinementName);
            Trace.WriteLine("Value: {0}", refinement.RefinementValue);

            // Generate a new token
            string newToken = RefinementTokenEncoder.GenerateToken(refinement);
            Trace.WriteLine(newToken);
```

```csharp
                // Compare the tokens
                Trace.WriteLine("Tokens are equal: " + token.Equals(newToken));
        }
    }

    public class Refinement
    {
        public string ManagedPropertyName { get; set; }
        public string RefinementName { get; set; }
        public string RefinementValue { get; set; }
    }

    public class RefinementTokenEncoder
    {
        public static string GenerateToken(Refinement refinement)
        {
            using (Serializer serializer = new Serializer())
            {
                serializer.WriteInt(1);
                serializer.WriteString(refinement.RefinementName);
                serializer.WriteString(refinement.ManagedPropertyName);
                int index = refinement.RefinementValue.IndexOf(refinement.RefinementName,
StringComparison.Ordinal);
                if ((refinement.RefinementName.Length > 0) && (index >= 0))
                {
                    serializer.WriteInt(1);
                    serializer.WriteString(refinement.RefinementValue.Substring(0, index));
                    serializer.WriteString(refinement.RefinementValue.Substring(index +
refinement.RefinementName.Length));
                }
                else
                {
                    serializer.WriteInt(0);
                    serializer.WriteString(refinement.RefinementValue);
                }
                return serializer.Token;
            }
        }

        public static Refinement Deserialize(string token)
        {
            Refinement refinement = new Refinement();
            using (Serializer serializer = new Serializer(token))
            {
                try
                {
                    if (serializer.ReadInt() != 1)
                    {
                        throw new ArgumentException("Token is not a valid refinement token.");
                    }
                    refinement.RefinementName = serializer.ReadString();
                    refinement.ManagedPropertyName = serializer.ReadString();
                    if (serializer.ReadInt() == 1)
                    {
                        refinement.RefinementValue = serializer.ReadString() + refinement.
RefinementName +
                                                    serializer.ReadString();
```

```csharp
            }
            else
            {
                refinement.RefinementValue = serializer.ReadString();
            }
        }
        catch (FormatException)
        {
            throw new ArgumentException("Token is not a valid refinement token.");
        }

        if (!serializer.IsAtEnd())
        {
            throw new ArgumentException("Token is not a valid refinement token.");
        }
    }
    return refinement;
}

private class Serializer : IDisposable
{
    private readonly MemoryStream _memoryStream;

    public Serializer()
    {
        _memoryStream = new MemoryStream();
    }

    public Serializer(string token)
    {
        _memoryStream = new MemoryStream(Convert.FromBase64String(token));
    }

    public bool IsAtEnd()
    {
        return (_memoryStream.Position == _memoryStream.Length);
    }

    private int ReadByte()
    {
        int num = _memoryStream.ReadByte();
        if (num == -1)
        {
            throw new FormatException("Token is invalid.");
        }
        return num;
    }

    private byte[] ReadBytes(int count)
    {
        byte[] buffer = new byte[count];
        if (_memoryStream.Read(buffer, 0, count) < count)
        {
            throw new FormatException("Token is invalid.");
        }
        return buffer;
    }
```

```
public int ReadInt()
{
    int num = ReadByte();
    bool flag = (num & 0x80) > 0;
    int num2 = (num & 0x70) >> 4;
    int num3 = num & 15;
    for (int i = 0; num2 > 0; i++)
    {
        num = ReadByte() << (4 + (i*8));
        num3 |= num;
        num2--;
    }
    if (flag)
    {
        num3 *= -1;
    }
    return num3;
}

public string ReadString()
{
    int count = ReadInt();
    byte[] bytes = ReadBytes(count);
    return new string(Encoding.UTF8.GetChars(bytes));
}

public void WriteInt(int value)
{
    bool flag = value < 0;
    if (flag)
    {
        value *= -1;
    }
    int num = 0;
    for (int i = value; i > 0; i = i >> 1)
    {
        num++;
    }

    int num3 = ((int) Math.Ceiling(((((num + 4))/8.0))) - 1;
    byte num4 = (byte) (((((byte) num3) << 4) | (flag ? 0x80 : 0));
    num4 = (byte) (num4 | ((byte) (value & 15)));

    _memoryStream.WriteByte(num4);
    value = value >> 4;

    while (num3 > 0)
    {
        _memoryStream.WriteByte((byte) (value & 0xff));
        value = value >> 8;
        num3--;
    }
}

public void WriteString(string value)
{
    int byteCount = Encoding.UTF8.GetByteCount(value);
```

```
            WriteInt(byteCount);
            _memoryStream.Write(Encoding.UTF8.GetBytes(value), 0, byteCount);
        }

        // Properties
        public string Token
        {
            get { return Convert.ToBase64String(_memoryStream.ToArray()); }
        }

        public void Dispose()
        {
            if (_memoryStream == null) return;
            _memoryStream.Close();
            _memoryStream.Dispose();
        }
    }
  }
}
```

Improving Query Suggestions

A great feature in SharePoint search is the ability to get query suggestions as you type your search query in the search box (automatic query completion) or displayed in the Related Searches Web Part. Displaying suggestions aids the user in picking a term that is known to have returned results in the past.

Query suggestions depend on previously executed searches. Only search queries that have been previously returned and then clicked through at least six times during the last 30 days appear in either the search box list or the Related Queries Web Part.

You can add search suggestions manually via Windows PowerShell, as detailed at *http:// technet.microsoft.com/en-us/library/hh148698.aspx*. This method is useful for a new installation because automatic suggestions have yet to be generated.

Let us assume that the query term *FAST Search Server for SharePoint* has been executed at least six times and that a result was clicked each time. When a user searches for *FAST*, the query suggestion *FAST Search Server for SharePoint* is displayed in the Related Queries Web Part on the Search Results page.

Adding, Removing, and Blocking Query Suggestions

In addition to the built-in functionality that adds query suggestions based on search usage over time is the ability to manually add query suggestions by using, for example, Windows PowerShell. Besides adding new terms, you can remove and block terms that you don't want to appear as search suggestions.

List all query suggestions

1. Open a SharePoint Management Shell.

2. Use the following command to list all available query suggestions.

```
Get-SPEnterpriseSearchQuerySuggestionCandidates -SearchApplication "<FAST Query SSA>"
```

Add a query suggestion

1. Open a SharePoint Management Shell.

2. Use the following command to add a new term to the suggestion list.

```
New-SPEnterpriseSearchLanguageResourcePhrase -SearchApplication "<FAST Query SSA>"
-Language en-us -Type QuerySuggestionAlwaysSuggest -Name "<term to suggest>"
```

3. Manually start the timer job to make the suggestions immediately available.

```
(Get-SPTimerJob -Identity "Prepare Query Suggestions").RunNow()
```

Important Be sure to set the language correctly when adding suggested terms because query suggestions are language-specific to either the user's browser setting or the language you have set your search page to use.

Block unwanted query suggestions

1. Open a SharePoint Management Shell.

2. Block terms from being added as search suggestions by using the following command.

```
New-SPEnterpriseSearchLanguageResourcePhrase -SearchApplication "<FAST Query SSA>"
-Language en-us -Type QuerySuggestionBlockList -Name "<term to suggest>"
```

3. Manually start the timer job to make the blocks immediately available.

```
(Get-SPTimerJob -Identity "Prepare Query Suggestions").RunNow()
```

1.   Open a SharePoint Management Shell.

2.   Use the following command to remove a search suggestion.

```
Remove-SPEnterpriseSearchLanguageResourcePhrase -SearchApplication "<FAST Query SSA>"
-Language en-us -Type QuerySuggestionAlwaysSuggest -Identity "<term to suggest>"
```

3.   Manually start the timer job to immediately remove the suggestion.

```
(Get-SPTimerJob -Identity "Prepare Query Suggestions").RunNow()
```

Security Trimming Search Suggestions

The query suggestion feature has a couple of shortcomings. One of them is that the returned suggestions are not security-trimmed. To exemplify this, consider this scenario: Within your company is a group of people working on a new project with a secret code name *Yooba*. They have added several documents with the code name and are frequently using it during search. After a short while, the code name is added to the automatic suggestion list.

If users outside the project go to the search page and start typing *yo*, a suggestion with *Yooba* will appear (as shown in Figure 9-9 and Figure 9-10), even if the users don't have access to any items with this word in it. Depending on your organization, this might not be a problem, but in many organizations, just exposing certain names is a breach of security.

FIGURE 9-9 Displaying search suggestions starting with *yo*.

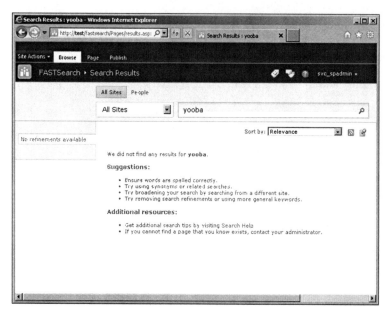

FIGURE 9-10 Executing a search with the term *yooba*. No results exist even though the term was suggested.

Fortunately, you can replace the default Search Box Web Part with a custom one that executes a search for each search suggestion in order to determine whether the user will get any results back at all. For suggestions that don't return a result, you can remove the term from the list returned to the user.

> **Important** Executing one search per query suggestion creates extra load on your FS4SP farm. Be sure to monitor your resources to ensure that your FS4SP deployment can handle the extra query load added by security-checking the suggestions. In the Search Box Web Part, you can tune how often the suggestion queries are executed.

Displaying Actual Results Instead of Suggestions

Instead of showing search suggestions when you start typing, you can display real results. For example, with e-commerce, you can start showing real products that guide the user immediately toward the right item.

For an intranet search, you can display the title and file type icon, giving an indication about what the first result page will return, as shown in Figure 9-11.

FIGURE 9-11 Search suggestions showing actual results instead of suggestions based on previous queries.

Creating a Custom Search Box and Search Suggestion Web Service

To control how search suggestions work, you can create a custom search box, inheriting from *SearchBoxEx*. You also need a custom Web Service deployed within SharePoint to handle the logic for your custom search suggestion queries.

SearchBoxEx uses an embedded version of the *AutoCompleteExtender* control found in the ASP.NET Ajax Control Toolkit. *AutoCompleteExtender* is the control that executes via JavaScript the suggestion queries from your browser. By default, it executes against the SharePoint Query Web Service *GetQuerySuggestions* method. Both the Web Service URL and the method can be changed, and this is what the following code sample does. This code sample creates a custom search box that has an additional Web Part setting to set the query suggestion mode, as shown in Figure 9-12. The modes are as follows:

- *Default*   Like the existing search box

- *SecurityTrimmed*   Same as default but each suggestion is security trimmed

- *Results*   Returns real search results instead of suggestions

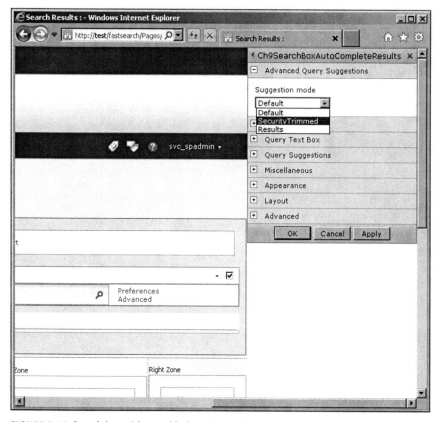

FIGURE 9-12 Search box with an added option to choose how query suggestions are returned.

The custom Web Service is created with the same web service signature as the SharePoint Query Web Service to ensure that the switch of Web Services is as seamless as possible. The Web Service contains two methods, *GetQuerySuggestionsFiltered* and *GetQueryResults*. In addition to these methods, there are some helper methods. All the code is commented inline.

After this Web Part is deployed, you can replace the search box on the default Search Center page and on the result page.

Custom Query Suggestion Web Service

```
using System;
using System.Collections.Generic;
using System.Data;
using System.Globalization;
using System.Linq;
using System.Security.Permissions;
using System.Web.Script.Services;
using System.Web.Services;
using System.Xml;
using Microsoft.Office.Server.Search.Query;
using Microsoft.SharePoint;
using Microsoft.SharePoint.Security;
```

```
[WebServiceBinding(ConformsTo = WsiProfiles.BasicProfile1_1),
 WebService(Namespace = "http://microsoft.com/webservices/OfficeServer/QueryService"),
ScriptService,
 SharePointPermission(SecurityAction.InheritanceDemand, ObjectModel = true),
 SharePointPermission(SecurityAction.Demand, ObjectModel = true)]
internal class SearchSuggestionService : WebService
{
    [ScriptMethod, WebMethod]
    public string[] GetQuerySuggestionsFiltered(string queryXml)
    {
        if (string.IsNullOrEmpty(queryXml))
        {
            throw new ArgumentNullException("queryXml");
        }

        // Use the Query Service internally to intercept the results
        // and reuse the original xml query packet
        QueryService service = new QueryService();
        string[] suggestions = service.GetQuerySuggestions(queryXml);
        if (suggestions.Length > 0)
        {
            bool[] validSuggestions = new bool[suggestions.Length];
            SPSite site = SPContext.Current.Site;

            XmlDocument queryDoc = new XmlDocument();
            queryDoc.LoadXml(queryXml);
            XmlNode textNode = queryDoc.SelectSingleNode("//*[local-name()='QueryText']");
            string language = textNode.Attributes["language"].Value;

            // For each suggestion, create an Action delegate which we can execute
            // in parallel to improve speed
            List<Action> actions = suggestions.Select((suggestion, index)
                => (Action)(()
                    =>
                {
                    // Create a query to search for the suggestion
                    KeywordQuery query = BuildKeywordQuery(language, site);
                    query.QueryText = suggestion;
                    // You only need one result to decide if you have any matches
                    query.RowLimit = 1;
                    // Turn on stemming to increase recall
                    query.EnableStemming = true;
                    // Execute the query
                    var result = query.Execute();
                    ResultTable resultTable = result[ResultType.RelevantResults];
                    // If there are no results, mark the suggestion as invalid
                    validSuggestions[index] = resultTable.TotalRows > 0;
                })).ToList();

            // If there is more than one suggestion, execute the filtering in parallel
            if (actions.Count > 1)
            {
                ThreadHelper.ExecuteParallel(actions);
            }
            else
            {
                ThreadHelper.ExecuteSynchronously(actions);
```

```
        }

        // Iterate the suggestions and create a new list with only
        // suggestions that return results for the current user
        List<string> trimmedSuggestions = new List<string>(suggestions.Length);
        for (int i = 0; i < validSuggestions.Length; i++)
        {
            var isValidSuggestion = validSuggestions[i];
            if (isValidSuggestion) trimmedSuggestions.Add(suggestions[i]);
        }
        return trimmedSuggestions.ToArray();
    }
    return suggestions;
}

[ScriptMethod, WebMethod]
public string[] GetQueryResults(string queryXml)
{
    if (string.IsNullOrEmpty(queryXml))
    {
        throw new ArgumentNullException("queryXml");
    }

    XmlDocument queryDoc = new XmlDocument();
    queryDoc.LoadXml(queryXml);

    // Pick out the query text, language and count from the query xml
    XmlNode textNode = queryDoc.SelectSingleNode("//*[local-name()='QueryText']");
    XmlNode countNode = queryDoc.SelectSingleNode("//*[local-name()='Count']");
    string language = textNode.Attributes["language"].Value;

    // Create a search query where we return title, file extension
    // and a highlighted title if it exists
    KeywordQuery query = BuildKeywordQuery(language, SPContext.Current.Site);
    query.QueryText = textNode.InnerText.Trim() + "*";
    query.SelectProperties.Add("title");
    query.SelectProperties.Add("fileextension");
    query.SelectProperties.Add("hithighlightedproperties");
    query.RowLimit = int.Parse(countNode.InnerText);

    // Execute a search
    ResultTableCollection resultTableCollection = query.Execute();
    ResultTable resultTable = resultTableCollection[ResultType.RelevantResults];

    string[] results = new string[resultTable.RowCount];
    for (int i = 0; i < resultTable.Table.Rows.Count; i++)
    {
        DataRow row = resultTable.Table.Rows[i];
        string title = GetTitle(row);
        results[i] = title;
    }
    return results.ToArray();
}
```

```
    /// <summary>
    /// Create a KeywordQuery object
    /// </summary>
    private static KeywordQuery BuildKeywordQuery(string language, SPSite site)
    {
        KeywordQuery query = new KeywordQuery(site);
        query.UserContextGroupID = site.ID.ToString();
        query.Culture = new CultureInfo(language);
        query.ResultTypes = ResultType.RelevantResults;
        return query;
    }


    /// <summary>
    /// Get the highlighted title if possible
    /// </summary>
    private static string GetTitle(DataRow row)
    {
        string title = (string)row["title"];
        string hh = "<root>" + row["hithighlightedproperties"] + "</root>";
        XmlDocument hhDoc = new XmlDocument();
        hhDoc.LoadXml(hh);
        XmlNode hhtitle = hhDoc.SelectSingleNode("//HHTitle");
        if (hhtitle != null && !string.IsNullOrEmpty(hhtitle.InnerText))
        {
            // Replace the default c0 with b to ensure it's displayed as bold
            title = hhtitle.InnerXml.Trim().Replace("c0", "b").Replace(" ", " ");
        }

        // Return icon and title
        string icon;
        string ext = ((string) row["fileextension"]).ToLower();
        if (ext.Contains("doc"))
            icon = "<img src=\"/_layouts/images/icdoc.png\" border=\"none\">";
        else if (ext.Contains("xls"))
            icon = "<img src=\"/_layouts/images/icxls.png\" border=\"none\">";
        else if (ext.Contains("ppt"))
            icon = "<img src=\"/_layouts/images/icppt.png\" border=\"none\">";
        else if (ext.Contains("pdf"))
            icon = "<img src=\"/_layouts/images/icpdf.png\" border=\"none\">";
        else
        {
            icon = "<img src=\"/_layouts/images/STS_ListItem16.gif\" border=\"none\">";
        }
        return icon + title;
    }
}
```

Custom search box

```
using System.Collections.Generic;
using System.ComponentModel;
using System.Linq;
using System.Web.UI;
using System.Web.UI.WebControls.WebParts;
using Microsoft.Office.Server.Search.WebControls;
using Microsoft.SharePoint.Portal.WebControls;
using Microsoft.SharePoint.WebPartPages;
```

```csharp
public enum QuerySuggestionMode
{
    Default,
    SecurityTrimmed,
    Results
}

[ToolboxItem(false)]
public class Ch9SearchBoxAutoCompleteResults : SearchBoxEx
{
    [WebBrowsable(true)]
    [Category("Advanced Query Suggestions")]
    [ReadOnly(false)]
    [FriendlyName("Suggestion mode")]
    [Description("Set the mode of the query suggestions")]
    [WebPartStorage(Storage.Shared)]
    public QuerySuggestionMode SuggestionMode { get; set; }

    protected override void CreateChildControls()
    {
        base.CreateChildControls();
        if (ShowQuerySuggestions && SuggestionMode != QuerySuggestionMode.Default)
        {
            // Get a reference to the AutoCompleteExtender class which
            // handles query suggestions
            var extender = this.FlattenChildren()
                            .OfType<AutoCompleteExtender>().FirstOrDefault();
            // Redirect the calls to your custom query suggestions Web Service
            extender.ServicePath = "/_layouts/FS4SP.Samples/SearchSuggestionService.asmx";
            if (SuggestionMode == QuerySuggestionMode.SecurityTrimmed)
            {
                // Security filter the search suggestion
                extender.ServiceMethod = "GetQuerySuggestionsFiltered";
            }
            else
            {
                // Return real results as search suggestions
                extender.ServiceMethod = "GetQueryResults";
            }
        }
    }
}

/// <summary>
/// Helper class to recursively find a control
/// </summary>
internal static class Helper
{
    public static IEnumerable<Control> FlattenChildren(this Control control)
    {
        var children = control.Controls.Cast<Control>();
        return children.SelectMany(c => FlattenChildren(c)).Concat(children);
    }
}
```

Helper class to execute queries in parallel

```csharp
using System;
using System.Collections.Generic;
using System.Threading;

public class ThreadHelper
{
    public static void ExecuteSynchronously(List<Action> actions)
    {
        foreach (var action in actions)
        {
            action();
        }
    }


    /// <summary>
    /// Executes a set of methods in parallel and returns the results
    /// from each in an array when all threads have completed.  The methods
    /// must take no parameters and have no return value.
    /// </summary>
    public static void ExecuteParallel(List<Action> actions)
    {
        // Initialize the reset events to keep track of completed threads
        ManualResetEvent[] resetEvents = new ManualResetEvent[actions.Count];

        // Launch each method in its own thread
        for (int i = 0; i < actions.Count; i++)
        {
            resetEvents[i] = new ManualResetEvent(false);
            ThreadPool.UnsafeQueueUserWorkItem(index =>
                {
                    int methodIndex = (int) index;

                    // Execute the method
                    actions[methodIndex]();

                    // Tell the calling thread that we're done
                    resetEvents[methodIndex].Set();
                }, i);
        }

        // Wait for all threads to execute
        WaitHandle.WaitAll(resetEvents);
    }
}
```

Preventing an Item from Being Indexed

It is fairly common that some items should not be indexed. The logic for this is more complex than what can be specified using crawl rules. The reason could be unwanted listing pages, printer-friendly views, old content, or poor content quality. No matter what the reason, any Enterprise Search system should ideally have the ability to prevent items from being indexed and made searchable based on custom logic that can examine the contents of the items being indexed.

The following sections outline the different ways you can prevent an item from being indexed using built-in SharePoint techniques and, by extension, capabilities unique to FS4SP.

Using List, Library, and Site Permission to Exclude Content

For SharePoint content, you can exclude whole lists, libraries, or sites. You configure whether the Share-Point crawler should skip indexing a particular list, library, or site via the settings pages in SharePoint, as shown in Figure 9-13 and Figure 9-14.

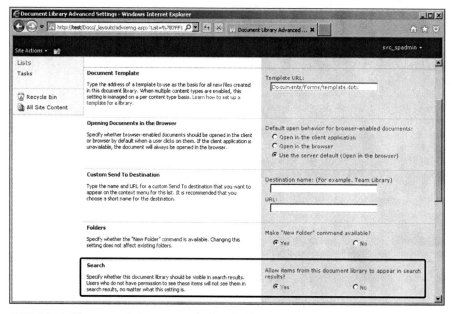

FIGURE 9-13 Library permissions to set whether the library or list is to be indexed.

FIGURE 9-14 Site permissions to set whether the site is to be indexed.

When you turn off search visibility on either of these settings pages, all items below the site or list/library are skipped during indexing.

Using Crawl Rules

For more fine-grained exclusion of content, you can set up crawl rules for your content sources as explained in the section "Crawl Rules Management" in Chapter 7. Basically, you can add a set of rules that either includes or excludes content based on pattern matching of the item path. For example, a rule of *http://intranet.contoso.com/personal/** matches all items starting with *http://intranet.contoso.com/ personal*, and the rule *file://*.pptx* matches all Microsoft PowerPoint files on file shares included as content sources.

Creating Custom Business Rules

So far, you've learned about rules that work on blocking whole libraries from being indexed or rules that can act on the URL of an item. But you might have the need for more complex rules to be applied to get even more control over what is indexed. These can be rules that exclude items based on SharePoint Content Types, prevent items written by a particular author from being skipped, or search for certain words inside of a document and skip the document if you have a match.

With FAST ESP, you had the ability to create custom document processing stages that not only could modify the data inside the pipeline, but also could employ rules that prevented an item from being indexed. The same capability exists in the item processing pipeline of FS4SP but it has not been exposed to the Custom Pipeline Extensibility stage.

Still, there is one stage in the item processing pipeline that applies logic to decide whether items should be dropped from indexing, and that is the Offensive Content Filter. This filter prevents an item from being indexed if it contains a certain amount of predefined offensive words.

More Info See Chapter 7 for more information about the Offensive Content Filter.

In addition to examining the default text in an item, you can include content to be considered when this filter is being run. You can create rules to act on all crawled properties for an item. Using this feature, you can prevent items from being indexed based on custom rules such as checking the date of an item or excluding items that contain sensitive or secret words for your business.

By creating an External Item Processing component, you can run custom business logic to decide whether an item should be indexed; if it should be skipped, you can add several offensive words that trigger the Offensive Content Filter later in the item processing pipeline.

Important By enabling the Offensive Content Filter, other items that include offensive words above the threshold defined in FS4SP are also dropped. It is a good idea to test content indexing with the Offensive Content Filter enabled to check whether it will trigger on items you actually want searchable.

Implement an External Item Processing component to drop items that include a specific word

The following sample shows how to enable the Offensive Content Filter, create the necessary managed property to hold your offensive trigger words, and create an External Item Processing component in Windows PowerShell that looks for the word *FS4SP* in the item text. If the text is present, the External Item Processing component adds enough offensive words to trigger the Offensive Content Filter to prevent the item from being indexed.

1. Enable the Offensive Content Filter by editing *<FASTSearchFolder>\etc\config_data\ DocumentProcessor\optionalprocessing.xml* as shown in the following code.

```
<processor name="OffensiveContentFilter" active="yes" />
```

2. The text you are adding to trigger the Offensive Content Filter has to reside in a managed property named *ocfcontribution*. This property has to be manually created. You cannot add data directly to a managed property in an External Item Processing component. Therefore, you must create a crawled property to hold your data and map the crawled property to the *ocfcontribution* managed property.

3. In an FS4SP shell, execute the following Windows PowerShell commands to create the crawled and managed property, and then map the properties.

```
$mp = New-FASTSearchMetadataManagedProperty -Name ocfcontribution -Type 1
$mp.SummaryType = 0
$mp.Queryable = $false
$mp.Update()
$cp = New-FASTSearchMetadataCrawledProperty -Name ocfcontribution  -Propset 48385c54-
cdfc-4e84-8117-c95b3cf8911c -VariantType 31
New-FASTSearchMetadataCrawledPropertyMapping -ManagedProperty $mp -CrawledProperty $cp
```

4. Create an External Item Processing component that searches for the word *fs4sp* in the item body text. If present, the External Item Processing component adds enough offensive words to trigger the Offensive Content Filter to prevent the item from being indexed. The following sample is a Windows PowerShell script that can be saved as *<FASTSearchFolder>\bin\itemdrop.ps1*.

 Important Remember to copy the script to all FS4SP servers configured to run the document processor component.

 Warning The use of Windows PowerShell in the sample is used to illustrate the logic of the item processor. Using Windows PowerShell for item processors should be used only for testing purposes because it will have an adverse impact on performance.

```
# <FASTSearchFolder>\bin\itemdrop.ps1
function DoWork()
{
    param ([string]$inputFile, [string]$outputFile)

    $template = @"
<?xml version="1.0" encoding="utf-8"?>
<Document>
  <CrawledProperty propertySet="{0}" propertyName="{1}" varType="{2}">{3}</
CrawledProperty>
</Document>
"@
```

```
$groupIn = "11280615-f653-448f-8ed8-2915008789f2" # FAST internal group
$nameIn = "body" # property name
$typeIn = 31 # text

$groupOut = "48385c54-cdfc-4e84-8117-c95b3cf8911c" # MESG Linguistics
$nameOut = "ocfcontribution" # property name
$typeOut = 31 # text

$xmldata = [xml](Get-Content $inputFile -Encoding UTF8) # read file
$node = $xmldata.Document.CrawledProperty | Where-Object {
    $_.propertySet -eq $groupIn -and
    $_.propertyName -eq $nameIn -and
    $_.varType -eq $typeIn }

# search for the word "fs4sp"
if( $node.innerText.ToLower().IndexOf("fs4sp") -ge 0 )
{
    # output off words
    $data = "crap porn ass screw dick"
}
else
{
    $data = ""
}

$resultXml = [string]::Format( $template, $groupOut, $nameOut, $typeOut, $data)
$resultXml | Out-File $outputFile -Encoding UTF8 # write file
}
DoWork $args[0] $args[1]
```

5. Open *<FASTSearchFolder>\etc\pipelineextensibility.xml* and add *itemdrop.ps1* as shown in the following code, where you add the *<Run>* node below the existing *<PipelineExtensibility>* node and replace *<FASTSearchFolder>* with the path where you saved your file.

```
<PipelineExtensibility>
    <Run command="C:\Windows\System32\WindowsPowerShell\v1.0\PowerShell.exe
<FASTSearchFolder> bin\itemdrop.ps1 %(input)s %(output)s">
        <Input>
            <CrawledProperty propertySet="11280615-f653-448f-8ed8-2915008789f2"
propertyName="body" varType="31"/>
        </Input>
        <Output>
            <CrawledProperty propertySet="48385c54-cdfc-4e84-8117-c95b3cf8911c"
propertyName="ocfcontribution" varType="31"/>
        </Output>
    </Run>
</PipelineExtensibility>
```

Important Depending on how much text your item contains, you might have to emit more words into *ocfcontribution* to make it trigger. However, testing shows that if you have more than ~2900 characters of text in your document, the filter will not trigger. You can fix this by modifying *pipelineconfig.xml*. Look for the line of XML listed after this paragraph and either put *ocfcontribution* as the first input parameter or remove *title* and *body*, leaving only *ocfcontribution* to be considered if you're using this stage only for preventing items from being index based on custom rules. If you need support from Microsoft, note that editing *pipelineconfig.xml* leaves your system in an unsupported state, but you can easily revert the change during the support process.

```
<param name="Input" value="title body ocfcontribution" type="str"/>
```

6. Issue **psctrl reset** to reload the document processor configuration files.

   During the next full crawl, items with the word *fs4sp* trigger the Offensive Content Filter and are not indexed. Items that are triggered by the Offensive Content Filter appear as errors in the crawl log, as shown in Figure 9-15.

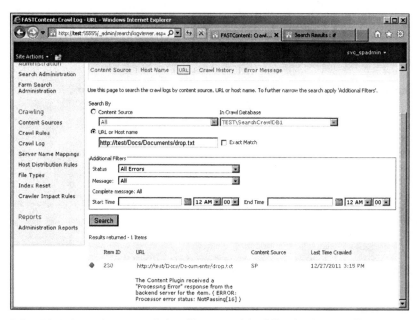

FIGURE 9-15 Items that are not indexed because of the Offensive Content Filter appear as errors in the SharePoint crawl log.

Creating a Custom Property Extractor Dictionary Based on a SharePoint List

One of the core features in FS4SP is the ability to examine the text of items being indexed and enrich the item with additional metadata. FS4SP comes with the ability to detect names, places, and company names, but you can also use your own property extractors based on custom dictionaries. The section "Custom Property Extraction" in Chapter 7 explains how you can create a custom dictionary and register it for use as a custom property extractor in the item processing pipeline.

Manually creating and maintaining an XML file for a dictionary is quite cumbersome. Because one of the core features of SharePoint is the ability to easily create and manage lists, it makes more sense to create the dictionary as a SharePoint list, as shown in Figure 9-16. Then create a custom application page that lets you upload the list as a dictionary file, as shown in Figure 9-17. You still must manually register the dictionary file with a custom property extractor, but you simplify the process of creating and editing the dictionary.

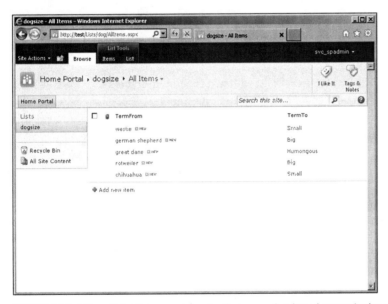

FIGURE 9-16 A SharePoint list named *dogsize* that maps dog breed names in the column TermFrom to the size of the dog in the column TermTo.

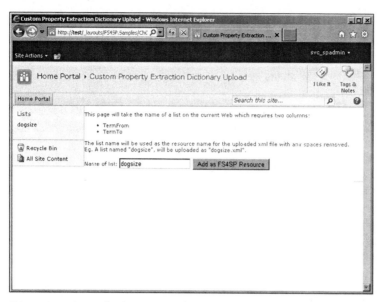

FIGURE 9-17 An application page used to upload the items of a SharePoint list as a dictionary to the FS4SP resource store.

The following code sample makes use of a list with two columns in SharePoint. One column is called *TermFrom*, which is the term you are looking for in the item text; the other column is called *TermTo*, which is what you want returned. The return value is assigned to a crawled property that again can be mapped to a managed property and used, for example, as a refiner.

Page markup

```
<%@ Assembly Name="$SharePoint.Project.AssemblyFullName$" %>
<%@ Import Namespace="Microsoft.SharePoint.ApplicationPages" %>
<%@ Register TagPrefix="SharePoint" Namespace="Microsoft.SharePoint.WebControls"
    Assembly="Microsoft.SharePoint, Version=14.0.0.0, Culture=neutral, PublicKeyToken=71e9bce11
1e9429c" %>
<%@ Register TagPrefix="Utilities" Namespace="Microsoft.SharePoint.Utilities"
Assembly="Microsoft.SharePoint, Version=14.0.0.0, Culture=neutral, PublicKeyToken=71e9bce111e94
29c" %>
<%@ Register TagPrefix="asp" Namespace="System.Web.UI" Assembly="System.Web.Extensions,
Version=3.5.0.0, Culture=neutral, PublicKeyToken=31bf3856ad364e35" %>
<%@ Import Namespace="Microsoft.SharePoint" %>
<%@ Assembly Name="Microsoft.Web.CommandUI, Version=14.0.0.0, Culture=neutral, PublicKeyToken=71
e9bce111e9429c" %>

<%@ Page Language="C#" AutoEventWireup="true" CodeBehind="Ch09UploadDictionaryBasedOnSPList.
aspx.cs"
    Inherits="FS4SP.Samples.Ch09UploadDictionaryBasedOnSPList"
    DynamicMasterPageFile="~masterurl/default.master" %>

<asp:Content ID="PageHead" ContentPlaceHolderID="PlaceHolderAdditionalPageHead" runat="server">
</asp:Content>
<asp:Content ID="Main" ContentPlaceHolderID="PlaceHolderMain" runat="server">
    <p>
        This page will take the name of a list on the current Web which
```

```
        requires two columns:
        <ul>
            <li>TermFrom</li>
            <li>TermTo</li>
        </ul>
        The list name will be used as the resource name for the uploaded xml file with any
        spaces removed.
        <br />
        Eg. A list named "dogsize", will be uploaded as "dogsize.xml".
    </p>
    <p>
        Name of list:
        <asp:TextBox ID="listName" runat="server"></asp:TextBox>
        <asp:Button ID="addBtn" Text="Add as FS4SP Resource" OnClick="AddResource_Click"
            runat="server" />
    </p>
    <p>
        <asp:Label ID="status" runat="server"></asp:Label>
    </p>
</asp:Content>
<asp:Content ID="PageTitle" ContentPlaceHolderID="PlaceHolderPageTitle" runat="server">
    Custom Property Extraction Dictionary Upload
</asp:Content>
<asp:Content ID="PageTitleInTitleArea" ContentPlaceHolderID="PlaceHolderPageTitleInTitleArea"
    runat="server">
    Custom Property Extraction Dictionary Upload
</asp:Content>
```

Page code-behind

```
using System;
using System.IO;
using System.Text;
using Microsoft.Office.Server.Search.Administration;
using Microsoft.SharePoint;
using Microsoft.SharePoint.Search.Extended.Administration.ResourceStorage;
using Microsoft.SharePoint.WebControls;

namespace FS4SP.Samples
{
    public partial class Ch09UploadDictionaryBasedOnSPList : LayoutsPageBase
    {
        protected void AddResource_Click(object sender, EventArgs e)
        {
            // Retrieve the list you want to save as a dictionary
            SPList spList = SPContext.Current.Web.Lists[listName.Text];

            // Initialize a MemoryStream to hold the dictionary
            MemoryStream ms = new MemoryStream();
            // Write the data as UTF-8 without a byte order mark (BOM)
            using (StreamWriter writer =
                new StreamWriter(ms, new UTF8Encoding(false)))
            {
                // Write the XML declaration and root node
                writer.WriteLine("<?xml version=\"1.0\"?><dictionary>");
                // Iterate the items in the list and write them to the stream
                foreach (SPItem item in spList.Items)
```

```
        {
            writer.WriteLine("<entry key=\"{0}\" value=\"{1}\"/>",
                    item["TermFrom"].ToString().ToLower(), item["TermTo"]);
        }
        // Write the end of the XML root node
        writer.WriteLine("</dictionary>");
        writer.Flush();

        // Get a reference to the FAST Query SSA proxy interfaces
        var ssaProxy =
            (SearchServiceApplicationProxy)SearchServiceApplicationProxy
                .GetProxy(SPServiceContext.Current);
        if (ssaProxy.FASTAdminProxy != null)
        {
            var fastProxy = ssaProxy.FASTAdminProxy;
            // Get a reference to the ResourceStorageContext
            ResourceStorageContext resourceContext = fastProxy.ResourceStorageContext;
            // Get a reference to the ResourceStore
            ResourceStore resourceStore = resourceContext.ResourceStore;
            // Rewind the position of our XML MemoryStream to allow reading it
            ms.Position = 0;
            // Create a filename and upload the dictionary to FS4SP
            string filename = listName.Text.Replace(" ", "");
            resourceStore.Upload(@"dictionaries\matching\" + filename + ".xml", ms);

            // Write out a status message
            status.Text = "Uploaded " + spList.Items.Count + " items";
        }
    }
}
}
}
```

Crawling a Password-Protected Site with the FAST Search Web Crawler

A common scenario when crawling web content is to be able log on to a protected site. When using the SharePoint built-in connectors, you do this by setting up a crawl rule, targeting a specific set of pages, and configuring which authentication method you want to use. This is all nicely laid out in a GUI in the FAST Content SSA.

If you're using the FAST Search Web crawler, the process is slightly more complex, although the possibilities and the level of control of the authentication process are greater. You configure the crawler to do this by working with the *<Login>* node in the crawl collection's XML configuration file.

> **Note** This section assumes you've already read the section "FAST Search Web Crawler" in Chapter 7 and have configured a crawl collection by using an associated XML file. If you have lost the XML configuration but already have configured the FAST Search Web crawler with this crawl collection, you can get back the XML by running the following command in an FS4SP shell.
>
> ```
> crawleradmin -G <crawl collection>
> ```

The *<Login>* node does not exist by default in any of the example configurations that come with FS4SP but is documented at *http://technet.microsoft.com/en-us/library/ff354932.aspx#element_login*. This page also provides an example configuration. The example is shown in the following code.

```xml
<?xml version="1.0" encoding="utf-8"?>
<CrawlerConfig>
    <DomainSpecification name="login_example">
        <Login name="mytestlogin">
            <attrib name="preload" type="string">http://preload.contoso.com/
            </attrib>
            <attrib name="scheme" type="string"> https </attrib>
            <attrib name="site" type="string"> login.contoso.com </attrib>
            <attrib name="form" type="string"> /path/to/some/form.cgi </attrib>
            <attrib name="action" type="string">POST</attrib>
            <section name="parameters">
                <attrib name="user" type="string"> username </attrib>
                <attrib name="password" type="string"> password </attrib>
            </section>
            <attrib name="sites" type="list-string">
                <member> site1.contoso.com </member>
                <member> site2.contoso.com </member>
            </attrib>
            <attrib name="ttl" type="integer"> 7200 </attrib>
            <attrib name="html_form" type="string">
                http://login.contoso.com/login.html
            </attrib>
            <attrib name="autofill" type="boolean"> yes </attrib>
            <attrib name="relogin_if_failed" type="boolean"> yes </attrib>
        </Login>
    </DomainSpecification>
</CrawlerConfig>
```

Not all of these parameters are required in all cases, but sometimes you may need to specify additional parameters, depending on the complexity of the site. Understanding which configuration parameters you need to use in the *<Login>* node usually involves some detective work of the targeted website. Luckily, there's a helpful tool that looks at the website and tries to figure out which configuration parameters must be defined in the *<Login>* node. This is far from a 100 percent–proof solution but usually takes you pretty close. The tool is invoked by running the following command in an FS4SP shell.

```
crawleradmin --getlogin [url]
```

Let's say you want to be able to crawl the contents of a (fictive) forum site page residing on *http://example.com/forum*. In order to get to the content, the crawler must first provide the appropriate credentials at *http://example.com/forum/login.html*. Targeting this webpage with *crawleradmin --getlogin* returns the following (also fictive) content.

```
PS C:\FASTSearch\bin> crawleradmin --getlogin "http://example.com/forum/login.html"
crawleradmin.exe 14.0.0325.0000 10091201

<login name="utf8">
  <attrib name="preload" type="string">  </attrib>
  <attrib name="scheme" type="string"> https </attrib>
  <attrib name="site" type="string"> example.com </attrib>
  <attrib name="form" type="string"> /sessions </attrib>
  <attrib name="action" type="string"> POST </attrib>
  <section name="parameters">
      <attrib name="utf8" type="string"> &#x2713; </attrib>
      <attrib name="authenticity_token" type="string"> 5b7zUvbKNIS2z7NkxyyoX3ems= </attrib>
      <attrib name="username" type="string"> ##undefined </attrib>
      <attrib name="password" type="string"> ##undefined </attrib>
      <attrib name="remember_me" type="string"> 1 </attrib>
  </section>
  <attrib name="sites" type="list-string">
      <member> </member>
  </attrib>
  <attrib name="ttl" type="integer"> 10080 </attrib>
</login>
```

The string *##undefined* indicates that the crawler couldn't fill in these HTML *<form>* elements by itself—not surprisingly, because it's in here, you enter the credentials for the user you want the crawler to impersonate.

After updating the credentials, as well as any other option you require, the XML is ready to be put into the configuration file for the crawl collection. Reload the configuration with the following.

```
Crawleradmin -f <configuration file>
```

Configuring the FAST Search Database Connector to Detect Database Changes

The FAST Search database connector can be configured for automatic change detection, making sure that both updates and removals from a database are synchronized into the index. Although you can achieve similar functionality by keeping track of updates to the database with triggers or status flags, you save both time and, potentially, a lot of headache if you use the FAST Search database connector and its module for change detection.

 Note This section assumes you've already read the section "FAST Search Database Connector" in Chapter 7 and have a working connector configuration up and running.

The FAST Search database connector is configured using XML configuration files. FS4SP provides a boilerplate configuration in the file *<FASTSearchFolder>\etc\jdbctemplate.xml*, which you can base your own configuration on. This file also contains a template configuration for the change detection functionality. This template is as follows.

```
<group name="ChangeDetection" expand="no">
  <parameter name="Enabled" type="boolean">
    <value>false</value>
  </parameter>
  <parameter name="ChangeDBPurge" type="boolean">
    <value>false</value>
  </parameter>
  <parameter name="ChangeDBAbortPercent" type="integer">
    <value>10</value>
  </parameter>
  <parameter name="ChangeDBIncludeFields" type="string">
    <value></value>
  </parameter>
  <parameter name="ChangeDBExcludeFields" type="string">
    <value></value>
  </parameter>
</group>
```

More Info The technical reference for all configuration options, including change detection, is available at *http://technet.microsoft.com/en-us/library/ff354942.aspx*.

To start using change detection, it's enough to edit the *Enabled* section to say *true* instead of the default *false*.

```
<parameter name="Enabled" type="boolean">
  <value>true</value>
</parameter>
```

Then rerun the connector by executing the following command in an FS4SP shell.

```
jdbcconnector.bat start -f <configuration file>
```

For each row that is pulled from the database, the FAST Search database connector now calculates and stores a checksum. Each time you rerun the connector with the same configuration, new checksums are calculated and compared to what was stored in the previous run. Unless there's a change in the checksum, no update is sent to the index.

Note If you ever want to throw away all the previously calculated checksums, you do so by setting the configuration option *ChangeDBPurge* to *true*, and then rerunning the connector. Be sure to swap back to *false* for subsequent runs.

By using the *ChangeDBAbortPercent* configuration option, you can specify an upper limit, in percentage, on how many changed rows you tolerate. If this limit is breached, the connector stops the current run without affecting the index. This is useful as a safety guard. If too many rows are changed, something might be wrong in the database and you might not want to have those changes replicated in the index.

You can use *ChangeDBIncludeFields* and *ChangeDBExcludeFields* to define which fields in the database result set should be taken into account when calculating the checksum.

Conclusion

This chapter explained how to perform tasks you may need when setting up FS4SP but are not apparent from TechNet documentation. Tasks that include doing an upgrade from SharePoint Search without downtime, configuring a custom property extractor dictionary in a SharePoint list, and many more have been outlined with simple, step-by-step instructions and code where necessary.

Some of the tasks, such as enabling searching inside nondefault file formats, are simply suggesting how to enhance search by enabling well-documented features. Others, such as upgrading without downtime and extending the *CoreResultsWebPart* to accept FQL, reach deep into the workings of FS4SP to turn some hidden knobs. These may even mean tweaking FS4SP in ways that its developers did not initially think of. But this is often what it takes to go from good to great, or to just turn a product into a useful solution to a business problem.

## CHAPTER 10

Search Scenarios

This chapter walks you through two search scenarios to show some of the capabilities of Microsoft FAST Search Server 2010 for SharePoint (FS4SP). The scenarios start from scratch and build two different search solutions in Microsoft SharePoint. This chapter focuses on how you tune for relevance with static and dynamic rank. The two scenarios are:

- Productivity search for an intranet site.

- E-commerce search.

Each scenario shows different capabilities of FS4SP; however, the techniques used in one scenario can be applied to the other, and vice versa. All techniques used are, in fact, potentially applicable to any search scenario.

> **Important** We highly recommend that you use a query monitoring tool such as the FS4SP Query Logger (*http://fs4splogger.codeplex.com/*) when trying out the scenarios to see how the rank changes during the tuning process.

Productivity Search

Search connects people to the information they need to get their jobs done. General productivity search solutions increase employee efficiency by connecting a broad set of people to a wide range of information, the most common examples being intranet and people search. In comparison, search-driven applications drive measurable return on investment by helping a well-defined set of people accomplish specific business tasks more efficiently. Search-driven applications, such as research portals and 360° customer insight solutions, aggregate information from a defined set of content repositories, add structure to unstructured information and provide a contextual, interactive, and actionable experience.

Introduction to Productivity Search

The key concept in productivity search is *user context*—providing users with results that are both meaningful and dynamically tailored to their jobs, roles, and functions within the organization. This means that your sales teams will be able to quickly find product information, collateral information, and answers to request for proposal (RFP) questions. In contrast, your engineering teams should see specification and requirement documents at the top of their result sets. But identifying user context is not easy. Using the FS4SP functionality of tapping into the fields of a user's profile page is a good starting place, but FS4SP provides tools that you can use to go even further in identifying user context.

When setting up SharePoint and FS4SP, you get access to a set of search functions such as synonyms, contextual search, and relevancy tuning. When you use these search functions via the FAST Search Center site template, you can deliver a solid search experience to your users with very little effort.

The sample productivity search scenario in this chapter shows you how to set up search experiences to capture user context so that you can bring the right content to the right user.

Important The boost values used for these examples were picked for testing. You should adjust the values to fit your particular scenario.

Contoso Productivity Search

This sample project covers the following:

- Set up a FAST Search Center in SharePoint with modifications.

- Set up contextual search.

- Add custom refiners.

- Use FQL-enabled Web Parts for item promotion.

- Use search scopes for item promotion.

- Use a managed property boost to demote content.

- Set up a custom property extractor.

- Use visual best bets with landing pages.

- Find relevant items based on enterprise keywords.

For this example, use the *2010 Information Worker Demonstration and Evaluation Virtual Machine (SP1)* download available at *http://www.microsoft.com/download/en/details.aspx?id=27417.* The password is *pass@word1* for all users for this download.

This example assumes that you installed the SharePoint 2010 ECM Resource Content Pack and the SharePoint 2010 Value Pillars Content Pack, both available for download from the link in the previous paragraph.

Setting Up a Search Center

For this example, you use and modify the existing FAST Search Center at the following link: *http://intranet.contoso.com/search/Pages/default.aspx*. Searching for the term *industry* shows a page similar to Figure 10-1. The result page is the default result page from the FAST Search Center site template with document thumbnails and Microsoft PowerPoint previews generated using Microsoft Office Web Apps.

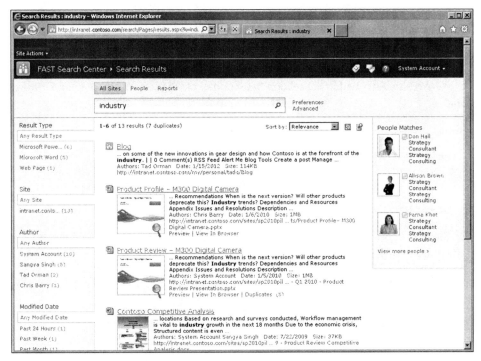

FIGURE 10-1 Default FAST Search Center with no customizations.

Setting Up Department User Context

In order to promote or demote items based on where in the organization users belong, you have to set up a user context. A *user context* is built by using any combination of properties from the user's profile page; however, by default, only the *Office Location* and *Ask Me About* properties are available when you create a new user context. In this example, you want to also enable the *Department* property for use within user contexts.

Add *Department* to the user context properties

1. Open a SharePoint 2010 Management Shell.

2. Execute the following commands to retrieve the existing properties *SPS-Location* and *SPS-Responsibility*, and add *Department* to the list. Note that the properties are separated with a comma.

```
$contextprops = Get-SPEnterpriseSearchExtendedQueryProperty -SearchApplication
"FASTQuery" -Identity "FASTSearchContextProperties"

$newprops = $contextprops.Value + ",Department"

Set-SPEnterpriseSearchExtendedQueryProperty -SearchApplication "FASTQuery" -Identity
"FASTSearchContextProperties" -Value $newprops
```

The new field should appear in the UI after a brief time. You can force it to be available by recycling the SharePoint web application pool.

Create a user context for the Strategy Consulting department

This procedure is also described in the section "User Context Management" in Chapter 6, "Search Configuration."

1. Go to Site Actions | Site Settings | Site Collection Administration.

2. Click FAST Search User Context or copy and paste the following URL:

    http://intranet.contoso.com/_layouts/usercontextmanagement.aspx

3. Click Add User Context.

4. In the User Context Name field, enter **Department**, and in the Department field, enter **Strategy Consulting**, as shown in Figure 10-2.

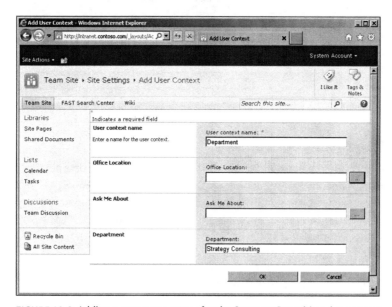

FIGURE 10-2 Adding a new user context for the Strategy Consulting department.

5. Click OK to save the new user context.

Use the Department user context in a site promotion

1. Go to Site Actions | Site Settings | Site Collection Administration.

2. Click FAST Search Site Promotion And Demotion.

3. Click Add Site Promotion.

4. Enter **Contoso** as the title.

5. Enter **http://intranet.contoso.com/sites/sp2010pillars** as a promoted site.

6. Enter **Department** as the user context.

   The filled-out form should look similar to Figure 10-3.

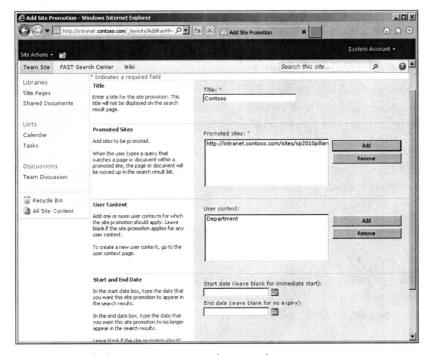

FIGURE 10-3 Assigning a user context to a site promotion.

7. Click OK to save your changes.

Test the new site promotion

1. Log in as **CONTOSO\administrator**.

2. Go to *http://intranet.contoso.com/search*.

3. Search for *analysis*.

   The top search result is a document named *M300 Market Analysis Report.docx* from the site *http://intranet.contoso.com/sites/pillarsbi*.

4. Log in as **CONTOSO\brads** (to indicate Brad Sutton, who works in the Strategy Consulting department), and then repeat steps 2 and 3 of this procedure.

5. The top search result now is a document named *Contoso Competitive Analysis* from the site *http://intranet.contoso.com/sites/sp2010pillars*, and the previous top search result is now in third place.

Creating a *Department* Refiner

When you navigate content, it can be useful to narrow down the results to items that either you or a colleague in your department have created. The Search Center includes a refiner for author, but you must create the *Created by department* refiner yourself.

To create a department refiner, you add an External Item Processing component that does author-to-department lookup and writes the department value to a crawled property. The value in the crawled property is mapped to a managed property used for the refiner.

Create an employee-to-department lookup list from Active Directory directory services

Instead of doing a lookup per author per item during indexing, you can prepopulate a lookup dictionary that the External Item Processing component will use. Doing this improves the lookup performance because you don't have to execute a Lightweight Directory Access Protocol (LDAP) call for every item.

1. Create a Windows PowerShell script by using the following code, and save it as **C:\FASTSearch\bin\extract-employees.ps1**.

```
# extract-employees.ps1
# Create a lookup list between employee and department
$filename = "C:\FASTSearch\bin\employee_list.txt"
$strFilter = "(&(objectCategory=User))"
$objDomain = New-Object System.DirectoryServices.DirectoryEntry
$objSearcher = New-Object System.DirectoryServices.DirectorySearcher
$objSearcher.SearchRoot = $objDomain
$objSearcher.PageSize = 1000
$objSearcher.Filter = $strFilter
$objSearcher.SearchScope = "Subtree"
```

```
foreach ($i in "name","department"){$objSearcher.PropertiesToLoad.Add($i) | Out-Null}
$results = $objSearcher.FindAll()
Remove-Item $filename -ErrorAction:SilentlyContinue
foreach ($result in $results)
{
    $item = $result.Properties
    if( $item.department.count -gt 0 -and $item.name.count -gt 0)
    {
        $entry = $item.name[0] + "," + $item.department[0]
        $entry | Out-File -encoding utf8 -append $filename
    }
}
```

2. Open an FS4SP shell.

3. Execute the script you just created by using the following command to generate the lookup list.

```
.\extract-employees.ps1
```

Create an external item processing component to assign the author's department

1. Using Microsoft Visual Studio, create an External Item Processing component with the following code and copy the compiled executable to C:\FASTSearch\bin.

```
using System;
using System.IO;
using System.Collections.Generic;
using System.Linq;
using System.Xml.Linq;

namespace FS4SP.Ch10.AuthorDepartment
{
  class Processor
  {
    static void Main(string[] args)
    {
      // Read the employee -> department lookup file
      string[] lines = File.ReadAllLines(@"C:\FASTSearch\bin\employee_list.txt");

      // Create a dictionary lookup
      Dictionary<string, string> departmentLookup = new Dictionary<string, string>();

      foreach (var line in lines)
      {
        string[] pair = line.Split(',');
        departmentLookup[pair[0]] = pair[1];
      }

      // Read the input XML file that was provided by FS4SP through %(input)s
      XDocument input = XDocument.Load(args[0]);

      // Fetch the crawled properties from the input file
      var inputCPs = from cp in input.Descendants("CrawledProperty") select cp;
```

```
      // Fetch the author from the first crawled property
      string department = string.Empty;
      var authorNode = inputCPs.Where(a =>
        !string.IsNullOrEmpty(a.Value)).FirstOrDefault();
      if (authorNode != null)
      {
        // Split on multi-field, and choose the first author to match
        var authors = authorNode.Value.Split(new char[] { '\u2029' },
          StringSplitOptions.RemoveEmptyEntries);
        foreach (string author in authors)
        {
          if (departmentLookup.TryGetValue(author.Trim(), out department))
          {
            break;
          }
        }
      }

      // Create an output XML file
      XElement output = new XElement("Document");

      // Add crawled property to the output file
      output.Add(
        new XElement("CrawledProperty",
          new XAttribute("propertySet", new Guid(
            "F29F85E0-4FF9-1068-AB91-08002B27B3D9")),
          new XAttribute("propertyName", "department"),
          new XAttribute("varType", "31"), department)
      );

      // Save the output XML where FS4SP designated through %(output)s
      output.Save(args[1]);
    }
  }
}
```

2. Open *C:\FASTSearch\etc\pipelineextensibility.xml*, and register your External Item Processing component as shown in the following XML, where you add the *<Run>* node below the existing *<PipelineExtensibility>* node. The crawled properties used as input are the default ones mapped to the managed property *author*.

> **Tip** You can retrieve the crawled property mappings for the managed property *author* by executing the following commands in an FS4SP shell.
>
> ```
> $mp = Get-FASTSearchMetadataManagedProperty author
> $mp.GetCrawledPropertyMappings()
> ```

```
<PipelineExtensibility>
    <Run command="C:\FASTSearch\bin\FS4SP.Ch10.AuthorDepartment.exe %(input)s %(output)s">
        <Input>
            <CrawledProperty propertySet="0f451d82-37a2-4831-a5d7-e5d57c3ad793"
                propertyName="Author" varType="31"/>
```

```
        <CrawledProperty propertySet="00020329-0000-0000-c000-000000000046"
            propertyName="urn:schemas:httpmail:fromname" varType="31"/>
        <CrawledProperty propertySet="00020386-0000-0000-c000-000000000046"
            propertyName="Item.Sender" varType="31"/>
        <CrawledProperty propertySet="a373e438-7a87-11d3-b1c1-00c04f68155c"
            propertyName="Author" varType="31"/>
        <CrawledProperty propertySet="0f451d82-37a2-4831-a5d7-e5d57c3ad793"
            propertyName="Artist" varType="31"/>
        <CrawledProperty propertySet="0f451d82-37a2-4831-a5d7-e5d57c3ad793"
            propertyName="primary_author" varType="31"/>
        <CrawledProperty propertySet="f29f85e0-4ff9-1068-ab91-08002b27b3d9"
            propertyId="4" varType="30"/>
        <CrawledProperty propertySet="f29f85e0-4ff9-1068-ab91-08002b27b3d9"
            propertyId="4" varType="31"/>
        <CrawledProperty propertySet="aa568eec-e0e5-11cf-8fda-00aa00a14f93"
            propertyId="6" varType="31"/>
    </Input>
    <Output>
        <CrawledProperty propertySet="f29f85e0-4ff9-1068-ab91-08002b27b3d9"
            propertyName="department" varType="31"/>
    </Output>
  </Run>
</PipelineExtensibility>
```

3. Open an FS4SP shell.

4. Create the new crawled property, the managed property, and the mapping between them by using the following code.

```
# Create properties for department
$department = New-FASTSearchMetadataManagedProperty -Name department -Type 1
$department.RefinementEnabled = $true
$department.Update()

$cDepartment = New-FASTSearchMetadataCrawledProperty -Name "department"
  -Propset " f29f85e0-4ff9-1068-ab91-08002b27b3d9" -VariantType 31

New-FASTSearchMetadataCrawledPropertyMapping -ManagedProperty $department
  -CrawledProperty $cDepartment
```

5. Edit the Refinement Panel Web Part in the Search Center, and add the following XML configuration to the existing category definition.

```
<Category    Title="Department"
  Description="Use this filter to restrict results by department"
  Type="Microsoft.Office.Server.Search.WebControls.ManagedPropertyFilterGenerator"
  MetadataThreshold="1"    NumberOfFiltersToDisplay="6"    MaxNumberOfFilters="20"
  ShowMoreLink="True"    MappedProperty="department"    MoreLinkText="show more"
  LessLinkText="show fewer"    ShowCounts="Count" />
```

6. Increase the Number Of Categories To Display value from 6 to **10**.

7. Clear the Use Default Configuration check box.

8. Save the changes to the Refinement Panel Web Part and to the result page.

9. Issue **psctrl reset** in an FS4SP shell to reload the indexing pipeline configuration.

10. Recrawl your content so that the *department* refiner is displayed in your search results, as shown in Figure 10-4.

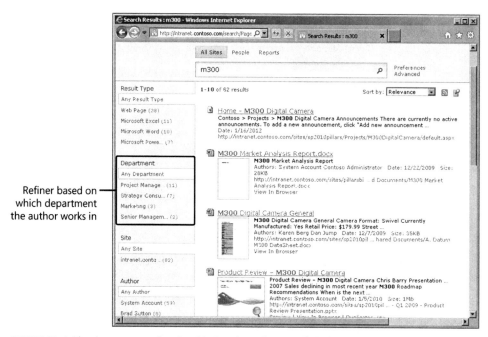

Refiner based on which department the author works in

FIGURE 10-4 The *department* refiner is added to the Refinement Panel Web Part.

Promoting Items for Coworkers by Using an FQL-Enabled Web Part

Content relevant to your work is often created by people close to you in your organization. This means that content created by someone in the same department as you might be more relevant for you. The further you move away from your position in the organization, the less relevant the information is likely to be for your work.

You can accomplish item promotion, or *item boosting*, by finding other employees in your department, such as your boss; however, boosting results that are based on people or content authors can easily generate quite large queries when manually crafting the FQL, easily hitting the 2,048 character limit for queries. Instead of boosting by author, you should boost by department because that aggregates the authors to fewer entities.

Tip Consider the following FAST Query Language (FQL) to boost one author.

```
xrank(string:"original query", author:"brad Sutton", boost=4000)
```

The query is 65 characters long. If you were to add 32 authors with similar statements, you would reach the 2,048 character limit of your query. Even if you optimize the query, you would stop at around 90 authors and you might have other logic included as well. So paying attention to the length of automatically generated FQL is a good idea to avoid errors.

Previously, you created a new user context to boost items from a site for members of the Strategy Consulting department. For the sample in this section, you create a custom Core Results Web Part that looks up the department of the signed-in user, and you add a boost for items created by members of that same department, regardless of where the item is stored or which department the user belongs to.

Warning The drawback of using FQL in a Core Results Web Part is that any property query added does not parse correctly without first modifying the query. Web Parts that include Keyword Query Language (KQL) to FQL conversion are available on CodePlex, courtesy of the SPSearchParts project team, at *http://spsearchparts.codeplex.com*.

The following code creates a custom Search Core Results Web Part that adds the department of the current user as a boost to the user query.

Note The following Custom Search Core Results Web Part is based on the code from "Creating an FQL-Enabled Core Results Web Part" in Chapter 9, "Useful Tips and Tricks," so only the code for the Core Result Web Part is included in this chapter.

Custom Search Core Results Web Part with FQL-enabled department boost

```
using System.ComponentModel;
using System.Web;
using Microsoft.SharePoint;
using Microsoft.Office.Server.Search.WebControls;

namespace FS4SP.Ch10.DepartmentBoost.FS4SP.Ch10.DepartmentBoost
{
    [ToolboxItem(false)]
    public class Ch10FQLEnabledCoreResults : CoreResultsWebPart
    {
        protected override void ConfigureDataSourceProperties()
        {
            FixedQuery = GetQuery();
            base.ConfigureDataSourceProperties();
        }
```

```csharp
        /// <summary>
        /// Executes a query where the entered keywords are evaluated as
        /// a simple-all query, and if the user is a member of a department,
        /// content from employees in that department will be promoted.
        /// </summary>
        /// <returns>FQL query</returns>
        private string GetQuery()
        {
            // Get the query terms from the search box
            string query = HttpUtility.UrlDecode(HttpContext.Current.Request["k"]);
            if (string.IsNullOrEmpty(query)) return null;

            string template;
            // Get the department for the logged in user
            string department = GetDepartment();
            if (string.IsNullOrEmpty(department))
            {
                // Execute a simple all query with the query terms
                template = @"string(""{0}"", mode=""simpleall"")";
            }
            else
            {
                // Add FQL boosting if the user belongs to a department
                // The filter operator is used to turn off linguistics because the value is
                // exact and there is no need to lemmatize the words
                template = @"xrank(string(""{0}"", mode=""simpleall""),
                            filter(department:""{1}""), boost=5000)";
            }
            string fql = string.Format(template, query, department);
            return fql;
        }

        private string GetDepartment()
        {
            SPUser currentUser = SPContext.Current.Web.CurrentUser;
            SPList userList = SPContext.Current.Web.SiteUserInfoList;
            SPListItem userListItem = userList.GetItemById(currentUser.ID);
            if (userListItem.Fields.ContainsField("Department"))
            {
                return userListItem["Department"] as string;
            }
            return string.Empty;
        }

        protected override void CreateDataSource()
        {
            // Create a custom DataSource and suppress calling
            // the base class method.
            DataSource = new CoreFqlResultsDataSource(this);
        }
    }
}
```

After deploying your new Web Part, replace the existing Search Core Results Web Part with your custom one in the Search Center.

To try out the boost effect for the *department* property, sign in as Tad Orman (**CONTOSO\tado**), who works in the CRM Strategy department, and search for *product cycle*. Next, sign in as Idan Rubin (**CONTOSO\idanr**) of the Strategy Consulting department, and perform the same search.

As shown in Figure 10-5, the top results for Idan are from a user named Brad Sutton (CONTOSO\ brads), who, coincidentally, also works in the Strategy Consulting department and is Idan's manager.

Results when logged in as Tad Orman
in the CRM Strategy department

Results when logged in as Idan Rubin
in the Strategy Consulting department

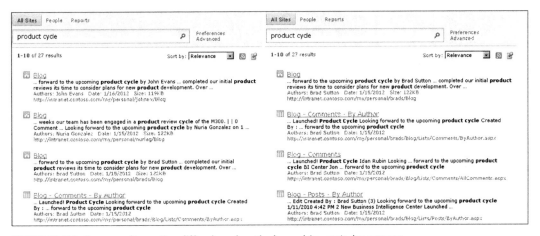

FIGURE 10-5 In these results, sorting differs based on the logged-in user's department.

You can expand the preceding Web Part to boost items in departments that are hierarchically close to the user as well. To do this, you can generate an organization chart and look up which departments have the same "parent," and then boost sibling departments with less of a boost than your own. How you build your boost expression depends on what content is relevant for different users, but using the FQL operator *xrank* together with user information is a powerful way to create contextual search.

Promoting Items for Coworkers by Using Predefined Scopes

In the previous sample, you created a custom Core Results Web Part that was FQL-enabled. The advantage of this is that you can create arbitrary FQL statements. The disadvantage is that you have to parse KQL syntax yourself for it to work 100 percent of the time, and you lose the keywords functionality with synonyms and best-bets.

Instead of creating the boost expression in FQL directly, you can precreate one for each department as a search scope and then append the scope to the query expression.

 More Info Read more about creating search scopes in Chapter 6.

The following Windows PowerShell code creates one search scope per department. Because *xrank* requires a matching expression as well as the boost expression, you can use *size:range(0,max)* as the matching expression to evaluate the boost expression on all items. The code should be run in a SharePoint Management Shell.

```
# employees-department-scopes.ps1
# Create a boost scope for each department

Add-Type -AssemblyName System.Core
$set = new-object 'System.Collections.Generic.HashSet[string]'
$strFilter = "(&(objectCategory=User))"
$objDomain = New-Object System.DirectoryServices.DirectoryEntry
$objSearcher = New-Object System.DirectoryServices.DirectorySearcher
$objSearcher.SearchRoot = $objDomain
$objSearcher.PageSize = 1000
$objSearcher.Filter = $strFilter
$objSearcher.SearchScope = "Subtree"
foreach ($i in "department"){$objSearcher.PropertiesToLoad.Add($i) | Out-Null}
$colResults = $objSearcher.FindAll()
foreach ($objResult in $colResults)
{
    $objItem = $objResult.Properties
    if( $objItem.department.count -gt 0)
    {
        $set.Add($objItem.department[0]) | Out-Null
    }
}
foreach ($department in $set)
{
    $name = $department.ToLower() -replace '\W'
    New-SPEnterpriseSearchQueryScope -Name "dept$name" -Description "Boost $department"
        -SearchApplication "FASTQuery" -DisplayInAdminUI 1 -ExtendedSearchFilter
        "xrank(size:range(0,max), filter(department:'"$department'"), boost=5000)"
}

# Compile scopes
(Get-SPEnterpriseSearchServiceApplication "FASTQuery").StartScopesCompilation()
```

After adding the scopes, use the following code to create a custom Core Results Web Part to programmatically add the boosting of the current user's department to the query.

Custom Search Core Results Web Part with department scope boost

```
using System.Text.RegularExpressions;
using System.ComponentModel;
using Microsoft.SharePoint;
using Microsoft.Office.Server.Search.WebControls;
```

```
namespace FS4SP.Ch10.DepartmentBoost.DepartmentScopeBoost
{
    [ToolboxItemAttribute(false)]
    public class DepartmentScopeBoost : CoreResultsWebPart
    {
        protected override void ConfigureDataSourceProperties()
        {
            // Add scope for the current user's department
            AppendedQuery = "scope:dept" + GetDepartment();
            base.ConfigureDataSourceProperties();
        }

        private string GetDepartment()
        {
            SPUser currentUser = SPContext.Current.Web.CurrentUser;
            SPList userList = SPContext.Current.Web.SiteUserInfoList;
            SPListItem userListItem = userList.GetItemById(currentUser.ID);
            string department = string.Empty;
            if (userListItem.Fields.ContainsField("Department"))
            {
                department = userListItem["Department"] as string;
                if (department == null) department = string.Empty;
            }
            return Regex.Replace(department, @"\W", "").ToLower();
        }
    }
}
```

After deploying your new Web Part, replace the existing Search Core Results Web Part with your custom one in the Search Center.

The results from this Web Part are similar to the previous sample with the FQL-enabled Core Result Web Part; fortunately, however, synonyms and property queries now also work.

Demoting Site Collection Root and Site Home

In larger organizations, you quickly end up with many site collections and sites. When searching, you also get hits in the titles and descriptions of your sites. If you are looking for a particular site, that can be useful, but when looking for documents, it's largely noise.

The default installation of FS4SP already demotes SharePoint list items by using managed property boosts, and you can use the same feature to demote site hits based on the content class of the item. Site collection roots have the content class *STS_Web*, whereas sites belong to the content class *STS_Site*.

More Info Read more about managed property boosts in Chapter 6.

Add a managed property boost

1. Execute a search for *Contoso* in your Search Center. Notice that hits 2, 3, and 4 are all sites, as shown in Figure 10-6.

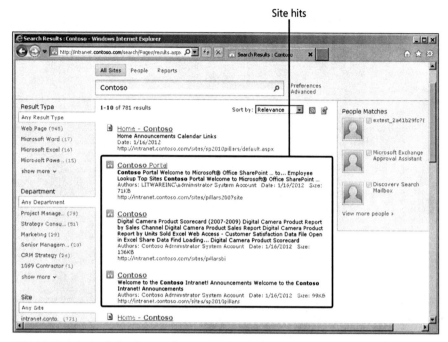

FIGURE 10-6 A search for *Contoso* that returns sites in the top results.

2. Open an FS4SP shell.

3. Execute the following Windows PowerShell commands to add two managed property boosts with a value of −4,000 to the default rank profile. Remember that boosts can be either positive or negative.

```
$RankProfile = Get-FASTSearchMetadataRankProfile -Name default
$Property = Get-FASTSearchMetadataManagedProperty -Name contentclass
$RankProfile.CreateManagedPropertyBoostComponent($Property, "STS_Web", -4000")
$RankProfile.CreateManagedPropertyBoostComponent($Property, "STS_Site", -4000")
```

4. Execute another search for *Contoso* in your Search Center, and verify that all the site hits have been pushed further down the result set, as shown in Figure 10-7. There might be a small delay before the demotion takes place because of caching.

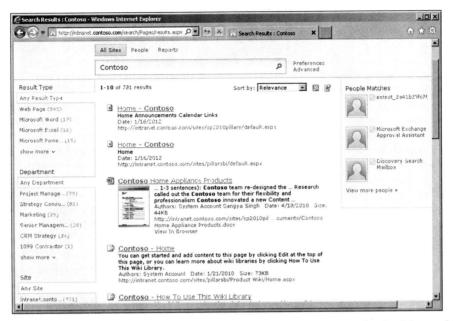

FIGURE 10-7 A search for *Contoso* now shows nonsite hits on the first page after the deboost of the content classes.

Demoting site hits to further down in the result set makes it easier to find documents on the result page, but finding sites is still useful. One way to list sites only is to add, via a search scope, a second Search Core Results Web Part in the column on the right side of the result page. Edit the Web Part settings and add a search scope to display only items of types *STS_Web* and *STS_Site*.

Set up a side search for site results

1. Open a SharePoint Management Shell.

2. Create a search scope to limit results to content classes *STS_Web* and *STS_Site* with the following Windows PowerShell command.

```
New-SPEnterpriseSearchQueryScope -Name "SiteScope" -Description
  "Scope on STSWeb and STSSite" -SearchApplication "FASTQuery"
  -DisplayInAdminUI 1 -ExtendedSearchFilter 'contentclass:or("STS_Web","STS_Site")'
```

3. Compile the scope in order for it to take effect right away.

```
(Get-SPEnterpriseSearchServiceApplication "FASTQuery").StartScopesCompilation()
```

4. Edit your search results page at *http://intranet.contoso.com/search/Pages/results.aspx*.

5. In the column on the right, add a Search Core Results Web Part.

6. Edit the second Search Core Results Web Part as shown in Figure 10-8.

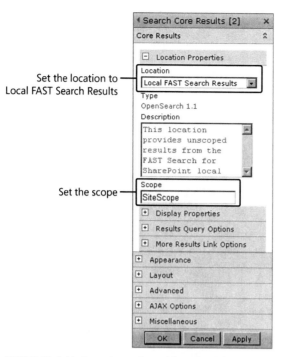

Set the location to Local FAST Search Results

Set the scope

FIGURE 10-8 Limit results to site results only with a search scope.

7. Expand Display Properties, and then clear the Use Location Visualization check box. Click the XSL Editor button and paste in the following XSLT.

```xml
<?xml version="1.0" encoding="UTF-8"?>
<xsl:stylesheet version="1.0" xmlns:xsl="http://www.w3.org/1999/XSL/Transform">
  <xsl:output method="xml" version="1.0" encoding="UTF-8" indent="yes"/>
  <xsl:template match="/">
    <div class="ms-searchChannelTitle">
      <span class="ms-searchChannelTitle">Site Matches</span>
    </div>
    <div class="ms-searchsummarybody">
      <xsl:for-each select="/All_Results/Result">
        <xsl:call-template name="Main" ></xsl:call-template>
      </xsl:for-each>
    </div>
  </xsl:template>
  <xsl:template name="Main">
    <div class="srch-Icon">
      <IMG border="0" align="absMiddle" src="/_layouts/images/siteicon_16x16.png" />
    </div>
    <div class="srch-Title3">
      <a href="{path}">
        <xsl:value-of select="title" />
      </a>
    </div>
    <div class="srch-Description2">
      <xsl:call-template name="TrimIfGreaterThanMax">
        <xsl:with-param name="Source" select="description"/>
        <xsl:with-param name="MaxLength" select="30"/>
```

```
          </xsl:call-template>
      </div>
      <div class="srch-Metadata2">
        <span class="srch-URL2">
          /<xsl:value-of select="substring-after(substring-after(path, 'http://'), '/')"/>
        </span>
      </div>
  </xsl:template>

  <xsl:template name="TrimIfGreaterThanMax">
    <xsl:param name="Source"/>
    <xsl:param name="MaxLength"/>
    <xsl:choose>
      <xsl:when test="string-length($Source) &gt; $MaxLength">
        <xsl:value-of select="substring($Source, 1, $MaxLength)"/>...
      </xsl:when>
      <xsl:otherwise>
        <xsl:value-of select="$Source"/>
      </xsl:otherwise>
    </xsl:choose>
  </xsl:template>
</xsl:stylesheet>
```

8. Expand Results Query Options, and then set Cross-Web Part Query ID to Query 2.

9. Save your changes to both the Web Part and the page.

10. Verify that the result page for *Contoso* now looks similar to Figure 10-9.

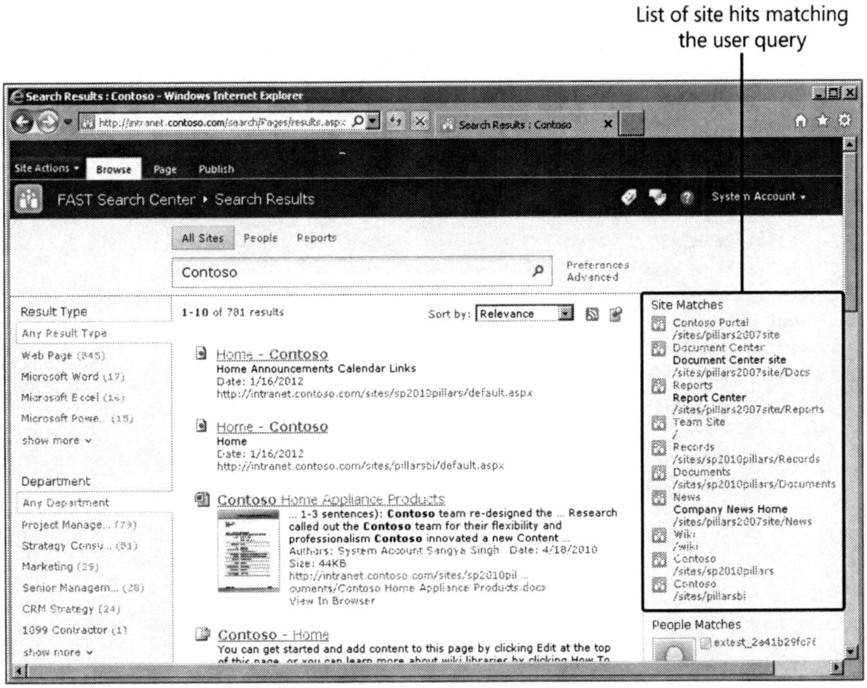

FIGURE 10-9 Search result screen with added side search for sites.

> **Tip** You can create the same search scope using the SharePoint UI and scope rules, and you can create it with SharePoint search as well as with FS4SP.

Adding a *Products* Refiner

If you search using the term # at *http://intranet.contoso.com/search*, you retrieve all items that the currently logged-in user is allowed to see. If you examine the refiners, you will find a refiner named *Products*, which contains only one refinement. This value comes from a list item that has been tagged with data from the managed metadata term store.

> **More Info** Read more about managed metadata and the manage metadata term store at *http://technet.microsoft.com/en-us/library/ee424402.aspx*.

For this next example, you create a list of known product names and set up custom property extraction to create a *products* refiner based on textual content inside the items being indexed, in addition to the one based on metadata assigned to the item. Unfortunately, it is not possible to add custom refiner data to the one based on managed metadata, nor can you merge the output of a managed metadata refiner with a custom one.

Register the products dictionary and set up a refiner

1. Create a dictionary to hold the product names in XML format like the following.

```xml
<dictionary>
  <entry key="m300" value="M300" />
  <entry key="m400" value="M400" />
  <entry key="m500" value="M500" />
  <entry key="x200" value="X200" />
  <entry key="x250" value="X250" />
  <entry key="x300" value="X300" />
  <entry key="x358" value="X358" />
  <entry key="x400" value="X400" />
  <entry key="x458" value="X458" />
  <entry key="x500" value="X500" />
  <entry key="z500" value="Z500" />
</dictionary>
```

2. Save the file as **C:\temp\products.xml**.

3. In an FS4SP shell, execute the following command.

```
# Normalize the file and save as UTF-8 without BOM
lowercase C:\temp\products.xml C:\temp\products_normalized.xml
# Register the dictionary
Add-FASTSearchResource -FilePath C:\temp\products_normalized.xml
  -Path dictionaries\matching\products.xml
```

4. With the following content, create an XML file at *C:\FASTSearch\etc\config_data\ DocumentProcessor\CustomPropertyExtractors.xml.*

```
<?xml version="1.0" encoding="UTF-8"?>
<extractors>
  <extractor name="product" type="Verbatim" property="product">
    <dictionary name="products" yield-values="yes"/>
  </extractor>
</extractors>
```

5. Create a crawled and managed property to hold the department values by using the following commands in an FS4SP shell:

```
$cp = New-FASTSearchMetadataCrawledProperty -Name product
  -Propset 48385c54-cdfc-4e84-8117-c95b3cf8911c -VariantType 31
$mp = New-FASTSearchMetadataManagedProperty -Name product -type 1
$mp.StemmingEnabled=0
$mp.RefinementEnabled=1
$mp.MergeCrawledProperties=1
$mp.Update()
New-FASTSearchMetadataCrawledPropertyMapping -ManagedProperty $mp -CrawledProperty $cp
```

6. Do a full crawl of your content in order to populate the refiner for products.

7. Edit the Refinement Panel Web Part in the Search Center and add the following XML configuration to the existing category definition.

```
<Category     Title="Products"
  Description="Use this filter to restrict results by product"
  Type="Microsoft.Office.Server.Search.WebControls.ManagedPropertyFilterGenerator"
  MetadataThreshold="1"     NumberOfFiltersToDisplay="5"     MaxNumberOfFilters="20"
  ShowMoreLink="True"     MappedProperty="product"     MoreLinkText="show more"
  LessLinkText="show fewer"     ShowCounts="Count" />
```

A search for *Contoso isdocument:true* now shows the *products* refiner for document type items such as Microsoft Word and Microsoft Excel files, as shown in Figure 10-10.

FIGURE 10-10 Result page showing the *products* refiner.

Using Visual Best Bets to Redirect to a Landing Page

Landing pages can display text, images, relevant links, or other elements related to the topic of the page. Landing pages are most common for online marketing but have use cases for intranets as well. The project home page of a product on the Contoso intranet can act as a landing page that shows all information related to the given product.

If a user searches for the term *M300*, the term is assumed to refer to the M300 digital camera, which has a project page at *http://intranet.contoso.com/sites/sp2010pillars/Projects/M300DigitalCamera*. The project page can then be seen as the best answer to the query, and instead of listing 10 results, you can automatically redirect the user to this page.

 Warning Doing an automated redirect has to be well–thought through to avoid unhappy users who might be browsing for content. You can also provide further search capabilities from the landing page to bring users back to the search page.

Add a redirecting visual best bet for the term *M300*

To create an automatic redirect, you take advantage of using the visual best bets feature. This feature loads an HTML file and displays it in an iframe. By uploading the HTML file in SharePoint, you are not blocked by cross-site scripting security because the HTML file and search page both reside on the same top-level domain.

1. Create a file **named m300landing.aspx** that has the following content.

```
<script>
// instruct the parent page to navigate to a new location
window.parent.location = "http://intranet.contoso.com/sites/sp2010pillars/Projects/
M300DigitalCamera/SitePages/
Home.aspx";
</script>
```

2. Upload the file to the SiteAssets library of the sp2010pillars site at *http://intranet.contoso.com/sites/sp2010pillars/SiteAssets*.

3. Go to the FAST Search Keywords page on the site collection root of the FAST Search Center, *http://intranet.contoso.com/_layouts/contextualkeywordmanagement.aspx*.

4. Add a new keyword for the term *M300*.

5. Add a visual best bet to the term, as shown in Figure 10-11, pointing to the file you just uploaded.

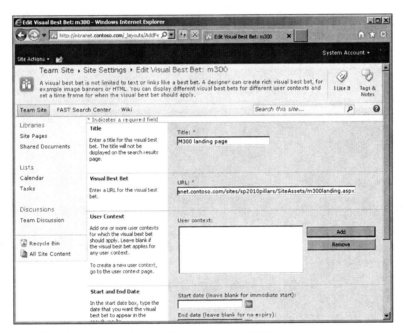

FIGURE 10-11 Adding a visual best bet to the term *M300*.

6. Go to the FAST Search Center, and search for the term *M300*. You will see a short flicker with the actual search results before the page is redirected to the project home page for the M300 digital camera.

Adding Relevant Documents to a Page by Using Enterprise Keywords

An *enterprise keyword* is a word or phrase added to items on a SharePoint site. Enterprise keywords are organized into a single, nonhierarchical term set within the managed metadata service, called the *keywords set*.

Using enterprise keywords from a page to pull in other relevant content is an easy way of enriching the user experience and navigation around a topic. For this sample, you create a custom Core Result Web Part to retrieve the enterprise keywords from the current page and use them in a query to show related documents based on these keywords.

Custom Web Part to display documents related to the page's enterprise keywords

```
using System.Collections.Generic;
using System.ComponentModel;
using Microsoft.SharePoint;
using Microsoft.SharePoint.Taxonomy;
using Microsoft.Office.Server.Search.WebControls;

namespace FS4SP.Ch10.DepartmentBoost.EnterpriseKeywords
{
    [ToolboxItemAttribute(false)]
    public class EnterpriseKeywords : CoreResultsWebPart
    {
        protected override void ConfigureDataSourceProperties()
        {
            string keywords = EnterpriseKeywordsQuery();
            if (!string.IsNullOrEmpty(keywords))
            {
                // Query for the keywords and filter to documents only
                FixedQuery = "isdocument:true " + keywords;
            }
            base.ConfigureDataSourceProperties();
        }

        private string EnterpriseKeywordsQuery()
        {
            List<string> keywords = new List<string>();
            SPListItem currentPage = SPContext.Current.ListItem;
            TaxonomyFieldValueCollection enterpriseKeywordCollection =
(TaxonomyFieldValueCollection)currentPage["TaxKeyword"];
            foreach (TaxonomyFieldValue enterpriseKeyword in enterpriseKeywordCollection)
            {
                keywords.Add(enterpriseKeyword.Label);
            }
            return string.Join(" OR ", keywords.ToArray());
        }
    }
}
```

Add enterprise keywords to a page

For the next sample to work, you have to follow the instructions in this procedure to add enterprise keywords to a page in the Contoso website.

1. Go to *http://intranet.contoso.com/sites/sp2010pillars/Projects/M300DigitalCamera/SitePages/Home.aspx*.

2. Click the Page tab on the ribbon, and then click Edit Properties.

3. Enter **M300** in the Enterprise Keywords field, and then click Save.

4. Edit the page.

5. Add your custom Web Part below the image in the column on the right, and limit the Web Part to display five results.

6. Save the page. It should look similar to Figure 10-12.

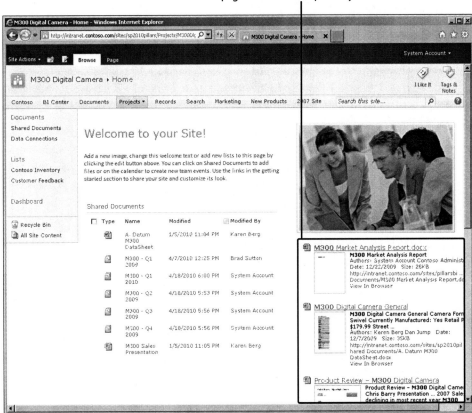

FIGURE 10-12 Listing relevant documents to the current page.

Productivity Search Example Wrap-Up

In this example, you modified the way search results are ranked based on the current user's department. Using FQL, you can expand on the boost query to also promote items created by employees in departments related to your own, or departments that are close in the organization chart. Those items could receive a lesser boost. A query might look like the following with nested *xrank* statements.

```
xrank(
    xrank(
        string("user query", mode="simpleall"),
        filter(department:"sibling department"),
        filter(department:"sibling department 2"),
        boost=2000
    ),
    filter(department:"your department"),
    boost=5000
)
```

It is also worth exploring other FQL operators such as *near* and *onear* for executing proximity searches where words must appear close to one other to get a match. Building contextual queries is not an easy task; matching your contextual requirements with the query capabilities of FS4SP requires analysis and testing.

Using the FAST Search Center site template gives you a good search page without you needing to do any customizations. But when you look more closely at your content and users, you will discover that they have different usage scenarios and search needs. Taking advantage of the contextual search and search scope capabilities that FS4SP introduces in SharePoint is a powerful way to customize the search experience for your users.

When the available configuration options fall short of solving your problems, you can either extend the existing Web Parts or build custom ones. When you use *xrank*, only your imagination, business requirements, and testing patience limit what you can achieve. But beware that tuning relevance with the use of *xrank* is not easy, and one change for some users can have an adverse effect on the results for other users.

This example showed how to add new profile parameters to the contextual search and how to add custom refiners to your Search Center. You were also shown different ways to boost items based on the department context of a user. The example also described the concept of side search, where you pull out a group of search results and present them alongside the main results. Taking this further, you were shown how to add a custom search Web Part to a wiki page to list documents relevant to that page based on enterprise keywords. And finally, you were shown how you can use visual best bets to redirect the user to a landing page for a particular query.

The goal of this scenario has been to show how you can start out with a default Search Center, expand on it, and then start using search to bring in relevant content to other parts of SharePoint.

E-Commerce Search

Most e-commerce search solutions on the Internet have at least two things in common:

- You can search for products.

- You can drill down in the result set by using product metadata refiners.

Both search and refiners are key features of FS4SP. When you think about SharePoint, e-commerce is probably not the first area that springs to mind, but the feature set offered with SharePoint and FS4SP makes it a good platform for building search-driven e-commerce solutions.

SharePoint and BCS can crawl your product inventories, often with surprisingly little effort. With FS4SP and SharePoint, you can create a good search experience that allows users to easily find the particular product they're looking for, as well as engage users in discovering your whole inventory. To top it off, FS4SP allows you to monitor and tune search queries so that you can maximize your profit, and form-based authentication in SharePoint makes it easy to manage your user base and make sure the right users are exposed to the right products and prices.

In addition to handling search, navigation, and users, you have to handle purchasing transactions. Purchasing transactions are not part of the SharePoint platform; you will either have to build them yourself or rely on third-party solutions such as Microsoft Commerce Server, which integrates well with SharePoint.

 More Info You can learn more about Microsoft Commerce Server at *http:// www.microsoft.com/commerceserver/en/us/default.aspx.*

Introduction to E-Commerce Search

The number one goal of e-commerce is to connect potential buyers with your products. This process should be as smooth and nonintrusive as possible for users; if it's not, users will surely move on to a competitor. Making the connection between users and products requires an intuitive user interface, sub-second search and navigation, and an ability to show the most desirable product at the top.

Navigation or refinements can be based on your product hierarchy. Searches, on the other hand, have to target multiple product metadata simultaneously, for example, the title, description, product number, and color. You also need to consider which metadata you get a match in when sorting your search results. For example, if a user searches for *LCD* in a consumer electronics store, he or she is more likely interested in an LCD TV than a washing machine with an LCD display even though the description of the washing machine contains a reference to the display. Therefore, matches in product titles, product numbers, and product group names should be prioritized above matches in a product description.

Other important issues to address are how to handle spelling mistakes, spelling variations, and differences in user and product vocabulary. If a user searches for *Mikrosoft* with a k, you should be able to show results for the correct spelling of *Microsoft*. In the sample e-commerce application in this chapter, you learn about possible solutions to these challenges.

 Important The boost values used for the samples are picked for testing. Be sure to adjust the values to fit your particular scenario.

Adventure Works E-Commerce

This sample project covers the following:

- Set up an external content type (ECT) connection to the *AdventureWorksLT2008R2* database via Microsoft SharePoint Designer.

- Set up a new content source.

- Create managed properties and map them to the crawled properties created during crawling of the ECT.

- Create a custom full-text index and rank profile.

- Set up a FAST Search Center in SharePoint with modifications.

- Sort items based on a formula.

- Promote items by using static rank.

- Provide search in both an English and French version of the products, with *price* refiner in both US dollars (USD) and euros (EUR).

For the sample application, use the Adventure Works database samples, and in particular the *AdventureWorksLT2008R2* database. The *AdventureWorks 2008R2* database samples can be downloaded from *http://msftdbprodsamples.codeplex.com/Releases/*.

Prerequisites for the sample are that you have installed the *AdventureWorksLT2008R2* database and configured BCS in SharePoint with a host site for BCS profile pages. Adventure Works is a fictive company selling bicycles and related merchandise.

 More Info For information about setting up the Adventure Works sample database, go to this URL: *http://msftdbprodsamples.codeplex.com/wikipage?title=Installing%20SQL%20 Server%202008R2%20Databases*. For a video tutorial about setting up BCS, go to this URL: *http://technet.microsoft.com/en-us/sharepoint/Video/ff680994*.

Add a custom view to the *AdventureWorksLT2008R2* database

For this sample application, you work with English and French product descriptions only and you want to avoid columns with *NULL* values returned from the database to make indexing easier. By creating a custom view, you can assign default values for *NULL* and filter on only English and French products.

The bold line in the following SQL statement encodes the binary images stored in the database to a base64-encoded string in order to easily show images in the search result.

■ In Microsoft SQL Server Management Studio, create a view named **vProductsAndInfo** in the *AdventureWorksLT2008R2* database.

```
USE [AdventureWorksLT2008R2]
GO
SET ANSI_NULLS ON
GO
SET QUOTED_IDENTIFIER ON
GO
CREATE VIEW [dbo].[vProductsAndInfo]
AS
SELECT CAST(p.ProductID AS varchar) + pmx.Culture AS ProductID,
    p.Name,
    pm.Name AS ProductModel,
    pmx.Culture,
    pd.Description,
    p.StandardCost,
    p.ListPrice,
    ISNULL(p.Color, 'na') AS Color,
    p.ProductNumber,
    ISNULL(p.Size, 0) AS Size,
    ISNULL(p.Weight, 0) AS Weight,
    SalesLT.ProductCategory.Name AS ProductCategory,
    (SELECT CAST(N'' AS XML).value('xs:base64Binary(xs:hexBinary(sql:column("bin")))',
'VARCHAR(MAX)') AS data
    FROM (SELECT CAST(p.ThumbNailPhoto AS VARBINARY(MAX)) AS bin) AS bin_sql_server_temp)
AS ThumbNailPhoto

FROM SalesLT.Product AS p
        INNER JOIN
    SalesLT.ProductModel AS pm ON p.ProductModelID = pm.ProductModelID INNER JOIN
    SalesLT.ProductModelProductDescription AS pmx ON pm.ProductModelID = pmx.
ProductModelID
        INNER JOIN
    SalesLT.ProductDescription AS pd ON pmx.ProductDescriptionID =
pd.ProductDescriptionID
        INNER JOIN
    SalesLT.ProductCategory ON p.ProductCategoryID = SalesLT.ProductCategory.
ProductCategoryID

WHERE (pmx.Culture = 'en') OR (pmx.Culture = 'fr')
GO
```

Setting Up an External Content Type for Indexing

In order to index the Adventure Works database, you have to create an external content type (ECT), which is used during crawling. You can set up the ECT manually by using SharePoint Designer as shown in Alternative 1, or you can import a premade Business Data Connectivity (BDC) model as described in Alternative 2.

Alternative 1   Create an ECT using SharePoint Designer

1. Start SharePoint Designer and open your SharePoint site.

2. Pick External Content Types in the Navigation pane, shown in Figure 10-13.

3. Click the External Content Type button on the ribbon.

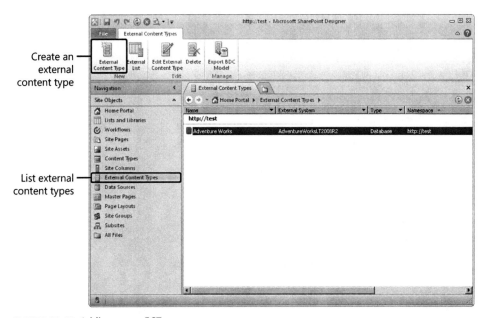

FIGURE 10-13 Adding a new ECT.

4. Name the ECT **AdventureWorks**, and connect it to the Adventure Works database by clicking the link next to External System, shown in Figure 10-14.

Enter a name ⌐   ⌐ Connect to the external source

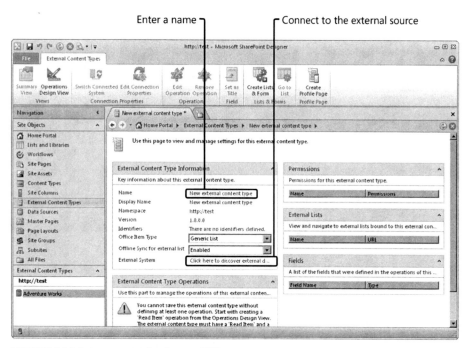

FIGURE 10-14 Set properties for the new ECT.

5. Add a connection to the *AdventureWorksLT2008R2* database. It is up to you to decide which credentials you want to use for the SQL connection. The different options shown in Figure 10-15 are out of scope for this sample.

FIGURE 10-15 Adding a SQL connection.

After the connection is established, you should see a view similar to Figure 10-16.

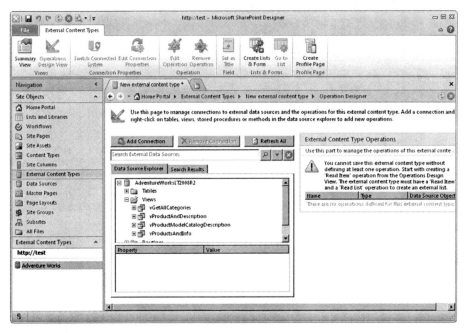

FIGURE 10-16 Connection view on your ECT.

6. Right-click vProductsAndInfo and choose New Read Item Operation.

7. Click Next.

8. Map ProductID as an identifier on the next two screens, and then click Finish.

9. Right-click vProductsAndInfo and choose New Read List Operation.

10. Click Next on the Name and Filter screens.

11. Map ProductID as an identifier, and then click Finish.

   Your ECT should look similar to Figure 10-17.

12. Create a profile page for the ECT by clicking Create Profile Page on the ribbon.

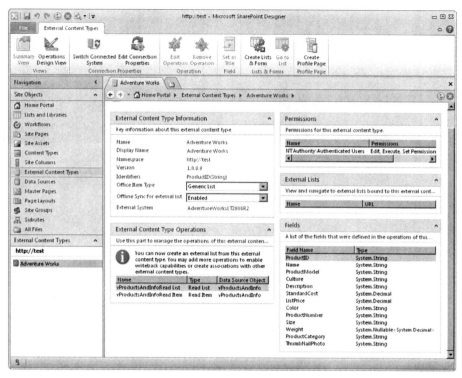

FIGURE 10-17 ECT summary page after operations are added.

Alternative 2   Import a predefined BDC model

Instead of going through the steps in SharePoint Designer, you can use a premade BDC model as described in the following steps.

1. Find the XML code in the file named *AdventureWorks.bdcm* in the downloadable code for this book. (The XML code is too long to show here.) In that file, replace *sql.contoso.com* with the name of your Microsoft SQL Server database, and replace *http://adventureworks.contoso.com:80/bcs/* with the SharePoint site hosting your BCS profile pages.

2. Open SharePoint Central Administration.

3. Go to Manage Service Applications and click your BCS service application.

4. Import the BDC model from step 1, as shown in Figure 10-18.

Import a BDC model

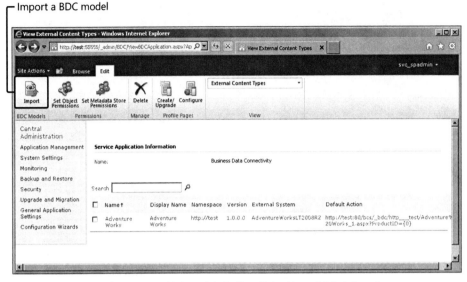

FIGURE 10-18 Import the ECT as a BDC model via SharePoint Central Administration.

Setting Up a New Content Source

After the ECT is set up, you have to index it to make the products from the Adventure Works database searchable. You do this by adding a new content source.

Set up crawling of the Adventure Works database

1. Open SharePoint Central Administration.

2. Go to your FAST Content SSA.

3. Add a new Line Of Business Data content source, as shown in Figure 10-19.

4. Crawl the new source to automatically generate the crawled properties.

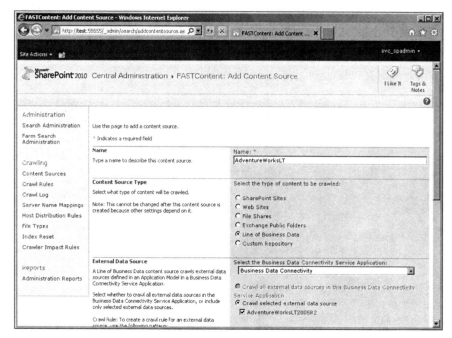

FIGURE 10-19 Setting up crawling of the Adventure Works database ECT.

Defining Properties, Full-Text Index, and Rank Profile

After the initial crawling of the Adventure Works database, each column in the database view has a corresponding crawled property. These crawled properties have to be mapped to managed properties used for searching and refining of the products.

Set up managed properties

1. For your search solution, use substring-enabled managed properties. You enable substring matching for the product name and the product number fields—both typical fields where the user might search for only parts of the text. Wildcards give a better recall. *Substrings* provide automatic wildcard search before and after the search terms by using bigrams.

> **More Info** Read more about enabling substring tokenization at *http://technet.microsoft.com/en-us/library/gg130819.aspx*. Read more about *n*-grams and bigrams in particular at *http://en.wikipedia.org/wiki/N-gram*.

2. Edit the file *<FASTSearchFolder>\components\admin-services\web.config* on your FS4SP administration server. Change *AllowIndexPurgeOnSchemaUpdate* to **yes**. This edit is needed in order to enable managed properties with substring search capabilities.

3. Open an FS4SP shell.

4. Run the following Windows PowerShell commands. Doing so creates managed properties that match the crawled properties created automatically during the crawl of the ECT and the mapping between the crawled properties and the managed properties.

```
$title = New-FASTSearchMetadataManagedProperty -Name advtitle -Type 1
$title.SubstringEnabled = $true
$title.Update()

$cTitle = Get-FASTSearchMetadataCrawledProperty "vProductsAndInfoRead ListElement.Name"
$cTitle.IsMappedToContents = $false
$cTitle.Update()
New-FASTSearchMetadataCrawledPropertyMapping -ManagedProperty $title -CrawledProperty
$cTitle

$desc = New-FASTSearchMetadataManagedProperty -Name advdesc -Type 1
$desc.SubstringEnabled = $true
$desc.Update()

$cDesc = Get-FASTSearchMetadataCrawledProperty "vProductsAndInfoRead ListElement.
Description"
$cDesc.IsMappedToContents = $false
$cDesc.Update()
New-FASTSearchMetadataCrawledPropertyMapping -ManagedProperty $desc -CrawledProperty
$cDesc

$cost = New-FASTSearchMetadataManagedProperty -Name advcost -Type 4
$cost.RefinementEnabled = $true
$cost.SortableType = "SortableEnabled"
$cost.Update()

$cCost = Get-FASTSearchMetadataCrawledProperty "vProductsAndInfoRead ListElement.
StandardCost"
$cCost.IsMappedToContents = $false
$cCost.Update()
New-FASTSearchMetadataCrawledPropertyMapping -ManagedProperty $cost -CrawledProperty
$cCost

$price = New-FASTSearchMetadataManagedProperty -Name advprice -Type 4
$price.RefinementEnabled = $true
$price.SortableType = "SortableEnabled"
$price.Update()

$cPrice = Get-FASTSearchMetadataCrawledProperty "vProductsAndInfoRead ListElement.
ListPrice"
$cPrice.IsMappedToContents = $false
$cPrice.Update()
New-FASTSearchMetadataCrawledPropertyMapping -ManagedProperty $price -CrawledProperty
$cPrice

$color = New-FASTSearchMetadataManagedProperty -Name advcolor -Type 1
$color.RefinementEnabled = $true
$color.Update()
```

```
$cColor = Get-FASTSearchMetadataCrawledProperty "vProductsAndInfoRead ListElement.Color"
$cColor.IsMappedToContents = $false
$cColor.Update()
New-FASTSearchMetadataCrawledPropertyMapping -ManagedProperty $color -CrawledProperty
$cColor


$pnumber = New-FASTSearchMetadataManagedProperty -Name advprodnumber -Type 1
$pnumber.SubstringEnabled = $true
$pnumber.Update()

$cPnumber = Get-FASTSearchMetadataCrawledProperty "vProductsAndInfoRead ListElement.
ProductNumber"
$cPnumber.IsMappedToContents = $false
$cPnumber.Update()
New-FASTSearchMetadataCrawledPropertyMapping -ManagedProperty $pnumber -CrawledProperty
$cPnumber


$size = New-FASTSearchMetadataManagedProperty -Name advsize -Type 1
$size.RefinementEnabled = $true
$size.Update()

$cSize = Get-FASTSearchMetadataCrawledProperty "vProductsAndInfoRead ListElement.Size"
$cSize.IsMappedToContents = $false
$cSize.Update()
New-FASTSearchMetadataCrawledPropertyMapping -ManagedProperty $size -CrawledProperty
$cSize


$weight = New-FASTSearchMetadataManagedProperty -Name advweight -Type 4
$weight.RefinementEnabled = $true
$weight.SortableType = "SortableEnabled"
$weight.Update()

$cWeight = Get-FASTSearchMetadataCrawledProperty "vProductsAndInfoRead ListElement.
Weight"
$cWeight.IsMappedToContents = $false
$cWeight.Update()
New-FASTSearchMetadataCrawledPropertyMapping -ManagedProperty $weight -CrawledProperty
$cWeight


$category = New-FASTSearchMetadataManagedProperty -Name advcategory -Type 1
$catgory.SubstringEnabled = $true
$category.RefinementEnabled = $true
$category.Update()

$cCategory = Get-FASTSearchMetadataCrawledProperty "vProductsAndInfoRead ListElement.
ProductCategory"
$cCategory.IsMappedToContents = $false
$cCategory.Update()
New-FASTSearchMetadataCrawledPropertyMapping -ManagedProperty $category -CrawledProperty
$cCategory


$thumb = New-FASTSearchMetadataManagedProperty -Name advthumbnail -Type 1
$thumb.Queryable = $false
$thumb.Update()
```

```
$cThumb = Get-FASTSearchMetadataCrawledProperty "vProductsAndInfoRead ListElement.
ThumbNailPhoto"
$cThumb.IsMappedToContents = $false
$cThumb.Update()
New-FASTSearchMetadataCrawledPropertyMapping -ManagedProperty $thumb -CrawledProperty
$cThumb

$lang = New-FASTSearchMetadataManagedProperty -Name advlang -Type 1
$lang.RefinementEnabled = $true
$lang.Update()

$cLang = Get-FASTSearchMetadataCrawledProperty "vProductsAndInfoRead ListElement.Culture"
$cLang.IsMappedToContents = $false
$cLang.Update()
New-FASTSearchMetadataCrawledPropertyMapping -ManagedProperty $lang -CrawledProperty
$cLang
```

Set up a custom full-text index and rank profile

For this example, you use a custom full-text index and rank profile, where you add only the searchable
fields for the product search and remove the freshness weight from the rank profile because the item
date is not important in this case.

1. Open an FS4SP shell, and then execute the following Windows PowerShell commands to
   create the full-text index and rank profile.

   ```
   # Create a new Full text index and rankprofile
   $advFTI = New-FASTSearchMetadataFullTextIndex -Name "adventureworks" -Description "Full
   text index for the Adventure Works LT database"
   # Set the new FTI as the default one for search
   $advFTI.MakeDefault()
   $advRP = New-FASTSearchMetadataRankProfile -Name "adventurerank"
   $RCList = $advRP.GetFullTextIndexRanks()
   $RCList.Create($advFTI)

   # Set FreshnessWeight to 0 as date is not important
   $advRP.FreshnessWeight = 0
   $advRP.Update()

   # Delete the reference for the "content" FTI which was added as default
   $contentRank = $RCList|where-Object -filterscript {$_.FullTextIndexReference.Name -eq
   "content"}
   $contentRank.Delete()

   $advRank = $RCList|where-Object -filterscript {$_.FullTextIndexReference.Name -eq
   "adventureworks"}
   ```

```
# Fix the rank per level as the default has a bug ranking level 1 above level 3
$advRank.SetImportanceLevelWeight(1,10)
$advRank.SetImportanceLevelWeight(2,20)
$advRank.SetImportanceLevelWeight(3,30)
$advRank.SetImportanceLevelWeight(4,40)
$advRank.SetImportanceLevelWeight(5,50)
$advRank.SetImportanceLevelWeight(6,60)
$advRank.SetImportanceLevelWeight(7,70)

New-FASTSearchMetadataFullTextIndexMapping -FullTextIndex $advFTI -Level 7
-ManagedProperty $title
New-FASTSearchMetadataFullTextIndexMapping -FullTextIndex $advFTI -Level 5
-ManagedProperty $category
New-FASTSearchMetadataFullTextIndexMapping -FullTextIndex $advFTI -Level 5
-ManagedProperty $desc
New-FASTSearchMetadataFullTextIndexMapping -FullTextIndex $advFTI -Level 4
-ManagedProperty $pnumber
```

 Warning By changing the default full-text index, all searches automatically use the new full-text index. If you have other content indexed and search solutions that are dependent on the default full-text index, you might not want to do this step; instead, you can customize the search site with code to search against the custom full-text index. You may also use the *FullTextIndex* parameter for search scopes—but then you cannot use substring-enabled managed properties in the nondefault full-text index (that has been verified not to work in SP1). See Chapter 6 for more information about defining full-text index limited search scopes.

2. Recrawl your content source.

Setting Up a Basic Search Storefront

For the product search page, use a FAST Search Center site. This site provides the basis for the search experience and shows off the different search features used for searching the products in the Adventure Works database.

Create a Search Center

1. Create a site based on the FAST Search Center site template.

2. Edit both the *default.aspx* and *results.aspx* pages and remove the tabs, as shown in Figure 10-20.

FIGURE 10-20 Remove the tabs from the search pages.

3. Edit the Search Action Links Web Part on the *results.aspx* page to enable sorting for *adventurerank* as shown in Figure 10-21, and then set that as the default sorting property. Remember, *adventurerank* is the rank profile you created earlier using Windows PowerShell.

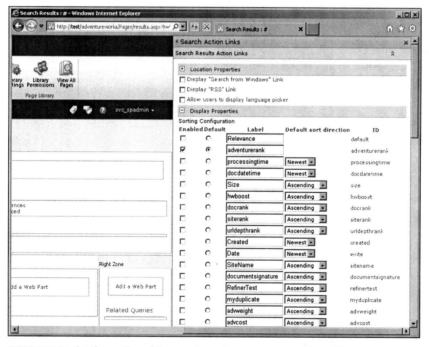

FIGURE 10-21 Set the sorting of the search results to your new rank profile.

4. Edit the Search Core Results Web Part.

5. Under Display Properties, clear the Use Location Visualization check box.

6. Add the following column definition to the Fetched Properties field.

```
<Columns>
    <Column Name="Url"/>
    <Column Name="docvector" />
    <Column Name="advtitle"/>
    <Column Name="advdesc"/>
    <Column Name="advprice"/>
    <Column Name="advcolor"/>
    <Column Name="advprodnumber"/>
    <Column Name="advsize"/>
    <Column Name="advweight"/>
    <Column Name="advthumbnail"/>
</Columns>
```

7. Click XSL Editor, and then paste in the contents of the *ch10-e-commerce-searchcenter.xslt* file, which you'll find in the downloadable code for this book.

8. Select the Enable Similar Results check box.

9. Clear the Enable Document Preview For PowerPoint and Enable Thumbnail Preview For Word check boxes.

10. Below the Result Query Options section, set Enable Spellchecking to Rewrite.

11. Select the Resubmit With Spellcheck and Suggest Spelling check boxes.

12. Make sure the Enable Search Term Stemming check box is selected because stemming and substring search don't work together.

13. Click OK to save your changes.

14. Edit the Refinement Panel Web Part.

15. Below the Refinement section, clear the Use Default Configuration check box, and then add the following Filter Category Definition.

```
<?xml version="1.0" encoding="utf-8"?>
<FilterCategories>
    Category    Title="Category"    Description="Product category"    Type="Microsoft.
Office.Server.Search.WebControls.ManagedPropertyFilterGenerator"    MetadataThreshold="1"
NumberOfFiltersToDisplay="5"    MaxNumberOfFilters="20"    ShowMoreLink="True"
MappedProperty="advcategory"    MoreLinkText="show more"    LessLinkText="show fewer"
ShowCounts="Count" />
    <Category    Title="Color"    Description="Product color"    Type="Microsoft.Office.
Server.Search.WebControls.ManagedPropertyFilterGenerator"    MetadataThreshold="1"
NumberOfFiltersToDisplay="5"    MaxNumberOfFilters="20"    ShowMoreLink="True"
MappedProperty="advcolor"    MoreLinkText="show more"    LessLinkText="show fewer"
```

```
ShowCounts="Count" />
    <Category    Title="Size"    Description="Product size"    Type="Microsoft.Office.
Server.Search.WebControls.ManagedPropertyFilterGenerator"    MetadataThreshold="1"
NumberOfFiltersToDisplay="5"    MaxNumberOfFilters="20"    ShowMoreLink="True"
MappedProperty="advsize"    MoreLinkText="show more"    LessLinkText="show fewer"
ShowCounts="Count" />
    <Category    Title="Language"    Description="Product language"    Type="Microsoft.
Office.Server.Search.WebControls.ManagedPropertyFilterGenerator"    MetadataThreshold="1"
NumberOfFiltersToDisplay="5"    MaxNumberOfFilters="20"    ShowMoreLink="True"
MappedProperty="advlang"    MoreLinkText="show more"    LessLinkText="show fewer"
ShowCounts="Count" />
</FilterCategories>
```

16. Click OK to save your changes.

17. Save your page.

18. Search for *shorts*. Your results should look similar to Figure 10-22.

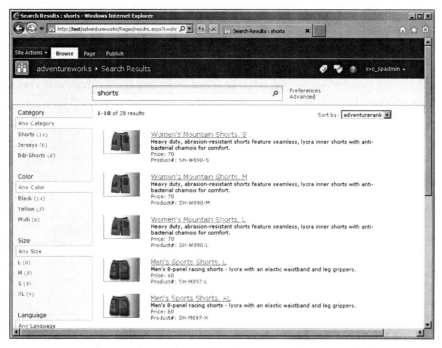

FIGURE 10-22 Result page after crawling and setting up a Search Center to display the results.

Important The image per search result is retrieved from the database in a base64-encoded format. The base64-encoded data is stored in the search index and is retrieved as part of the search result. In a production scenario, this is not an optimal way to handle images because you do not get any caching of the images and you store unnecessary data in the FS4SP search index.

The rendering is done via the data URI scheme directly on the page itself and is supported in Windows Internet Explorer 9. The data URI scheme is described at *http://en.wikipedia.org/wiki/Data_URI_scheme*.

Promoting High-Margin Products

At this point, you have a search page where items are ranked based on how the search terms match the textual content of your products defined in the *adventurerank* rank profile.

While you are creating an e-commerce application, you want to maximize profit and promote products on which you have the largest margin. One way of achieving these goals is to sort the results based on a sort formula. You use the product data in the Adventure Works database and sort on the difference between the price and cost fields for each product.

More Info Read more about sort formulas in Chapter 8, "Querying the Index."

On the other hand, if you don't want to do absolute sorting, you can create a separate managed property that is populated with the margin during item processing, and include this property as part of the static rank in the rank profile.

Alternative 1: Extend the Search Core Results Web Part with formula sort   So far the Search Core Results Web Part is set up to sort on the *adventurerank* rank profile. This model takes the matching of search terms and item text into account when ranking the results. Support for sort formulas is not built into the Core Results Web Part or the Search Action Links Web Part by default and you have to extend the Search Core Results Web Part in order to include this functionality.

The following code creates a custom Search Core Results Web Part with functionality to add a custom sort formula to be used as the primary sorter for your results. The *adventurerank* rank profile is used as a secondary sort for items having an equal formula sort value.

Custom Search Core Results Web Part

```
using System.ComponentModel;
using System.Web.UI.WebControls.WebParts;
using Microsoft.Office.Server.Search.Query;
using Microsoft.Office.Server.Search.WebControls;

namespace FS4SP.Samples.Ch10CustomSortCoreResults
{
    public enum Sorting
    {
```

```
        Ascending,
        Descending
    }

    [ToolboxItem(false)]
    public class Ch10CustomSortCoreResults : CoreResultsWebPart
    {
        [WebBrowsable(true)]
        [Category("Custom Sorting")]
        [WebDisplayName("Sort Formula")]
        [WebDescription("Set the formula which you want to order the results by")]
        [Personalizable(PersonalizationScope.Shared)]
        public string SortFormula { get; set; }

        [WebBrowsable(true)]
        [Category("Custom Sorting")]
        [WebDisplayName("Sort Order")]
        [WebDescription("Sort ascending or descending")]
        [Personalizable(PersonalizationScope.Shared)]
        public Sorting SortOrder { get; set; }

        protected override void CreateDataSource()
        {
            base.CreateDataSource();
            if (!string.IsNullOrEmpty(SortFormula))
            {
                // Add the custom sorting. Any other sorting will be added after this one
                // and used as secondary sorting
                SortDirection direction = SortDirection.Ascending;
                if (SortOrder == Sorting.Descending) direction = SortDirection.Descending;
                ((CoreResultsDatasource)this.DataSource).SortOrder.Add("[formula:" + SortFormula
+ "]", direction);
            }
        }
    }
}
```

Set up the custom Search Core Results Web Part

1. After deploying your new Web Part, replace the existing Search Core Results Web Part with your custom one and configure it the same way you did in the section "Setting Up a Basic Search Storefront" earlier in this chapter.

2. Configure the sort formula to be used. Use the formula *(advprice-advcost)*10000/advcost*, as shown in Figure 10-23.

Note Although it is possible to use decimals in sort formulas, the result of the formula has to be a 32-bit signed integer, as described at *http://msdn.microsoft.com/en-us/library/ff394654.aspx#ranking_sorting_algorithmic*. When dividing the difference between price and cost on the cost, you get a decimal number representing the difference as a percentage. By multiplying that number by 10,000, the outcome is a positive integer including four decimal places from the original number, for example, *(103-99)/99 = 0,04040 * 10000 = 404.*

3. Click OK to save your changes.

4. Save your page.

Added section for defining
a custom sort formula

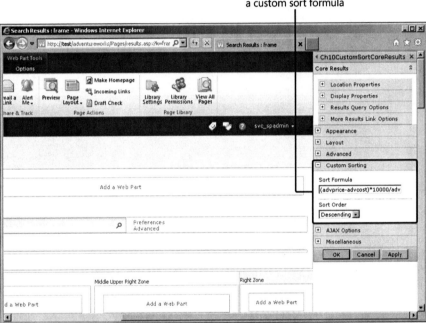

FIGURE 10-23 Sort results based on a custom sort formula, yielding items with a high profit margin on top.

Alternative 2: Add the product margin as a static rank component   In Alternative 1, you added a sort formula that, for any given query, returns items with the highest profit margin at the top of the results. Such sorting is absolute because rank is not calculated for items when using a sort formula. This is probably not an ideal solution in an e-commerce scenario. (See the discussion about searching for *LCD* in the section "Introduction to E-Commerce Search" earlier in this chapter.

If you want to employ a softer promotion, you can add the profit margin as part of the rank profile. This addition gives you the opportunity to tune how much weight is to be put on the search terms and how much on the profit margin.

Add profit margin as part of the *adventurerank* rank profile

In this procedure, you add profit margin as a static rank component. Any managed property of type *integer* can be used as input to the static rank. For this procedure, you create an External Item Processing component that uses the same formula as in Alternative 1 but writes the calculated value to a crawled property that you map to a new managed property. This managed property is then used as part of the rank profile.

1. Using Visual Studio, create a custom component similar to the following code and copy it to <FASTSearchFolder>\bin.

```
using System;
using System.Linq;
using System.Xml.Linq;

namespace FS4SP.Ch10.ProfitMargin
{
    class Processor
    {
        static void Main(string[] args)
        {
            // Read the input XML file that was provided by FS4SP through %(input)s
            XDocument input = XDocument.Load(args[0]);

            // Fetch the crawled properties from the input file
            var inputCPs = from cp in input.Descendants("CrawledProperty") select cp;

            var p = inputCPs.Where(cp => cp.Attribute("propertyName").Value ==
                "vProductsAndInfoRead ListElement.ListPrice").First().Value;
            var c = inputCPs.Where(cp => cp.Attribute("propertyName").Value ==
                "vProductsAndInfoRead ListElement.StandardCost").First().Value;

            int profitMargin = 0;
            if (!string.IsNullOrEmpty(p) && !string.IsNullOrEmpty(c))
            {
                int price = int.Parse(p);
                int cost = int.Parse(c);
                profitMargin = (price - cost) * 10000 / cost;
            }

            // Create an output XML file
            XElement output = new XElement("Document");
```

```
                        // Add crawled property to the output file
                        output.Add(
                            new XElement("CrawledProperty",
                                new XAttribute("propertySet",
                                        new Guid("2EDEBA9A-0FA8-4020-8A8B-30C3CDF34CCD")),
                                new XAttribute("propertyName", "advprofitmargin"),
                                new XAttribute("varType", "20"), profitMargin)
                        );

                        // Save the output XML where FS4SP designated through %(output)s
                        output.Save(args[1]);
                    }
                }
            }
```

2. Open *<FASTSearchFolder>\etc\pipelineextensibility.xml* and register your custom
   component as shown in the following code, where you add the *<Run>* node below the
   existing *<PipelineExtensibility>* node.

```
<PipelineExtensibility>
    <Run command="C:\FASTSearch\bin\FS4SP.Ch10.ProfitMargin.exe %(input)s %(output)s">
        <Input>
            <CrawledProperty propertySet="2edeba9a-0fa8-4020-8a8b-30c3cdf34ccd"
                propertyName="vProductsAndInfoRead ListElement.ListPrice" varType="20"/>
            <CrawledProperty propertySet="2edeba9a-0fa8-4020-8a8b-30c3cdf34ccd"
                propertyName="vProductsAndInfoRead ListElement.StandardCost" varType="20"/>
        </Input>
        <Output>
            <CrawledProperty propertySet="2edeba9a-0fa8-4020-8a8b-30c3cdf34ccd"
                propertyName="advprofitmargin" varType="20"/>
        </Output>
    </Run>
</PipelineExtensibility>
```

3. Open an FS4SP shell.

4. Create the crawled property, the managed property, and the mapping between them.

```
# Create properties for profit margin
$margin = New-FASTSearchMetadataManagedProperty -Name advprofitmargin -Type 2
$margin.SortableType = "SortableEnabled"
$margin.Update()

$cMargin = New-FASTSearchMetadataCrawledProperty -Name "advprofitmargin" -Propset
"2edeba9a-0fa8-4020-8a8b-30c3cdf34ccd" -VariantType 20

New-FASTSearchMetadataCrawledPropertyMapping -ManagedProperty $margin -CrawledProperty
$cMargin
```

5. Add the *advprofitmargin* managed property as a static rank component.

```
# Add profit margin as a static rank component
$RankProfile = Get-FASTSearchMetadataRankProfile -Name adventureworks
$QualityComponents = $RankProfile.GetQualityComponents()
$QualityComponents.Create($margin, 10)
```

6. Issue **psctrl reset** in an FS4SP shell to reload the indexing pipeline configuration.

7. Recrawl your content for the profit margin to take effect on your search results. (See Figure 10-24.)

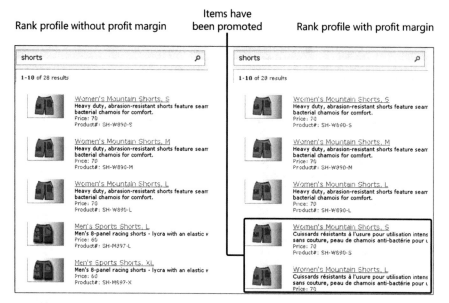

FIGURE 10-24 Searching for *shorts* before and after profit margin has been added as a component to the rank profile.

Tip Using the FS4SP Query Logger (*http://fs4splogger.codeplex.com/*) when comparing results, and including the managed properties *rank* and *profitmargin* in your XSLT to display the values, are both useful for gaining an understanding of how the rank changes are affecting the result.

Setting Up a Price Refiner Conditional on the Product Language

The current search page does not include the ability to filter on price ranges. Adding that capability is fairly easy because you already have a managed property that contains item prices, and the Refinement Panel Web Part supports setting up ranges for refiners. By adding the following XML to the filter category definition in the Refinement Panel Web Part, you get four different price ranges.

```
<Category   Title="Price"    Description="Item Price"
  Type="Microsoft.Office.Server.Search.WebControls.ManagedPropertyFilterGenerator"
  MetadataThreshold="2"    NumberOfFiltersToDisplay="0"    SortBy="Custom"
  ShowMoreLink="False"    MappedProperty="advprice"    ShowCounts="Count" >
  <CustomFilters MappingType="RangeMapping" DataType="Numeric" ValueReference="Absolute"
    ShowAllInMore="False">
    <CustomFilter CustomValue="$0-$249">
       <OriginalValue>..249</OriginalValue>
    </CustomFilter>
    <CustomFilter CustomValue="$250-$499">
       <OriginalValue>250..499</OriginalValue>
    </CustomFilter>
    <CustomFilter CustomValue="$500-$999">
       <OriginalValue>500..999</OriginalValue>
    </CustomFilter>
    <CustomFilter CustomValue="Over $1000">
       <OriginalValue>1000..</OriginalValue>
    </CustomFilter>
  </CustomFilters>
</Category>
```

The default prices are in U.S. dollars (USD), but for products with French text, it would be better to display the values in EUR instead. There are several ways to accomplish this:

- Modify the database view to include prices in EUR as well as USD.

- Add an External Item Processing component, which calculates the EUR price and adds it to each item.

- Modify the value at run time when it's displayed on your search page.

For the following procedure, you use the last option from the previous list, modifying the value as the currency at run time. This option provides the flexibility to change the price in the user interface as the currency conversion rate changes without having to reindex the items.

However, there's a problem: The filter category definition is static. You can solve this problem by creating a custom Refinement Panel Web Part that, upon initialization, changes the price ranges according to a currency conversion rate. To trigger the currency conversion, you check which language is being displayed. For the sample, you add a search scope for each product language, a scope drop-down to reflect the language options, and a custom Refinement Panel Web Part; and you modify the Core Results Web Part XSLT to display the price for each product in EUR as well as in USD.

Add language-specific search scopes and scope drop-down menus

1. Open a SharePoint Management Shell.

2. Run the following Windows PowerShell commands to create one scope per language.

```
# Get a reference to the Query SSA
$ssa = Get-SPEnterpriseSearchServiceApplication "<FAST Query SSA>"
# Create scope for English
```

```
New-SPEnterpriseSearchQueryScope -Name "advenglish" -Description "English"
-SearchApplication $ssa -DisplayInAdminUI 1 -ExtendedSearchFilter 'advlang:en'
# Create scope for French
New-SPEnterpriseSearchQueryScope -Name "advfrench" -Description "French"
-SearchApplication $ssa -DisplayInAdminUI 1 -ExtendedSearchFilter 'advlang:fr'
# Start scope compilation
$ssa.StartScopesCompilation()
```

3. On your SharePoint top-site, click Search Scopes below Site Collection Administration for your Site Settings.

4. Click Display Group and New Display Group, and then create a display group named **Adventureworks**. Add the *advenglish* and *advfrench* scopes as shown in Figure 10-25.

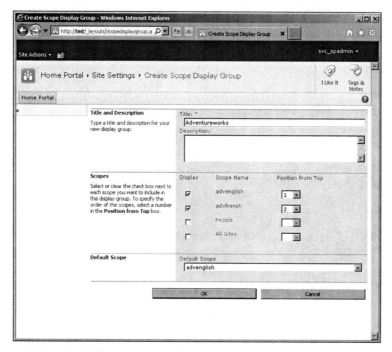

FIGURE 10-25 Adding a new scope display group with the English and French scopes.

5. Edit the result page of your FAST Search Center.

6. Edit the Search Box Web Part and enable scope drop-down menus. Set the scope display group you just created as shown in Figure 10-26.

You can now choose to search in either English or French on the result search page.

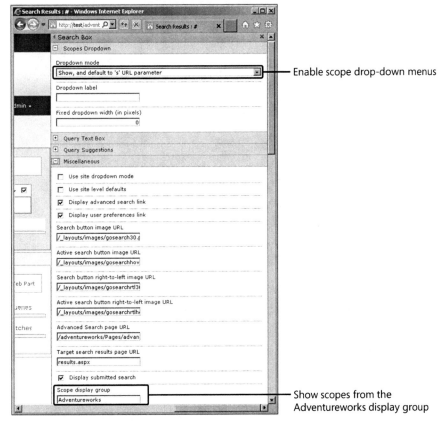

FIGURE 10-26 Enable scope drop-down menus and display the scopes from the *Adventureworks* scope display group.

Add a Custom Refinement Panel Web Part

The custom Refinement Panel Web Part reads the existing filter category definition and recalculates the price ranges. For example, the range 250–499 is rewritten to retrieve 200–399 with a USD-to-EUR conversion rate of 0.8.

Custom Refinement Panel Web Part

```
using System;
using System.ComponentModel;
using System.Text.RegularExpressions;
using System.Web;
using System.Xml;
using Microsoft.Office.Server.Search.WebControls;
```

```csharp
namespace FS4SP.Samples.Ch10CustomRefinementPanel
{
    [ToolboxItem(false)]
    public class Ch10CustomRefinementPanel : RefinementWebPart
    {
        protected override void OnInit(EventArgs e)
        {
            // Retrieve scope parameter from the URL
            string scope = HttpContext.Current.Request["s"];

            // If scope is French and you have filter categories defined
            if (scope == "advfrench" && !string.IsNullOrEmpty(FilterCategoriesDefinition))
            {
                // Load the filter category definition in an XmlDocument
                XmlDocument document = new XmlDocument();
                document.LoadXml(FilterCategoriesDefinition);

                // Regular expression to match numbers
                Regex reNum = new Regex(@"\d+");

                // Iterate all CustomFilter nodes
                foreach (
                    XmlNode parentNode in document.SelectNodes(
                        "//Category[@MappedProperty='advprice']//CustomFilter"))
                {
                    XmlNode node = parentNode.SelectSingleNode("OriginalValue");
                    foreach (Match m in reNum.Matches(node.InnerText))
                    {
                        // Conversion rate USD->EUR = 0.8 - Could retrieve externally
                        double euroPrice = int.Parse(m.Value) / 0.8;
                        int newVal = (int)Math.Floor(euroPrice);

                        // Replace filter value numbers with USD->EUR converted number
                        node.InnerText = node.InnerText.Replace(m.Value, newVal.ToString());
                    }
                    // Replace currency symbols in the refinement text
                    string text = parentNode.Attributes["CustomValue"].Value;
                    text = text.Replace("$", "€");
                    parentNode.Attributes["CustomValue"].Value = text;
                }
                // Set the modified filter category definition
                FilterCategoriesDefinition = document.OuterXml;
            }
            // Call base initialization
            base.OnInit(e);
        }
    }
}
```

1. Edit the Search Result page.

2. Copy your existing filter category definition from the Refinement Panel Web Part.

3. Remove the existing Refinement Panel Web Part.

4. Add your custom Refinement Panel Web Part.

5. Set the Filter Category Definition as described in step 15 of "Setting Up a Basic Search Storefront" with the XML copied in step 2.

6. Edit the Core Results Web Part and edit the XSLT.

   Replace this:

   ```
   <div>
       Price: <xsl:value-of select="advprice"/>
   </div>
   ```

   with the following:

   ```
   <div>
       <xsl:choose>
         <!-- Check if the URL contains the French scope name -->
         <xsl:when test="contains($SimilarFindBaseURL,'advfrench')">
            <!-- Convert USD to EUR -->
            Price: €<xsl:value-of select="format-number(advprice * 0.8,'0.00')"/>
         </xsl:when>
         <xsl:otherwise>
            Price: $<xsl:value-of select="format-number(advprice,'0.00')"/>
         </xsl:otherwise>
       </xsl:choose>
   </div>
   ```

7. Save the page.

8. Change the language in the scope drop-down menus to view the currency change in the Refinement Panel. Figure 10-27 shows the English with USD and French with EUR.

Prices converted
from USD to EUR

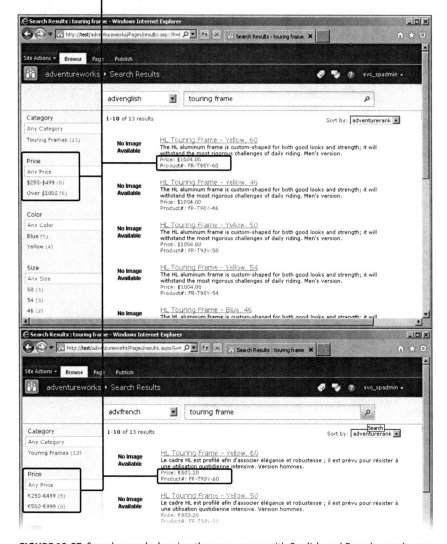

FIGURE 10-27 Sample search showing the same query with English and French search scope.

Promoting Items

A standard feature of an e-commerce solution is product promotions. FS4SP supports promotions by using the keyword functionality and document promotions. The keyword functionality and document promotion let you define certain search terms to trigger on and promote specific items to the top of the result list if the search term matches. You can also define start and end dates for your promotions.

 More Info See the section "Keyword, Synonym, and Best Bet Management" in Chapter 6 for more information about document promotions.

For the following procedure, you do not use the document promotion functionality accessible via SharePoint administration, but instead add a promotion. This promotion is not tied to a particular search term. It provides extra boost based on a criterion rather than boosting a specific item. This functions much like promoting high-margin products, but it is evaluated at run time. Internally, it uses the FQL *xrank* operator for the promotion.

Promote items in English that have a red color

For this procedure, you add a product promotion that boosts all red English products until the end of December 2012. This can be useful, for example, if a color is going out of fashion and you want to clear those products from your inventory.

1. Open an FS4SP shell.

2. Run the following Windows PowerShell commands to create the promotion.

```
# Get a reference to the search settings group
$searchSettingGroup = Get-FASTSearchSearchSettingGroup -Name <SiteCollectionID>
# Get a reference to the promotions collection without keywords
$globalPromotions = $searchSettingGroup.PromotionsWithoutKeyword
# Create a promotion
$globalPromotion = $globalPromotions.AddPromotion("FQL Red English Promotion")
# Set the boost value
$globalPromotion.BoostValue = "4000"
# Set the end date for the promotion
$globalPromotion.EndDate = "2012-12-31"
# Create the filter to trigger the promotion
$fql = 'and(advlang:"en",advcolor:"red")'
# Add the filter to the promotion
$globalPromotion.PromotedItems.AddPromotedExpression($fql)
```

 Note The site collection ID to be used with the *Get-FASTSearchSearchSettingGroup* can be retrieved from a SharePoint Management Shell by using the following command.

```
(Get-SPSite -Identity "http://<site collection root>").ID
```

All search queries will now be appended with an *xrank* statement. If, for example, you search for *frame*, the generated FQL looks like the following sample.

```
xrank(
    string(
        "frame",                    # Search term
        annotation_class="user",
        mode="simpleall"
    ),
    and(
        advlang:"en",               # Promotion filter for English
        advcolor:"red"              # Promotion filter for the color red
    ),
```

```
        boost=4000
) AND filter(
    and(
        advlang:en                          # Filter applied by the search scope
    )
)
```

Multiple Search Setting Groups

The keyword functionality in SharePoint is, by default, using settings that are global to a site collection. This means that if you add a keyword and a synonym, these additions will affect all searches executed from a Search Center on that particular site collection. The keywords for FS4SP are related to a search setting group where the default group has a one-to-one relationship with the site collection.

It is possible to create more than one search settings group using Windows PowerShell or code. The drawback with creating more search setting groups is that SharePoint provides an administration user interface for only the default one. All other usage has to be done either via code or Windows PowerShell, which makes it hard to administer without creating a custom administration user interface.

Furthermore, setting the search settings group on the Core Results Web Part is not easily done because you have to create a custom Core Results Web Part to do so, as shown in the section "Creating an FQL-Enabled Core Results Web Part" in Chapter 9. Basically, you have to get access to the *FAST-SearchRuntime* object and assign your custom search settings group name to the *UserContextGroupID* property.

E-Commerce Example Wrap-Up

The Adventure Works e-commerce example illustrates a variety of techniques that you can use to start customizing your search solutions. You started off by connecting a SQL Server database to a standard FAST Search Center, which you then modified by configuring Web Parts.

You also saw how you can achieve various ways of sorting search results by using custom sort formulas, working with rank profile, and by capitalizing on dynamic boosting based on context and business rules.

This scenario's last procedure showed you how to create custom Web Parts to handle nonconfigurable logic, such as adding multiple sort levels and changing the refinement panel dynamically based on user choices.

The goal of this scenario has been to show the relevant features of FS4SP and how you can take advantage of them in a realistic e-commerce solution.

Index

Symbols

360° customer insight solutions
    productivity search and, 389
2010 Information Worker Demonstration and Evaluation Virtual Machine (SP1), 390
<FASTSearchFolder>\bin folder
    command-line tools in, 117
    nctrl.exe command, 118
<FASTSearchFolder>\etc\CrawlerConfigTemplate-Advanced.xml, 255
<FASTSearchFolder>\etc\CrawlerConfigTemplate-RSS.xml, 255
<FASTSearchFolder>\etc\CrawlerConfigTemplate-Simple.xml, 255
.NET
    API, 164
    class entry points for administration, 165
    collection management in, 197–198
    crawled and managed properties in, 179–181
    creating custom property extractors, 276
    full-text indexes in, 189–191
    keyword management in, 225–227
    managed property boosts in, 193–195
    scopes management in, 203–205
    similarity to PowerShell code, 162
    site promotions and demotions in, 229

A

Access Control List (ACL)
    security trimming and, 51
Active Directory
    accounts, 243
    security trimming and, 51
Add Content Source page, 246
Add Crawler Impact Rule page, 249
Add Crawl Rule page, 247
administration. *See also* Central Administration
    FS4SP architecture and, 58
    other means of, 166
    overview, 115–117
administration page
    FAST Content SSA v. SP SSA, 61, 63–64
administrative privileges
    opening shells with, 88, 98
advanced filter pack. *See also* filters/filtering; IFilters
    deployment and, 101–103
    document conversion and, 281
    document conversion filters in, 42
    legacy document formats and, 329–330
advanced query language
    feature explained, 14
Adventure Works search example, 416
All Sites search tab, 47, 48
anchor text weight
    in dynamic rank tuning, 33
AND operator, 46
anti-phrasing
    feature described, 15
APIs
    choosing, 327–328
    common for FAST and SP, 290
    for searching, 303–328
application proxy group, 104
Asian languages
    substring matching for, 170
Augmented Backus-Naur Form (ABNF), 295
authorization tokens, 51

Windows PowerShell (*continued*)

About the Authors

 MIKAEL SVENSON is currently a principal consultant for a SharePoint consultancy and software vendor that creates shrink-wrapped productivity applications for SharePoint, and a Microsoft MVP focused on search within SharePoint. He has worked in the search field for over 10 years, focusing on the development of search engines and content connectors as well on search usability. He has created media monitoring software and led the development of an Enterprise Search Engine built on Microsoft .NET. Mikael has implemented search solutions on several different platforms, most recently focusing on Microsoft FAST Search for SharePoint, for major international corporations, and for several Nordic governmental institutions.

 MARCUS JOHANSSON has spent the last six years working with search solutions, both in academia and industry. He has implemented search technology for a wide range of clients, ranging from large Fortune 100 financial companies to some of the world's largest real-estate agents and leading media conglomerates. Marcus holds an MSc in Computer Science & Engineering. He lives in Stockholm, Sweden.

 ROBERT PIDDOCKE has worked with search technology for over a decade and has implemented hundreds of site and enterprise search solutions, including solutions for The Holy See, The London Stock Exchange, Lloyds of London, Microsoft Xbox, Metlife, and many more. He co-authored the book *Pro SharePoint 2010 Search*. Originally from Vancouver, British Columbia, where he currently lives with his wife and two children, Robert has also worked in Japan, and Denmark, and speaks English, Danish, and Japanese. He holds a degree from the University of Victoria, in Victoria, British Columbia. Currently, Robert is a director of business development for a global leader in search infrastructure software.

What do you think of this book?

We want to hear from you!

To participate in a brief online survey, please visit:

microsoft.com/learning/booksurvey

Tell us how well this book meets your needs—what works effectively, and what we can do better. Your feedback will help us continually improve our books and learning resources for you.

Thank you in advance for your input!

CPSIA information can be obtained at www.ICGtesting.com
Printed in the USA
BVOW052159190412

288155BV00002B/2/P